HANDBOOK OF
Training Evaluation
and
MEASUREMENT
METHODS
third edition

IMPROVING HUMAN PERFORMANCE SERIES

Series Editor: Jack J. Phillips, Ph.D.

Corporate Performance Management
David Wade and Ronald Recardo

Developing Supervisors and Team Leaders
Donald L. Kirkpatrick

Handbook of Training Evaluation and Measurement Methods, 3rd Edition
Jack J. Phillips

Human Performance Consulting
James S. Pepitone

Human Performance Improvement
William J. Rothwell, Carolyn K. Hohne, and Stephen B. King

The Human Resources Scorecard
Jack J. Phillips, Patricia Pulliam Phillips, and Ron D. Stone

Linking Learning and Performance
Toni Krucky Hodges

Managing Change Effectively
Donald L. Kirkpatrick

The Project Management Scorecard
Jack J. Phillips, G. Lynne Snead, and Timothy W. Bothell

Managing Employee Retention
Jack J. Phillips and Adele O. Connell

HANDBOOK OF
Training Evaluation
and
MEASUREMENT METHODS

third edition

jack j. phillips

IMPROVING
HUMAN
PERFORMANCE
SERIES

HANDBOOK OF TRAINING EVALUATION AND MEASUREMENT METHODS

Third Edition

Permissions may be sought directly from Elsevier's Science and Technology Rights Department in Oxford, UK. Phone: (44) 1865 843830, Fax: (44) 1865 853333, e-mail: permissions@elsevier.co.uk. You may also complete your request on-line via the Elsevier homepage: http://www.elsevier.com by selecting "Customer Support" and then "Obtaining Permissions".

Originally published by Gulf Publishing Company, Houston, TX.

10 9 8 7 6

Library of Congress Cataloging-in-Publication Data

Phillips, Jack J., 1945–
    Handbook of training evaluation and measurement methods / Jack J. Phillips.—3rd ed.
      p. cm.
    Includes index.
    ISBN 0-88415-387-8
    1. Employees—Training of—Evaluation.   I. Title.
HF5549.5.T7P43   1997
658.3'12404—dc21
                                  97-16782
                                     CIP

For information, please contact:
Manager of Special Sales
Butterworth–Heinemann
An Imprint of Elsevier
225 Wildwood Avenue
Woburn, MA 01801–2041
Tel: 781-904-2500
Fax: 781-904-2620
For information on all Butterworth–Heinemann publications available, contact our World Wide Web home page at:
http://www.bh.com

Contents

About the Author

Jack J. Phillips, Ph.D., received his B.S. in physics and mathematics from Oglethorpe University, his M.A. in decision sciences from Georgia State University, and his Ph.D. in human resources development from the University of Alabama. Dr. Phillips has 25 years of human resources management experience and is president of Performance Resources Organization, an international consulting firm in Birmingham, Alabama.

Preface

The Importance of Evaluation

Since the first two editions of this book were published, the Human Resource Development (HRD) field continues to grow at a phenomenal rate. The exact amount of growth and the size of the industry are difficult to pinpoint, but one report has placed the total dollars budgeted for formal training by U.S. organizations at $59.8 billion.[*] When participants' salaries for the time in training are added, the number should double. Informal training would account for an equal amount, bringing the total to over $200 billion. The total number of employees who receive formal, employer-sponsored training annually is about 58.6 million. The total dollars budgeted by HRD departments for outside expenditures, such as seminars and packaged training programs, stands at $13 billion. This brief profile shows how dramatically the HRD field has increased and the tremendous potential impact it can have on U.S. organizations. Other industrialized nations and developing countries have experienced similar growth rates.

Among the hottest issues in the HRD field are evaluation, results-based training, and ROI (Return On Investment) analysis. When any of these topics are discussed, they attract attention. Why? Because there is more pressure today than ever before to produce results with HRD programs. Training and development departments are struggling to meet demands from management for profit contributions and from participants who want a program that produces results.

This trend toward accountability is one of the most significant developments in the HRD field in recent years. Yet many HRD professionals are reluctant to change, contending that evaluation and measurement are too difficult or too costly. Some evaluation models may appear that way, but evaluation can be simple and inexpensive. Practical ideas can work for any training and development department. With all the tremendous growth and expenditures in this field, today's HRD professionals can no longer ignore their basic responsibility to evaluate programs and measure the results of their department's efforts.

[*] Industry Report, *Training,* 33(10), 1996, pp. 42–54.

Progress with ROI

No part of measurement and evaluation has generated more interest and received more attention than the topic of measuring the return on investment (ROI) in training and development. Fueled by a variety of influences, HRD professionals are seeking specific techniques and processes to measure the actual ROI with the same formulas used to evaluate other investments in an organization. Because of this development, several chapters have been added to increase the coverage of ROI. This enhanced coverage makes the third edition a more practical and useful reference for the HRD professional. The additional material on ROI is taken primarily from a new publication at Gulf Publishing, *Return on Investment in Training and Performance Improvement Programs.*

Major Revisions for the Third Edition

Each chapter has been revised and updated to include additional research, expanded coverage, and new examples of my case studies. In addition, seven new chapters have been added. More specifically, the following changes have been made:

☐ A chapter has been added to describe a model for developing the ROI in HRD programs.
☐ The chapter on data collection has been divided into two chapters: Measuring Reaction and Learning, and Measuring Application and Impact.
☐ A chapter has been added on isolating the effects of training.
☐ A chapter had been added on converting data to monetary values.
☐ A chapter has been included on identifying intangible benefits.
☐ A chapter has been added describing how to calculate the ROI at different levels of evaluation.
☐ A chapter has been included on implementation issues for measurement and evaluation.
☐ Also, the chapter on computers and HRD evaluation has been deleted. Relevant material from that chapter has been integrated into other chapters.

These changes are significant and substantially increase the size and scope of the handbook. With these additions, it becomes a valuable reference on how to evaluate and measure the success of HRD.

Success of Early Editions

By all measures, the first and second editions of this handbook were very successful. It has become the standard evaluation reference in major human resource development and training and development departments all over the globe.

Its use outside the U.S.A. has been impressive, with international orders accounting for about 40% of sales. A British edition has been developed, portions of the handbook have been translated into several foreign languages, and it has been used as a textbook at almost 50 universities and colleges. Because of the important updates and additions, the third edition should even surpass previous successes.

Target Audiences

Although this book's target audience can be broadly defined as HRD professionals and students in formal HRD programs, the audience can be further divided into five key groups.

1. The handbook is designed to be a significant resource for those individuals involved in evaluating HRD and training and development, organizational development, and a variety of HR and change programs. It is an indispensable reference for any program evaluator.
2. The handbook is designed to be a quick reference for all HRD professionals involved in the needs assessment, design, development, delivery, coordination, administrative support, or management of the HRD process. It provides complete coverage of evaluation topics for these individuals.
3. The handbook is valuable as a primary or supplemental text for college and university courses on measurement and evaluation, training and development, human resource development and special topics in HRD. It provides students with a practical and realistic perspective on important issues in measurement and evaluation.
4. The handbook is a useful and practical tool for consultants and training supply firms struggling to measure the success of their programs. The third edition contains all the information necessary to conduct an evaluation and report the results.
5. The handbook is a practical guide for managers who are supporting, advising, and reinforcing training and development in the organization. It shows how to design programs that focus on results and how to monitor, evaluate, and report success.

The third edition will become a valuable reference and text for these important target audiences.

Practical Approach

This handbook equips HRD professionals with the tools necessary to evaluate programs. Presented in a systematic format with many examples and illustrations, it is based on actual experiences. Each technique or idea has been tested and proven.

I have been fortunate to experience evaluation from four important perspectives. First, and most important, I have been directly involved in the evaluation process for many years as a full-time trainer and HRD manager. As part of this experience, I served as training manager for two Fortune 500 firms. In these roles, I applied and refined many of the concepts reported in this book.

Second, while serving as a key staff executive, the HRD department reported directly to me. In this role, I required the HRD staff to emphasize evaluation in a results-based approach.

Third, as a line executive and bank president, I frequently made use of HRD services. In this role, I insisted that the HRD staff show contributions for their programs, which could only be derived from a comprehensive approach to evaluation. I often required that specific evaluation techniques be implemented.

Last, but not least, I have had the opportunity to provide consulting assistance to help organizations revamp their evaluation processes. In this role, I have helped organizations improve evaluation techniques and strategies.

General Considerations

This book is designed to be a valuable reference both for individuals new to the field and seasoned professionals. The simplistic presentation, with examples, will provide the novice with the foundation to develop a sound program of evaluation. For the seasoned professional, the book contains numerous ideas that can add to the evaluation effort in a fully functioning HRD department. The information presented applies equally to small or large HRD staffs. Even a one-person department can find many ideas to evaluate the HRD effort in the organization.

An important strength of this book is the many examples taken from a variety of settings. Because so much of HRD occurs in business and industry, most examples come from the private sector. However, examples are also included from government, health care, and education. They cover a broad range of different types of programs, although the emphasis is on management and supervision, an area of HRD that is difficult to evaluate.

Some additional explanation is necessary for the terminology used throughout the book. The term "human resource development (HRD)" is generally used instead of training, training and development, manpower development, or management development. "Participant" is used instead of trainee or conferee. "Program" is used instead of course, and in most cases the term "HRD professional" is used in place of trainer, training specialist, or instructor.

The Structure of the Book

The book is divided into four major parts.

Part I, The Measurement Imperative, outlines the importance of measurement and the need for evaluating HRD programs. Recent trends toward measurement are documented to set the proper perspective for evaluation. Chapter 3, the last chapter in Part I, offers useful techniques for developing a results-based approach.

Part II, Evaluation Models and Design Issues, offers five chapters to provide the appropriate framework and design considerations necessary to develop a complete evaluation system. The first chapter presents an 18-step results-based model and shows how a program should be developed to focus on application and business impact objectives. The next chapter presents an ROI process model with additional steps that must be taken to calculate the return on investment. More detailed parts of the model are presented in other chapters. Evaluation design is covered in two chapters, one covering evaluation instrument design issues, and the other covering overall evaluation design.

Part III, Data Collection and Analysis, comprises nine chapters and is the heart of the book. The first two chapters focus on data collection; the first presents techniques for measuring reaction and learning, while the second covers techniques to measure application and business impact. The next chapter tackles one of the most critical issues in post-program evaluation: isolating the effects of the training program. Ten ways to isolate various factors that influence output measures are presented. The next chapter covers the critical issue of converting data to monetary values, which is necessary to calculate the ROI. A brief chapter is presented on identifying intangible measures that are not converted to economic benefits, while another chapter explores a variety of data analysis techniques. Another important chapter focuses directly on how to calculate the return on investment, covering the various issues involved in developing and reporting the ROI. The next chapter focuses on special issues involved in evaluating outside resources, including external seminars, purchased programs, consultants, and outside conference facilities. The final chapter explores the ROI at multiple levels, showing how it can be developed at different evaluation levels.

Part IV, Implementation Issues, focuses on those factors that will influence the implementation of a comprehensive measurement and evaluation process. The first chapter describes the influence of the management group and explores what must be done to ensure that managers support HRD and provide the appropriate commitment of resources. The next chapter describes how program results are communicated, which is an extremely important step to ensure that the appropriate target audience receives evaluation information. The final chapter focuses on other key issues necessary for a comprehensive measurement and evaluation process to be fully integrated into the human resource development process.

Seven appendices give additional information and examples related to the chapters.

Generally, each chapter is self-contained, although some build on the information of others. It is not required that the chapters be read in the sequence presented. Experienced professionals may want to refer to selected chapters, depending on their individual evaluation needs.

What This Handbook Will Do for You

This book explores the key issues of HRD program evaluation and measurement. It will show you how to

☐ Assess the status of HRD program results in your organization.
☐ Define the purposes of evaluation.
☐ Develop programs with an emphasis on achieving results.
☐ Select the optimum evaluation strategy.
☐ Design instruments to use in program evaluation and measurement.
☐ Compare and select the most effective and efficient data-collection methods.
☐ Isolate the effects of the program.
☐ Convert data to monetary values.
☐ Determine the costs of HRD programs.
☐ Analyze evaluation data collected from HRD programs.
☐ Identify intangible benefits from HRD programs.
☐ Calculate the ROI for HRD programs.
☐ Illustrate how ROI can be developed at different levels of evaluation.
☐ Evaluate the use of outside resources such as seminars, consultants, and packaged programs.
☐ Improve management commitment and support for the HRD function.
☐ Obtain management involvement in the HRD process.
☐ Communicate the results of HRD programs.
☐ Implement a comprehensive measurement and evaluation process.

In summary, this is the only book presenting concise, practical methods to evaluate any type of HRD program. Ranging from determining the purposes of evaluation to communicating the results of an evaluation, it is designed to be a standard reference and text on evaluation and measurement. I welcome comments, criticisms, and any suggestions for improvement.

Acknowledgments

No book represents the work of the author alone. Many people contribute to the final product, and this book is no exception. Many colleagues and clients have shared their thoughts, which have been refined, developed, and ultimately presented here. The many organizations that supplied material for this book are given credit throughout the publication.

The individuals who have influenced, supported, or encouraged me in this effort are almost too numerous to mention, but some deserve special attention. Ron Stone, an officer in our consulting firm and colleague for almost 30 years, has utilized and refined many of the techniques in this book.

Through the years, I have worked with several colleagues who share an equal interest in evaluation. Jac Fitz-Enz is one of those individuals. Through his work at the Saratoga Institute and his publications, he has heightened the interest in evaluation. His encouragement and support are appreciated.

Special thanks go to all the professors who have used this book in their classes. Their collective feedback has helped to improve the final product.

Much gratitude goes to Leonard and Zeace Nadler, for their encouragement to develop the initial manuscript and for their thoughtful suggestions for improvement. Len has rightfully earned his place in the HRD Hall of Fame for his contributions to the profession. He has an extraordinary insight into the HRD field.

My editorial assistant, Tammy Bush, has accomplished the almost insurmountable task of typing and editing this revised edition in a short time frame. Her diligence, patience, and expertise are always appreciated.

And finally, I owe much appreciation to my wife, Johnnie, who always provides encouragement, support, and assistance in my work. She continues to make many sacrifices so that I may develop books and conduct research.

Jack J. Phillips, Ph.D.
Birmingham, Alabama

CHAPTER 1

The Need for Results-Based HRD

Much has been written about the need for the human resource development function to become more accountable and measure its contribution. In essence, the function must be a business partner in the organization. Most observers of training and development, human resource development, and performance improvement have indicated that for HRD to become a true business partner, three things must be in place:

1. Human resource development must be integrated into the overall strategic and operational framework of the organization. It cannot be an isolated, event-based activity, unrelated to the mainstream functions of the business.
2. Partnerships must be established with key operating managers. These key clients are crucial to the overall success and well-being of the HRD function.
3. There must be a comprehensive measurement and evaluation process to capture the contribution of human resource development. The process must be comprehensive yet practical and feasible as a routine function in the organization.

Most HRD executives believe that human resource development is an important part of strategy, and it has become a mainstream function in many organizations. The same executives give good marks to the successful establishment of partnerships with key management in item number two. Tremendous strides have been made in working with managers to build the relationships that are necessary. However, the executives also indicate that there has not been similar progress in measurement and evaluation in most organizations. This book focuses on how to develop a comprehensive, feasible measurement and evaluation process for almost any type of organization. In reality the three issues cannot be separated, and must work together to produce a dynamic results-based HRD process.

Evaluation Myths

There are many faulty assumptions about the mysterious process of evaluation that have kept HRD professionals from measuring the contribution of their efforts. Ten myths are presented here, and each deserves a few comments.

Myth #1: I can't measure the results of my training effort. A persistent myth about training is that the value of a training program cannot be quantitatively measured. Although myth makers concede that the effects of training may be measurable, they continue to insist that the value of professional and management development programs can't be identified and calculated. This is simply not true. Recent years have seen the proliferation of technology and methods to measure the impact of almost any program.[1] The primary decision is not so much whether results should be measured, but rather how to identify the most appropriate method. Perhaps today's paradigm shift toward quality management will increase the focus on the importance of evaluation.

Myth #2: 1 don't know what information to collect. If a program is properly designed and has precise and measurable objectives, there should be some idea about what type of information to collect to ascertain if the program worked. When training focuses on performance, much of the confusion about data collection evaporates. Today there is more information available on performance measurement than ever before. Well-conceived needs assessments also reveal some quantifiable measures of performance.

Myth #3: If I can't calculate the return on investment, then it is useless to evaluate the program. Determining the return on investment (ROI) should be a priority for every HRD professional. In addition to exhibiting good stewardship toward the organization's financial resources, it is simply sound human resource management. However, the ROI of a training effort is usually based on a few subjective premises and, consequently, its calculation may not be as specific as the ROI of a capital expenditure. Also, there may be reasons other than economics for implementing a training program.[2]

For some programs, the cost of an objective and precise evaluation may outweigh the program's cost. In these situations, evaluations do not make economic sense and a brief, subjective program appraisal may be more appropriate. The following example illustrates this approach:

> A 15-hour listening course, intended to build effective listening skills, was conducted for 10 supervisors. The total cost of the course—including participants' time, materials, instructor salaries, and administrative expenses—was $5,000. The program's impact can be measured by direct observation of all participants over a period of time, extensive interviews with each participant, follow-up testing, and interviews and surveys of the participants' subordinates. The resulting information can then be combined in a detailed study that gives a fairly reliable estimate of the change, if any, the 10 supervisors experienced. Although the approximate economic impact of that change can be calculated, an evaluation of this type can easily cost $50,000. No organization can justify spending $50,000 to determine the impact of a $5,000 course.

This extreme example points to the key question that should always be asked before undertaking an evaluation: "Is it worth it?" The amount of useful information you expect to obtain should be identified and considered in the evaluation-consideration process. It may be worthwhile, for example, to spend $50,000 to evaluate a course that costs $750,000 annually to conduct.

Myth #4: Measurement is only effective in the production and financial arenas. Today, the accountability spotlight is focused on every functional area of business. Functional specialists who prospered during good economic times and survived the threat of corporate downsizing during recessionary periods are scurrying to find ways to show their contribution. Because HRD is one of these areas, creative minds in the field have produced an abundance of meaningful and realistic measurements.

Myth #5: My chief executive officer (CEO) does not require evaluation, so why should I do it? This is an easy trap. If top management does not demand measurable results, and no evaluation takes place, the HRD department is very likely heading for trouble. The CEO may suddenly demand justification for the department's existence, or a new CEO can assume command and require measurement.

More importantly, although measurement may not be required, key decisions affecting the HRD department are routinely made. Savvy chief executives evaluate the efforts of all departments, either explicitly or implicitly, and will use any information available to assign a value to their efforts. In the absence of realistic evaluation data, a CEO may draw erroneous conclusions about the HRD department based on inaccurate or incomplete information. It is dangerous to wait until a top executive forces evaluation.

Myth #6: There are too many variables affecting the behavior change for me to evaluate the impact of training. Many research studies have been conducted that show the impact of training when other variables remain fairly constant. It is possible to isolate the variables for which the HRD staff has primary control, namely those involved in the learning process.

On the job, many variables can affect performance after a program is completed. Common among these are the participant's self-motivation, work environment, peer pressure, and on-going or non-existent reinforcement from his or her supervisor. While these are significant factors not directly under the control of most HRD departments, they should not be the basis for discarding evaluation.

Wishing for less complex duties and responsibilities is like hoping taxes will go away—it will never happen. Jobs are becoming more complicated and require analyzing many interrelated variables. Although measurements of change may not be precise, they are better than no measurement at all.

Myth #7: Evaluation will lead to criticism. Evaluation results can reflect unfavorably on those who designed the program, those who conducted it, and possibly even on the participants' supervisors who may have failed to support it. Unless an organization is ready for criticism, evaluation should not be undertaken. Comments and feedback will not always be positive, particularly when reactions and observations are solicited. For a light-hearted look at criticism and evaluation, see Appendix 1 at the back of this book.

Myth #8: I don't need to justify my existence, I have a proven track record. Many HRD professionals have established an excellent reputation for their individual efforts and do not have to justify their existence. However, the effectiveness of the HRD function still needs consideration, because the HRD department's reputation is at stake. Individual contributions are usually short-lived and forgotten during economic crises. Management needs clear-cut data to show the value of a department or section, and the contribution it makes to its objectives.

Myth #9: Measuring progress toward learning objectives is an adequate evaluation strategy. Training program objectives are typically narrowly focused on course content, learning activities, and immediate end-of-program improvements. In today's competitive environment, simply measuring progress toward these objectives is inadequate. Evaluation strategies must include the impact of programs measured in terms of organizational change, ultimate outcomes, or business results. Measurements of the on-the-job impact of training and education are an important part of the evaluation process.

Myth #10: Evaluation would probably cost too much. Evaluation represents only a small part of the total cost of a program. If integrated into program conception, design, development, and delivery, the evaluation process can be quick and inexpensive. The key issue is this: If evaluation is necessary to determine a payoff from training, how can an HRD department afford not to allocate expenses for evaluation?

These myths should not hinder the evaluation efforts of any HRD department. The chapters ahead expose these faulty assumptions and pave the way for a successful evaluation program. The next section examines why a change in approach is needed.

Needed: A Change in Approach

More Talk Than Action

When it comes to measurement and evaluation, there is still more talk than action. HRD executives are reluctant to disclose their approaches to evaluation and admit to few bottom-line ties to their training efforts. In a meeting with several training directors, a human resource director (who refused to be quoted by name) offered the following comment:

> ". . . I can't win," he said. "If I tell you we don't measure bottom-line benefits, you run a headline that says 'XYZ Corporation Doesn't Evaluate Its Training.' If I say we do, you ask me how, and I can't answer because I don't believe you can hang dollar signs on the value of professional or management training."

Even prestigious companies with extensive training budgets do not always have a comprehensive approach to tying their training investment to bottom-line results.

Consider IBM. When the company was spending $2 billion a year, 4% of its total operating budget, on education, IBM was hitting a plateau in growth. In an attempt to control expenses, a management committee asked the education division to give back $200 million. Jack Bowsher, former director of education, told them it would be difficult to know what to cut without damaging the company. No one knew which education and training programs were working, which ones needed to be revamped, or which ones were ineffective. According to Bowsher, "All we knew was that we were doing a lot of it. My message to the directors of education was that either we were going to show that education had value or it would be taken down $200 million."[3] Ultimately, IBM downsized its education division into two entities: Skill Dynamics and Work Force Solutions. Both are expected to keep balance sheets and report profit and loss statements to IBM headquarters, as do other operating units. IBM officials are tacitly acknowledging that their old approach to education and development was, if not wrong, at least unsuited to the kind of organization IBM wanted to become.

It is increasingly common to read in-depth stories of successful programs and discuss them at professional meetings. However, when some programs are examined in detail to secure evidence of success, there appears to be more talk than action. In an attempt to improve employee basic skills, the Brenlin Group, an Akron, Ohio-based industrial products company, implemented site-based learning centers to focus on improving reading and math skills.[4] They reported that the learning centers "yielded strong, if indirect, indicators that literacy training pays off in greater productivity, increased sales, and a more stable work force." The goals of the learning center are to

☐ Generate employee interest in life-long learning
☐ Upgrade employees' educational levels
☐ Enhance employees' thinking, communication, and math skills

To encourage use of the centers, the Brenlin Group gave employees who participated compensatory time off and gift certificates. The company spent about $600,000 to establish the four centers, and operating costs for each center, including lost production time, run about $300,000 annually. Brenlin reports that it is still difficult to show a direct link between learning centers and plant productivity, but officials cite the following indicators as evidence of the project's success:

☐ One manufacturing facility reported a 21% increase in productivity since the training began in 1989.
☐ Sales per employee at one plant increased by 88%.
☐ Sales per employee at another plant increased by 30%.
☐ Turnover in one facility has dropped from 26% to 7% since the learning centers opened.
☐ Managers report increased desire and willingness of employees to seek promotions and participate on employee-involvement teams.
☐ Employee-opinion surveys in at least one plant show that most employees feel better about the workplace after training.
☐ Some of the plants are reporting lower scrap and waste rates.

Although these performance indicators are impressive, there is little concrete evidence to indicate a connection between the program and these results.

Fortune magazine reported that "Motorola calculates that every $1 it spends on training delivers $30 in productivity gains within three years."[5] An article in *Training* stated that "Since 1987 the company has cut costs by $3.3 billion—not by the normal expedient of firing workers, but by training them to simplify processes and reduce waste. Sales per employee have doubled in the past five years, and profits have increased 47%." Unfortunately, Motorola officials indicate that by policy they do not connect training to business results.[1]

Other examples of more talk than action occur when impressive results are attributed to a program with no explanation of how the results are calculated. For example, Frito-Lay attributed a substantial savings to the implementation of three creative problem-solving courses. According to Frito-Lay's group manager, Dave Morrison, ". . . we saved major dollars—-more than $500 million during the first six years."[6] Morrison asserts that there is a direct connection between employees learning and using creative problem-solving techniques and profit. He does not indicate how the savings were generated, and provides no additional details about the connection between the training programs and profitability. While there may be some connection, there is no hint of how the $500 million was tabulated. It is admittedly difficult to evaluate the many intangible benefits of creativity training and problem-solving programs. However, when bold claims are not substantiated, it places the entire evaluation process in jeopardy.

Training Magazine conducts an extensive annual industry report. For the last three years, the comprehensive report on the status of training and development in the U.S.A. has also collected information regarding the extent of training evaluation.[7] Table 1-1 shows study results from the 1,456 responses tabulated in the 1996 report. The most surprising issue is the extent to which behavior and business results are evaluated in organizations. The percent of organizations representing evaluations of training based on business results is 49%. Those same organizations indicated that 44% of their programs are evaluated at that level. These data appear to be out of line with earlier studies.[8] When questioned about the survey results, the sponsors indicated that the data may be exaggerated because many respondents provided answers about what they wish were present instead of reality. Also, sometimes the questions' phrasing provides much latitude in the interpretation of responses. Although the table shows that tremendous strides have been made, it is perhaps an overstatement of the actual progress achieved.

Table 1-1
Annual Industry Report—Status of Training Evaluation

	All Industries	Manufac- turing	Transpor- tation/ Communi- cations/ Utilities	Wholesale/ Retail Trade	Finance/ Insurance/ Banking	Business Services	Health Services	Educa- tional Services	Public Admini- stration
Trainees' REACTIONS to the course will be measured . . .									
Percent Measuring Reactions[1]	86	74	86	85	97	86	91	97	95
Percent of Courses[2]	83	76	82	88	85	84	86	91	84
Trainees will be TESTED to determine what they learned . . .									
Percent Testing[1]	71	73	77	59	87	64	92	54	75
Percent of Courses[2]	51	51	56	52	52	55	52	41	45
Trainees' BEHAVIOR will be evaluated when they return to the job									
Percent Evaluating Behavior[1]	65	67	64	55	81	60	73	59	52
Percent of Courses[2]	50	50	48	56	58	55	42	41	42
Changes in BUSINESS RESULTS attributable to the training will be measured . . .									
Percent Measuring Business Results[1]	49	59	44	43	47	48	51	45	30
Percent of Courses[2]	44	45	40	57	48	51	36	39	36

Under pressure to justify budgets in an era of downsizing and doing more with less, nearly half of the respondents in this year's survey claim they attempt to measure training's effect on business results.

[1] *Of organizations with 100 or more employees, percentage that evaluate any of their training courses in this way.*
[2] *Average percentage of all courses in an organization's curriculum that are evaluated in this way (considering only organizations that evaluate some courses).*
Source: *Industry Report, Training, 33(10), 1996, p. 63.*

Painful Lessons

Unfortunately, the following scene has repeated itself many times:

A phone call is received from an acquaintance employed in the HRD field. The caller asks if there are any vacancies, explaining: "Business is down with my company, and they're cutting back on the training and development department. I'm looking for a job." A few questions reveal the cause. Top management of the organization felt that the training and development department could be cut without seriously affecting the company. In other words, there was little bottom-line contribution.

Management training and development has received much criticism in recent years. In most organizations, teaching managers how to manage has been a difficult, haphazard, and often unsuccessful exercise. After years of observing corporations, business and industry still struggle with a variety of approaches to management training. Some researchers suggest that management training has failed because it has no connection to real life in the company.[9] Ask a manager six months after completing a program how it changed his or her behavior, and you will probably get a vague answer.

Each year, companies spend millions of dollars on programs to help supervisors, managers, and executives become more competent. How many such programs really affect the organization's ability to compete? Not very many, according to one leader, who claims that management development programs fail to add value to corporate strategy.[10] The five most common reasons for failure include:

1. Programs are not linked specifically to strategies, challenges, or problems in the organization.
2. Programs are designed to create awareness and understanding, but not competence.
3. Programs focus on individuals rather than operating units.
4. Participants attend programs for reasons other than personal or organizational need.
5. Programs fail to help participants confront reality.

Such painful lessons appear across all types of industries. One situation involved an alliance between two major organizations. A large engineering and construction firm joined forces with a major paper company to create an academy to train their managers. In the beginning, the paper company insisted on measurement and evaluation systems to include a linkage with business results. The engineering and construction firm was uninterested in pursuing results and, consequently, no evaluation was undertaken beyond the standard reaction evaluation. The concern for results eventually became a larger issue, and the paper company pulled out of the project, dissolving the alliance. The focus on results with specific on-the-job measures could have made a difference in the success of this project.

These problems can be partially overcome with a comprehensive, results-based approach using measurement and evaluation.

For years many HRD observers have suspected a direct correlation between a lack of evaluation and measurement and training departments that suffer cutbacks during recessions. One large defense contractor with an education and training staff of almost 300 instructors, specialists, coordinators, artists, supervisors, and managers faced a severe reduction of employment when defense spending was reduced at its primary facility. No other department suffered reductions of the magnitude and frequency of the education and training department. The staff was cut from 300 to under 30 within 2 years, with most of the reductions taking place in the first few months. Only essential, required training was retained. The primary reason: Among hundreds of courses and programs, not one could be tied to a direct bottom-line contribution. There were few attempts to evaluate any of the programs, and although they may have been effective, there was no evidence to prove it.

It is understandable that management, when faced with severe reductions, will chop away those functions that can be eliminated with the least amount of disruption in the operation. Had the training department's programs shown a strong contribution, it would have been more difficult to cancel them. The timing and number of the reductions probably would have been vastly different had data been available to substantiate the positive effect the training and development curricula had on the bottom line.

It is a difficult lesson to learn. Unfortunately, this situation has occurred in many organizations. HRD departments are placed in the same category as public relations and government affairs—nice to have, but trimmed when times are tough. It is a lesson that need not be repeated.

Sometimes the cutback of staff is not precipitated by a reduction in business. For example, in a major midwestern city, the local chapter of the American Society for Training and Development gave its annual employer award to an organization that appeared to support training in an exceptional way. The award was designed to recognize employers that provided positive support and commitment to the training and development process. Soon after the award was given, the entire training and development function was abolished. The primary reason, according to internal sources, was that top executives could not see any measurable contribution from the training function.

These painful lessons often have a devastating effect on individuals in HRD. For example, a training manager terminated from a large motel chain offered little explanation as to why he left, saying "things just didn't work out." Later, in a conversation with his former boss, some of the specifics on the termination were uncovered. More than any other reason, he was terminated because he could not justify the existence of his department. To quote his former boss,

> "He had some good ideas, some popular programs, and he seemed to enjoy what he was doing. But, he could not show us how effective his programs were and what they were doing for the company. We need someone who can make a contribution and let us know about it."

That is indeed a painful lesson for anyone to learn.

Why Change?

Why should HRD departments change their approach? While some reasons are rather obvious, there are more far-reaching reasons to reexamine traditional beliefs and actions.

It just makes good economic sense. Evaluation should be required of any activity that represents a significant expenditure of funds from the organization. The pressures of cost-cutting, scarce resources, and highly competitive industries have led to increased pressure on HRD departments to make a bottom-line contribution.

Accountability is an important trend. In almost every function, staff members are attempting to quantify the impact of their efforts. Most executives want to know how departments, programs, and services contribute to clients, consumers, and customers. This trend toward measurement applies to the HRD profession as well.

Increased scrutiny of HRD budgets. Securing budget approval is a difficult task facing HRD managers. Specific measurements of a past program's success can help secure additional funds in the future. With the popularity of zero-based budgeting, departments must justify their existence to obtain funds for next year's operation. Without evaluation, this is almost impossible.

Pressure from the top to make a contribution. It is becoming increasingly common for chief executives to express the need for HRD departments to achieve results. Many say it is now time for HRD departments to show what they can do in hard, indisputable facts. Some require it now. More will require it in the future.

Peer pressure from HRD professionals. Peer pressure causes some departments to strengthen their efforts in evaluation and measurement. When the

HRD department in one organization sees another HRD department making progress in this fertile field; others feel obligated to try to do the same. This pressure is a healthy part of any professional organization.

Self-satisfaction. There is a certain sense of self-satisfaction when a person sees the results of his efforts. Also, learning new skills and knowledge can lead to high levels of job satisfaction. A training and development manager, who wishes to remain anonymous, described this issue best:

> "I once accepted a training manager's job that had been previously occupied by a line manager. That line manager wrestled with the job unsuccessfully for about three years. Finally, in a fit of frustration, he gave it up and went back to the line organization as a plant manager. His biggest frustration as a training manager, which he shared with me later, was the fact that he never had a feeling of accomplishment. While in line management, he could go home each day and see how much work had been accomplished by counting the tons of production. But in the training assignment, it was different. He would go home frustrated, not knowing whether his programs worked or if he was doing the right thing. He never knew the extent of the programs' contribution, because no effort was made to evaluate them or measure their results. He did not know the difference between evaluating learning and job performance."

More information is available. Although the field of measurement and evaluation is embryonic, it is indeed mushrooming, as described in Chapter 2. Information is shared in professional journals, meetings, and books, although much of it is still theory. Although each situation is different, techniques used in one situation may apply to another. Techniques can be borrowed, results cannot.

Professionalism. The extent to which measurement and evaluation are conducted differentiates an amateur function from a professional team. Part of the process of professionalism in any field is to show the worth of the function. Measurement and evaluation have become an integral part of the HRD profession, and are becoming part of beginning professionals' career development. Many professional development courses for HRD personnel cover evaluation strategies and techniques.

Survival. One final reason for changing is survival. In the future, those who do not evaluate their efforts may be left behind. Organizations are reaching the point where they will not hire or promote HRD staff members who do not show their contributions and justify their existence.

How Results-Based Are Your HRD Programs?
A Quick Check for the HRD Manager

Before pursuing the topic of results-based HRD, a review of the status of HRD departments is in order. The following instrument should be taken by each staff member involved in HRD. It is brief and can be taken in just a few minutes. Responses should be candid and accurately reflect the organization's present approach to training and development. Complete the instrument now, before reading the analysis that follows. Select the most correct response.

To fully understand the incident, a few definitions are needed. **"Human Resource Development"** refers to education, training, and development as a combined function. The term **"program"** refers to a series of courses or learning solutions, or other events that are educational or developmental in nature. The term **"participant"** is used to reflect the individual directly involved in the program. This is preferred over the term student or trainee. The **"Chief Executive Officer (CEO)"** is the top executive in the organization. **"Top management"** refers usually to the senior management level in the headquarters, division, or regional operations.

1. HRD programs are
   a. Activity-oriented. (All team leaders attend the "Performance Appraisal Workshop".)
   b. Individual results-based. (The participant will reduce his or her error rate by at least 20%.)
   c. Organizational results-based. (The cost of quality will decrease by 25%.)
2. The investment in HRD is measured primarily by
   a. Accident; there is no consistent measurement.
   b. Observations by management, reactions from participants.
   c. Monetary benefits through increased productivity, reduced costs, or improved quality.
3. The concern for the method of evaluation in the design and implementation of HRD programs occurs
   a. After a program is completed.
   b. After a program is developed; before it is conducted.
   c. Before a program is developed.
4. HRD efforts usually consist of
   a. One-shot, seminar-type approaches.
   b. A full array of courses to meet individual needs.
   c. A variety of education and training programs designed to change the organization.

5. Cost/benefit comparisons of HRD programs are
   a. Never developed.
   b. Occasionally developed.
   c. Frequently developed.
6. HRD programs without some formal method of evaluation are implemented
   a. Regularly.
   b. Seldom.
   c. Never.
7. The results of HRD programs are communicated
   a. When requested, to those who have a need to know.
   b. Occasionally, to members of management only.
   c. Routinely, to a variety of selected target audiences.
8. The HRD staff's involvement in evaluation consists of
   a. No specific responsibilities, with no formal training in evaluation methods.
   b. Part of the staff has responsibilities for evaluation, with some formal training.
   c. All members of the staff have been trained and have some responsibilities in evaluation; some are devoted full time to the effort.
9. In an economic downturn the HRD function will
   a. Be the first to have its staff reduced.
   b. Be retained at the same staffing level.
   c. Go untouched in staff reductions, and possibly be beefed up.
10. Budgeting for HRD is based on
    a. Whatever is left over.
    b. Whatever the department head can "sell."
    c. A zero-based budgeting system.
11. HRD is funded through
    a. The training department budget.
    b. The administrative budget.
    c. Line operating budgets.
12. The principal group that must justify HRD expenditures is
    a. The training department.
    b. Various staff areas, including HR and industrial relations.
    c. Line management.
13. Over the last two years, the HRD budget as a percent of operating expenses has
    a. Decreased.
    b. Remained stable.
    c. Increased.

14. The CEO interfaces with the manager responsible for HRD
    a. Never; it is a delegated responsibility.
    b. Occasionally, when someone recommends it.
    c. Frequently, to know what is going on.
15. The CEO's involvement in the implementation of HRD programs is primarily
    a. Limited to sending invitations, extending congratulations, handing out certificates, etc.
    b. Monitoring progress, opening/closing speeches, presentations on the outlook of the organization, etc.
    c. Program participation to see what's covered, conducting major segments of the program, requiring key executives to be involved, etc.
16. On the organization chart, the HRD manager
    a. Is more than two levels removed from the CEO.
    b. Is two levels below the CEO.
    c. Reports directly to the CEO.
17. Line management involvement in implementing HRD programs is
    a. Nil; only HRD specialists conduct programs.
    b. Limited to a few operating specialists conducting programs in their areas of expertise.
    c. Significant; on the average, over half of the programs are conducted by line managers.
18. When an employee completes an HRD program and returns to the job, his or her supervisor usually
    a. Makes no reference to the program.
    b. Asks questions about the program and encourages the use of the material.
    c. Requires use of the program material and gives positive rewards when the material is used successfully.
19. When an employee attends an external training program and returns to the job, he or she is required to
    a. Do nothing.
    b. Submit a report summarizing the program.
    c. Evaluate the seminar, outline plans for implementing the material covered, and estimate the benefits.
20. With the present HRD philosophy and practice, the HRD function's impact on profit
    a. Can never be assessed accurately.
    b. Can be estimated, but probably at a significant cost.
    c. Can be estimated (or is being estimated) with little cost.

Analysis of Test Scores

Score the test as follows. Allow:
1 point for each (A) response.
3 points for each (B) response.
5 points for each (C) response.

The total is in the range of 20–100 points.

The score can reveal much about HRD in an organization, and, in particular, the attitude toward evaluation and measurement. A perfect score of 100, which is probably unachievable, represents utopia and is the ultimate goal of many HRD departments. Conversely, a score of 20 reveals an ineffective organization, with inappropriate methods, that probably will not exist for very long. The instrument has been administered to several thousand HRD managers who were primarily responsible for the HRD function. The average score has been 53, with a standard deviation of 9. A score can be best analyzed by examining four ranges:

Score Range	Analysis of Score
81–100	This organization represents results-based education and training in action. There is little room for improvement, and no additional concentrated efforts to improve evaluation of the HRD function are needed. HRD departments with this rating are leaders in the important field of evaluation, and are setting examples for others. An organization with this attitude toward HRD and evaluation is likely to be extremely effective.
61–80	This organization is probably better than average in HRD evaluation. There is room for improvement, but efforts appear to be headed in the right direction. Several methods and strategies appear to be appropriate. Although there is some attention to obtaining results from programs, additional emphasis is needed to make the department more effective in the future.
41–60	Ths organization needs improvement. The attitude about, and approach to, HRD and evaluation are less than desirable. Most methods are ineffective. Emphasis needs to be placed on securing the appropriate management involvement in changing the philosophy of the organization.
20–40	This organization shows little or no concern for measuring results of the HRD function. The department is very ineffective and needs improvement if it is to survive. Urgent attention is needed from top management to change the approach and status of the HRD function.

This score analysis is simplistic and may not be exact, but the point is obvious. Achieving results from HRD is more than just evaluating a single program. It is a philosophy that involves the active participation of many, with attention to evaluation at several stages in the process. The remainder of this book is devoted to practically every area covered on this instrument.

The rationale for selecting what is considered the best response will become obvious in the chapters ahead.

Discussion Questions

---

1. How realistic are the myths presented in this chapter? Please elaborate.
2. Cite specific examples of the myths in action (i.e., situations when the myths inhibited a comprehensive evaluation process).
3. Review these myths with your organization's HRD staff, or one with which you are familiar. Discuss the level of attachment to these myths.
4. Which myths cause the greatest number of problems in the evaluation process? Why?
5. Why are HRD practitioners reluctant to change their approaches to evaluation?
6. Why is there more talk than action when examining the success of the evaluation process?
7. Is there really a need to have monetary results from the evaluation processes? Please explain.
8. Should the government agency and a large manufacturing company approach evaluation in the same way?
9. What is considered an adequate score on the results-based status check?
10. Compare the test scores in your organization (or one with which you are familiar) to other organizations. Explain the differences.
11. In what ways can the results-based status instrument be used in an organization?
12. What is the greatest obstacle that keeps organizations from evaluating HRD programs?

References

---

1. Geber, B. "Does Training Make a Difference? Prove It!" *Training,* March 1995, pp. 27–34.
2. Lewis, T. "A Model for Thinking About the Evaluation of Training," *Performance Improvement Quarterly,* Vol. 9, No. 1, 1996, pp. 3–22.
3. Geber, B. "A Clean Break for Education at IBM," *Training,* February 1994, pp. 33–36.
4. O'Connor, P. J. "Getting Down to Basics," *Training & Development,* July 1993, pp. 62–64.
5. Henkoff, R. "Companies that Train Best," *Fortune,* March 22, 1993, pp. 62–75.

6. Solomon, C. M. "What an Idea: Creativity Training," *Personnel Journal,* May 1990, p. 68.

7. Industry Report, *Training,* 33(10), 1996, pp. 36–79.

8. Shelton, S. and Alliger, G. "Who's Afraid of Level 4 Evaluation? A Practical Approach," *Training & Development,* June 1993, pp. 43–46.

9. Carlisle, K. E. and Henrie, D. "Are You Doing High-Impact HR?" *Training & Development,* August 1993, pp. 47–53.

10. Berry, J. K. "Linking Management Development to Business Strategies," *Training and Development,* August 1990, pp. 20–21.

The Trend Toward Measurement

Now for the good news. There is an important and steady trend in the HRD field: a move toward more relevant programs whose impact and results are monitored, evaluated, and reported. The entire human resources management function is responding to demands to measure its impact, and training and development appear to be taking the lead. This is probably one of the most difficult and challenging changes occurring in this profession, and there is growing evidence of this trend in every direction. Some HRD professionals, already aware of this trend, may find Chapter 2 elementary and wish to proceed to Chapter 3.

Top Management Interest

Chief executives' requirement that HRD programs show evidence of their effectiveness indicates a new and persistent trend toward measurement. A few years ago, it was difficult to find comments from chief executives on whether results should be achieved from the HRD function. This new trend is significant because the view from the top determines to what extent the HRD department will evaluate its efforts. When a CEO expects results and communicates that expectation, the HRD department will usually produce those results. This action can have a tremendous impact on the organization.

Top management's interest in HRD evaluation is reflected in the publications targeting that group. For example, the *William and Mary Business Review* publishes a special edition for top executives each summer. The editors select a topic they consider critical. Reengineering was the topic in 1994, while 1995's focus was "Corporate Training, Does it Pay Off?" In this special edition, ten experts presented different perspectives on how corporate training should be measured.[1]

Significant publications in the HRD field have solicited comments from chief executives. *Training and Development* regularly features interviews with chief executives. The interviews use a standard set of questions, several of which focus on measurement and evaluation. Although many of the interview responses are probably prepared in part by HRD professionals, the process serves the purpose of defining and clarifying what the CEO expects from the HRD function. CEO responses are important and affect other executives. *Training* magazine features many articles of interest to top management, as well as interviews with chief executives who have demonstrated strong support for and involvement with the HRD function. Many stories detail explanations from chief executives as to how HRD is evaluated in their organizations. These independent efforts by two leading publications in the HRD field have been instrumental in helping chief executives become more familiar with the importance of the HRD process. Other HR and HRD publications regularly report CEO viewpoints about training results.

Just what did these chief executives say about evaluating training? An analysis shows that responses vary from vague and noncommittal to strong, specific statements. For instance, one CEO offered this comment, "While we can't measure the absolute results of training programs, our record as an organization indicates we're doing something right."[2] The message is unclear— except that training seems to be difficult to measure at this company. This comment also gives the HRD department little incentive to attempt evaluation. Fortunately, it was not representative of all the comments. Most were more specific and supportive, such as "you can demonstrate the dollar value of training without spending all of your time on elaborate evaluations."[3]

These examples are only two of hundreds of statements about measurement and evaluation of HRD from the profession's largest organizations. Public comments illustrate a definite trend to encourage—and demand— measurable results from HRD programs.[4]

Perhaps the CEO viewpoint is best described in an editorial by the CEO of the American Management Association, a large organization whose members are primarily CEOs of major firms all over the world. The editorial, titled "Making Training Quantifiable," ended with this paragraph:

> In the final analysis, however, the only measurements that may matter are those that relate to organizational performance—growth, profit, market share, etc. We may, in fact, be watching the macros results of these investments right now. Throughout AMA's 70-plus-year history, we have seen training budgets slashed in each recession except the most recent one. This time around, U.S. companies did more than just pay lip

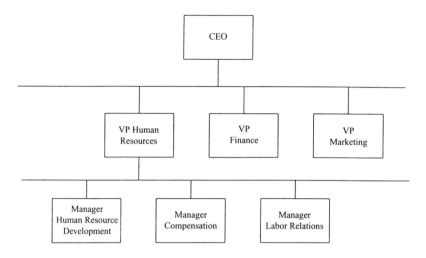

Figure 2-1. A typical HRD organization.

service to the value of training as they sustained investments in education. Perhaps the gathering strength of the economy can be attributed to the wisdom of that decision.[5]

The HRM Perspective

The HRD function may fit into an organization in one of several different ways. Figure 2-1 illustrates a common approach for medium-to-large organizations. The HRD manager reports to a vice-president of human resources, who usually reports to the chief executive. The human resource management (HRM) perspective is important to the results-based approach, not only because of the reporting relationship, but also because of concerns about the overall HRM function's contribution. In recent years there has been much concern about, and criticism of, the lack of accountability of overall HR. A very critical article in *Fortune* magazine brought the issue clearly into focus when it suggested, among other things, that the HRM function should be abolished because of its inefficiency, lack of direction, and overall lack of accountability.[6] The interesting point about this assessment is that it was misguided. Professional organizations such as the Society for Human Resource Management and the International Personnel Management Association quickly responded with information and statistics to show how the HR function contributes to organizational performance. In addition, major publications such as *Personnel Journal, HRMagazine,* and *Public Personnel Management* responded with additional evidence of this important trend. Several major works have carefully documented the progress made in measuring HR.[7, 8]

It is increasingly common to find a vice-president of human resources with a background in training and development. In years past, in a traditional unionized setting, the vice-president of industrial relations or personnel, as it was called, historically had progressed through the labor relations field. Because labor relations were regarded as crucial to the organization, it was assumed that any manager responsible for the entire HRM function had to have a strong background in that area. In a non-union setting, the HR manager would typically be a generalist, with exposure to all functions in a smaller environment, or a specialist in employment or employee relations. Rarely did you see a training director fill this top personnel job.

HR managers who were formerly training managers will require measurement and evaluation from their current HRD managers if they believe evaluation is an integral part of the HRD function. One HR manager, who was formerly a training manager, characterized it this way:

> I now require the training and development department to submit plans for evaluation along with their plans for conducting a program. I send the proposal to our chief executive. This process is followed without exception. It continues to position the training and development department as a successful, contributing unit in the organization.

Also, the HRD department is sometimes regarded as one of the most dispensable functions of HRM. Without adequate measurement of results, the justification for a formal training and development department is difficult. Compensation and benefits administration are necessary to provide employee payroll and benefits. Labor relations support is required for a unionized facility. Recruitment is essential when new employees are needed. But training may be considered unnecessary as a formal activity, because it could occur directly on the job under management's direction. In the past, without evaluation, training and development departments grew and diminished along with good and bad economic times. Now, HR vice-presidents are demanding HRD evaluation to keep the current staff intact during restructuring and downsizing.

While the most common arrangement for the HRD reporting relationship was depicted earlier, an increasingly common arrangement places the individual responsible for HRD on the same level as the human resources manager. For example, many of the more than 1,000 corporate universities established in recent years do not report to human resources, but report directly to an operating executive and sometimes to the chief executive officer.[9] Some experts argue that HRD should be separated from the traditional HRM, because HRD focuses on change and improvement, whereas other HR functions do not have this responsibility. Compensation and benefits, labor relations, EEO, and recruiting are not designed to produce major change.

This reporting arrangement enhances the overall influence of the HRD department and increases the prospect for accountability. As a general rule, the higher the reporting level of a function in an organization, the greater the expectations from the function. As a result, top executives have clearly defined accountability measures for HRD, along with similar expectations from the human resources function.[10]

Growth and Status of the HRD Function

In some organizations, the status of the training and development function has been enhanced enough in recent years that it has become an integral part of their competitive strategies. Some organizations have credited training the workforce as a major ingredient in achieving organizational objectives and overall success.[11] Training and development are regularly included in organizational goals and strategies. Because visibility demands accountability, the same organizations have stepped up their measurement and evaluation processes to measure the success of this critical function.[12]

The growth of training and development has also contributed to accountability. In organizations in almost every major country, budgets for formal training and development continue to grow. In the U.S.A. alone, each year sees a significant growth in the overall function.

One of the most significant jumps in formal training and development budgets occurred in 1996, with a 16% increase reflected in a major magainze's annual industry report.[13] As budgets continue to grow, so does the concern for accountability. Larger budgets mean increased attention and accountability, along with a necessity to show a contribution to the organization. Budgets' growth should cause many organizations to step up to the challenge and measure the success of the training function.

The training and development function has played a significant role in the implementation of major change programs such as total quality management, reengineering, and continuous process improvement. The training and development function has been an integral part of the process, serving initially in a support role and eventually, in some organizations, as a driver of the change. Since measurement and evaluation is an important part of these change efforts, the HRD function has been required to measure its own effort as its function was reengineered and improved with new processes. The training and development department had to take its own advice and explore ways to measure its impact and show its contribution to prevent being radically restructured or downsized in the organization.[14]

Professional Exposure

In the past it was difficult to find an article, or even references, on the evaluation process. Today, articles on evaluation appear in almost every issue of *Training and Development, Training, Technical and Skills Training, PI* (Performance Improvement), *Human Resource Development Quarterly,* and *Performance Improvement Quarterly.* These publications regularly feature evaluation as one of their key areas of coverage. The programs described in these publications contain information on how they were evaluated and, in many cases, the actual results are included. One publication, *Evaluation: The International Journal of Theory, Research, and Practice,* is devoted exclusively to this topic. *HRMagazine,* the magazine of the Society for Human Resource Management, *Personnel Journal, Public Personnel, Personnel Psychology,* and *Human Resource Management* frequently contain HRD evaluation articles.

Training and development organizations and associations support the trend toward evaluation by offering insight into evaluation processes at their own professional meetings. Measurement and evaluation has become a common topic in meetings of the American Society for Training and Development and the International Society for Performance Improvement. Also, the American Society for Healthcare Education and Training, the Society for Human Resource Management, and the American Management Association are increasing the scope and depth of sessions devoted to training and development evaluations. Some annual conferences have been created around evaluation themes such as the Annual Assessment, Measurement, and Evaluation Conference sponsored by Linkage, Inc. Video conferences, seminars, and short courses on evaluation are also available. One of the most successful seminars, organized by the International Quality and Productivity Center, is a program on "Performance Measurements for Training." College-level courses on measurement and evaluation are now required for HRD degrees. This handbook has been adopted for use in several college and university courses on evaluation.

The interest in evaluation has increased to the point that professional organizations have been developed to focus directly on the issue. The American Evaluation Association was created for persons across a variety of disciplines interested in evaluation, with a primary focus on the social sciences. Recently, a new organization was developed specifically for human resource development professionals interested in measuring the return on investment in training. The HRD-ROI Network is a group of HRD managers and specialists who are pursuing a comprehensive measurement and evaluation process in their organizations, including measuring the actual return on investment.[15]

Competencies for HRD Staff

The American Society for Training and Development (ASTD) has analyzed the roles of HRD practitioners, including competencies needed for success on the job. After two years of research, ASTD published the models for practice that focus on these important issues.[16] As part of this study, ASTD identified eleven key roles of HRD personnel. One of these roles is the evaluator. In this role, the evaluator identifies the impact of an intervention on individual or organizational effectiveness. The output from this role are evaluation designs and plans, instruments, findings, processes, feedback, and conclusions and recommendations.

The study identified HRD competencies in four areas: technical, business, interpersonal, and intellectual. Some of these are closely related to measurement and evaluation. Among the technical competencies are

☐ **Objective preparation skills:** preparing clear statements that describe desired output.

☐ **Performance observation skills:** tracking and describing behaviors and their effects.

☐ **Research skills:** selecting, developing, and using methodologies such as statistical and data-collection techniques for formal inquiry.

Among the business competencies are

☐ **Cost/benefit analysis skills:** assessing alternatives in terms of their financial, psychological, and strategic advantages and disadvantages.

☐ **Record management skills:** storing data in an easily retrievable form.

Among the interpersonal competencies are

☐ **Feedback skills:** communicating information, opinions, observations, and conclusions so that they are understood and can be acted upon.

☐ **Questioning skills:** gathering information from and stimulating insight in individuals and groups through the use of interviews, questionnaires, and other probing methods.

Among the intellectual competencies are

☐ **Data reduction skills:** scanning, synthesizing and drawing conclusions from data.

☐ **Model building skills:** conceptualizing and developing theoretical or practical frameworks that describe complex ideas in understandable, usable ways.

☐ **Observing skills:** recognizing objectively what is happening in or across situations.

These competencies and the role of an evaluator clearly place measurement and evaluation as a key part of an HRD specialist's job.

In 1996, ASTD updated their model to include the paradigm shift to performance improvement. In the new model for human performance improvement, four roles were identified including analyst, intervention specialist, change manager, and evaluator.[17] The evaluator role contains six competencies:

1. Performance gap evaluation skills
2. The ability to evaluate results against organizational goals
3. Standard-setting skills
4. The ability to assess impact on culture
5. Human performance improvement intervention reviewing skills
6. Feedback skills

This new model not only updates the roles and competencies previously published, but also reflects the shifting focus of the HRD focus to human performance improvement.

Some competencies have been developed around the more narrowly focused process of measuring the contribution of HRD. One organization has developed ten specific skill sets illustrating the competencies necessary to develop and implement the ROI process in an organization. These skills are

1. Planning for ROI calculations
2. Collecting evaluation data
3. Isolating the effects of the program
4. Converting data to monetary values
5. Monitoring program costs
6. Analyzing data including calculating the ROI
7. Presenting evaluation data
8. Implementing the ROI process
9. Providing internal consulting on ROI
10. Teaching others the ROI process

These skill sets were developed with the input of dozens of HRD managers and specialists working on this important aspect of evaluation.[18] The skill sets are actually used in a certification process in which individuals develop and demonstrate competencies for each of the ten areas. Demonstrations occur during a one-week workshop in which exercises and cases are analyzed and discussed. In addition, on-the-job projects and action plans provide the final evidence of success with the competencies.

Successful experience in evaluation is becoming more important in an HRD professional's list of credentials. One human resource vice-president responsible for hiring an HRD manager in his organization put it this way:

> I would virtually disregard any resume for our HRD manager position that did not address the issue of evaluation. I would like to know what the candidate has accomplished and what was done to evaluate the most significant programs.

It is not unusual to see an ad for a training manager that refers to evaluation. An informal analysis of newspaper help-wanted ads for training/HRD positions revealed that approximately 60% mentioned the word "evaluation" either in the skills and experience required, or in the duties and responsibilities of the position.

HRD professionals must be prepared to discuss experiences in evaluation. Job requirements for future HRD positions will likely require more experience in evaluation because of the trend toward accountability. Any individual seeking opportunities in this field would be wise to include references to either knowledge, skill, or experience in the evaluation process. Even if it is not required for the job, this experience will impress executives recruiting HRD professionals.

Also, job descriptions of many HRD specialists, coordinators, instructors, and other positions now include evaluation duties as part of their key responsibilities. Figure 2-2 is a job description for a training advisor who designs, develops, conducts, and evaluates the HRD process. Several key responsibilities are in the area of evaluation.

HRD Structure and Practice Within the Organization

In many organizations, particularly larger ones, the HRD function is structured with a department or unit devoted to evaluation, providing additional evidence of the trend toward measurement. As Figure 2-3 shows, sometimes evaluation and research are performed by the same group.

Figure 2-4 shows the functions and responsibilities of a research and evaluation section.

More company policy statements on HRD contain references to training evaluation. Aetna Life and Casualty's statement contains one example:

> Training evaluation and monitoring go beyond simple evaluation of a course or instructor. From the beginning, both the trainer and the client

Job Description

Job Title: Training Advisor.

Summary: Plan, develop, conduct, and evaluate training and education programs for all functions and business units in the company.

Work Performed:

1. Determine training needs in various functional areas of the company and develop appropriate learning, application, and business impact objectives for programs.
2. Plan and develop training and education programs, on-the-job training, and special seminars as required for employees.
3. Prepare or procure training materials, visual aids, software, and other support materials needed to implement training and education programs.
4. Develop program content, determine methodology, develop schedules, and select media for the effective implementation of training and education programs.
5. Plan and develop methods, techniques, and criteria for evaluating the effectiveness of training and education programs.
6. Collaborate with program participants, supervisors, and other appropriate staff members to assist in the evaluation of the impact of training and education programs.
7. Identify and select additional sources of support for training and education, such as external vendors, adjunct facilitators, and consultants.
8. Counsel employees on training needs and career development plans.

Figure 2-2. Job description for a training advisor.

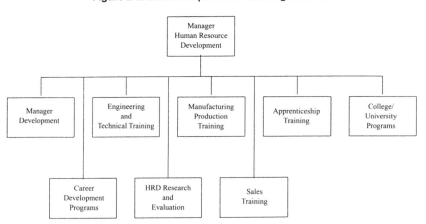

Figure 2-3. Organization chart for an HRD Department.

Functions and Responsibilities

Human Resource Development Research and Evaluation

Reports To: Manager, Human Resource Development.

Summary: In collaboration with all sections within the HRD department, provide basic research, needs assessment, and evaluation assistance for all current and proposed HRD programs. In an advisory capacity, make recommendations as to specific methods, techniques, and strategies for needs assessment and program evaluation. Provide necessary assistance to initiate and complete needs assessment and evaluation projects.

Specific Responsibilities:

1. Explore, investigate, and keep abreast of new HRD innovations and techniques.
2. Establish HRD standards, policy, needs assessment guidelines, and measurement and evaluation guidelines.
3. Provide research and analysis to develop and implement HRD programs.
4. Conduct needs assessments to determine overall direction of new HRD programs.
5. Develop and implement systems for collecting data for needs assessment and evaluation.
6. Design and develop instruments used in needs assessment and evaluation.
7. Plan evaluation strategy for specific programs.
8. Assist HRD staff in preparing and presenting proposals for new projects.
9. Develop systems for estimating, monitoring, and reporting HRD program costs.
10. Assist HRD staff in testing programs on a pilot basis to make adjustments and evaluate their results.
11. Analyze and interpret evaluation data, and report conclusions to appropriate target audience.
12. Recommend program adjustments based on evaluation data.
13. As requested, calculate cost/benefit ratios, returns on investment, and other measures of economic justification for HRD programs.
14. Develop guidelines for communicating HRD needs assessment and program results to appropriate decision managers.
15. Keep abreast of the latest software designed for research and analysis applications.

Figure 2-4. Functions and responsibilities of a research and evaluation section.

must ask "How will we know if we made a difference?" There is no shortage of methods and techniques for evaluating training, but what is missing too often is the evaluation mindset. Evaluation is not merely a last step to the training process but a continual concern of the trainer.[19]

Some policy statements are very stern and explicit. Consider the policy NCR, a former unit of AT&T,[20] adopted:

One sunny morning back in the 1890s, John H. Patterson, founder of National Cash Register Corp., decided to fire one of his executives. The unlucky exec arrived at work that day to find his desk and chair out on the front lawn, set ablaze. It was a business decision.

Today, 100 years later, if you want to conduct training at NCR, you've got two options: 1) make sure the training represents a good business decision, or 2) expect to receive a similar incendiary reception.

Finally, some organizations have developed standard procedures for conducting evaluations. Appendix 2 presents a condensed table of contents of detailed procedures for measurement and evaluation at a large global company.

More Evidence of Progress

Surveys and Case Studies

Surveys are routinely conducted with HRD professionals to determine the status of the profession. Although the surveys vary with the purpose and type of questions, many of them gather information on the status of evaluation because of the subject's popularity. As discussed in the previous chapter, a survey a few years ago would reveal almost no effort at evaluation and would contain almost no references to evaluation success stories. Lip service was the order of the day. Recent surveys have shown a significant increase in evaluation activity.[21]

There is a consensus among HRD professionals that when times get tough in an organization, the training staff is first to be cut. It is assumed that cuts are taken because there is no clear-cut connection between training efforts and bottom-line results. Now, there is evidence to suggest that the trend does not exist to the extent that it did previously.[22]

Government and Non-Profit Applications

Another significant piece of evidence about trends in evaluation involves recent efforts of governmental organizations. The federal government has been creative and diligent in its evaluation efforts, despite facing persistent budget reductions. Under the auspices of the Office of Personnel Management, several research and development efforts have been undertaken to assist various government agencies to develop procedures and models for evaluating their training programs. This provided a systematic approach for formulating and implementing an overall evaluation plan.

At state and local levels, the evaluation of training and development programs has increased dramatically. Driven by cost-cutting measures, competition for scarce resources, and elected officials' promises to be more efficient with governmental resources, training and development functions are increasingly measuring the contribution of the training programs. An example illustrates the increased pressures facing these organizations. The management controls of a large state agency were audited by the state. The auditors examined the training and development function, among others, paying particular attention to its efficiency and effectiveness. The following comments are taken from the auditor's report:

"Although the agency has expressed its intention of having a well-trained staff, management of the training function is fragmented and incomplete:

☐ The training function was reorganized at least four times in the last two years.
☐ A comprehensive training plan does not exist.
☐ The last comprehensive training needs assessment was done in November 1992.
☐ Actual training costs, both direct and indirect, are not routinely collected or analyzed.
☐ Although participant evaluations are collected, no further system exists for assessing if the knowledge gained is actually used or if the training is effective.
☐ A system for tracking training agency-wide is still being implemented.

As a result of these problems, the agency cannot provide assurance that:

☐ Training benefits exceed costs.
☐ The training provided is effective, efficient, or properly used to enhance agency management, administration, and operations.
☐ Training most appropriate to employee needs is available."

Vendors and Suppliers

Finally, additional evidence of the trend toward measurement appears in programs available from suppliers and vendors. The marketing strategy, at least of the more innovative firms, is to show tangible results achieved from the application of their programs. Many ads now show how the program was evaluated and what results were achieved. An excerpt from a recent ad from Development Dimensions International:

> Since the Reynolds Metals Bellwood Reclamation Plan put a team in place to improve total quality, plant output has gone up by 30% and cycle time has gone down by 94%. Profit sharing and morale are up. Grievances and waste product are down. And that has everyone—union and nonunion—smiling.
>
> Industrial engineer Jim Adee says, 'Not long ago we were considered marginally productive and being challenged by new competitors in the worldwide aluminum market. We knew we had to make some major changes—and involve everyone. We initiated a culture change effort and implemented TQM, which led us to teams and, as our HR consultant, DDI.'[23]

This trend toward more responsible evaluation by program developers is in response to the hard questions HRD professionals have been asking in recent years. Potential purchasers want to know what results have been achieved and how they were developed. Effective sales representatives must provide specific answers and not vague, general responses to evaluation questions. There was a time when testimonials and an impressive client list were convincing enough that the program was successful. This is no longer the case. Programs have failed in the most prestigious companies. Furthermore, just because a program works in one organization does not mean that it will work in another. Many suppliers of training programs are now developing ROI studies of their products to validate the success of their programs. Among these suppliers are Development Dimensions International, Zenger-Miller, Blanchard Training & Development, Covey Leadership Center, Dale Carnegie Training, and Huthewaite.

Summary

This chapter presented the good news. There is growing evidence of more evaluation in every aspect of the HRD field, from those directly involved in the process to those working on the sidelines. It is a trend that should continue in the future. Chapter 3 explores ways in which an organization can develop and practice a results-based HRD philosophy.

Discussion Questions

1. Have you noticed a trend toward measurement and evaluation in the HRD field? If so, please cite specific examples. What developments have occurred in your organization (or one with which you are familiar)?
2. Why is it important for a CEO to communicate expectations for the HRD function—both privately and publicly?
3. How does the reporting relationship affect the accountability of the HRD function?
4. Do the requirements for HRD jobs in your organization (or one with which you are familiar) contain specific statements about measurement and evaluation? Please explain.
5. Discuss the relationship between the models for HRD practice and evaluation.
6. Although more want-ads for training positions require evaluation experience, some still do not. Why?
7. Most organizations measure participant reaction to training programs, yet few measure the actual results. Why?
8. Why are training suppliers more responsive to requests for measurable results from their programs?

References

1. Phillips, J. J. "Measuring Training's ROI: It Can Be Done." *William and Mary Business Review,* Summer 1995, pp. 6–10.
2. Barron, T. "A New Wave in Training Funding," *Training and Development,* August 1996, pp. 28–33.
3. Noonan, J. V. "How to Escape Corporate America's Basement," *Training,* December 1993, pp. 39–42.
4. Thornburg, L. "Training in a Changing World," *HRMagazine,* August 1992, pp. 44–47.
5. Fagiano, D. "Making Training Quantifiable," *Management Review,* April 1994, p. 4.
6. Stewart, T. A. "Taking on the Last Bureaucracy," *Fortune,* January 15, 1996, pp. 105–106.
7. Fitz-enz, J. *How to Measure Human Resources Management,* 2nd Edition. New York, NY: McGraw-Hill, Inc., 1995.

8. Phillips, J. J. *Accountability in Human Resource Management.* Houston, TX: Gulf Publishing, 1996.
9. Downs, A. "Mervyn's U to the Rescue," *Training & Development,* June 1995, pp. 59–62.
10. Dixon, N. M. "New Routes to Evaluation," *Training & Development,* May 1996, pp. 82–85.
11. King, J. P. "Union Pacific Gets Back on Track with Customers," *Training & Development,* August 1993, pp. 30–40.
12. Chaddock, P. "Building Value with Training," *Training & Development,* July 1995, pp. 22–26.
13. Industry Report, *Training,* 33(10), 1996, pp. 36–79.
14. Biech, E. *TQM for Training.* New York, NY: McGraw-Hill, Inc., 1994.
15. HRD-ROI Network, P.O. Box 380637, Birmingham, AL 35238-0637.
16. McLagan, P. A. "Models for HRD Practice," *Training and Development,* September 1989, pp. 54–57.
17. Rothwell, W. J. *ASTD Models for Human Performance Improvement.* Alexandria, VA: American Society for Training and Development, 1996.
18. Performance Resources Organization, P.O. Box 380637, Birmingham, AL 35238-0637.
19. Craig, R. L. *The ASTD Training & Development Handbook,* New York, NY: McGraw-Hill, 1996.
20. Filipczak, B. "The Business of Training at NCR," *Training,* February 1992, pp. 55–59.
21. Lyau, N. M. and Pucel, D. J. "Economic Return on Training Investment at the Organization Level," *Performance Improvement Quarterly,* 8(3), 1995, pp. 68–79.
22. Fagiano, D. "Making Training Quantifiable," *Management Review,* April 1994, p. 4.
23. Development Dimensions International ad. This ad appeared on the back cover of the January 1997 issue of *Training and Development.*

CHAPTER 3

Developing a Results-Based Approach

What Is Results-Based HRD?

Results-based HRD is a term that will be used throughout this book. What does it mean? It represents a philosophy and practice that emphasize results, and is characterized in the following ways:

HRD programs are not usually undertaken unless tangible results can be measured. If the impact of the program cannot be measured, then perhaps the program should not be implemented. HRD programs that represent a significant effort or cost should begin with the end in mind. While there are many reasons for proceeding with a planned program, a results-based philosophy may cause a review of the process and possibly the creation of additional evaluation approaches if the potential impact cannot be identified.

The program design includes at least one method of evaluation. The evaluation strategy is usually determined when program objectives are established. With the results-based HRD philosophy, evaluation strategy is placed on a level of equal importance with the program's content, objectives, delivery system, and coordination.

Each HRD staff member should have some responsibility for evaluation. The HRD staff must see the importance of evaluation and the necessity of including the process as an integral part of the HRD cycle. If possible, each staff member should participate directly in some phase of the evaluation process.

Management is involved in all phases of the HRD process. From inception through evaluation and follow-up, management's active involvement is critical to the success of any program. This active participation will enhance the success of the HRD program, and facilitate the communication of results to the management group.

A proactive effort is under way to increase management commitment and support of the HRD effort. Management support is critical for the allocation of resources to the HRD department. Obtaining results and properly communicating them to managers will increase support, which will in turn enhance programs' results. It is a continuous cycle, and a very important part of a results-based HRD philosophy.

A comprehensive measurement and evaluation plan is in place. A key to obtaining consistent success with training and development programs is to have a systematic approach to measurement and evaluation. This often involves setting targets, goals, and objectives for the implementation of the process, and deciding how and at what level each new program will be evaluated.

The participants understand their role to achieve results. Too often participants are unsure of expectations from management, facilitators, and program designers as to what business measures they should derive from the program. Under the results-based approach, participants have a clear understanding of their expectations, communicated at a variety of critical points in the process.

Programs are connected to strategic initiatives. Each program should be related to major strategic goals, objectives, and initiatives. In a direct or supporting role, each program should enhance the contribution of training and development to the organization's strategic direction and effectiveness.

Purposes and Uses of Evaluation

Evaluation is a systematic process to determine the worth, value, or meaning of an activity or process. In a broad sense, evaluation is undertaken to improve HRD processes, or to decide the future of a program. These broad purposes can be divided into ten evaluation purposes, identified and described below:

To determine success in accomplishing program objectives. Every HRD program should state objectives in a generally accepted format (i.e., measurable, specific, challenging, etc.). Evaluation provides input to determine if objectives are being (or have been) met.

To identify the strengths and weaknesses in the HRD process. Probably the most common purpose of evaluation is to determine the effectiveness of an HRD program's various elements and activities. Program components include, but are not limited to, methods of presentation, learning environment, program content, learning aids, schedule, and the facilitator. Each component makes a difference in the HRD effort and must be evaluated to make improvements in the program.

To compare the costs to the benefits of an HRD program. With today's business focus on the bottom line, determining a program's cost-effectiveness is crucial. This evaluation compares the cost of a program to its usefulness or value, measured in monetary benefits. The return on investment is the most common measure. This evaluation measure provides management with information needed to eliminate an unproductive program, increase support for programs which yield a high payoff, or to make adjustments in a program to increase benefits.

To decide who should participate in future programs. Sometimes evaluation provides information to help prospective participants decide if they should be involved in the program. This type of evaluation explores the application of the program to determine success and barriers to implementation. Communicating this information to other potential participants helps decide participation.

To test the clarity and validity of tests, cases, and exercises. Evaluation sometimes provides a testing and validating instrument. Interactive activities, case studies, and tests used in the learning process must be relevant. They must measure the skills, knowledge, and abilities the program is designed to teach.

To identify which participants were the most successful with the program. An evaluation may identify which participants excelled or failed at learning and implementing skills or knowledge from the program. This information can be helpful to determine if an individual should be promoted, transferred, moved up the career ladder, or given additional assignments. This type of evaluation yields information on the individual, in addition to the effectiveness of the HRD program.

To reinforce major points made to the participant. A follow-up evaluation can reinforce the information covered in a program by attempting to measure the participants' results. The evaluation process reminds participants what they should have applied on the job and the subsequent results that should be realized. This follow-up evaluation serves to reinforce to participants the actions they should be taking.

To gather data to assist in marketing future programs. In many situations, HRD departments are interested in knowing why participants attend a specific program, particularly if many programs are offered. An evaluation can provide information to develop the marketing strategy for future programs by determining why participants attended the program, who made the decision to attend, how participants found out about the program, and if participants would recommend it to others.

To determine if the program was the appropriate solution for the specific need. Sometimes evaluation can determine if the original problem needed a training solution. Too often, a training program is conducted to correct problems that cannot be corrected by training. There may be other reasons for performance deficiencies such as procedures, work flow, or the quality of supervision. An evaluation may yield insight into whether or not the training program was necessary, and possibly even point management toward the source of the problem.

To establish a database that can assist management in making decisions. The central theme in many evaluations is to make a decision about the future of an HRD program. This information can be used by those in positions of responsibility, including instructors, HRD staff members, managers (who approve programs), and executives (who allocate resources for future training and development). A comprehensive evaluation system can build a database to help make these decisions.

Levels of Evaluation

The question of what to evaluate is crucial to evaluation strategy. The answer depends on the type of HRD program, the organization, and the purposes of evaluation. The information collected and used for evaluation can usually be grouped into different categories or levels. For a given category, or level, some methods of evaluation are more appropriate than others. The types of groupings vary slightly with the different experts in the HRD field. The following section presents five models. The specific evaluation techniques mentioned here will be discussed later.

The Kirkpatrick Four-Level Approach

Probably the most well-known framework for classifying areas of evaluation,[1] developed by Kirkpatrick, contains four levels of evaluation. This conceptual framework assists in determining the types of data to collect and answers four very important questions, as shown in Table 3-1.

Reaction is defined as what the participants thought of the program, including materials, instructors, facilities, methodology, content, etc. Participant reaction is sometimes a critical factor in redesigning or continuing HRD programs. Responses on reaction questionnaires help ensure against decisions based on the comments of a few very satisfied or disgruntled participants.

Table 3-1
Kirkpatrick's Four Levels of Evaluation

Level	Questions
1. Reaction	Were the participants pleased with the program?
2. Learning	What did the participants learn in the program?
3. Behavior	Did the participants change their behavior based on what was learned?
4. Results	Did the change in behavior positively affect the organization?

Learning evaluation is concerned with measuring the extent to which principles, facts, techniques, and skills have been acquired. There are many different measures of learning, including paper-and-pencil tests, skill practices, and job simulations.

Behavioral change is measured to determine the extent to which skills and knowledge learned in the program have translated into improved behavior on the job. Evaluations in this category may include before-and-after comparisons of observations from the participant's superiors, subordinates, and peers, and self-assessments.

Evaluation of results involves monitoring organizational improvement such as cost savings, work output changes, and quality changes.

Kaufman's Five Levels of Evaluation

Some researchers, recognizing some shortcomings of Kirkpatrick's four-level approach, have attempted to modify and add to this basic framework. Kaufman offers one such presentation.[2] As shown in Table 3-2, Kaufman has expanded the definition of Level 1 and added a fifth level addressing societal issues. At Level 1, the factor of the concept of enabling addresses the availability of various resource inputs necessary for a successful intervention. At Level 5 is the evaluation of societal and client responsiveness, and consequences in payoff. This moves evaluation beyond the organization, and examines the extent to which the performance improvement program has enhanced society and the environment surrounding the organization.

Table 3-2
Five Levels for Evaluation of Interventions for Human Performance
Improvement

Level	Evaluation	Focus
5	Societal outcomes	Societal and client responsiveness, consequences and payoffs.
4	Organizational output	Organizational contributions and payoffs.
3	Application	Individual and small group (products) utilization within the organization.
2	Acquisition	Individual and small group mastery and competency.
1b	Reaction	Methods', means', and processes' acceptability and efficiency.
1a	Enabling	Availability and quality of human, financial, and physical resources input.

The CIRO Approach

Another four-level approach, originally developed by Warr, Bird, and Rackham, is a rather unique way to classify evaluation processes. Originally used in Europe, this framework has a much broader scope than the traditional use of the term "evaluation" in the United States.[3]

As with other approaches, four general categories of evaluation are described, which form the letters C I R O.

1. Context evaluation
2. Input evaluation
3. Reaction evaluation
4. Outcome evaluation

Context evaluation involves obtaining and using information about the current operational situation (or context) to determine training needs and objectives. This evaluation determines if training is needed. During this process, three types of objectives may be evaluated:

1. Ultimate objectives (the particular deficiency in the organization that the program will eliminate or overcome).
2. Intermediate objectives (the changes in employees' work behavior that will be necessary for the ultimate objectives to be attained).
3. Immediate objectives (the new knowledge, skills, or attitudes that employees must acquire to change their behavior and reach the intermediate objective).

Context evaluation involves collecting information about a performance deficiency, assessing the information to establish HRD needs and, on the basis of those findings, setting objectives at three levels.

Input evaluation involves obtaining and using information about possible training resources to choose between alternative inputs to HRD. This type of evaluation involves analyzing the resources available (both internal and external) and determining how they can be deployed so that there is a maximum chance of achieving the desired objectives. Factors such as budget and management requirements may limit the options available. Thus, input evaluation refers to the process of collecting evidence and using it to decide on the HRD methods.

Reaction evaluation involves obtaining and using information about participants' reactions to improve the HRD process. The distinguishing feature of this type of evaluation is that it relies on the subjective input of the participants. Their views can prove extremely helpful when collected and used in a systematic and objective manner.

Outcome evaluation involves obtaining and using information about the results or outcomes of HRD, and is usually regarded as the most important part of evaluation. If outcome evaluation is to be successful, it requires careful preparation before the program begins. There are four stages that form outcome evaluation.

1. Defining trend objectives.
2. Selecting or constructing some measures of those objectives.
3. Making the measurements at the appropriate time.
4. Assessing the results and using them to improve later programs.

In determining the results of an HRD program, it is helpful to think in terms of a hierarchy of HRD outcomes that correspond to the three levels of objectives presented earlier: immediate, intermediate, and ultimate. A successful HRD program produces some initial change in a participant, an immediate outcome, which is reflected in changes of knowledge, skills, or attitudes. These changes can be measured during or at the end of the program.

HRD programs are not conducted primarily for the sake of learning. The main concern is to bring about positive change in the participant on the job, an intermediate outcome often referred to as a change in job performance.

If changes occur in the performance of the participants on the job, the organization will be influenced in some way. The impact on the organization is the ultimate outcome of any HRD program. For example, there may be improvements in a department's output, cost, scrap rates, accident frequencies, etc. This measurement represents one of the most difficult areas to evaluate.

CIPP Model

Another evaluation framework, similar to CIRO, is the CIPP Model, an acronym for the four basic types of evaluation in the model—context, input, process, and product. Developed by educators, the CIPP model is useful to evaluate management training and development.[4] Its developers claim it is practical, effective, efficient, comprehensive, and balanced.

Context evaluation defines the relevant environment, identifies needs and opportunities, and diagnoses specific problems. A needs analysis is a common example of context evaluation.

Input evaluation provides information to determine how resources can be best used to meet program goals. Information from input evaluation helps determine the general strategy for program planning and design, and if outside assistance is necessary. Common results of input evaluation are policies, budgets, schedules, proposals, and procedures.

Process evaluation provides feedback to the individuals responsible for implementation. It is accomplished by monitoring potential sources for failure, providing information for preplanned decisions during implementation, and describing what actually occurs. Both formal and informal approaches are used in data collection. These include reaction sheets, rating scales, and analysis of existing records.

Product evaluation measures and interprets the results of objectives, including both intended and unintended outcomes. Evaluation at this level can take place both during and after the program, and any traditional evaluation procedure may be used at this level, provided it is a good fit for the situation.

In summary, context evaluation assists in forming goals; input evaluation aids in planning programs; process evaluation guides implementation; and product evaluation helps review decisions.

The Phillips Five-Level ROI Framework

The ROI process adds a fifth level to the four levels of evaluation developed by Kirkpatrick. Table 3-3 shows the five-level framework used in this book.[5] At Level 1, Reaction and Planned Action, program participants' satisfaction is measured, along with a listing of how they plan to apply what they have learned. Almost all organizations evaluate at Level 1, usually with a generic end-of-program questionnaire. While this level of evaluation is important as a participant satisfaction measure, a favorable reaction does not ensure that participants have learned new skills or knowledge.[6] At Level 2, Learning, measurements focus on what participants learned during the program using tests, skill practices, role plays, simulations, group evaluations, and other assessment tools. A learning check is helpful to ensure that participants have absorbed the material and know how to use it. However, a posi-

Table 3-3
Five-Level ROI Framework

Level	Brief Description
1 Reaction & Planned Action	Measures participant's reaction to the program and outlines specific plans for implementation.
2 Learning	Measures skills, knowledge, or attitude changes.
3 Job Applications	Measures change in behavior on the job and specific application of the training material.
4 Business Results	Measures business impact of the program.
5 Return on Investment	Measures the monetary value of the results and costs for the program, usually expressed as a percentage.

tive measure at this level is no guarantee that the material will be used on the job. The literature is laced with studies that show the failure of learning to be transferred to the job.[7] At Level 3, Job Applications, a variety of follow-up methods are used to determine if participants apply what they learned on the job. While Level 3 evaluations such as frequency and use of skills are important to gauge the success of the program's application, it still does not guarantee that there will be a positive impact in the organization. At Level 4, Business Results, the measurement focuses on the actual results program participants achieve as they successfully apply the program material. Typical Level 4 measures include output, quality, costs, time, and customer satisfaction. Although the program may produce a measurable business impact, there is still a concern that the program may have cost too much. At Level 5, Return on Investment, the measurement goes further, comparing the monetary benefits from the program with its costs. Although the ROI can be expressed in several ways, it is usually presented as a percent or cost/benefit ratio. The evaluation cycle is not complete until the Level 5 evaluation is conducted.

While almost all HRD organizations conduct evaluations to measure satisfaction, very few actually conduct evaluations at the ROI level, perhaps because ROI evaluation is often characterized as a difficult and expensive process. Although business results and ROI are desired, it is very important to evaluate the other levels. A chain of impact should occur through the levels as the skills and knowledge learned (Level 2) are applied on the job (Level 3) to produce business results (Level 4). If measurements are not taken at each level, it is difficult to conclude that the results achieved were actually caused by the HRD program.[8] Because of this, it is recommended that evaluation be conducted at all levels when a level-five evaluation is planned. This practice is consistent with the practices of ASTD's benchmarking forum members.[9]

Which Model Is Best?

With so many frameworks for evaluation, the question becomes, "Which one is best?" There is no right answer. What is best for one organization may be inappropriate for another. The most important course of action is to select a model around which the organization will focus its evaluation. The framework developed by Kirpatrick has been the most widely used approach in organizations.[10] The five-level ROI framework, an update of Kirkpatrick's approach, is rapidly gaining acceptance. Reference will be made to the five-level framework throughout the remainder of this book.

In a comprehensive evaluation process, evaluation should occur at each of the five levels. The common thread among most evaluation models and frameworks is an emphasis on ultimate outcomes of improved group or organization performance. This is the most difficult to obtain, document, and measure. The first three levels are not enough when an ultimate evaluation is needed. Studies indicate that evaluations at the fourth level, Business Impact, and fifth level, ROI, are the most desired and receive the most support.[11]

What is needed from most evaluation processes is customer satisfaction. Two major groups of customers are served in most programs. The first group are the participants who attend, or become involved with, an HRD program. The participants, as customers, must be satisfied with the process. They must see some value of participating in the program, and some usefulness of the skills and knowledge that they can learn. Levels 1 and 2 provide information to judge the extent to which this group of customers is satisfied. Another important group is the managers. Whether they are the immediate managers, senior managers, or top executives, they are all concerned about the value of training. They want to observe behavior changes as participants apply new skills. They want their investment in training and development to yield a measurable impact on business performance measures and, more importantly, an appropriate return. The data collected at Levels 3, 4, and 5 provide the information desired by the management team, when deciding to continue or justify future HRD programs—two of the most important purposes for undertaking evaluation. Table 3-4 illustrates this process of using evaluation to satisfy customers.

Developing a Results-Based Focus

The focus on business results should be integrated throughout the HRD cycle, as is presented in the next chapter. Newly developed programs should be linked to business results. For example, a review of Motorola's catalog of training programs reveals the name of the program, the target audience, the overall goal of the program, the method of delivery, and, probably most

Table 3-4
The Evaluation Process as a Customer Satisfaction Tool

Evaluation Level		Customer Satisfaction Target
Level 1	Reaction/Planned Action	Participants
Level 2	Learning	Participants
Level 3	Job Applications	Immediate Managers
Level 4	Business Impact	Immediate Managers/Senior Managers
Level 5	ROI	Senior Managers/Top Executives

importantly, the business issue addressed.[12] Among the issues addressed in a sampling of courses are

☐ Total quality improvement
☐ Planning product marketing strategy
☐ Improving organizational productivity
☐ Ten-fold quality improvement
☐ Return on net assets
☐ Business planning

To help eliminate confusion over the outcome that can be expected from an evaluation program, this book examines ways to measure business results. The term "evaluation" will be used as an all-inclusive term and, occasionally, "measuring results" will refer to the measurement aspect of the evaluation. In some situations, these results will be converted to a monetary value to develop the return on investment.

HRD Staff Perception

Developing results-based HRD greatly depends on the proper philosophy and attitude among HRD staff and the employees. Evaluation goes beyond reaction forms, measuring output data, and presenting statistical analyses of improved performance. So many factors can affect the outcome of HRD programs that evaluation must be a part of the culture.

The HRD staff's attitude toward evaluation is an important part of this culture. It involves

☐ How they feel about measurement and evaluation. Are they threatened by it?
☐ How they plan for evaluation, implement the process, and use evaluation data.
☐ How much time they are willing to allocate to evaluation.
☐ How they feel about the relative value/priority of evaluation.

The HRD staff member who asks the question, "Do we really have to develop an evaluation plan before the program is conducted?" does not have the proper attitude for an effective evaluation. This attitude may be based on a lack of understanding, lack of information, or lack of skills. HRD staff members must be committed to the evaluation process to make it effective.

A key to the proper evaluation culture is the HRD staff's involvement. The simplest option for improving a process is to be involved and take responsibility for a part of the process.

Attitude and Performance

The link between attitude and performance is an important issue, as a positive attitude may produce more results than a negative attitude. Sometimes referred to as the Pygmalion Effect or the self-fulfilling prophecy, this phenomenon is best described as the powerful influence of one person's expectations on another person's behavior. If a manager's expectations are high, productivity is likely to be excellent. If expectations are low, productivity is likely to be sub-standard. Case studies on the self-fulfilling prophecy, prepared during the past decade for major industrial concerns, have revealed the following:[13]

☐ What a manager expects of his subordinates and the way he or she treats them largely determine their work performance and career progress.

☐ A unique characteristic of superior managers is their ability to create high performance expectations, which subordinates fulfill.

☐ Less effective managers fail to develop similar expectations and, consequently, the productivity of their subordinates suffers.

☐ Subordinates, more often than not, do what they believe they are expected to do.

An example of the Pygmalion Effect in action comes from the fast-food industry in an experimental program in Philadelphia.[14] An extremely high turnover rate has plagued the industry in an area where there is a shortage of entry-level workers. A program called Project Transition used the Pygmalion Effect to develop entry-level training programs for welfare recipients, the program's employee base. Using Pygmalion techniques, none of the 57 participants in the first year of Program Transition returned to welfare. Program designers credit Pygmalion factors such as gut reaction, work ethic, initiative, work quality, reliability, and availability as being the key to the program's success.

The relationship of this phenomenon to HRD program results should be apparent. If participants are expected to obtain results from applying knowledge and skills acquired in an HRD program, that expectation enhances the results achieved. An active effort undertaken to develop a results-based attitude among participants should improve results.

This phenomenon can be reinforced with an experiment using a control group and an experimental group. In the control group the HRD program is presented in its usual manner, with little emphasis on what is expected of participants. There is no pressure to apply what they have learned, other than the knowledge that a follow-up will be conducted to measure the program's effectiveness. In the experimental group, discussions on expectations and the achievements of previous attendees are held at periodic intervals in the program with the participants. The planned follow-up is announced in the same way, but with the addition of a statement that participants are expected to improve performance beyond what others have achieved. This expectation of exceptional results is reinforced throughout the program. If the two groups have approximately the same ability and experience, program content is the same (except for communicating desired results to the experimental group), and the work environment of the two groups is similar, the experimental group should obtain greater results.

Communicating Expectations

Discussions about program results should be routine. Participants must understand expected performance; there should be no doubt that they should apply, on the job, what they have learned. Discussions are held at the beginning, end, and at other appropriate times, depending on the type and duration of the HRD program. Some specific evaluation methods include an explanation of the requirements. This explanation, when coupled with a reminder about expected results, enhances the evaluation effort and helps to ensure that what is taught is applied on the job.

If possible, participants should be made aware of what others in previous programs accomplished. Knowing about tangible results can motivate participants to meet or exceed those results. If previous results are unavailable, discussing what can be accomplished by applying the program material can be helpful. As a matter of practice, follow-up evaluations should be discussed thoroughly with participants.

The power of discussions about expectations is illustrated in the remarks of a chief executive at the beginning of a supervisory training program:

> The participants who have preceded you have achieved excellent results by applying what they have learned from this program. In follow-up surveys, those supervisors who have utilized the safety practices, rules, and tips presented in this program have reduced, on a combined basis, the accident frequency rate from 2.2 to 1.5 over a period of 6 months after attending the training program. This represents a 32%

reduction, a significant result when you consider the average cost of an accident and the human suffering involved. Those statistics represent only the supervisors who used the material in the program. Not all did, and that's disappointing. The follow-up survey revealed that 20% did not use it. With improvements in our training program, and when considering the ability of this particular group, I am sure that you can beat both records. It can be done, and we expect you to do it.

That introduction leaves no doubt as to what is expected after completing the program. It would be difficult for anyone to ignore the material in the course.

Responsibility for Results

Achieving results from HRD programs is a multiple responsibility shared by several groups. An important part of the responsibility rests with the participants, who must understand the material, apply it on the job, and obtain the desired results.

The reinforcement (or lack of reinforcement) from a participant's supervisor (team leader) can have a significant effect on results. Studies have revealed that one of the most critical barriers to the transfer of learning to the job is supervisor support. The supervisor must show support for the HRD effort and make a commitment to help achieve the expected results. Positive supervisor reinforcement is a key part of results-based HRD, and will be discussed in more detail in a later chapter.

Discussion leaders have an important role in achieving results. They must conduct programs effectively so that the content is understood and relevant. Program designers and subject-matter experts also share in the responsibility, since they must develop a program that is relevant to the needs of the participants.

Last, but not least, top management shares in the responsibility for results. When top management demands results-based HRD programs, requires evaluation of all programs, and communicates expectations, program results will be enhanced. It is only through shared responsibility, with each party accepting their respective roles, that maximum results will be obtained from HRD programs.

Policy Statements

Another factor in developing a results-based approach is the organization's intentions, which must be clearly defined and communicated. Functions and responsibilities, practices and procedures, and policy statements can have an influence on the results of an HRD effort. A results-based philosophy must be communicated to management and, in some cases, to all employees. Chevron's policy statement for training and development sets the tone for evaluation: "If no measurement can be developed, training is not undertaken. Measurement can be either objective or subjective, but is based on observable data, preferably in dollars of cost reduction or productivity increase." There can be little doubt in the minds of the HRD staff and management about the importance of evaluation at Chevron.

When defining the responsibilities for training and development it is appropriate to detail roles and responsibilities for evaluation. The HRD staff, the line organization, and the support functions all have evaluation responsibilities. This communication puts a proper emphasis on evaluation and defines the responsibilities. The impact on program results may be surprising. Additional information on policy, procedures, and guidelines is presented in another chapter.

Summary

This chapter presented the information necessary to understand and develop a results-based approach to HRD in an organization. It began with a thorough definition of results-based HRD. Next, it presented the purposes and uses of evaluation in detail. Several common approaches for placing evaluation into categories or levels were outlined, which helps develop a better understanding of the full scope of the evaluation process. Finally, the chapter presented the factors necessary to develop a results-based approach. This approach is communicated to all who have a responsibility for results. The next chapter presents a results-based HRD model.

Discussion Questions

1. Why is the results-based approach advocated as a necessary philosophy in an organization?
2. How much of a results-based approach does your organization (or one with which you are familiar) have?
3. Which purposes of evaluation are the most commonly used? Which are most important? Least important?
4. Discuss a recent evaluation project. What were the purposes of evaluation?
5. Contrast the basic frameworks for the levels of evaluation. Which one is best suited for your organization (or one with which you are familiar)?
6. Why is the Kirkpatrick Model (or variations thereof) so popular?
7. How can HRD staff members be motivated to pursue evaluation?
8. Cite examples or personal experiences of the self-fulfilling prophecy.

9. Why is it important to communicate performance expectations to program participants?
10. Examine the training policy statement from your organization (or another organization). What does it reveal about obtaining results? Why?
11. Why are long-term results from a program difficult to achieve?

References

1. Kirkpatrick, D. L. "Techniques for Evaluating Training Programs," in *Evaluating Training Programs*. Alexandria, VA: American Society for Training and Development, 1975, pp. 1–17.
2. Kaufman, P. and Keller, J. M. "Levels of Evaluation: Beyond Kirkpatrick," *HRD Quarterly,* 5(4), Winter 1994, pp. 371–380.
3. Warr, P., Bird, M., and Rackham, N. *Evaluation of Management Training*. London, U.K.: Gower Press, 1970.
4. Galvin, J. G. "What Can Trainers Learn from Educators about Evaluating Management Training?" *Training and Development Journal,* August 1983, p. 52.
5. Phillips, J. "Return on Investment—Beyond the Four Levels," in *Academy of HRD 1995 Conference Proceedings*. E. Holton (Ed.), 1995.
6. Dixon, N. M. *Evaluation: A Tool for Improving HRD Quality*. San Diego, CA: University Associates, Inc., 1990.
7. Broad, M. L. and Newstrom, J. W. *Transfer of Training*. Reading, MA: Addison-Wesley, 1992.
8. Alliger, G. M. and Janak, E. A. "Kirkpatrick's Levels of Training Criteria: Thirty Years Later," *Personnel Psychology,* 42, 1989, pp. 331–342.
9. Kimmerling, G. "Gathering Best Practices," *Training and Development,* 47, No. 3, September 1993, pp. 28–36.
10. Kirkpatrick, D. L. *Evaluating Training Programs*. San Francisco, CA: Berrett-Koehler Publishers, 1994.
11. McCune, J. C. "Measuring the Value of Employee Education," *Management Review,* April 1994, pp. 10–15.
12. Galagan, P. "Focus on Results at Motorola," *Training & Development Journal,* May 1994, p. 45.
13. Eden, D. *Pygmalion in Management: Productivity as a Self-Fulfilling Prophecy*. Lexington Books: Lexington, MA, 1990.
14. Shimko, B. W. "The McPygmalion Effect," *Training and Development Journal,* June 1990, pp. 64–70.

CHAPTER 4

A Results-Based HRD Model

A variety of models are available for the design and implementation of HRD programs.[1] Most are sound, logical, and produce effective programs. Some focus on impact instead of activity[2]; others focus on efficiency and effectiveness.[3] However, most lack steps that emphasize evaluation throughout the design process and, more specifically, do not provide the framework to identify the desired results. A model can be very useful to observe the total HRD process and examine the relationship of one step to another. The model in this chapter, appropriate for almost any HRD activity, contains 18 logical steps, 10 of which directly involve evaluation. The reaction to this model in earlier editions of this Handbook was very favorable.[4]

Evaluation is a systematic process with several key components. Most successful evaluations are planned at the beginning of the needs-assessment process, when the questions that will shape the training program are asked. Evaluation efforts must be initiated before, during, and after a program. Before a program is developed, several key questions must be answered to ensure that it meets objectives and the evaluation progresses logically.

☐ Who will collect the data?
☐ What data will be collected?
☐ Where will the data be collected?
☐ When will the data be collected?
☐ How will the data be collected?

During the program, exercises and activities are geared toward achieving results, and sometimes the data are collected. After the program, additional data are collected, analyzed, and reported.

Table 4-1 shows the complete HRD process model that emphasizes evaluation throughout the steps. Because the complete model may be too detailed for some organizations, it can be shortened or terminated as needed. However, for a results-based approach the steps directly related to evaluation are necessary and must be included to improve the evaluation process and enhance results.

A Complete Results-Based HRD Model

1. Conduct a Needs Assessment and Develop Tentative Objectives

A needs assessment is the first step for any HRD program design. This step could be triggered by one of several events such as discovering a performance deficiency, fulfilling a request for training from top management, observing a problem, responding to the need to improve productivity, satisfying a government regulation, or addressing a need to improve employee job satisfaction. Regardless of what triggered the program, a needs assessment should be conducted to determine specific deficiencies in knowledge, skills, or attitudes. Needs assessments are typically conducted through interviews with participants or their managers, or by administering surveys and

Table 4-1
A Complete Results-Based HRD Model

1. Conduct a Needs Assessment and Develop Tentative Objectives
2. Identify Purposes of Evaluation
3. Establish Baseline Data, If Available
4. Select Evaluation Method/Design
5. Determine Evaluation Strategy
6. Finalize Program Objectives
7. Estimate Program Costs/Benefits
8. Prepare and Present Proposal
9. Design Evaluation Instruments
10. Determine and Develop Program Content
11. Design or Select Delivery Methods
12. Test Program and Make Revisions
13. Implement or Conduct Program
14. Collect Data at Proper Stages
15. Analyze and Interpret Data
16. Make Program Adjustments
17. Calculate Return on Investment
18. Communicate Program Results

questionnaires. To the extent feasible, the environment surrounding the performance deficiency should be examined to identify any other circumstances affecting performance. This may involve procedures, systems, leadership climate, compensation, or other factors.

Typical questions that might be appropriate for a detailed needs assessment are

☐ Is there a performance problem?
☐ What is the gap between desired and actual performance?
☐ How important is the problem?
☐ What happens if we do nothing?
☐ Does a lack of skill contribute to the problem?
☐ Do attitudes need to be improved?
☐ Is the program designed to meet an outside requirement or to satisfy an external influence? If so, define.
☐ Which employees will need the training?
☐ Are there alternative ways to satisfy the need?
☐ To what extent will other departments be involved?
☐ Are there natural barriers to accomplishing the program?
☐ Who supports this new program?

These and other questions will help HRD professionals focus more specifically on the need for the new program. In reality, this becomes a performance audit and several models have been developed to focus exclusively on this process.[5]

The output of the needs assessment is a description of the performance deficiencies of the target employees (i.e., skills, knowledge, or abilities). At this point, the effort could be terminated if it is determined that not enough deficiencies exist to justify designing and implementing the HRD program.

The second part of this step involves developing tentative program objectives. The needs assessment should reveal information that can be used to develop objectives; specifically, what the new program must accomplish. The objectives are only tentative and will be finalized in Step 6, after determining if data are available and can be collected.

2. Identify Purposes of Evaluation

Before pursuing program development, the purposes of evaluation must be determined. In most cases, evaluation will be undertaken to assist in making a decision about the future of the program. In practice, there are other reasons for evaluation, and these reasons will affect the type of data and the data-collection method(s) chosen. For example, if evaluation is undertaken to improve the learning process, a questionnaire at the end of the program would be appropriate.

3. Establish Baseline Data, If Available

Before comparisons can be made, data must be collected both prior to the program and after its completion. Data may exist in a variety of forms and generally reflect the conditions that have created the need for training. Ideally, data should be collected for a finite amount of time to provide a realistic comparison. The data-collection method answers the basic question of what to evaluate. Typical examples are the number of grievances in the last six months, how many errors in processing claims in the past year, the accident frequency rate for the last quarter, or the average monthly sales cost for the previous year. Baseline data reflect the information that is most important and represent the performance deficiency.

Establishing baseline data after the needs assessment enables the HRD professional to focus more clearly on the changes the program should deliver. This process is relatively easy when specific baseline data exist. Difficulty arises when a program is being designed to improve something for which there is no clear evidence of an existing problem or deficiency. In this case, it might be appropriate to begin this step of the model by again asking the question, "Is this training really necessary?" If the current performance level cannot be clearly defined, is there any need for improvement? And, more importantly, how can we tell if there has been improvement?

Most of the difficulty in establishing baseline data occurs in supervisory and management programs. These programs are designed to improve the effectiveness of supervisors and team leaders, and very little baseline data have traditionally been available on their current level of effectiveness. While evaluation is difficult, many progressive organizations have made significant improvements in developing individualized performance data such as absenteeism, turnover, grievances, etc. for supervisors and team leaders. In addition, work unit output, quality, costs, and time delays are group outputs directly linked to those supervisors.

If supervisors or team leaders do not have appropriate measures of their effectiveness, perhaps such measures should be developed to determine which areas need improvement. Alternatives include

☐ Asking the question, "What necessitated the training program?" If a needs assessment was conducted and performance deficiencies were identified, the analysis may contain measurements of the current situation. It may involve soft data such as making improper decisions or a lack of open communication between the employee and the supervisor. Ultimately, deficiencies must be tied to measurable items, although the estimate of that baseline might be subjective.

☐ Developing baseline data. If deficiencies exist, but no data are present to measure the level, data should be developed for a short period to provide a baseline. For example, suppose there is an indication that employee complaints are increasing, but there is no mechanism in the organization to trace the number of complaints. If this is a serious problem, it might be appropriate to ask supervisors to note the frequency and types of employee complaints over a specific period of time. With this new baseline data, the HRD program could focus on reducing those complaints.

4. Select Evaluation Method/Design

The next step is to select the evaluation method(s) and design. It may seem illogical for this to precede the step of finalizing program objectives, but the choice of evaluation method may influence the objectives established for the program. It is pointless to set an objective for a program if there is no way of collecting information to measure progress toward the objective. Therefore, if the methods of collecting data are finalized first, then objectives can be tailored to those methods. Some might disagree with this approach, thinking that the objectives should be set first and the methods to evaluate those objectives selected afterward. While that approach may seem logical, there are only a finite number of evaluation methods, and these methods must be tailored to the organization and to the proposed program. Selecting the method before finalizing objectives can make a difference in thought processes. It is possible to perform the two steps concurrently.

Selecting the evaluation method answers the question of how to evaluate, as the method must be appropriate for the type of data, learning environment, participants, and program content. The types of evaluation methods include pre- and post-course examinations, participant feedback, participant follow-up, action planning, and performance contracts.

As part of this step, the evaluation design must also be selected—a decision equally as important as selecting the evaluation method. Several possible designs are available, all of which will be discussed later.

5. Determine Evaluation Strategy

This step in the process answers *who, where,* and *when* as they relate to the evaluation. The answers to these key questions are important in planning the evaluation. Because both the HRD department and the program participants have significant roles in evaluation, questions about responsibility for assignments (*who*) need to be addressed.

☐ Will a facilitator conduct the evaluation? If not, who will?
☐ Will information be collected from supervisors of the participants?
☐ Will information be collected from participants' team members or subordinates?
☐ Who will analyze the data?
☐ Who will interpret the data?
☐ Who will conduct the follow-up evaluation?

☐ Who will make the decision to stop or alter the evaluation process?

These questions should be answered before taking any further action. In most cases, one individual or a small team will be responsible for collecting data, analyzing results, and communicating them to the appropriate target audience.

The *where* refers to the location for the evaluation. Some relevant questions are

☐ Will all the evaluations occur in a classroom, on the job, or a combination of the two?
☐ Will the participants need to be taken off the job a few months after the program to conduct a follow-up?
☐ Will it be necessary to observe employees at their work stations?

The question of *when* involves timing and requires careful planning. Generally, an evaluation can occur

☐ During the program (to gather reaction and measure learning).
☐ At the end of the program (to gather reaction and measure learning).
☐ On the job (to observe behavior change).
☐ At a specified follow-up date (to measure the results achieved by the individual or the group).

A thorough evaluation and measurement system will collect data at each of these time intervals. When combined with previous steps, this step covers all the questions that form the initial approach to evaluation.

6. Finalize Program Objectives

The next step is to finalize the program's objectives. This step is made after all questions regarding the evaluation plans have been answered, since evaluation plans may influence the final selection of objectives. Ideally, each objective should be related to baseline data that have been collected. For example, suppose an HRD program is conducted to improve the relationship between supervisors and employees. The baseline data might include the number of grievances in the last six months. One objective, therefore, might be to reduce grievances by 20% in the next six-month period. A more complete training objective then becomes:

> To prepare supervisors to conduct effective disciplinary discussions and administer the labor contract so that the number of grievances is reduced by 20% in the next six-month period.

Program objectives provide direction to course developers and program participants, as well as to management, who must determine whether or not the program should be conducted. HRD program objectives should follow the normal criteria for all sound objectives. They should be challenging, precise, dated, achievable, and easily understood.

To meet these criteria, it is important for all stake holders to participate in setting objectives. This helps to ensure that the objectives are precisely what management wants and are relevant to the jobs performed in the organization. This process is essential to the production of a high-quality training system.[6]

It is sometimes useful to consider objectives at different levels or hierarchies. For example, specific end-of-course objectives may define what learning should occur. On-the-job performance objectives might define what will change on the job as a result of the program (Level 3 evaluation). Finally, business impact or outcome objectives focus on the business results of the program. On rare occasions, objectives may be set at the ultimate level of evaluation, return on investment (Level 5 evaluation) This approach ties objectives to the framework of different levels of evaluation.

7. Estimate Program Costs/Benefits

The next step is to calculate the approximate cost of developing and conducting the program. This step is undertaken before any development work is initiated to see if a "go/no-go" decision is in order. Up to this point, a needs analysis could reveal a definite performance deficiency. After baseline data are established, the evaluation strategy determined, and program objectives finalized, the cost for developing and conducting the program is estimated and compared to anticipated benefits. The return on investment can then be forecast.[7]

These are only cost estimates, but will satisfy the need. Costs can be tabulated in standard categories such as analysis, development, delivery, and evaluation. After these costs are tabulated, the potential monetary benefits are estimated. For example, if $2000 can be saved for each participant who completes the program and there are 100 people to be trained, then there is a potential cost savings of $200,000.

This step, however, may be unnecessary in some situations. If, in the opinion of the program designers, the program will be conducted regardless of the cost, there is little need for a forecast of the ROI. Implementing a program without ROI considerations does not mean that costs are unimportant, but rather that the need is driven by factors other than economics.[8] Efforts should then concentrate on efficient program development and delivery. The HRD manager should still calculate costs to keep the staff aware of the magnitude of their efforts and the expense of their function to the entire organization, and to generate historical data.

8. Prepare and Present Proposal

At this stage, a formal proposal is recommended to management prior to implementing the program. The proposal should present, in a professional manner, an unbiased summary of the information collected. There are many ways to prepare a proposal. Investing time in preparation and presentation ensures that it will receive the appropriate attention. The following action checklist is useful when preparing a proposal for a significant training project:

☐ Develop an audience profile. Determine who will receive and approve the proposal.

☐ Determine the proper timing to present the proposal. Make sure all appropriate individuals have concurred with its contents.

☐ Select the location for the presentation. Is the HRD conference room suitable or would an executive conference room be more appropriate?

☐ Arrange the audience carefully. Strategically place key decision makers where they can best see the presentation to ask questions as necessary.

☐ Rehearse the delivery.

☐ Make notes and stay focused on the outcome.

☐ Consider appropriate visual aids. Charts, graphs and slides are very helpful in developing audience understanding.

☐ Anticipate questions from the audience and be prepared with responses. Expect difficult questions and be prepared to tactfully and firmly counteract individuals who may be biased against the proposal.

☐ Understand the calculations in the financial justification portion of the proposal. Be prepared to explain the rationale for the assumptions.

☐ Discuss advantages and disadvantages candidly and truthfully.

☐ Explain what can happen if the program is not conducted, particularly in terms of losses.

☐ Present the proposed implementation schedule for the program with estimated completion dates.

☐ Discuss follow-up sessions at which updated data will be presented.

☐ Ask for approval to proceed with the program.

☐ Leave a copy of the report.

Following these steps will help ensure that the proposal is presented accurately and professionally, and receives the proper consideration.[9]

9. Design Evaluation Instruments

This step involves the design and selection of specific instruments to be used in the evaluation process. In the context of evaluation, an instrument is a data-gathering tool that collects data to describe changes in attitudes, learning, behavior, or other results achieved from the program. Instruments may include record-keeping systems, questionnaires, examinations, attitude surveys, interviews, focus groups, observations, or job simulations.[10] The instrument should be statistically reliable and easy to use. It is important for the instrument to be designed before the program is developed, as additional information might be uncovered that will alter course development and content.

10. Determine and Develop Program Content

Probably the most time-consuming step of this model is determining and developing the program's content. The content may be determined by subject matter experts who decide what participants need to know (such as principles, facts, and skills) to meet the program objectives. This step requires careful review by appropriate management. Reviewing and revising should continue throughout the design process. Program developers may rely on previous programs or similar programs conducted with other groups. For example, a training session on safety improvement designed by one organization may be adapted for use in another. Steps 1–10 of the Results-Based Model will focus attention only on those areas that will produce the desired results. Program material that is nice to know but not related to objectives will probably be excluded. Program development is beyond the scope of this book, but other works provide detail on this topic.[11]

11. Design or Select Delivery Methods

Selecting delivery methods to meet the program's objective is the next step. Instructional systems and audiovisual tools are frequently used because they are readily available and encourage participant interaction. Mayo and Dubois[12] have identified fourteen methods of training delivery:

1. Presentation-discussion (including lectures and listening and questioning)
2. Conference (including seminars)
3. Case study
4. Role play
5. Workshop
6. Computer-based instruction (including computer-assisted instruction and computer-managed instruction)
7. Simulations and games
8. On-the-job training
9. Peer training
10. Programmed instruction
11. Team teaching/training
12. Demonstration
13. Field trips
14. Preparatory (short-course) format

The effectiveness of these methods varies. Lectures are considered to be among the least effective, while methods that require extensive participant interaction are the most effective.[13] For example, participants in behavior-modeling training significantly outperform those who only attend lectures. Although lectures have value, there is some evidence to suggest that their use is declining.[14] The selection of a method (or methods) depends on such factors as

☐ Budget
☐ Available resources
☐ Program objectives
☐ Time frame
☐ Ability of participants
☐ Ability of program developers
☐ Ability of instructors
☐ Location of training

Presentation methods can exert considerable influence on the outcome of the program. Just as businesses and individuals are becoming more and more reliant on cutting-edge technology, savvy HRD managers are integrating new media into programs to satisfy today's increasingly sophisticated and demanding seminar attendees.

12. Test Program and Make Revisions

After the program is developed, a run-through may be appropriate. Pilot testing is often overlooked in the HRD process. It is particularly useful when the program will be repeated with many participants; there is little reason to test a one-time program on an experimental basis unless there are unusual circumstances. This step also gives the program developers an opportunity to test, to a certain extent, some of the evaluation methods. Pre-program and post-program evaluations, participants' reactions, and behavior simulations can be observed on a test basis and adjusted as necessary.

A well-planned pilot program can help make the months of analysis, interviews, and program development pay off. Taking appropriate steps before, during, and after the pilot provides an opportunity to analyze the program's strengths and weaknesses, and improves the chances of a flawless, fail-safe program.[15] This fail-safe approach involves choosing the test audience carefully, establishing ground rules, developing group cohesiveness, and watching for warning signals as the program is delivered.

13. Implement or Conduct Program

Of course, implementing or conducting the actual program is an integral part of the HRD evaluation process. This step needs little comment except that participants should be made aware of what results are expected. As discussed in the previous chapter, communicating expectations can influence the results achieved.

Note that this step does not specifically deal with classroom training programs. The HRD model may involve programs that are not of the traditional classroom variety. For instance, an on-the-job management development program should be subjected to the same development process and evaluation model.[16]

14. Collect Data at Proper Stages

Another logical and critical step of evaluation is the collection of data. A system to accomplish data collection must be implemented at the appropriate time, and the predetermined schedule for data collection must be closely followed. It is easy to establish elaborate plans for an evaluation and have them fall short of expectations because of failure to collect the data at proper intervals. A variety of data-collection methods appropriate for any type of data are available.[17]

15. Analyze and Interpret Data

Data analysis involves a sometimes difficult challenge. All data are collected for a predetermined purpose; this step involves the analysis of the data and the interpretation of that analysis. Responses to questionnaires should be tabulated and prepared for presentation. Variances need to be analyzed.

When analyzing data, statistics are usually needed. There are three general groups of statistical analysis that are particularly useful when analyzing evaluation data: measures of central tendency, measures of dispersion, and measures of association.

Measures of central tendency include the mean, median, and mode. They convey the general idea of the impact on participants as a group. For example, "the average error rate is now 5.2, compared to 9.5 before the HRD program."

Measures of dispersion, which use standard deviations and analysis of variance, calculate how widely the performance of the participants varies when compared with each other and over time. Individuals with different levels of performance can be compared to determine whether or not there was an actual improvement of the group.

Measures of association use correlation to show a quantitative relationship between different elements of the HRD program and performance. For example, comparing a participant's performance on the job with test scores at the end of the program can reveal the correlation between the two items. Also, a comparison can be useful in drawing conclusions about other participants in the future, based on their examination scores.

If appropriate for the analysis, the monetary value of the results is calculated at this step. Judgmental factors may be involved in arriving at these values. Also, the analysis and interpretation of results may be done in different stages. For example, data collected during the program will usually be evaluated at that time to provide information for possible program adjustments. On-the-job performance data or follow-up data will be collected later and combined with the initial data analysis for a complete program evaluation.[18]

16. Make Program Adjustments

Changes in the program may be necessary, based on the analysis of the information collected. If the program did not produce results, something went wrong, and adjustments or cancellation of the program may be in order. If the evaluation indicates that parts of the program are not effective, those parts must be redesigned or improved.

Unacceptable results should be examined to determine the cause of failure. Some common reasons for failure are improper content, inappropriate delivery, inadequate reinforcement on the job, or lack of motivation of the participants. Every part of the program should be examined.

17. Calculate Return on Investment (ROI)

If an economic justification is planned, the next step in the sequence is to calculate the ROI. Although the ROI should be calculated whenever possible, it may be unnecessary in some instances, or it may be too unreliable to be useful. The basic ROI formula is:

$$ROI(\%) = \frac{\text{Net Program Benefits}}{\text{Program Costs}} \times 100$$

When ROIs are calculated, they should be compared to targets for HRD programs. Sometimes these targets are determined based on company standards for capital expenditures. Others are based on what management expects from an HRD program, or what level they would require to approve implementation of a program. The calculation of the ROI deserves much attention, because it represents the ultimate approach to evaluation and is becoming an increasingly important part of the HRD function as business, industry, and the government become more bottom-line oriented. It provides a sound basis for calculating the efficient use of financial resources allocated to HRD activities.[19]

18. Communicate Program Results

The final step in developing a results-based HRD model involves communicating the results of the program. While there is a large audience that should receive evaluation information, four groups are imperative. One of the most important groups is the HRD staff, which needs this information to make improvements in the program. Only through refinement, based on feedback, will programs be improved.

Management is another important group because it includes key decision-makers who determine the future of the program. A fundamental purpose of evaluation is to provide the basis for sound decisions. Should funds be expended to continue this effort? Was the program worthwhile? Answers to these questions should be communicated to the management group.

The third major group is the participants, who need to know how well they have done in the program and compare their performance to others. This feedback can enhance their efforts, as well as the efforts of others who will be involved in future programs.

A fourth group is participants' immediate managers. This group must make adjustments when participants attend programs, and is accordingly very interested in their success.

Communicating results is an often overlooked step in HRD. Although evaluation data that has been analyzed and interpreted will usually be given to someone, problems occur when others who need the information do not receive it. Care must be taken to present information in an unbiased, effective manner.[20] Because of its importance, an entire chapter is devoted to ways to communicate HRD program results successfully.

Summary

The HRD model represents an effective results-based approach to designing, developing, and implementing an HRD program. Evaluation is emphasized at different stages in the process. These steps are necessary to produce HRD programs that focus on results.

When implementing this process, Murphy's Law, or variations thereof, should be considered:

☐ If things can go wrong, they will.
☐ Nothing is as easy as it looks.
☐ Every step takes longer than you expect.
☐ Projects take longer than they do.

Armed with this knowledge, an HRD professional can develop a results-based program.

Discussion Questions

1. Why is it important to focus on evaluation at virtually all stages of the HRD process?
2. Is there a need for another model for developing a new HRD program? Please explain.
3. Contrast the results-based model with other models with which you are familiar.

4. In this model, program objectives are not established in final form until Step 6. Why does this occur so late in the process?
5. Examine the objectives of a training program. At what level of evaluation are these objectives aimed?
6. A training-needs assessment is sometimes regarded as a performance audit. Please explain.
7. In what types of programs would a cost/benefit analysis be appropriate in the proposal stage, prior to development of the program?
8. One HRD executive stated, "Few proposals for new training programs contain the right types of information." What do you think is the problem?
9. How can the design and selection of the methods of delivery have an impact on program results? Please explain.
10. When is pilot testing appropriate for a new program?
11. Examine a data-collection scheme for a training evaluation project. At what point is data collected? Why?
12. Why is the return on investment important in this model?
13. Examine an evaluation project. How were the results communicated? To what audiences and why?

References

1. Ford, D. (Ed.) *In Action: Designing Training Programs.* Alexandria, VA: American Society for Training and Development, 1996.
2. Robinson, D. G. and Robinson, J. C. *Training for Impact: How to Link Training to Business Needs and Measure the Results.* San Francisco, CA: Jossey-Bass, 1989.
3. Pepitone, J. S. *Future Training.* Dallas, TX: AddVantage Learning Press, 1995.
4. Phillips, J. J. "Training Programs: A Results-Based Model for Managing the Development of Human Resources," *Personnel,* May/June 1983, pp. 11–18.
5. Robinson, D. C. and Robinson, J. C. *Performance Consulting.* San Francisco, CA: Berrett-Koehler Publishers, 1995.
6. Shelton, S. and Alliger, G. "Who's Afraid of Level 4 Evaluation? A Practical Approach," *Training & Development,* June 1993, pp. 43–46.
7. Tracey, W. R. "How to Weigh the Costs and Benefits of Training," *Solutions,* December 1995, pp. 52–56.
8. Hequet, M. "Beyond Dollars," *Training,* March 1996, pp. 40–42.
9. Birnbrauer, H. "How to Get Accountability and Commitment for Training Programs," *P&I,* 33(5), May/June 1994, pp. 17–19.
10. Marrelli, A. F. "Ten Evaluation Instruments for Technical Training," *Technical & Skills Training,* July 1993, pp. 7–14.

11. Nadler, L. and Nadler, Z. *Designing Training Programs,* Houston, TX: Gulf Publishing Company, 1994.
12. Mayo, G. and Dubois, P. H. *The Complete Book of Training: Theory, Principles and Techniques,* University Associates, Inc.: San Diego, CA, 1989.
13. Dionne, P. "The Evaluation of Training Activities: A Complex Issue Involving Different Stakes," *Human Resource Development Quarterly,* 7(3), Fall 1996, pp. 279–286.
14. Estrada, V. F. "Functional Training Builds Knowledge Workers," *Quality Digest,* July 1995, pp. 51–53.
15. Chernick, J. "Keeping Your Pilots on Course," *Training & Development,* April 1992, pp. 69–73.
16. Rothwell, W. J. and Kazanas, H. C. *Improving On-the-Job Training.* San Francisco, CA: Jossey-Bass Publishers, 1994.
17. Phillips, J. J. "Measuring ROI: The Fifth Level of Evaluation," *Technical and Skills Training,* Vol. 3, April 1996, pp. 10–13.
18. Williams, L. A. "Measurement Made Simple," *Training & Development,* July 1996, pp. 43–45.
19. Davidove, E. A. and Shroeder, P. A. "Demonstrating ROI of Training," *Training & Development,* August 1992, pp. 70–71.
20. McIntosh, S. S., Page, S., and Hall, K. B. "Adding Value through Training," *Training & Development,* July 1993, pp. 39–44.

CHAPTER 5

The ROI Process Model

The previous chapter presented a comprehensive HRD process model that began with needs assessment and ended with communicating program results. The model can be shortened as necessary, as emphasis on program results and scarce resources may alter the planned evaluation.

In recent years there has been a tremendous increase in emphasis on the development of the return on investment for training and development.[1] This emphasis has caused HRD practitioners to seek a rational process that would enable them to develop the ROI for a specific program. Thus, the ROI process has become an important and essential part of evaluation.

This chapter presents a practical logical model in summary form. This model has been adopted by thousands of organizations and enjoys a high level of acceptance with practitioners and researchers.[2] The process begins with data collection after the program has been implemented, and ends with an ROI calculation. Traditionally Level 4 data is used to develop the economic benefits for the ROI formula, but in some cases Level 3 data can be used. There may be overlap between this model and the results-based HRD model presented in Chapter 4, but this is necessary to have a complete process model. Accordingly, this presentation becomes a stand-alone chapter that presents a rational, practical approach to developing the ROI using post-program data. The material in this chapter is a slightly modified version of the ROI process presented in another publication.[3]

The basic model, illustrated in Figure 5-1, simplifies a potentially complicated process. A step-by-step approach keeps the process manageable so users can tackle one issue at a time. The model also emphasizes the fact that this is a logical, systematic process that flows from one step to another. Application of the model, each step of which is briefly described in this chapter, provides consistency from one ROI calculation to another.

Preliminary Evaluation Information

Several pieces of the evaluation puzzle must be explained when developing the evaluation plan for an ROI calculation; four specific elements are briefly described here.

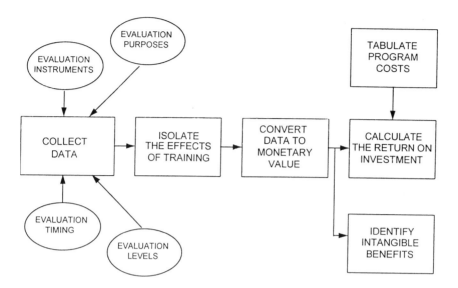

Figure 5-1. ROI process model.

Evaluation purposes should be considered prior to developing the evaluation plan because they will often determine the scope of the evaluation, the types of instruments used, and the type of data collected. For example, when an ROI calculation is planned, one of the purposes would be to compare the cost and benefits of the program. This purpose has implications for the type of data collected (hard data), type of data-collection method (performance monitoring), the type of analysis (thorough), and the communication medium for results (formal evaluation report). Multiple evaluation purposes are pursued for most programs.

A variety of instruments are used to collect data. The appropriate instruments should be considered in the early stages of developing the ROI. The seven most common instruments used to collect data are

1. Surveys
2. Questionnaires
3. Interviews
4. Focus Groups
5. Tests
6. Observation
7. Performance Records

The instruments most familiar to the culture of the organization and appropriate for the setting and evaluation requirements should be used in the data-collection process. Additional information on evaluation instruments is covered in Chapter 6.

Training programs are evaluated at five different levels.

1. Level 1: Measuring Reaction and Identifying Planned Actions
2. Level 2: Measuring Learning
3. Level 3: Assessing Application of the Program on the Job
4. Level 4: Identifying Business Results from the Program
5. Level 5: Calculating Return on Investment

Data should be collected at Levels 1, 2, 3, and 4 if an ROI analysis is planned. This helps ensure that the chain of impact occurs as participants learn the skills and knowledge, apply them on the job, and obtain business results.

A final aspect of the evaluation plan is the timing of the data collection, discussed more thoroughly in a later chapter. In some cases, pre-program measurements are taken to compare with post-program measurements, while others take multiple measurements. Sometimes, pre-program measurements are not available but specific follow-ups are still taken after the program. The important issue is to determine the timing for the follow-up evaluation. For example, evaluations can be made as early as three weeks after a customer service skills training program for a major airline. However, five years may be required to measure the return for an employee to attend an MBA program sponsored by an Indonesian company. For most professional and supervisory training, a follow-up is usually conducted in the range of 3–6 months.

These four elements—evaluation purposes, instruments, levels, and timing—are all considerations in selecting data-collection methods and developing a data-collection plan.

Collecting Post-Program Data

Data collection is central to the ROI process. In some situations, post-program data are collected and compared to pre-program situations, control group differences, and expectations. Both hard data, representing output, quality, cost, and time; and soft data, including work habits, work climate, and attitudes, are collected. Data are collected using a variety of methods including the following:

☐ Follow-up **surveys** are taken to determine the degree to which participants have utilized various aspects of the program. Survey responses are often developed on a sliding scale and usually represent attitudinal data. Surveys are useful for Level 3 data.

☐ Follow-up **questionnaires** are administered to uncover specific applications of training. Participants provide responses to a variety of open-ended and forced-response questions. Questionnaires can be used to capture both Level 3 and Level 4 data.

☐ On-the-job **observation** captures actual skill application and use. Observations are particularly useful in customer service training and are more effective when the observer is either invisible or transparent. Observations are appropriate for Level 3 data.

☐ Post-program **interviews** are conducted with participants to determine the extent to which learning has been utilized on the job. Interviews allow probing to uncover specific applications and are appropriate with Level 3 data.

☐ **Focus groups** are conducted to determine the degree to which a group of participants have applied the training to job situations. Focus groups are appropriate with Level 3 data.

☐ **Program assignments** are useful for simple short-term projects. Participants complete the assignment on the job, utilizing skills or knowledge learned in the program. Completed assignments can often contain both Level 3 and Level 4 data.

☐ **Action plans** are developed in training programs and implemented on the job after the program is completed. A follow-up of the plans provides evidence of a training program's success. Level 3 and Level 4 data can be collected with action plans.

☐ **Performance contracts** are developed when the participant, the participant's supervisor, and the instructor all agree on specific outcomes from training. Performance contracts are appropriate for both Level 3 and Level 4 data.

☐ Programs are sometimes designed with a **follow-up session**, which is utilized to capture evaluation data and present additional learning material. In the follow-up session, participants discuss their successes with the program. Follow-up sessions are appropriate for both Level 3 and Level 4 data.

☐ **Performance monitoring** is useful when various performance records and operational data are examined for improvement. This method is particularly useful for Level 4 data. The important challenge in this step is to select data-collection methods appropriate for the setting and the specific program, within the time and budget constraints of the organization. Because of the importance of post-program data collection, a chapter is devoted to the topic.

Isolating the Effects of the Program

An often overlooked issue in many evaluation studies is the process by which the effects of training are isolated. This is also referred to as evaluation design or research design. In this step of the process, specific strategies are explored that determine the amount of output performance directly related to the program. Because many factors will influence performance data after training, this step is essential. It will pinpoint the amount of improvement directly related to the training program. The result is increased accuracy and credibility of the ROI calculation. The following strategies have been utilized by organizations to tackle this important issue:

☐ A **control group** arrangement is used to isolate training impact. With this strategy, one group receives training while another similar group does not. The difference in the performance of the two groups is attributed to the training program. When properly set up and implemented, a control group arrangement is the most effective way to isolate the effects of training.

☐ **Trend lines** are used to project the value-specific output variables if training had not been undertaken. The projection is then compared to the actual data after training, and the difference represents the estimate of the impact of training. Under certain conditions, this strategy can be an accurate way to isolate the impact of training.

☐ When mathematical relationships between input and output variables are known, a **forecasting model** is used to isolate the effects of training. With this approach, the output variable is predicted using the forecasting model, with the assumption that no training is conducted. The actual performance of the variable after training is then compared with the forecasted value to estimate the impact of training.

☐ **Participants estimate** the amount of improvement related to training. With this approach, participants are provided with the total amount of improvement (on a pre- and post-program basis) and are asked to indicate the percent of the improvement that is actually related to the training program.

☐ **Participants' supervisors estimate** the impact of training on the output variables. With this approach, participants' supervisors are presented with the total amount of improvement and are asked to indicate the percent related to training.

☐ **Senior management estimates** the impact of training. In these cases, managers provide an estimate or adjustment to reflect the portion of the improvement related to the training program. While perhaps inaccurate, there are some advantages to having senior management involved in this process.

☐ **Experts provide estimates** of the impact of training on the performance variable. Because the estimates are based on previous experience, the experts must be familiar with the type of training and the specific situation.

☐ In supervisory and management training, the **participants' subordinates identify changes in the work climate** that could influence the output variables. With this approach, the subordinates of the supervisors receiving training determine if other changing variables in the work climate could have influenced output performance.

☐ When feasible, **other influencing factors are identified and their impact is estimated or calculated, attributing the remaining unexplained improvement to training.** In this case, the influences of all other factors are developed, and training remains the one variable not accounted for in the analysis. The unexplained portion of the output is attributed to training.

☐ In some situations, **customers provide input on the extent to which training has influenced their decision** to use a product or service. Although this strategy has limited applications, it can be quite useful in customer service and sales training.

Collectively, these ten strategies provide a comprehensive set of tools to tackle the important and critical issue of isolating the effects of training. Because this topic is critical to an evaluation's success, a full chapter is devoted to the ten methods listed previously.

Converting Data to Monetary Values

To calculate the return on investment, data collected in a Level 4 evaluation are converted to monetary values and compared to program costs. This requires a value to be placed on each unit of data connected with the program. Ten strategies are available to convert data to monetary values; the specific strategy selected usually depends on the type of data and the situation.

☐ **Output data is converted to profit contribution or cost savings.** In this strategy, output increases are converted to monetary value based on their unit contribution to profit or the unit of cost reduction. These values are readily available in most organizations.

☐ The **cost of quality is calculated** and quality improvements are directly converted to cost savings. This value is also available in many organizations.

☐ For programs in which employee time is saved, a participant's **wages and benefits are used for the value for time.** Because a variety of programs focus on improving the time required to complete projects, processes, or daily activities, the value of time becomes an important and necessary issue.

☐ **Historical costs** are used when they are available for a specific variable. In this case, organizational cost data are used to establish the specific value of an improvement.

☐ When available, **internal and external experts** may be used to estimate a value for an improvement. In this situation, the credibility of the estimate hinges on the individual's expertise and reputation.

☐ **External databases** are sometimes available to estimate the value or cost of data items. Research, government, and industry databases can provide important information for these values. The challenge lies in finding a specific database related to the situation.

☐ **Participants estimate** the value of the data item. For this approach to be effective, participants must be capable of providing a value for the improvement.

☐ **Participants' supervisors provide estimates** when they are both willing and capable of assigning values to the improvement. This approach is especially useful when participants are not fully capable of providing this input, or in situations in which supervisors need to confirm or adjust the participant's estimate.

☐ **Senior management provides estimates** on the value of an improvement when they are willing to do so. This approach is particularly helpful in establishing values for performance measures that are important to senior management.

☐ **HRD staff estimates** may be used to determine the value of an output data item. In these cases it is essential that the estimates be provided on an unbiased basis.

This step in the ROI model is very important, as it is absolutely necessary to determine the monetary benefits from a training program. The process is challenging, particularly with soft data, but can be methodically accomplished using one or more of the above strategies. To fully cover these techniques, an entire chapter is devoted to this topic.

Tabulating Program Costs

The other part of a cost/benefit analysis equation is the cost of the program. Tabulating the costs involves monitoring or developing all related costs of the program targeted for ROI calculation. Among the cost components that should be included are

☐ The cost to design and develop the program, possibly prorated over the expected life of the program.

☐ The cost of all program materials provided to each participant.

☐ The cost for the instructor/facilitator, including preparation and delivery time.

☐ The cost of facilities for the training program.

☐ Travel, lodging, and meal costs for the participants, if applicable.

☐ Salaries plus employee benefit costs of the participants attending the training.

☐ Administrative and overhead costs allocated to the training program.

In addition, any specific costs related to the needs assessment and evaluation should be included, if appropriate. The conservative approach is to include all of these costs so that the total is fully loaded. To highlight the various schemes for tabulating and classifying costs, a complete chapter is devoted to the topic.

Calculating the Return on Investment

The return on investment is calculated using the program benefits and costs. The cost/benefit ratio is the program benefits divided by cost. In formula form it is:

$$CBR = \frac{\text{Program Benefits}}{\text{Program Costs}}$$

The return on investment uses the net benefits divided by program costs. The net benefits are the program benefits minus the costs. In formula form, the ROI becomes:

$$ROI(\%) = \frac{\text{Net Program Benefits}}{\text{Program Costs}} \times 100$$

This is the same basic formula used in evaluating other investments in which the ROI is traditionally reported as earnings divided by investment. The ROI from some training programs is high. For example, in sales training, supervisory training, and managerial training, the ROI can be quite large, frequently over 100%, while the ROI value for technical and operator training may be lower.

Identifying Intangible Benefits

In addition to tangible, monetary benefits, most training programs will have intangible, non-monetary benefits. The ROI calculation is based on converting both hard and soft data to monetary values. Other data items are identified but are not converted to monetary values. These intangible benefits include items such as

☐ Increased job satisfaction
☐ Increased organizational commitment
☐ Improved teamwork
☐ Improved customer service
☐ Reduced complaints
☐ Reduced conflicts

During data analysis, every attempt is made to convert all data to monetary values. All hard data such as output, quality, and time are converted to monetary values. The conversion of soft data is attempted for each data item. However, if the process used for conversion is too subjective or inaccurate and the resulting values lose credibility in the process, then the data are listed as an intangible benefit with the appropriate explanation. For some programs intangible, non-monetary benefits are extremely valuable, often carrying as much influence as the hard data items. To underscore the importance of intangible benefits, an entire chapter is devoted to the topic.

Implementation Issues

A variety of environmental issues and events will influence successful implementation of the ROI process. These issues must be addressed early to ensure that the ROI process is successful. Specific topics or actions include:

☐ A policy statement concerning results-based training and development.
☐ Procedures and guidelines for different elements and techniques of the evaluation process.
☐ Meetings and formal sessions to develop staff skills with the ROI process.
☐ Strategies to improve management commitment and support for the ROI process.
☐ Mechanisms to provide technical support for questionnaire design, data analysis, and evaluation strategy.
☐ Specific techniques to change or improve the organizational culture to place more attention on results.

The ROI process can fail or succeed based on the success of these implementation issues. Because implementation is crucial to a successful measurement and evaluation process, the last chapter is devoted to this issue.

Planning for the ROI

Proper planning for ROI early in the training and development cycle is an important ingredient in the ultimate success of the ROI process. Appropriate upfront attention will save time later when data are actually collected and analyzed, thus improving accuracy and reducing the cost of the ROI process. It also avoids any confusion as to what will be accomplished, by whom, and at what time. Two planning documents are key to the upfront analysis, and should be completed before the program is designed or developed. Each document is briefly described as follows:

Data-Collection Plan

Figure 5-2 shows a completed form for planning data collection for an interactive selling-skills program. The three-day training program was designed for retail sales associates in the electronics department of a major retail store chain. An ROI calculation was planned for a pilot of three groups.

This document provides a place for the major elements and issues regarding collecting data for the four levels of evaluation. Broad objectives are appropriate for planning. Specific, detailed objectives are developed later, before the program is designed.

The objectives for Level 1 usually include positive reactions to the training program and presence of completed action plans. If it is a new program, as is the example in Figure 5-2, another category for suggested improvements may be included.

Level 2 evaluation focuses on the measures of learning. The specific objectives include those areas where participants are expected to change knowledge, skills, or attitudes. The method is the specific way in which learning is assessed, whether as a test, simulation, skill practice, or facilitator assessment. Level 2 evaluation is usually held during or at the end of the program, and the responsibility usually rests with the instructor or facilitator.

For Level 3 evaluation, the objectives represent broad areas of application of the program, including significant on-the-job activities. The evaluation method includes one of the post-program methods described earlier. The timing is usually a matter of weeks or months after the program is completed. Because responsibilities are often shared among several groups including

Program: Interactive Selling Skills   **Responsibility:** _____   **Date:** _____

Evaluation Plan: Data Collection

Level	Objective(s)	Evaluation Method	Timing	Responsibilities
I Reaction, Satisfaction and Planned Actions	■ Positive Reaction ■ Recommended Improvements ■ Action Items	■ Reaction Questionnaire	■ End of 2nd Day ■ End of 3rd Day	■ Facilitator
II Learning	■ Acquisition of Skills ■ Selection of Skills	■ Skill Practice	■ During Program	■ Facilitator
III Job Application	■ Use of Skills ■ Frequency of Skill Use ■ Barriers	■ Questionnaire ■ Follow-up Session	■ 3 Months After Program ■ 3 Weeks After the First Two Days	■ Training Coordinator ■ Facilitator
IV Business Results	■ Increase of Sales	■ Performance Monitoring	■ 3 Months After Program	■ Training Coordinator

Figure 5-2. Data-collection plan for an interactive selling-skills program.

the training and development staff, division trainers, or local managers, it is important to clarify this issue early in the process.

For Level 4 evaluation, objectives focus on business impact variables influenced by the program. The objectives may include the way in which each item is measured. For example, if one of the objectives is to improve quality, a specific measure would indicate how that quality is actually measured, such as defects per thousand units produced. While the preferred evaluation method is performance monitoring, other methods such as action planning may be appropriate. The timing depends on how quickly participants can generate a sustained business impact. It is usually a matter of months after training. Responsibility for Level 4 data collection can vary significantly, including the participants themselves, supervisors, division training coordinators, or perhaps an external evaluator.

The data-collection plan is an important part of the evaluation strategy, and should be completed prior to moving forward with the training program. For existing training programs, the plan is completed before pursuing the ROI evaluation. The plan provides clear direction as to what type of data will be collected, how it will be collected, when it will be collected, and who will collect it.

ROI Analysis Plan

Figure 5-3 shows a completed plan for calculating the ROI for the interactive selling-skills program described earlier. This planning document is the continuation of the data-collection plan presented in Figure 5-2, and captures information on several key items necessary to develop the actual ROI calculation. In the first column, significant data items are listed. These are usually Level 4 data items, but in some cases Level 3 items could be included. These items will be used in the ROI analysis.

In the second column, the method used to isolate the effects of training is listed next to each data item. The method will usually be the same for each data item, but there could be variations. For example, if no historical data are available for one data item, then trend-line analysis is not possible for that item, although it may be appropriate for others.

The third column includes the method of converting data to monetary values using one of the ten strategies outlined earlier. The fourth column outlines the categories of costs that will be captured for the training program. Instructions about how certain costs should be prorated would be noted here. Normally the cost categories will be consistent from one program to another. However, a specific cost that is unique to the program would also be noted. The fifth column outlines intangible benefits expected from the program. This list is generated from discussions about the program with sponsors and subject matter experts.

Program: <u>Interactive Selling Skills</u>   Responsibility_____   Date:_____

Evaluation Strategy: ROI Analysis

Data Items	Methods of Isolating the Effects of the Program	Methods of Converting Data	Cost Categories	Intangible Benefits	Other Influences/Issues	Communication Targets
■ Weekly Sales Per Employee	■ Control Group Analysis	■ Direct Conversion Using Profit Contribution	■ Facilitation Fees ■ Program Materials ■ Meals/ Refreshments ■ Facilities ■ Participant Salaries/Benefits ■ Cost of Coordination/ Evaluation	■ Customer Satisfaction ■ Employee Satisfaction	■ Must Have Job Coverage During Training ■ No Communication With Control Group ■ Seasonal Fluctuations Should be Avoided	■ Program Participants ■ Electronics Dept. Managers-Target Stores ■ Store Managers-Target Stores ■ Senior Store Executives District, Region, Headquarters ■ Training Staff: Instructors, Coordinators, Designers and Managers

Figure 5-3. ROI analysis for an interactive selling-skills program.

Other issues or events that might influence the implementation of the program would be highlighted in the sixth column. Typical items include the capability of participants, the degree of access to data sources, and unique data analysis issues. Finally, the last column outlines communication targets. Although there could be many groups that should receive the information, four target groups are always recommended.

1. Senior management
2. Participants' supervisors
3. Program participants
4. Training and development staff

All four of these groups need to know the results of ROI analysis.

When combined with the data-collection plan, the ROI analysis plan provides the detailed information needed to develop the ROI, illustrating how the steps will be accomplished from beginning to end. When thoroughly completed, these two plans provide the direction necessary to develop the ROI calculation.

Summary

This chapter presented a rational ROI process model for calculating a training program's return on investment. The process takes the complicated issue of calculating ROI and breaks it into simple steps. When the process is thoroughly planned, taking all potential strategies and techniques into consideration, the process becomes manageable and achievable.

Discussion Questions

1. What are the advantages of a systematic, step-by-step approach to developing the ROI?
2. Why is a model needed for the ROI process? Contrast this model with the one presented in the previous chapter.
3. What are the most difficult parts of this model? Why?
4. Why does the ROI process appear to be confusing?
5. Some organizations need an ROI process that will look forward (forecast) and backward (ROI results). Can this model be used in both scenarios? Explain.
6. How does this model compare with other approaches to measuring ROI?
7. Can this ROI process model be used with all types of performance interventions? Provide examples of diverse applications, addressing the first three blocks in the model.
8. One criticism of an ROI measurement is that it does not present a "balanced" view of results. How does this model address this issue?
9. Why is sampling necessary for ROI calculations?
10. Detailed planning is essential for an effective evaluation. Why?

References

1. Phillips, J. J. "ROI: The Search for Best Practices," *Training & Development,* Vol. 50, No. 2, February 1996, pp. 42–47.
2. Phillips, J. J. "Meeting the ROI Challenge: A Practical Approach to Measuring the Return on Investment in Training and Development," *European Forum for Management Development,* January 1997, pp. 24–28.
3. Phillips, J. J. *Return on Investment in Training and Performance Improvement Programs,* Houston, TX: Gulf Publishing Company, 1997.

CHAPTER 6

Evaluation Instrument Design

Types of Data

Evaluation's fundamental premise is to collect data directly related to the objectives of the HRD program. HRD professionals are sometimes concerned that appropriate data are not available in the organization; fortunately, this is not the case. The data needed to evaluate training are already being collected in the vast majority of settings. The confusion sometimes stems from the different types of outcomes planned for training programs. Often, programs' skill and behavioral outcomes reflect what participants will be able to do after completing the program. The outcomes of some programs, such as technical training programs, are easy to observe and evaluate. For example, it is easy to measure the speed and quality of an assembly line operator before, during, and after a training program. However, behavioral outcomes associated with effective management are not nearly so obvious or measurable. Demonstrating that a manager is an effective delegator or motivator is much more difficult than demonstrating that an assembly line operator is maintaining quality and quantity standards.

To help focus on the desired measures, a distinction is made in two general categories of data—hard data and soft data. Hard data are the primary measurement of improvement, presented in rational, undisputed facts that are easily accumulated. They are the most desired type of data to collect. The ultimate criteria for measuring the effectiveness of management rest on hard data items, such as return on investment, productivity, profitability, cost control and quality control.

Hard data are

☐ Easy to measure and quantify.
☐ Relatively easy to convert to monetary values.

☐ Objectively based.
☐ Common measures of organizational performance.
☐ Very credible with management.

Because changes in these data may lag behind changes in the condition of the human organization by many months, it is useful for management planning and control to supplement these measures with interim assessments of soft data such as attitude, motivation, satisfaction, and skill usage.[1] Although a supervisory program designed to enhance delegation and motivation skills should have an ultimate impact on hard data items, it may be best measured by soft data items. Soft data are more difficult to collect and analyze, and are therefore used when hard data are not available.

Soft data are

☐ Sometimes difficult to measure or quantify directly.
☐ Difficult to convert to monetary values.
☐ Subjectively based, in many cases.
☐ Less credible as a performance measurement.
☐ Usually behaviorally oriented.

Hard Data

Hard data can be grouped into four categories (or subdivisions), as shown in Figure 6-1. These categories—output, quality, cost, and time—are typical performance measures in almost every organization. When they are not available, the basic approach is to convert soft data to one of the four basic measurements.

Output. Probably the most visible hard data results achieved from training are those involving improvements in the output of the work unit. Every organization, regardless of type, has basic measurements of work output. Table 6-1 outlines some common measurements. Since these factors are monitored by organizations, changes can be easily measured by comparing before-and-after work output.

Quality. One of the most significant hard data results is quality. Every organization is concerned with quality; therefore, processes are usually in place to measure and monitor it. Many HRD programs are designed to improve quality, and results can be easily documented using a variety of the quality improvement measurements illustrated in Table 6-1.

Cost. Another significant hard data results area is improvement in costs. HRD programs that produce a direct cost savings can easily show a bottom-line contribution. A few examples of types of costs are shown in Table 6-1.

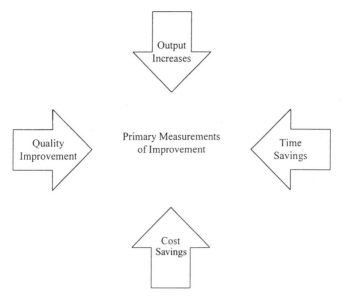

Figure 6-1. The four major categories of hard data.

There can be as many cost items as there are accounts in a cost accounting system. In addition, costs can be combined to develop any number of combinations needed for evaluation.

Time. The fourth hard data results area is time. Easy to measure and just as critical as cost or quality, a time savings may mean that a project was completed faster than initially planned, a new product was introduced earlier, or the time to repair equipment was reduced. The savings translates into additional output or lower operating costs. Examples of time savings generated by HRD programs are shown in Table 6-1.

The distinction among these four groups of hard data is sometimes unclear, as there are some overlapping factors. For example, accident costs may be listed under the cost category, the number of accidents listed under quality, and the lost-time days due to an accident listed under the time category. The rationale? Accidents represent a cost that can easily be determined. Accidents are usually caused by someone making a mistake and are a reflection of the quality of employee efforts. The days lost from the job represents time lost to the organization. In another example, an incentive bonus may be listed as output, since the amount of bonus is usually tied directly to the output of an employee or group of employees. However, the bonus is usually presented in cash, which represents a cost to the organization. The distinction among the different subdivisions is not so important as an awareness of the vast number of measurements in these four areas.

Table 6-1
Examples of Hard Data

OUTPUT	TIME
Units Produced	Cycle Time
Tons Manufactured	Response Time for Complaint
Items Assembled	Equipment Downtime
Items Sold	Overtime
Sales	Average Delay Time
Forms Processed	Time to Project Completion
Loans Approved	Processing Time
Inventory Turnover	Supervisory Time
Patients Visited	Training Time
Applications Processed	Meeting Time
Students Graduated	Repair Time
Tasks Completed	Efficiency (Time-Based)
Productivity	Work Stoppages
Work Backlog	Order Response Time
Incentive Bonus	Late Reporting
Shipments	Lost-Time Days
New Accounts Generated	

COSTS	QUALITY
Budget Variances	Scrap
Unit Costs	Waste
Cost by Account	Rejects
Variable Costs	Error Rates
Fixed Costs	Rework
Overhead Costs	Shortages
Operating Costs	Product Defects
Delay Costs	Deviation from Standard
Penalties/Fines	Product Failures
Project Cost Savings	Inventory Adjustments
Accident Costs	Percent of Tasks Completed Properly
Program Costs	Number of Accidents
Sales Expense	Customer Complaints
Administrative Costs	
Average Cost Reduction	

Soft Data

There are times when hard, rational numbers just do not exist. When this is the case, soft data may be meaningful in evaluating HRD programs. Table 6-2 shows common types of soft data, categorized or subdivided into six areas: work habits, climate, new skills, development, satisfaction, and initiative. Because there can be many other types of soft data, the possibilities are almost limitless. While there are other ways to divide soft data into categories, this grouping of six categories makes the presentation easier to follow.

Table 6-2
Examples of Soft Data

WORK HABITS	NEW SKILLS
Absenteeism	Decision Made
Tardiness	Problem Solved
Visits to the Dispensary	Conflicts Avoided
First Aid Treatments	Grievances Resolved
Violations of Safety Rules	Counseling Successes
Number of Communication Break-downs	Listening Comprehension
Excessive Breaks	Reading Speed
	Use of New Skills
	Intention to Use New Skills
	Frequency of Use of New Skills
	Importance of New Skills

CLIMATE	DEVELOPMENT
Number of Grievances	Number of Promotions
Number of Discrimination Charges	Number of Pay Increases
Employee Complaints	Number of Training Programs Attended
Job Satisfaction	Requests for Transfer
Organizational Commitment	Performance Appraisal Ratings
Employee Turnover	Increase in Job Effectiveness

SATISFACTION	INITIATIVE
Favorable Reactions	Implementation of New Ideas
Job Satisfaction	Successful Completion of Projects
Attitude Changes	Number of Suggestions Implemented
Perceptions of Job Responsibilities	Setting Goals and Objectives
Perceived Changes in Performance	
Employee Loyalty	
Increased Confidence	
Customer/Client Satisfaction	

Work habits. Employee work habits are critical to the success of a work group. Dysfunctional work habits can lead to an unproductive and ineffective work group, while productive work habits can boost the group's output and morale. The most common and easily documented unproductive work habits include absenteeism and tardiness, which can be tied to cost savings much more easily than other types of soft data. HRD programs for supervisors frequently contain modules to improve the work habits of employees. In most organizations, measurement systems are in place to record employee's problematic work habits such as absenteeism, tardiness, and visits to the first aid station. In others situations, the employee's supervisor may have to document the work habits.

Climate. The climate of the work group is another area of importance in team effectiveness. Grievances, discrimination charges, complaints, and job dissatisfaction are often linked to the work climate. The result: less efficiency, less output, unionization drives, and possibly even employee resignations. Many HRD and organizational development programs are designed to improve work climate.

New skills. Employee skill-building is critical for most organizations. Although the successful application of new skills may result in hard data measurements such as a new employee learning a production process, they may also involve soft data measurements which are intangible in nature and difficult to relate to a monetary savings. Examples of soft data skills are making decisions, solving problems, resolving conflicts, settling grievances, and improving listening. An important measure is the frequency with which the new skill is employed. The success of many skill-based HRD programs lies in the frequency of use after the program was completed. With proper preplanning, the frequency and extent of the use of new skills can be monitored and documented, thus providing additional data for a program evaluation.

Development. Another important type of soft data is employee development and/or advancement. Promotions, transfers, pay increases, and performance ratings are typical data that indicate improvement in this area. In the case of managers/supervisors, measurements focus on the extent to which they provide developmental opportunities for their employees.

Satisfaction. Almost every HRD program is designed to improve satisfaction with the subject, work, environment, or customers. Some programs are conducted to change attitudes toward customers, the job, or the organization. A few programs are designed to change participants' perception of the work. In all these situations, feelings and attitudes are relatively easy to document with reaction questionnaires and attitude surveys.

Initiative. The final category of soft data involves initiative. In some HRD programs participants are encouraged to try new ideas and techniques. The extent to which employees accomplish what they plan provides additional evidence of the program's success. Also, the employee's initiative to generate ideas and submit suggestions are further indications of improvement.

As with hard data, these subdivisions have some overlap. Some items listed under one category could appropriately be listed in another. For instance, consider employee loyalty. Loyalty is related both to the feelings and attitudes of an employee as well as work habits. An employee exhibits loyalty through attitudes and feelings in these situations:

☐ Placing the organization's goals above personal non-work goals.
☐ Choosing to purchase the company's products rather than those of a competitor.

Loyalty may also surface in these work habits of an employee:

☐ Returning to work promptly after break.
☐ Studying job information on his or her own time.
☐ Taking work home when necessary to finish the job.

Soft Data versus Hard Data

The preference for hard data in program evaluation does not mean that soft data are not valuable. In fact, soft data are essential for a complete evaluation of an HRD program. A program's total success may rest on soft data measurements. For example, in a program designed to reduce turnover at a fast food restaurant, four key measures of success were identified in the program evaluation: trainee turnover, interview-to-hire ratios, participants' evaluation, and reduced litigation.

Most programs use a combination of hard and soft data items in the evaluation. A comprehensive evaluation would use several hard data and soft data measurements. For example, a maintenance supervisors' training program used the following measures of success:

☐ A reduction of costs associated with specific maintenance activities
☐ Improvement in production equipment and processes
☐ Changes in maintenance responsibilities and procedures
☐ Improvement in training of maintenance employees
☐ Changes in organization and personnel

These changes included both hard data (production and costs) and soft data (increased training, changes in procedures, and changes in the organization).

Soft data are usually best when evaluating behavioral and skill outcomes. For example, in behavior modeling, which has proven to be a very effective approach to building supervisory skills, the evaluation of behavioral and skill outcomes rests almost entirely on soft data.

The important point is that there is a place for both hard and soft data in program evaluation. A comprehensive program will use both types of data.[2] Some programs will rely on soft data as primary measures, while others will rely on hard data as primary measures. Hard data are preferred because of their distinct advantages and level of credibility.

Sources of Data

When considering possible sources of data to provide input on the success of an HRD program, the categories are easily defined. The six major categories are briefly described below.

Organizational Performance Records

The most useful and credible sources of data for ROI analysis are the organization's records and reports. Whether individualized or group-based, the records reflect performance in a work unit, department, division, region, or company overall. This source can include many types of measures, which are usually available in abundance throughout the organization. Data from these sources is preferred for Level 4 evaluation because it is easy to obtain and usually reflects business impact data.[3] The difficulty lies in locating the particular reports for the data if the organization has been inconsistent in record keeping.

Participants

One of the most widely used sources of data for an ROI analysis is the participants in the program. Participants are frequently asked to provide input on how skills and knowledge acquired in a program have been applied on the job. Sometimes they are asked to explain the impact of those actions as well. Participants are a rich source of data for Level 1, 2, 3 and 4 evaluations. Most participants are credible because they are the individuals who have achieved the performance improvement and possess knowledge of processes and other influencing factors. The challenge is to find an effective and efficient way to capture data in a consistent manner among participants.

Supervisors of Participants

Those individuals who directly supervise or lead program participants are another important source of data. This group will often have a vested interest in the evaluation process since they probably approved participants' attendance at the program. Also, in many situations, they have observed the participants as they attempted to use the knowledge and skills acquired in the program. Consequently, they can report on successes linked to the program as well as any difficulties and problems associated with application. Although supervisor input is usually best for Level 3 data, it can be useful for Level 4 data. It is important, however, for supervisors to maintain objectivity in assessing the program participants.

Subordinates of Participants

In situations in which supervisors and managers are being trained, their subordinates can provide information about changes in behavior that have occurred since the program was conducted. Input from subordinates is appropriate for Level 3 data, but usually not for Level 4 data. While collecting data from this source can be very helpful and instructive, it is often avoided because of the potential biases that can enter into the feedback process.

Team/Peer Group

Those individuals who serve as the participants' team members or occupy a peer position in the organization are another source of data in a few types of programs. In these situations, peer group members provide input on the change in the participants' behavior. Using this source of data is more appropriate when all team members have participated in the program and are reporting on changes in behavior of specific individuals or the collective efforts of the group. The subjective nature of this process and the lack of opportunity to fully evaluate the application of skills make this source of data somewhat limited.

Internal/External Groups

In some situations, internal or external groups such as the training and development staff, program facilitators, or external consultants may provide input on a participant's success at applying the skills and knowledge acquired in the program. The input from this source may be based on on-the-job observation after the training program has been completed. Collecting data from this source has limited uses. Because internal groups may have a vested interest in the outcome of evaluation, their input may lose credibility. Input from external groups is appropriate with certain types of observations of on-the-job performance.

Data-Collection Instrument Design

Instruments are used to collect data. The remainder of this chapter presents preliminary instrument design issues. Although instrument design occurs after the decision has been made to develop the program, it is more appropriate to consider it in conjunction with developing the evaluation strategy.

Types of Instruments

An evaluation instrument is a data-gathering device administered at the appropriate stages in the HRD process. Instruments come in a variety of forms and are usually divided into the following categories:[4]

☐ Questionnaires
☐ Surveys
☐ Tests
☐ Interviews
☐ Focus groups
☐ Observations
☐ Performance records

After reviewing a few general design considerations in this chapter, Chapters 9 and 10 will present each of these types of instruments along with advantages, disadvantages, and specific design considerations.

Preliminary Questions

Before designing an instrument, several issues need to be addressed. Answers to the following questions provide input on the instrument's optimum design to serve its planned function to collect soft or hard data.[5]

How will the data be used? Before selecting or designing an instrument, the basic purpose(s) of evaluation should be reviewed. Will the data be used to calculate ROI? Will it be used to strengthen the HRD process? Will it be used to attract new participants? The answers to these questions will have an impact on the type of instrument needed.

What types of data are needed? Hard data are needed for higher-level evaluations. Opinions, reactions, attitudes, and other soft data may also be needed. Which ones are best for the evaluation? What is available? The instrument may collect specific costs, output, time and quality data, and observations and perceptions.

How will the data be analyzed? Data are usually collected to be tabulated, summarized, and reported to others. The planned analyses, including statistical comparisons, should be considered when the instrument is designed.

Who will use the information? The target audience is another important consideration. Who will review the data, in either its raw state or in a summary? Who will see the full report? How will the report be used? This determination can lead to specific questions for the instrument.

Should the instrument be tested? When a program represents a significant investment or will be repeated many times, it may be appropriate to test an instrument before using it to evaluate the program. Pilot testing provides an opportunity to analyze the data to see if there are any problems with the instrument.

Is there a standard instrument? In some cases standard instruments can be equally effective and less expensive than custom-designed ones. Broad areas such as communications, human relations, or leadership may be suitable for standard instruments. Of course, the program content and objectives must be appropriate for the areas covered in the instrument. For example, in a general communications course for supervisors, an inventory on communications may be an appropriate standard instrument for evaluating the program.

What are the consequences of biased information? The consequence of participants supplying biased information on the instrument is an often overlooked part of this process. Sometimes, evaluation data are supplied on a voluntary basis—even anonymously. The participants' biases can then enter into the information. Unless opinions and attitudes are sought out, the information will not be reliable. Purposeful wrong answers can possibly have a significant influence on an individual, a budget, or a group of employees. If so, preventative measures must be taken. One technique involves asking similar questions at different times and cross-checking the answers. Similar answers to similar questions can show whether or not the information is consistent.

Characteristics of Effective Evaluation Instruments

Regardless of the type of instrument, several basic design principles lead to a more effective instrument. The most common of these principles follow.

Validity

Probably the most important characteristic of an evaluation instrument is validity. A valid instrument measures what it is designed to measure. The degree to which it performs this function satisfactorily is usually called the relative validity. The HRD professional should be concerned with validity when there is a question about the appropriateness of a particular instrument. The economic consideration of design may dictate that little time is spent with the subject, but the evaluation of elaborate programs will demand more attention to validity.

There are four basic approaches to determining if an instrument is valid. These approaches, adopted by the American Psychological Association, are (1) content validity, (2) construct validity, (3) concurrent validity, and (4) predictive validity.[6] The actions taken to make the instrument valid are usually referred to as "defending" the validity of the instrument. The term "correlation" is used in several of these methods. Correlation refers to the strength of the relationship between two measures. It is expressed in terms of a correlation coefficient and can be positive or negative, ranging from -1 to $+1$.

Content validity. Content validity refers to the extent to which the instrument represents the content of the program. Content validity is the most common and cost-effective approach. One or more individuals who are very knowledgeable about the program's content would be asked if the instrument is a representative sample of the skill, knowledge, or ability presented in the HRD program. Low content validity means that the instrument does not represent a true sample of what was covered. High content validity means that the instrument represents a good balance of all the information presented. To ensure content validity, all important items, behaviors, or information covered in the program should be included proportionately in the instrument. The number of items or questions in the instrument should correspond roughly with the amount of time, exposure, or importance of the material presented. A seven-step procedure for ensuring content validity is contained in Smith and Merchant.[7]

Construct validity. Construct validity refers to the extent to which an instrument represents the construct it purports to measure. A construct is an abstract variable such as a skill, attitude, or ability. Examples of constructs follow:

☐ Attitude toward supervisor
☐ Ability to read a scale
☐ Skill in conducting an effective performance discussion

As a first step in defending construct validity, all parts of the construct must be defined and a logical case should be made showing that the instrument is an adequate measure of that construct. The definition of the construct should be as detailed as possible so that it is easy to understand. Construct validity can be defended in one or more ways.

☐ Expert opinion
☐ Correlations
☐ Logical deductions
☐ Criterion group studies

Expert opinion is a relatively easy approach in which a group of experts agree that the instrument, in their opinion, is an accurate measurement of the construct. Correlations are more complex. In this case, another instrument is used to measure the same or a similar construct, and the results are correlated with the first instrument. Statistically significant positive correlations could show construct validity. Another, more subjective, option is logical deduction. In this case, the instrument designer must logically conclude through a series of deductions that the instrument represents a measure of the construct. Criterion group studies can be more useful. A group of people who possess an abundance or deficiency of the construct in question are administered the instrument. If the results agree with the existing knowledge about the group, then it helps make the case for construct validity.

Construct validity is indeed a complex matter. Perhaps an example can help illustrate the process. An HRD program is conducted to improve company loyalty in a group of employees. Therefore, an instrument must be designed to measure loyalty before and after the program. During the program analysis, it is concluded that employees with high levels of company loyalty

☐ Have a desire to work hard for the organization (high productivity).

☐ Become part of the organization's goals and values (high job satisfaction, job involvement).

☐ Have a strong desire to remain with the organization (low turnover, low absenteeism).

The construct in this example is company loyalty. Job satisfaction and involvement are measured with a standard instrument. Data are also collected on productivity, absenteeism, and turnover. Employees who are perceived to have a high degree of company loyalty are administered the instrument. Data collected from the instruments show a positive relationship between company loyalty and job satisfaction, involvement, and productivity, and a negative correlation between company loyalty and absenteeism and turnover. This provides necessary support for the validity of the company loyalty construct.

Concurrent validity. Concurrent validity refers to the extent to which an instrument agrees with the results of other instruments administered at approximately the same time to measure the same characteristics. For example, a survey is conducted with team members to measure the effectiveness of the team. Another survey, designed for the same purpose, is administered to the same group. If both instruments show the same results, it can be argued that the instrument is valid based on concurrent validity. Concurrent validity is determined by calculating the correlation coefficient between the results of the two instruments. Calculating the correlation coefficient will be discussed further in Chapter 14.

Predictive validity. Predictive validity refers to the extent to which an instrument can predict future behaviors or results. For example, the results obtained from an end-of-program evaluation may be used to predict future behavior and performance on the job. If an instrument predicts certain levels of performance and behavior, and a significant number of participants exhibit that performance and behavior level, then the instrument possesses predictive validity. Predictive validity can be expressed as a correlation coefficient relating performance on the instrument in question to the measure of the predicted results or behavior. For example, in a sales training program an end-of-program test is administered that reflects the skills and knowledge gained in the program. Test scores are compared to actual sales performance three months after the program, and correlation coefficients are developed. A significant positive correlation indicates that the test has predictive validity.

Methods to Improve Validity. There are no magic formulas to ensure that an instrument is valid when it is designed. However, a few simple guidelines may help improve validity.[8]

Include an appropriate number of items on an instrument. Too few items can hamper the validity, while too many can be cumbersome and time-consuming. Strive for the right balance to improve the validity.

Reduce response bias when possible. Participants may respond in the way they think administrators want them to respond, which can make an instrument invalid. Participants should be encouraged to provide candid responses. In some cases the staff administering the instrument may be biased in their expectations of the outcome. For instance, revealing that one group is expected to outperform another can sometimes influence results. Participants may provide responses that are interpreted as showing improvement when actually those improvements do not exist.

Reliability

Reliability, another important characteristic of an evaluation instrument, refers to the consistency and stability of an instrument. A reliable instrument is one that is consistent enough to provide approximately the same results in subsequent measurements of an item. For example, if an attitude survey is administered to an employee and the same survey is administered to the same employee two days later, the results should be the same (assuming that nothing happens in the interim to change the employee's attitude). A reliable instrument will provide the same results. If there is a significant difference, the instrument is unreliable, because the results fluctuated without additional effort to change the employee's attitude.

The causes of these potential fluctuations are called errors. There are a number of sources of errors that affect instruments' reliability. They include

☐ Fluctuations in the mental alertness of the participants.
☐ Variations in the conditions under which the instrument is administered.
☐ Differences in the interpretation of results from the instrument.
☐ Random effects caused by the personal motivation of the participants.
☐ The length of the instrument. With a longer instrument, more data are collected, but reliability may be increased at the expense of other factors.

It is essential to have reliable instruments in examinations in which data are collected from participants before and after a program; otherwise, the changes in scores cannot be attributed to the HRD program. Four procedures that can help ensure an instrument's reliability are (1) test/retest, (2) alternate-form, (3) split-half and (4) inter-item correlations. For more information on reliability, see other references.[10]

Test/retest. This procedure involves administering the same test or survey to the same group of employees at two different time periods. The correlation of the scores is then calculated; if there is a significant positive correlation, the test is reliable.

Alternate-form method. This procedure involves constructing two similar instruments, administering them to employees at the same time, and analyzing the correlation between the two scores. If there is a significant positive correlation, the instrument is considered reliable. Bear in mind that constructing a similar instrument is time consuming, which may make this approach impractical.

Split-half procedure. This method involves splitting the instrument into two equal parts and comparing the results. For example, it might be appropriate to compare the even-numbered questions with the odd-numbered questions. The scores of the two halves are compared, and the correlation is developed. A significant correlation indicates a reliable instrument.

Inter-item correlations. This procedure involves calculating correlations between each of the items on the instrument. For example, a test with 25 items is divided into 25 parts. A correlation is developed to compare each item to the others.

Ease of Administration

An instrument should be easy to administer. Directions and instructions should be simple and straightforward, increasing the likelihood that it will be administered consistently among different participants. Clear written instructions to participants, as well as verbal explanations, will help ensure consistent application.

Simple and Brief

An effective instrument will be simple and brief. The readability level should be appropriate for the participants' knowledge, ability, and background. Short objective responses should be sought whenever practical, as long responses and essay answers detract from the simplistic approach. The fewest number of questions necessary to cover a particular topic is recommended. There is a natural tendency to ask more questions than necessary, which adds to the instrument's length and possibly frustrates the participants.

Economical

As with every other stage of the HRD process, economics must be considered in the design, development, or purchase of an instrument. An effective instrument will be one that is economical for its planned use. The length of time needed to administer an instrument is another cost consideration, as well as the time necessary to analyze the data collected and present it in a meaningful format.

Summary

This chapter presented introductory information concerning the data-collection phase of evaluation, which will be continued in other chapters. This chapter also described the two major categories of data and the sources of data for an evaluation. Preliminary issues concerning instrument design were presented, which must be addressed regardless of which instrument is being designed and developed for data collection. Subsequent chapters will focus on overall evaluation design as well as specific uses of these instruments to collect data.

Discussion Questions

1. Before selecting an evaluation instrument, why is it important to analyze the types of data needed and examine how the data will be used in the evaluation?

2. Can all data be grouped into either hard data or soft data? Explain.
3. Identify additional hard data and soft data measurements from your organization (or one with which you are familiar).
4. What problems occur in collecting feedback from groups other than participants' supervisors?
5. What are the advantages and disadvantages of using standard instruments versus customized instruments?
6. What types of validity would be of most concern for HRD program evaluators? Why?
7. What represents a good validity coefficient? Is the development of a validity coefficient necessary in program evaluation? Explain.
8. How does reliability differ from validity? What represents a good reliability coefficient? Is it necessary to develop a reliability coefficient for an instrument used in evaluation?
9. How could administrative problems cause errors in the use of evaluation instruments?

References

1. Pine, J. and Tingley, J. "ROI of Soft-Skills Training," *Training,* February 1993, pp. 55–60.
2. Fitz-enz, J. "Yes . . . You Can Weigh In Training's Value," *Training,* July 1994, pp. 54–58.
3. Bramley, P. and Kitson, B. "Evaluating Training Against Business Criteria," *Journal of European Industrial Training,* 18(1), pp. 10–14.
4. Marshall, V. and Schriver, R. "Using Evaluation to Improve Performance," *Technical & Skills Training,* January 1994, pp. 6–9.
5. Rea, L. M. and Parker, R. A. *Designing and Conducting Survey Research.* San Francisco, CA: Jossey-Bass Publishers, 1992.
6. Gatewood, R. D. and Field, H. S., *Human Resource Selection,* 3rd Edition. Chicago, IL.: Dryden Press, 1995.
7. Smith, J. E. and Merchant, S. "Using Competency Exams for Evaluating Training," *Training and Development Journal,* August 1990, pp. 65–71.
8. Aiken, L. R. *Psychological Testing and Assessment,* 7th Edition. Boston, MA: Allyn and Bacon, 1991.
9. Morris, L. L., Fitz-Gibbon, C. T., and Lindheim, E. *How to Measure Performance and Use Tests,* 2nd Edition. Beverly Hills, CA: Sage Publications, Inc., 1993.
10. Litwin, M. S. *How to Measure Survey Reliability and Validity.* Thousand Oaks, CA: Sage Publications, Inc., 1995.

CHAPTER 7

Evaluation Design

The Results-Based HRD Model presented in Chapter 4 devoted several steps to the evaluation process. One step involved selecting the evaluation method and design, perhaps one of the most important steps among those directly involved with evaluation. Sometimes the methods of evaluation are difficult to separate from the evaluation design. Evaluation methods concern data collection and are presented as data-collection methods in two chapters. Evaluation design presents a more general view of the evaluation. It is concerned with the development of a system or overall scheme to obtain the desired measurements at the appropriate time. Proper design is imperative for effective evaluation.

The research designs presented in this chapter are classic designs found in most references.[1] From a practical perspective, these designs attempt to isolate the amount of output performance directly associated with the program. They are commonly used when the performance is stated in terms of skill and knowledge acquisition (Level 2), skill and knowledge use and application (Level 3), or business impact (Level 4). In recent years, additional methods to isolate the impact of performance have been developed that extend beyond the classic research design.[2] These methods are presented in a later chapter on isolating the effects of the program.

Elements of Design

In many HRD program evaluations, performance comparisons are made. The performance of a group of program participants can be compared to

☐ Performance prior to the program.
☐ Another group who did not receive the same program.
☐ The remainder of the population of potential participants.
☐ Management's or the client's expectation.
☐ Industry or benchmarking data.

Various combinations of comparisons are important factors in evaluation design. This section covers the elements of design with emphasis on various design approaches.

Control Groups

Control groups and experimental groups frequently appear in designs. A control group is a group of participants who have characteristics similar to those in the experimental group but do not attend the HRD program that is being evaluated. It represents pre-course conditions. The experimental group participates in training. Ideally, the only difference between the two groups is that one participates in the program and the other does not. Therefore, a performance comparison of the two groups should indicate the impact or success of the HRD program. Appendix 3 presents the selection of control groups, along with guidelines for determining the appropriate sample size.

In a control-group arrangement, it is important that the two groups be equivalent in their job settings, skills, abilities, and demographic characteristics. The true control group is formed by random assignment. If possible, the identity of the control group should not be revealed, as it could affect their performance. With these requirements, control groups may not be practical in real work situations. However, for critical evaluations affecting many participants, control groups are almost essential.

Timing of Measurements

A critical issue in evaluation is the timing of measurements. A measurement is defined as the application of a data-collection instrument such as a questionnaire, survey, test, or interview. These measurements, sometimes referred to as tests, may be taken before the program, during the program, and at subsequent intervals after the program. The post-test portion of a design is never omitted, because it directly measures the results of the program.

Pre-Tests. Careful attention should be given to determining when and how pre- and post-tests are conducted. When conducting pre-tests, (or pre-program measurements), four general guidelines are recommended.

1. **Avoid pre-tests when they alter the participant's performance.** Pre-tests are intended to measure the state of the situation before the HRD program begins. The test itself should not influence performance. If there is evidence that the testing procedure will affect performance, the pre-test should possibly be modified, given far enough in advance of the program to minimize its effect, or omitted.
2. **Do not use pre-tests when they are meaningless.** If teaching completely new material or providing information participants do not yet know, pre-test results may be meaningless. Results would simply show an absence of the knowledge, skill, or ability. For example, in a foreign language program, it is meaningless to conduct a pre-test in the foreign

language if the participants do not know the language. Instead, a post-program measurement of proficiency in acquiring foreign language skills after the program is more appropriate.

3. **Pre-tests and post-tests should be identical or approximately equivalent.** Scores should have a common base for comparison. Identical tests may be used for pre-tests and post-tests, although this may influence results when they are taken the second time. Similar but equivalent tests may be more appropriate for the post-test.

4. **Pre-testing and post-testing should be conducted under the same or similar conditions.** The time allowed for the test and the conditions under which each test is taken should be approximately the same.

Measurement During the Program. While pre- and post-testing generally refer to measuring the level of performance just prior to the program and at the very end of the program, it is sometimes helpful to take measurements during the program itself. In some cases, these measurements capture the extent to which knowledge, skills, and attitudes have been acquired or changed. In other cases, they measure the reaction to the program as it progresses. Progress toward objectives may be measured and feedback data may be obtained to make adjustments in the program. Measurements taken during the program often focus on measures of reaction and learning.

Time Series. There are times when multiple measures are taken before and after a program is conducted. These time series measurements are recommended when feasible, and if data are readily available. Time series tests taken before a program is conducted measure trends prior to the program. They typically focus on Level 3 and 4 data to determine the extent to which skills and knowledge are presently applied on the job and the changes in business performance. Time series measures after the program show the extent of skill use and application, the progress being made toward overall application of the program, and the long-term effects of the program. Time series measures are important to see if trends are developing both before and after the program so that projections or comparisons can be made. This process is explained in more detail in the chapter on isolating the effects of the program.

Timing of Post-Program Follow-Ups. Perhaps the most important measures are taken, at a predetermined time, after the program is completed. This allows participants an opportunity to apply on the job what has been learned in the program. Three types of data can be measured in a follow-up. First, Level 2 data can be obtained to determine the extent to which participants have retained the knowledge and/or skills learned in the program. Learning retention is important, particularly when it is critical for participants to have the knowledge and skills necessary to perform a task. For example, in critical job functions (particularly those involving safety and health) it is essential that participants always know how to perform the tasks. The timing of the learning retention follow-up depends on the feasibility of the evaluation and resources available to continue to test participants.

A Level 3 follow-up determines the extent to which knowledge and/or skills have been applied on the job. For new skills, it is important for them to be used quickly and reinforced regularly. Thus, the timing for a Level 3 follow-up is usually very soon after the program, often in a matter of weeks. For example, in a customer service training program, it might be helpful to determine the extent to which the skills have been applied on the job in a 2–3 week time period. Research has shown that if skills are not used quickly, retention decreases significantly and the likelihood of skills actually being applied will diminish dramatically.[3] In some programs, the timing of the Level 3 follow-up depends on the opportunity to use the skills. For example, if participants are taught a skill that is only used at intervals of 1–2 months, follow-up must be timed so that the participants will have had an opportunity to use the skills and are able to report the progress made. For example, in a negotiation skills training program for managers at Texas Instruments, a follow-up was conducted one year after the program was completed.[4] It was determined that it would take at least a one-year period for the participants to use the negotiation skills and be able to report progress in the application.

A Level 4 follow-up usually requires a longer time period than Level 3. Changes in business performance measures are a consequence of the application of the skills and knowledge learned (Level 3). Thus, there is often lag time between skill application and movement of impact data. In some situations, the lag time is significant and may be dependent on the data-collection process. For example, in a customer service training program, skill application could occur quickly within a 2–3 week time frame, but the actual impact on customers (obtained in a customer satisfaction survey) may not be noticeable for six months. Thus, a Level 4 follow-up must take into consideration the time needed for data collection and the lag time for the application of skills to produce a business performance change. In most situations, a Level 4 follow-up occurs within a 3–6 month time frame.

Table 7-1 shows a summary of the timing of various potential measurements. It contains the common terminology used to describe different measurements, along with the appropriate timing, typical level of data, and the measurement focus.

Threats to Validity

When discussing the merits of various evaluation designs, it is appropriate to return to the subject of validity. Several problems may develop that can

Table 7-1
Timing of Measurements

Description	Timing	Target Data Levels	Measurement Focus
Pre-Test	Taken just before program begins	2, 3, & 4	Level of performance before the program
Post-Test	Taken at the end of the program	1, 2, & 4	Level of performance immediately after the program
Time Series Before the Program	Taken at a predetermined time prior to the program	3 & 4	Changes or trends with on-the-job performance (Level 3) and business performance measures (Level 4), prior to the program
Time Series After the Program	Taken at predetermined times after the program	3 & 4	Changes or trends with on-the-job performance (Level 3) and business performance measures (Level 4) after the program
Measures During the Program	Taken at predetermined times during the program, sometimes daily	1 & 2	Reaction to the program (Level 1) and progress toward skill and knowledge acquisition (Level 2)
Post-Program Follow-up	Taken at a predetermined time after the program has been completed, usually a different time period for each type of data	2, 3, & 4	Learning retention (Level 2), job performance (Level 3), and business impact (Level 4) after the program

reduce the validity of an evaluation design and, consequently, alter the results of the program. Different designs can counteract or offset the effects of these threats.

Time or history. Time has a way of changing things. With the passage of time, performance can improve and attitudes can change—even without an HRD program. When observing output measurements of an HRD program, this question should always be asked: "Would the same results have occurred without the program?" This threat to validity can be isolated by modifying the evaluation design.

Effects of testing. It is possible that the actual experience of a test or other instrument can have an effect on performance or attitude even if no HRD program is undertaken. This effect is more likely to occur when pre-tests and post-tests are identical. Participants reflect on the pre-test material and possibly seek answers to questions that attract their curiosity. Also, after participants know the full scope and purpose of a program, they may provide more favorable responses on the post-test, based on their knowledge of what is expected—not what was learned. The effects of testing can be eliminated with a specific evaluation design.

Selection. The selection of the group participating in an HRD program can possibly have an effect on the outcome. Naturally, some individuals will perform better than others. If a large number of high achievers or underachievers are selected for one group, the results will be distorted and atypical. The problem can be resolved by using random selection when feasible.

Mortality. Participants may drop out of the program for various reasons. If pre- and post-tests are used, the number of participants in the group may have changed from one testing to another. This change makes it difficult to compare the results of the two, and is compounded by the fact that lower-level performers are usually the ones who drop out of a program. The evaluation is compromised when a significant number of participants are not in the same job when the follow-up is conducted.

These are the most common internal threats to validity.[5] The following designs overcome these threats in varying degrees. Additional information on this issue may be found in other references.[6]

Selecting the Appropriate Design

Selecting the appropriate evaluation design is an important part of the evaluation strategy. This section presents common evaluation designs and the relative advantages and disadvantages of each.

One-Shot Program Design

One of the most common designs involves the "one-shot" program measurement. This technique involves a single group that is evaluated only once after an HRD program is completed. No data are collected prior to the program. There are many uncontrolled factors that might influence the measurement and invalidate conclusions based on results achieved through this design. However, to increase the validity of this process, the information obtained in this one-shot evaluation can be adjusted and analyzed using one of the strategies outlined in a later chapter on isolating the effects of the program.

This design can be useful for measuring the performance of a group when there is no way to measure performance beforehand or, possibly, when there is no significant knowledge, skill, or ability existing before the program is conducted. For example, a group of international sales representatives attend a program to learn about a completely new product to be sold on the Mexican market. It makes little sense to evaluate their current understanding of the product before the program is conducted. A measurement at the end of the program to measure their understanding is a more appropriate evaluation.

The one-shot program evaluation design, illustrated in Figure 7-1, is useful when financial, organizational, or time constraints prohibit the use of pre-program data collection. Since it is the least effective design, it should be a minimum reference point for evaluation and used only when necessary.

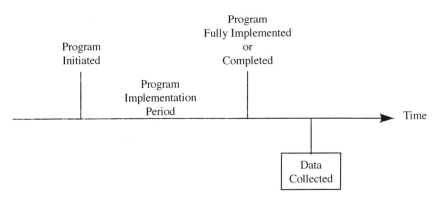

Figure 7-1. One-shot program evaluation design.

Single Group, Pre-Test, and Post-Test Design

The single group, pre-test, and post-test design, as shown in Figure 7-2, remedies the problem of no data for comparisons. This design goes one step beyond the one-shot design by collecting data before and after the HRD program. The pre-program level of knowledge, skills, or attitudes can be compared to post-program levels of knowledge, skills, or activities to detect improvements.

The effect of a pre-test is one disadvantage of this design. The pre-test may encourage participants to explore and examine the topics and questions presented. Consequently, the changes measured by the post-test may result not only from the HRD program, but also from the fact that the pre-test was taken. The effect of external factors is another disadvantage to this design. Changes in the organization, environment, work setting, or other factors may cause changes in performance. It is difficult to isolate the effects of testing and external factors.

Single Group, Time Series Design

One popular design for evaluating an HRD program involves a series of measurements both before and after the program. This is referred to as a sin-

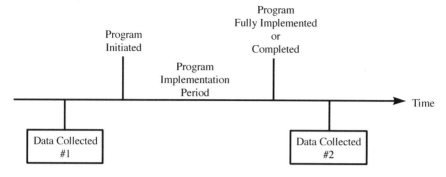

Figure 7-2. Single group, pre-test, and post-test design.

gle group, time series design. In this design, the experimental group serves as its own control group. Multiple measurements taken before the program eliminate some of the problems incurred when a separate control group is not used. Repeated measurements after the program not only allow for comparison with the initial results, but also enable measurement of the long-term effects of the program. This design, illustrated in Figure 7-3, may involve any number of measurements practical for the setting. The single group, time series design eliminates many time and selection threats to validity, but the mortality threat is not counteracted.

There can be a number of outcomes in a time series design, as illustrated in Figure 7-4. In Outcome A, the HRD program apparently had no effect. There was no change in what was measured. Outcome B had a change in output, apparently as a result of the program. Outcome C shows a brief change in output as a result of the program; however, the participants returned to the previous level of measurement. There were apparently no lasting effects from the program.

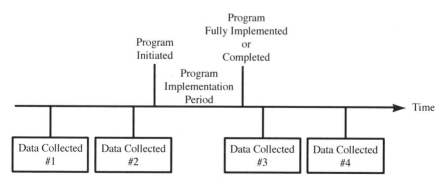

Figure 7-3. Single group, time series design.

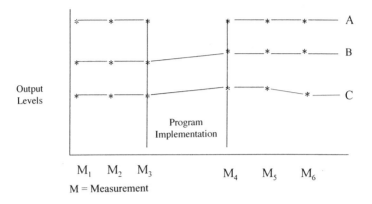

Figure 7-4. Outcomes from a time series design. M series represents test intervals.

The time series design is extremely useful when measurement data are readily available as part of the organization's performance reporting. With this design, the impact of HRD programs can be compared with previous performance over a prolonged time period.

Control Group Design

The next design involves a comparison between two groups: an experimental group and a control group. This is referred to as a control group design and is illustrated in Figure 7-5.

The experimental group receives the HRD program, while the control group does not. Data are gathered on both groups before and after the pro-

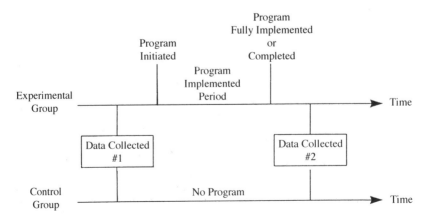

Figure 7-5. Control group design.

gram. The results of the experimental group, when compared to the control group, reveal the impact of the HRD program.

This design is acceptable only when the two groups are quite similar with respect to the appropriate selection criteria. The participants in each group should be at approximately the same job level, with similar experience, ability, working conditions, and possibly even location. For example, it is improper to compare first-line supervisors with middle-level managers. This difference makes any sensible analysis of the post-program performance almost impossible.

The ideal way to select control groups is on a random basis. If the participants for the two groups come from the same population, and can be randomly assigned, then this evaluation design becomes a true control group arrangement. Random selection not only tends to equalize the groups prior to the program, it also promotes a generalization of the evaluation results to other groups and situations. However, from a practical standpoint, it may be difficult to select participants on a random basis. If this is the case, the shortcomings of the design need to be recognized when reporting results.

The true control group design is one of the most powerful evaluation designs available, because it combines random selection and the use of a control group. Threats to validity are controlled with this design, except the effects of testing. Since both groups are subjected to the pre-test, it can have an indeterminate effect on performance. The next design will eliminate the most common threats to validity.

Ideal Experimental Design

Figure 7-6 shows an evaluation design that represents a more idealistic situation. This comprehensive design involves three groups, random selection of participants, and pre- and post-testing on selected groups. As Figure 7-6 illustrates, Group A is pre-tested, participates in the program, and has a post-test. The control group is pre-tested, does not participate in the program, but does have a post-test. Group B has no pre-test, participates in the program, and does have a post-test.

The control group isolates the time and mortality threats to validity. If pre-test and post-test results are equal for the control group, then it follows that neither of these factors influenced the result. The random selection isolates the selection threat.

Group B is used to rule out the interaction of the pre-test with the effects of the HRD program, a weakness in the true control group design presented previously. If post-test results for Groups A and B are identical, then the pre-test had no effect on performance.

This design approaches the ultimate in experimental designs. However, from a practical standpoint, obtaining three randomly selected groups may be difficult. The time, expense, inconvenience, and administrative proce-

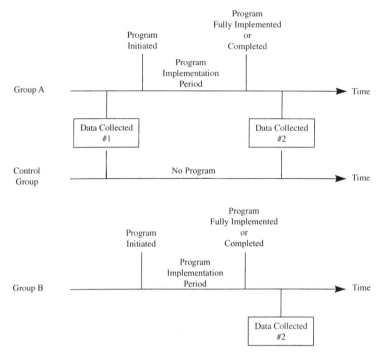

Figure 7-6. Ideal experimental design.

dures required for this arrangement may prohibit its use. Alternate designs, such as the one presented next, can yield similarly reliable results.

Post-Test Only, Control Group Design

Figure 7-7 shows a more practical and less expensive alternative to the ideal experimental design called the post-test only, control group design.

Only a post-test is used on the randomly-selected experimental and control groups. This reduces the effects of a pre-test on the participants. In addition, this design isolates almost all threats to validity.[7] Elimination of the pre-test reduces the time and expense of the previous evaluation design.

Which Design to Choose

With several basic types of evaluation designs, there are many possible constructions of an evaluation system for an HRD program. These designs can also be combined to form alternate designs. The question of which design to use depends on several factors. In most cases, the availability of appropriate data to measure HRD program results and the practical considerations of the working environment may dictate the appropriate design. The

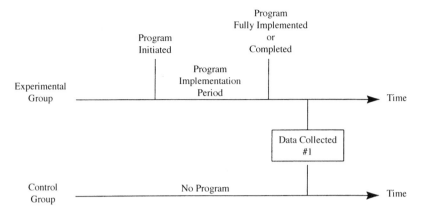

Figure 7-7. Post-test only, control group design.

more complex the design, the more costly (and valid) the evaluation effort. The availability of control groups and the ease of randomization are other factors that enter into the decision. And finally, there is no way to completely isolate the effects of factors outside the learning situation. If a design is less than optimum, the HRD professional should be prepared to defend the selection in terms of trade-offs.

On a practical basis, some designs are not feasible in organizational settings. Thus, other approaches must be explored to address the same issue of isolating the effects of the program on performance. The trade-off often pits research principles vs. feasibility. Unfortunately, most decisions made by managers are not based on valid and reliable data. Instead, they are often made on an intuitive assessment of the data presented to them. In recent years, much progress has been made in developing innovative ways to isolate the effects of the program on output performance. Another chapter presents recommended approaches to isolating the effects of a program, using the classical designs in this chapter plus other innovative and creative techniques to arrive at ten strategies for accomplishing this important goal.

Summary

This chapter has presented the basic research designs that are primarily concerned with the availability of groups (particularly control groups) to compare performance. Selecting the research design involves determining the timing of measures that are critical to making the appropriate comparisons. Several important designs considered to be classics were presented, ranging from a single group post-test only to a post-test only, control group design. Each design has its own advantages and disadvantages.

Discussion Questions

1. When is it important to use control groups in the evaluation process? Is this a common practice? Explain.
2. What factors affect the timing of measurements in an evaluation process?
3. Are the threats to validity usually considered in most evaluation schemes? Explain.
4. What types of evaluation designs are used in your organization (or one with which you are familiar)?
5. Which evaluation design is most commonly used? Why?
6. Suppose you are developing a training program for sales representatives in an effort to boost sales in a medium-sized organization. Which evaluation design may be appropriate? Explain.
7. In a single-group time series design, how many measurements are necessary? Explain.
8. Why is the ideal experimental design rarely used in evaluation projects?
9. One HRD executive stated, ". . . although we try to show the results of our programs, we are not concerned that much with evaluation designs." What is the basis for this comment?
10. When classic evaluation designs are not feasible, how can the influence of the program be isolated? Explain.

References

1. Pedhazur, E. J. and Schmelkin, L. P. *Measurement, Design, and Analysis: An Integrated Approach.* Hillsdale, NJ: Lawrence Erlbaum Associates, 1991.
2. Phillips, J. J. "Was It the Training?" *Training & Development,* Vol. 50, No. 3, March 1996, pp. 28–32.
3. Broad, M. L. and Newstrom, J. W. *Transfer of Training.* Reading, MA: Addison-Wesley, 1992.
4. Phillips, J. J. (Ed.), in *In Action: Measuring Return on Investment.* Alexandria, VA: American Society for Training and Development, 1994.
5. Swanson, R. A. "Backyard Research in Human Resource Development," in *The ASTD Training & Development Handbook,* 4th Edition, R.L. Craig (Ed.), New York, NY: McGraw-Hill, 1996, pp. 357–369.
6. Denzin, N. K. and Lincoln, Y. S. (Eds.). *Handbook of Qualitative Research,* Thousand Oaks, CA: Sage Publications, 1994.
7. Aiken, L. R. *Psychological Testing and Assessment,* 7th Edition. Boston, MA: Allyn and Bacon, Inc., 1991.

CHAPTER 8

Collecting Data: Reaction and Learning Evaluation

Importance of Reaction and Learning Evaluation

Because of the complexity and variety of approaches to collecting data at all four levels (reaction, learning, application, and impact), two chapters are devoted to presenting the techniques and issues surrounding this critical phase of evaluation. This chapter focuses on measuring reaction and learning while the next chapter focuses on measuring application and business impact. Participant reaction can represent instrumental feedback that can drive important changes in any part of the training delivery process. Measuring learning demonstrates the effectiveness of the program in meeting its critical learning objectives. Ensuring that participants have learned new knowledge or skills is the first step to measuring the ultimate success of the program.

Collecting data at all four levels is critically important for several reasons. First, it is essential to have data collection at all four levels to satisfy the two principal customers for programs. One group of customers is the participants, who must be pleased with the program and see its potential for application. In addition, they must feel a sense of accomplishment as they learn skills and knowledge. Level 1 and 2 evaluations provide input to satisfy the participants.

The other group of customers is the sponsors of the program. These are the managers who allocate resources to training, request training programs, approve training budgets, and send participants to attend the programs. They are very interested in the success of the program in terms of on-the-job behavior, business impact, and return on investment. In short, they want to know if the program has made a difference. For this group of customers, Level 3 and 4 data are necessary to provide on-the-job behavior change and business impact.

Collecting data at all four levels is also necessary because of the chain of impact that must exist for a program to be successful. Participants should experience a positive reaction to the material and its potential application, and learn new skills or knowledge. There should be changes in on-the-job behavior, and this should in turn cause a positive change in business performance. The only way to know if the chain has occurred is to collect data at all four levels.

Collecting data at Levels 1 and 2 is much easier than at 3 and 4. Thus, with budget constraints and scarce resources, many organizations stop evaluation prior to Level 3, placing more emphasis on Level 1 and 2 evaluations.

Questionnaires

The questionnaire is probably the most common form of program evaluation. Questionnaires come in all sizes, ranging from short reaction forms to detailed follow-up instruments. They can be used to obtain subjective information about participants' feelings as well as document measurable results for use in an ROI analysis. With this versatility and popularity, it is important that questionnaires be designed properly to satisfy their intended purposes.

Types of Questions

Five basic types of questions are available. Depending on the purpose of the evaluation, the questionnaire may contain any or all of the following types of questions:

1. Open-ended question—has an unlimited answer. The question is followed by ample blank space for the response.
2. Checklist—a list of items. A participant is asked to check those that apply to the situation.
3. Two-way question—has alternate responses, a yes/no, or other possibilities. This type of question can also include a range of responses from disagree to agree.
4. Multiple-choice question—has several choices, and the participant is asked to select the most correct one.
5. Ranking scales—requires the participant to rank a list of items.

Figure 8-1 shows examples of each of these types of questions.

1. Open-Ended Question:

   What problems will you encounter when attempting to use the customer service skills presented in the program?

2. Checklist:

   For the following list, check all of the output measures that may be influenced by the application of the knowledge and skills learned in this program.

   ☐ Responsibility   ☐ Cost Control
   ☐ Productivity   ☐ Response Time
   ☐ Quality   ☐ Customer Satisfaction
   ☐ Efficiency   ☐ Job Satisfaction

3. Two-Way Question:

   As a result of this program, I have a better understanding of my job as an air traffic controller.

   YES ☐   NO ☐

4. Multiple-Choice Question:

   The absenteeism rate for our company last year was:

   a. 2.0%   c. 3.2%
   b. 2.8%   d. 4.1%

5. Ranking Scales:

   The following list contains five important factors that will affect team leader performance. Place a one (1) by the item that is most important to you, a two (2) by the item that is second most important, and so on. The item ranked five (5) will be the least important item on the list.

   Reward Systems   _____   Training   _____
   Responsibility Levels _____   Management Support _____
   Communication   _____   Compensation _____

Figure 8-1. Types of questions.

Questionnaire Design

Questionnaire design is a simple and logical process. An improperly designed or worded questionnaire is confusing, frustrating, and potentially embarrassing. The following steps will help ensure that a valid, reliable, and effective instrument is developed.

Determine the information needed. The first step of any instrument design is itemizing the subjects, skills, or abilities presented in the program, along with other factors related to the success of the program. Questions are developed later. It might be helpful to develop this information in outline form so that related questions can be grouped together.

Select the type(s) of questions. Determine whether open-ended questions, checklists, two-way questions, multiple-choice questions, or a ranking scale is most appropriate for the intended purpose. Take the planned data analysis and variety of data to be collected into consideration.

Develop the questions. The next step is to develop the questions based on the type of question(s) planned and the information needed. The questions should be simple and straightforward enough to avoid confusion or leading the participant to a desired response. Terms or expressions unfamiliar to the participant should be avoided. Develop the appropriate number and variety of questions consistent with the validity and reliability discussions presented in an earlier chapter.

Test the questions. After the questions are developed, they should be tested for understanding. Ideally, the questions should be tested on a group of participants in a pilot program. If this is not feasible, the questions should be tested on employees at approximately the same job level as the potential participants. Collect as much input and criticism as possible, and revise the questions as necessary.

Prepare a data summary. A data summary sheet should be developed so that data can be tabulated quickly for summary and interpretation. This step will help ensure that the data can be analyzed quickly and presented in a meaningful way.

Develop the completed questionnaire. The questions should be finalized in a professional questionnaire with proper instructions.

After completing these steps, the questionnaire is ready to be administered. Because questionnaire administration is a critical element in follow-up evaluation, several ideas will be presented on this topic in the next chapter.

Attitude Surveys

Attitude surveys represent a specific type of questionnaire with several applications for measuring learning and attitude changes. A program may be designed to change employee attitudes toward work, policies, procedures, the organization, and even the immediate supervisor. Before-and-after program measurements are required to show changes in attitude. Sometimes an organization will conduct a survey to assess employee attitude toward one of the areas listed previously. Then, based on these results, HRD programs are undertaken to change attitudes in areas where improvement is needed.

Measuring attitudes is a complex task. It is impossible to measure an attitude precisely, since information gathered may not represent a participant's true feelings. Also, the behavior, beliefs, and feelings of an individual will not always correlate. Attitudes tend to change with time, and several factors can form an individual's attitude. Recognizing these shortcomings, it is possible to get a reasonable assessment of an individual's attitude.

Surveys are not the only way to measure attitudes. Interviews and observations, two other ways to check attitudes, are discussed in the next chapter.

Guidelines for Developing Attitude Surveys

The principles of attitude survey construction are similar to those of questionnaire design, which were discussed earlier. However, there are a few guidelines unique to the design or purchase of an attitude survey.

Involve appropriate management. The executives involved in this process must be committed to taking action based on survey results. Involve them early in the process, before the survey is constructed. Address management concerns, issues, and suggestions, and try to win commitment.

Determine precisely the attitudes that must be measured. While this is obvious, it is easy to stray into areas unrelated to the subject. "Let's check their attitude on this" is a familiar trap. While it may be interesting information, it should be omitted if it is not related.

Keep survey statements as simple as possible. Participants need to understand the meaning of a statement or question. There should be little room for differing interpretations.

Ensure that participant responses are anonymous. If feasible, participants must feel free to respond openly to statements or questions. The confidentiality of their responses is of the utmost importance. If data are collected that can identify a respondent, then a neutral third party should collect and process the data.

Communicate the purpose of the survey. Participants cooperate in an activity when they understand its purpose. When a survey is administered, participants should be given an explanation of its purpose and told what will be done with the information. Also, they should be encouraged to give correct and proper statements or answers.

Identify survey comparisons. Attitudes by themselves are virtually meaningless. They need to be compared to attitudes before or after the HRD program or compared to another group. A group of employees may be compared to all employees, a division, or a department. For purchased surveys, information may be available on a national scale in similar industries. In any case, specific comparisons should be planned before administering the survey.

Design for easy tabulation. In an attitude survey, yes/no remarks or varying degrees of agreement and disagreement are the usual responses. Figure 8-2 illustrates these two kinds of responses.

Uniform types of responses make it easier for tabulation and comparisons. On a scale of strongly agree to strongly disagree, numbers are usually assigned to reflect their response. For instance, a one (1) may represent strongly disagree and a five (5) strongly agree. An average response of 2.2 on a pre-program survey followed by a post-program average response of 4.3 shows a significant change in attitude. Some argue that a five-point scale merely permits the respondent to select the midpoint and not be forced to make a choice. If this is a concern, an even-numbered scale should be used.

Purchasing an Existing Survey

Many organizations purchase existing surveys to use in program evaluation. There can be several advantages. They can save time in development and pilot testing. Most of the reputable companies producing and marketing surveys have designed them to be reliable and valid for their intended purposes. Also, outside surveys make it easy to compare your results with others. For example, a team-effectiveness survey is administered prior to a

Yes/No Responses	**Yes**	**No**
1) My supervisor gives us credit for work well done.	☐	☐
2) My supervisor secures our ideas about our job.	☐	☐

Agreement/Disagreement Responses

	Strongly Agree	Agree	Neutral	Disagree	Strongly Disagree
1) My work environment is free of offensive language.	☐	☐	☐	☐	☐
2) Management provides adequate resources for me to do my job.	☐	☐	☐	☐	☐

Figure 8-2. Typical attitude survey questions.

team-building session. The survey is administered again at the end of the program. Pre- and post-program results can also be compared with other organizations within the same industry or in similar industries.

Participant Feedback

Feedback from program participants is the most frequently used, and least reliable, method of collecting data for evaluation.[1] The popularity of this form of data collection is astounding. Ratings from reaction questionnaires can be so critical that a person's job may be at stake, as in the case of instructor ratings in some education and training departments.

Feedback forms are used in many places outside the HRD area, particularly in customer service settings. Any organization that provides a service or product is usually interested in feedback from those who use the service or product. While participant feedback is popular, it is also subject to misuse. Sometimes referred to as a "happiness rating," it has come under fire from many HRD professionals because it is considered worthless. The primary criticism concerns the subjectivity of the data.[2] A positive reaction at the end of the program is no assurance that learning has occurred or that there will be a change in on-the-job performance.[3]

While there is no good substitute for follow-up data in evaluating programs, a carefully designed, properly used participant feedback questionnaire at the end of an HRD program might suffice. There is a definite place for feedback questionnaires in HRD evaluation. A high-quality evaluation would be difficult to achieve without feedback questionnaires.[4]

Areas of Feedback

The areas of feedback used on reaction forms depend to a large extent on the organization and the purpose of the evaluation. Some forms are simple while others are detailed and require a considerable amount of time to complete. A feedback questionnaire should be designed to supply the information necessary to satisfy the purpose of evaluation. The following is a comprehensive listing of the most common types of feedback solicited:

☐ Progress with objectives. To what degree were the objectives met?
☐ Program content. Was the content appropriate?
☐ Instructional materials. Were the materials useful?
☐ Pre-work materials. Were the pre-work materials necessary? Helpful?
☐ Assignments. Were the out-of-class assignments helpful?
☐ Method of delivery. Was the method of delivery appropriate for the objectives?
☐ Instructor/facilitator. Was the facilitator effective?

☐ Motivation to learn. Were you motivated to learn this material?
☐ Program relevance. Was the program relevant to your needs?
☐ Registration/logistics. Were the scheduling and registration smooth?
☐ Facilities. Did the facilities enhance the learning environment?
☐ Overall evaluation. What is your overall rating of the program?
☐ Potential barriers. What potential barriers exist for the application of the material?
☐ Planned improvements/use of material. How will you apply what you have learned?
☐ Recommendations for target audiences. What is the appropriate audience for this program?

Objective questions covering each of these areas will ensure thorough feedback from participants. This feedback can be extremely useful in making adjustments in a program and/or assist in predicting performance after the program. The instructor/facilitator evaluation deserves additional comments. In some organizations the primary evaluation centers on the facilitator (a separate form may be used for each facilitator if there are several) covering a variety of areas such as the following:

☐ Preparation for sessions
☐ Knowledge of the subject matter, including familiarity with content and depth of understanding
☐ Presentation skills, including clarity of the presentation, pacing of material, and eye contact
☐ Communication skills, including the use of understandable language, real-life examples, and the promotion of discussion
☐ Assessing learner understanding and responding appropriately to learner needs and questions
☐ Use of appropriate technology and responding effectively to technical requirements of learners
☐ Encouraging application of learning through the use of real-life examples, job-related discussions, and relevant exercises.

In most medium- to large-size organizations where there is significant training and development activity, the Level 1 instrument is usually automated for computerized scanning and reporting. Typical Level 1 questions can easily be developed for a scan sheet and programmed to present reports to help understand and use the data. Some organizations use automated processing to develop not only detailed reports, but also to develop databases, allowing feedback data to be compared to other programs or the same program with other instructors.

Appendix 4 provides a detailed participant feedback questionnaire that covers most of the previously listed areas. It was used at the end of a program for new supervisors.

Useful Administrative Guidelines

In addition to the questionnaire design principles presented earlier, several helpful administrative guidelines can improve the effectiveness of this data-collection method. Each is briefly described in the next section.

Keep responses anonymous. Anonymous feedback is highly recommended. It allows the participants to be open with comments that can be helpful and constructive. Otherwise, the input can be extremely biased and perhaps stifled because of concern about the direct reaction from the facilitator.

Have a neutral person collect the forms. In addition to anonymous responses, it is helpful to have a neutral person collect the feedback questionnaires. In some organizations, the program coordinator or sponsor will conduct the evaluation at the end, independent of the facilitator. This action increases the objectivity of the input and decreases the likelihood of the instructor/facilitator reacting unfavorably to criticism contained in the feedback.

Provide a copy in advance. For lengthy evaluation forms covering programs that span several days, it is helpful to distribute the feedback questionnaire early in the program so that participants can familiarize themselves with the questions and statements. Participants can also address specific topics as they are covered, and are provided more time to think through particular issues. They should be cautioned, however, not to reach a final conclusion on general issues until the end of the program.

Explain the purpose of the feedback and how it will be used. Although this is sometimes understood, it is best to repeat where the information goes and how it is used in the organization. There is still some mystery surrounding the use of feedback data. Restating the process in terms of the flow and use of data can help clarify this issue.

Explore an ongoing evaluation. For lengthy programs, an end-of-program evaluation may leave participants unable to remember what was covered at what time. An ongoing evaluation can be used to improve this situation. One approach is to distribute evaluation forms at the beginning of the program and instruct participants when and how to supply the information. After each topic is presented, participants evaluate the topic and facilitator. The information can be easily recalled by participants and the feedback is more useful to program evaluators. Another approach is to use a daily feedback form to collect input on program pacing, degree of involvement, unclear items, etc. Figure 8-3 shows a recommended daily feedback form.

Consider quantifying course ratings. Some organizations attempt to solicit feedback in terms of numerical ratings. Although still subjective, overall ratings can be useful in monitoring performance and making com-

---

1. What issues presented today still remain confusing and/or unclear?

_____

_____

_____

2. The most useful topics presented today were

_____

_____

_____

3. It would help me if you would

_____

_____

_____

4. The pacing of the program is:
   ☐ Just right
   ☐ Too slow
   ☐ Too fast

5. The degree of involvement of participants is:
   ☐ Not enough
   ☐ Too much
   ☐ Just right

6. Three very important items that you should cover tomorrow are
   1. _____
   2. _____
   3. _____

7. Comments

_____

_____

Figure 8-3. A recommended daily feedback form.

parisons. For example, the American Management Association collects an overall rating in their public seminars. AMA monitors these overall ratings to compare them with similar programs and track changes over time. With a large number of programs repeated several times, these ratings can be useful in making comparisons. In some cases, targets or norms are established to compare ratings. When using a norm scale, a rating that is normally considered good may prove to be quite low when compared to the norm of the factor being rated. Another caution is needed since these ratings are subjective: Comparing numerical values may create an impression that the data are objective. This point should be underscored in evaluation communications.

Collect information related to improvement. Although it is difficult to get realistic input related to cost reductions or savings on a feedback form, it is worth a try. The response may be surprising. Just a simple question will sometimes cause participants to concentrate on cost savings. A possible statement might be

Please estimate the savings in monetary values that will be realized (i.e., increased productivity, improved methods, reduced costs, etc.) as a result of this program over a period of one year. $ _____.

Please explain the basis of your estimate.

Express as a percent the confidence you place on your estimate.

(0% = no confidence, 100% = certainty) _____.%

Allow ample time for completing the form. A time crunch can cause problems if participants are asked to complete a feedback form at the end of a program, particularly if they are in a hurry to leave. Consequently, participants may provide incomplete information in an effort to finish and leave. A possible alternative is to allow ample time for evaluation as a scheduled session before the end of the program. This evaluation session could be followed by a wrap-up of the program and the last speaker. A 30-minute session will provide much opportunity to enhance the quality and quantity of information.

Use of Reaction Data

Sometimes participant feedback is solicited, tabulated, summarized, and then disregarded. The information must be collected and used for one or more of the purposes of evaluation. Otherwise, the exercise is a waste of the participants' time. Too often instructors or program evaluators use the material to feed their egos and let it quietly disappear in their files, forgetting the original purposes for its collection.

Monitoring customer satisfaction. Because this input is the principal measure taken from the participants, it provides a good indication of their overall reaction to, and satisfaction with, the program. Thus, program developers and owners will know how well the customers are actually satisfied with the product.

Identify strengths and weaknesses of the HRD process. Feedback is extremely helpful in identifying weaknesses as well as strengths in the HRD process. Participant feedback on weaknesses can often lead to adjustments and changes. Identifying strengths can be helpful in future design so that they can be replicated.

Develop norms and standards. Because Level 1 evaluation data can be automated and is usually collected with 100% of programs, it becomes relatively easy to develop norms and standards throughout the organization. Target ratings can be set for expectations; particular course results are then compared to those norms and standards.

Evaluate instructors. Perhaps one of the most common uses of Level 1 data is instructor evaluation. If properly constructed and collected, helpful feedback data can be provided to instructors so that adjustments can be made to increase effectiveness. Some caution needs to be taken since instructor evaluations can sometimes be biased and other evidence may be necessary to provide an overall assessment of instructor performance.

Evaluate planned improvements. Feedback data from the Level 1 questionnaire can provide a profile of planned actions and improvements. This can be compared with on-the-job actions as a result of the program. This provides a rich source of data in terms of what participants may be changing or implementing because of what they have learned.

Link with follow-up data. If a follow-up evaluation is planned, it may be helpful to link Level 1 data with follow-up data to see if planned improvements became reality. In most cases, planned actions are often inhibited in some way through on-the-job barriers.

Marketing programs. For some organizations, participant feedback data provides helpful marketing information. Participants' quotes and reactions provide information that may be convincing to potential participants. Program brochures often contain quotes and summaries of data from Level 1 feedback in the marketing material.

Advantages/Disadvantages

Several important advantages are inherent in the use of feedback questionnaires. Two important ones are

1. Reaction questionnaires provide a quick reaction from participants while information is still fresh in their minds. By the end of the program, participants have formed an opinion about its effectiveness and the usefulness of program materials. This reaction can help make adjustments and provide evidence of the program's effectiveness.
2. They are easy to administer, usually taking only a few minutes. And, if constructed properly, they can be easily analyzed, tabulated, and summarized.

Three disadvantages to feedback questionnaires are

1. The data are subjective, based on the opinions and feelings of the participants at the time of testing. Personal bias may exaggerate the ratings.
2. Participants often are too polite in their ratings. At the end of a program, they are often pleased and may be happy to get it out of the way. Therefore, a positive rating may be given when they actually feel differently.
3. A good rating at the end of a program is no assurance that the participants will practice what has been taught in the program.

In summary, there is a definite place for feedback questionnaires in HRD program evaluation. They can provide a very convenient method of data collection. Ideally, however, it should be only a part of the total evaluation process.

Measuring Learning with Tests

Testing is important for measuring learning in program evaluations. Precourse and post-course comparisons using tests are very common. An improvement in test scores shows the change in skill, knowledge, or attitude attributed to the program. By any measure, there was a dramatic increase in the use of tests in the U.S.A. throughout the 1990s.[5] The principles of test development are similar to those for the design and development of questionnaires and attitude surveys. This section presents additional information on types of tests and test construction.

Types of Tests

Several types of tests, which can be classified in three ways, are used in HRD. The first is based upon the medium used for administering the test.

The most common media for training tests are paper-and-pencil performance tests, using simulated tools or the actual equipment; and computer-based tests, using computers and video displays. Knowledge-and-skills tests are usually written, because performance tests are more costly to develop and administer. Computer-based tests and those using interactive video are gaining popularity. In these tests, a computer monitor or video screen presents the test questions or situations, and trainees respond by typing on a keyboard or touching the screen. Interactive videos have a strong element of realism because the person being tested can react to images, often moving pictures and video vignettes, that reproduce real job situations.

The second way to classify tests is by purpose and content. In this context, tests can be divided into aptitude tests or achievement tests. Aptitude tests measure basic skills or innate or acquired capacity to learn an occupation. An achievement test assesses a person's knowledge or competence in a particular subject, the end result of education and training.

A third way in which to classify tests is by test design. The most common are oral examinations, essay tests, objective tests, norm-referenced tests, criterion-referenced tests, and performance tests. Oral examinations and essay tests are probably more useful in academic settings, and have limited use in HRD program evaluation. Objective tests have answers that are specific and precise, based on the objectives of a program. However, attitudes, feelings, creativity, problem-solving processes, and other intangible skills and abilities cannot be measured accurately with objective tests. A more useful form of objective test is the criterion-referenced test. The last three types of tests listed above are more common in HRD evaluation efforts, and are described in more detail as follows:

Norm-referenced test. Norm-referenced tests compare participants with each other or to other groups rather than to specific instructional objectives. They are characterized by using data to compare the participants to the "norm" or average. Although norm-referenced tests have only limited use in some HRD evaluations, they may be useful in programs involving large numbers of participants in which average scores and relative rankings are important. In some situations participants who score highest on the exams are given special recognition or awards or made eligible for other special activities.

In an example, suppose the top 50% of the graduates from an HRD program are selected for promotion. The measurement would be norm-referenced so that participants are ranked rather than held to a specific cut-off score. If, rather, a minimum passing score is established and participants are selected on that basis, then the measurement device is a criterion-referenced measurement, discussed next.

Criterion-referenced test. The criterion-referenced test (CRT) is an objective test with a predetermined cut-off score. The CRT is a measure against carefully written objectives for the HRD program. In a CRT, the interest lies in whether or not participants meet the desired minimum standards, not how that participant ranks with others. The primary concern is to measure, report, and analyze participant performance as it relates to the instructional objectives.

Table 8-1 examines a reporting format based on criterion-referenced testing. This format helps explain how a CRT is applied to an evaluation effort. Four participants have completed a program with three measurable objectives. Actual test scores are reported, and the minimum standard is shown. For example, on the first objective, Participant 4 received a pass rating for a test that has no numerical value and is simply rated pass or fail. The same participant passed objective 2 with a score of 14 (10 was listed as the minimum passing score). Participant 4 scored 88 on objective 3, but failed because the standard was 90. Overall, Participant 4 satisfactorily completed the program of study. The grid on the far right shows that the minimum passing standard for the program is at least two of the three objectives. Participant 4 achieved two objectives, the required minimum.

Criterion-referenced testing is a popular measurement instrument in HRD. Its use is becoming widespread and is frequently computer-based. It has the advantage of being objective-based, precise, and relatively easy to administer. It does require programs with clearly defined objectives that can be measured by tests.

Performance testing. Performance testing allows the participant to exhibit a skill (and occasionally knowledge or attitudes) that has been learned in an HRD program. The skill can be manual, verbal, analytical, or a combination of the three. Performance testing is used frequently in job-related training where the participants are allowed to demonstrate what they have learned. In supervisory and management training, performance testing comes in the form of skill practices or role plays. Participants are asked to demonstrate discussion or problem-solving skills they have acquired. To illustrate the possibilities of performance testing, three examples are presented.

Example 1: New computer science engineers are required to attend a course on systems engineering. As a final exam for the program, participants are asked to design, build, and test a basic system. The instructor observes participants as they check out the system, then carefully builds the same design and compares his results with those of the participants. These comparisons and the performance of the design provide an evaluation of the program and represent an adequate reflection of the skills learned in the course.

Example 2: As part of a management training program, participants learn how to motivate an average performer. Part of the course evaluation requires managers to write a skill practice session for an actual situation involving an average performer in their work unit. Then, participants are asked to conduct the skill practice on another member of the group using the real situation and

Table 8-1
Reporting Format for CRT Test Data

	Objective 1		Objective 2			Objective 3			Total Obj's Passed	Minimum Program Standard	Overall Program Score
	P/F	Raw Score	Std	Raw Score	P/F	Std	Raw Score	P/F			
Participant 1	P	4	10	87	F	90		F	1	2 of 3	Fail
Participant 2	F	12	10	110	P	90		P	2	2 of 3	Pass
Participant 3	P	10	10	100	P	90		P	3	2 of 3	Pass
Participant 4	P	14	10	88	P	90		F	2	2 of 3	Pass
Totals 4	3 Pass 1 Fail		3 Pass 1 Fail			2 Pass 2 Fail			8 Pass 4 Fail		3 Pass 1 Fail

applying principles and steps taught in the program. The skill practice is observed by the facilitator, and a written critique is provided at the end of the practice. These critiques provide part of the evaluation of the program.

Example 3: Potential aircraft assemblers attend a course on basic aircraft production assembly techniques. At the end of the course, trainees are required to complete a special assembly project. Each is provided with a blueprint and a list of materials and asked to build the item according to the specifications outlined on the blueprint. The time needed for completion and the quality and accuracy of the construction of the project comprise the evaluation. A successful combination is necessary for the potential employee to advance to a permanent job as an aircraft assembler.

Design and administration of a performance test. For a performance test to be effective, the following steps are recommended for its design and administration.

☐ The test should be a representative sample of the HRD program, and should allow the participant to demonstrate as many skills as possible that are taught in the program. This increases the validity of the test and makes it more meaningful to the participant.

☐ Every phase of the test should be thoroughly planned, including the timing, the preparation of the participant, the collection of necessary materials and tools, and the evaluation of the results.

☐ Thorough and consistent instructions are necessary. As with other tests, the quality of the instructions can influence the outcome of a performance test. All participants should be given the same instructions. They should be clear, concise, and to the point. Charts, diagrams, blueprints, and other supporting information should be provided if they are normally provided in the work setting. If appropriate and feasible, the test should be demonstrated by the instructor so that participants observe how the skill is practiced.

☐ Procedures should be developed for objective evaluation. Acceptable standards must be developed for a performance test. These are sometimes difficult to develop because there can be varying degrees of speed, skill, and quality associated with test outcomes. Predetermined standards must be developed so that employees know in advance what has to be accomplished to be considered satisfactory and acceptable for test completion.

☐ Information that may lead participants astray should not be included. The program is conducted to train participants in a particular skill. They should not be led astray or tricked into obvious wrong answers unless they face the same obstacles in the real-world environment.

With these general guidelines, performance tests can be developed into effective tools for program evaluation. Although more costly than written tests, performance tests are essential in situations where a high degree of fidelity is required between work and test conditions.[6]

Measuring Learning with Simulation

Another technique to measure learning is a job simulation. This method involves the construction and application of a procedure or task that simulates or models the activity for which the HRD program is being conducted. The simulation is designed to represent, as closely as possible, the actual job situation. Simulation may be used as an integral part of the HRD program as well as for evaluation. In evaluation, participants are provided an opportunity to try out their performance in the simulated activity and have it evaluated based on how well the task was accomplished. Simulations may be used during the program, at the end of the program, or as part of the follow-up evaluation.

Advantages of Simulations

Simulations offer several advantages for the HRD professional. Several are highlighted below.

Reproducibility. Simulations permit a job or part of a job to be reproduced in a manner almost identical to the real setting. Through careful planning and design, the simulation can have all of the central characteristics of the real situation. Even complex jobs, such as that of the manager, can be simulated adequately. In addition, simulation can allow the HRD professional to shorten the time required to perform a task in an actual environment.

Cost effectiveness. Although sometimes expensive to construct, simulations can be cost effective in the long run. For example, it is cost prohibitive to train airline pilots using a $50 million aircraft. Therefore, an aircraft simulator is used to simulate flying conditions and enable the pilot to learn to fly before boarding the actual vehicle. The cost involved in learning on the job becomes prohibitive in many situations, making simulation much more attractive.

Safety considerations. Safety is another advantage of using simulations. In the aircraft simulator example, safety is an important consideration. It would be too dangerous for the pilot to learn how to fly an airplane without the use of a simulator. The nature of many other jobs requires participants to be trained in simulated conditions instead of real situations. For example, in training emergency medical technicians, the possible risk of life is too great to have someone learn how to administer emergency medical techniques on a victim as part of the training process. Similarly, firemen are trained on simulated conditions prior to being exposed to actual fires and CIA agents are trained in simulated conditions prior to being exposed to their real-world environment. Safety is an important consideration.

Simulation Techniques

There are a variety of simulation techniques used to evaluate program results. The most common techniques are briefly described as follows:

Electrical/mechanical simulation. This technique uses a combination of electronics and mechanical devices to simulate real-life situations, and is used in conjunction with programs to develop operational and diagnostic skills. Expensive examples include simulated "patients" or a simulator for a nuclear power plant operator. Other less-expensive types of simulators have been developed to simulate equipment operation.

Task simulation. Another approach involves the performance of a simulated task as part of an evaluation. For example, in an aircraft company technicians are trained on the safe removal, handling, and installation of a radioactive source used in a nucleonic oil-quantity indicator gauge. These technicians attend a thorough training program on all of the procedures necessary for this important assignment. To become certified to perform this task, technicians are observed in a simulation in which they perform all the necessary steps on a checkoff card. After they have demonstrated that they possess the skills necessary for the safe performance of this assignment, they become certified by the instructor. This task simulation serves as the program's evaluation.

Business games. Business games have grown in popularity in recent years. They represent simulations of part or all of a business enterprise in which participants change the variables of the business and observe the effect of those changes. The game not only reflects the real-world situation but represents the synopsis of the HRD program of which it is a part. The participants are given certain objectives, play the game, and have their output monitored. Their performance can usually be documented and measured. Typical objectives are to maximize profit, sales, market share, or return on investment. Those participants who attain the objectives are those who usually have the highest performance in the program.

In-basket. Another simulation technique, called an in-basket, is particularly useful in supervisory and management training programs. Portions of a supervisor's job are simulated through a series of items that normally appear in the in-basket. These items are typically memos, notes, letters, and reports, which create realistic conditions facing the supervisor. The participant must decide what to do with each item while taking into consideration the principles taught in the HRD program. The participant's performance in the in-basket represents an evaluation of the program. In some situations the course of action chosen for each item in the in-basket is rated, and a combination of the chosen alternatives provides an overall rating on the in-basket. This provides a performance score representing the participant's ability to handle the program material.

Case study. A possibly less-effective, but still popular, technique of simulation is a case study. A case study gives a detailed description of a problem and usually contains a list of several questions. The participant is asked to analyze the case and determine the best course of action. The problem should reflect the content in an HRD program and the conditions in the real-world setting.

The most common categories of case studies include

☐ Exercise case studies, which provide an opportunity for participants to practice the application of specific procedures.
☐ Situation case studies, which provide participants the opportunity to analyze information and make decisions about their particular situation.
☐ Complex case studies, an extension of the situation case study, in which the participant is required to handle a large amount of data and information, some of which may be irrelevant.
☐ Decision case studies, which require the participant to go a step further than the previous categories and present plans for solving a particular problem.
☐ Critical incident case studies, which provide the participant with a certain amount of information but withhold other information until it is requested by the participant.
☐ Action maze case studies, which present a large case in a series of smaller units. The participant is required to predict, at each stage, what will happen next.

The difficulty in a case study lies in the objective evaluation of the participants' performance. Frequently, there can be many possible courses of action, some equally as effective as others, making it extremely difficult to obtain an objective measurable performance rating for the analysis and interpretation of the case.

Role playing. In role playing, sometimes referred to as skill practice, participants practice a newly learned skill as they are observed by other individuals. Participants are given their assigned role with specific instructions, which sometimes include an ultimate course of action. The participant then practices the skill with other individuals to accomplish the desired objectives. This is intended to simulate the real-world setting to the greatest extent possible. Difficulty sometimes arises when other participants involved in the skill practice make the practice unrealistic by not reacting the way individuals would in an actual situation. To help overcome this obstacle, trained role players (non-participants trained for the role) may be used in all roles except that of the participant. This can provide a more objective evaluation. The success of this technique also lies in the judgment of those observing the role plays. The skill of effective observation is as critical as the skill of the role player. Also, the success of this method depends on the participants' willingness to participate in and adjust to the planned role. If participant resistance is extremely high, the performance in the skill practice may not reflect the actual performance on the job. Nevertheless, these skill practices can be very useful, particularly in supervisory and sales training, to enable participants to practice discussion skills.[7]

Assessment Center Method. The final method of Level 2 data collection is a formal procedure called the assessment center method. The feedback is provided by a group of specially trained observers (called assessors), not HRD staff members as in the previous section. For years the assessment center approach has been a very effective tool for employee selection. It now shows great promise as a tool for evaluating the effectiveness of an HRD program.[8]

Assessment centers are not actually centers, that is, a location or building. The term refers to a procedure for evaluating the performance of individuals. In a typical assessment center the individuals being assessed participate in a variety of exercises that enable them to demonstrate a particular skill, knowledge, or ability, usually called job dimensions. These dimensions are important to on-the-job success of individuals for whom the program was developed. For example, one organization identified the following job dimensions for first-line supervisors:

☐ Oral communication
☐ Planning and organizing
☐ Written communication
☐ Analysis
☐ Reading skills
☐ Judgment
☐ Initiative
☐ Sensitivity
☐ Leadership

☐ Management identification
☐ Delegation
☐ Technical knowledge

It may take anywhere from four hours to three days for the participants to complete all the exercises. The assessors evaluate the participants by assigning a rating for each dimension. They then combine individual ratings to remove subjectivity and reach a final rating for each participant.

In HRD program evaluation, the assessment center process gives a rating of the participants prior to the HRD program. After the program is conducted, the participants are assessed again to see if there are improvements in their performance of the job dimensions. The use of a control group in an evaluation design helps to produce evidence of the impact of training.

Although the popularity of this method seems to be growing, it still may not be feasible in some organizations. The use of an assessment center is quite involved and time consuming for both the participants and the assessors. The assessors have to be carefully trained to be objective and reliable. However, for programs that represent large expenditures aimed at making improvements in soft data, the assessment center approach may be the most promising way to measure the impact of the program. This is particularly true of an organization where the assessment center process is already in use for selection purposes.

In summary, simulations come in a wide variety. They offer an opportunity for participants to practice what is being taught in an HRD program and have their performance observed in a simulated job condition. They can provide extremely accurate evaluations if the performance in the simulation is objective and can be clearly measured.

Measuring Learning with Less-Structured Activities

In some situations, it is important to have an informal check of learning that provides some assurance that participants have acquired skills, knowledge, or perhaps some changes in attitudes. This approach is appropriate when other levels of evaluation are pursued. For example, if a Level 3 on-the-job application evaluation is planned, it might not be critical to have a comprehensive Level 2. An informal assessment of learning may be sufficient. After all, resources are scarce and a comprehensive evaluation at all levels becomes quite expensive. The following are some alternative approaches to measuring learning that might suffice when inexpensive, low-key, informal assessments are needed.

Exercises/Activities

Many HRD programs contain specific activities, exercises, or problems that must be explored, developed, or solved during the program. Some of these are constructed in terms of involvement exercises, while others require individual problem-solving skills. When these are integrated into the program, there are several specific ways in which to measure learning.

The results of the exercise can be submitted for review and possible scoring by the instructor. This becomes a measure of learning and part of the overall score for the course.

The results can be discussed in a group with a comparison of various approaches and solutions. The group can reach an assessment of how much each individual has learned. This may not be practical in many settings, but can work in a few narrowly focused applications.

The solutions to the problem or exercises can be shared with the group and the participant can provide a self-assessment indicating the degree to which skills and/or knowledge have been obtained from the exercise. This also has some reinforcement value in that participants quickly see the correct solution.

The instructor can review the individual progress or success of each participant to determine the relative success. This will work for small groups but could be very cumbersome and time consuming in larger groups.

Self-Assessment

In many applications, a self-assessment may be appropriate, by which participants are provided an opportunity to assess the extent of skills and knowledge acquisition. This is particularly applicable when Level 3, 4, and 5 evaluations are planned, and it is important to know if actual learning is taking place. A few techniques can ensure that the process is effective:

☐ The self-assessment should be made on an anonymous basis so that individuals feel free to express a realistic and accurate assessment of what they have learned.

☐ The purpose of the self-assessment should be explained, along with the plans for the data. Specifically, if there are implications for course design or individual re-testing, this should be discussed.

☐ If there has been no improvement or the self-assessment is unsatisfactory, there should be some explanation as to what that means and what the implications will be. This will help to ensure that accurate and credible information is provided.

Instructor Assessment

A final technique is for the instructors and facilitators to provide an assessment of the learning that has taken place. Although this approach is very subjective, it may be appropriate when a Level 3, 4, or 5 evaluation is planned. One of the most effective ways to accomplish this is to provide a checklist of the specific skills that need to be acquired in the course. Instructors can then check off their assessment of the skills individually. Also, if there is a particular body of knowledge that needs to be acquired, the categories could be listed with a checklist for assurance that the individual has a good understanding of those items. This could create a problem if the participants have not had the appropriate time and opportunity to demonstrate skills or knowledge acquisition, and the instructor may have a difficult time in providing appropriate responses. There is also the question of what to do if there is no evidence of learning. The specific consequences need to be considered and addressed before the method is used.

Administrative Issues

There are several administrative issues surrounding the use of processes to measure learning. Each of these is briefly discussed as follows and should be addressed in the overall plan for administering a Level 2 measurement:

Consistency

It is extremely important that different tests, exercises, or processes to measure learning are administered consistently from one group to another. This includes issues such as the time required for response, the actual learning conditions in which participants complete the process, the amount of resources available to them, and the assistance from other members of the group. These issues can easily be addressed by the test instructions.

Monitoring

In some situations, it is important for participants to be monitored as they are completing the test or other measurement process. This ensures that each individual is working independently but has someone there to provide assistance or answer questions as necessary. This may not be an issue in all situations, but should be addressed in the overall plan.

Scoring

Scoring instructions need to be developed for the measurement process so that the person evaluating the responses will be objective and provide consistent scores. Ideally, the potential bias from the individual scoring the instrument will be completely removed through proper scoring instructions and other information necessary to provide an objective evaluation.

Reporting

A final issue is reporting the results. In some situations, the participants are provided with the results immediately, particularly with self-scoring tests or with group-based scoring mechanisms. In other situations, the actual results may not be known until a later time frame. In these situations, some mechanism for providing scoring data should be built into the evaluation plan unless it has been predetermined that participants will not know the scores. The worst case situation is to promise test scores and not deliver them either on time or at all.

Using Level 2 Data

Although there can be several uses of Level 2 data, the following three uses are most common:

Providing Individual Feedback

Level 2 data, when provided directly to participants, provides reinforcement for correct answers and enhances learning for those solutions that were less than desirable. This reinforces the learning process and provides much-needed feedback to participants in some situations.

Improving Training Programs

Perhaps the most important use of Level 2 data is to improve the design of the program. Consistently low responses in certain parts of a Level 2 measure may indicate that inadequate coverage has been provided on that particular topic. Consistently low scores by all participants may indicate that the objectives and scope of coverage are too ambitious for the time allotted.

Evaluating Instructors

Just as Level 1 data is used to evaluate instructors, Level 2 provides additional evidence of the success of the program. The instructor has a significant responsibility to ensure that the participants have learned the material, and that the testing is a reflection of the degree to which the material has been acquired and internalized.

Summary

This chapter presented data-collection methods and issues for measuring reaction and learning. These two levels of evaluation are important to satisfy a key group of customers, the program participants. The questionnaire, the most common instrument to measure reaction, was described in detail including specific ways in which the process can be improved. Measuring learning involves the use of tests, simulations, and other exercises to capture the amount of knowledge and skill acquisition.

Discussion Questions

1. Why is it important to obtain participant feedback in training programs?
2. One HRD manager commented ". . . Smile sheets (participant feedback forms) are not worth the time it takes to complete them. These happiness ratings do nothing but feed the ego of the instructor." Is this true? Explain.
3. Design a participant feedback form for a one-day workshop on improving interviewing skills.
4. Secure a sample questionnaire and critique its design, following the principles in this chapter.
5. What are the advantages and disadvantages of attitude surveys in evaluation?
6. Is it important to compare survey results with norms from other industries or other organizations in the same industry? Explain.
7. Critique the design and use of a test to measure learning.
8. Why are performance tests important to HRD evaluation?
9. Design and describe a performance test to measure the effectiveness of a training program designed to improve interviewing skills.
10. How have computers influenced the use of simulations in the evaluation process?

References

1. Phillips, J. J. "Return on Investment—Beyond the Four Levels," in *Academy of HRD 1995 Conference Proceedings*, E. Holton (Ed.), 1995.
2. Erickson, P. R. "Evaluating Training Results," *Training and Development Journal*, January 1990, p. 57.
3. Dixon, N. M. *Evaluation: A Tool for Improving HRD Quality*. San Diego, CA: University Associates, Inc., 1990.

4. Marshall, V. and Schriver, R. "Using Evaluation to Improve Performance," *Technical & Skills Training,* January 1994, pp. 6–9.

5. Jacobs, L. C. and Chase, C. I. *Developing and Using Tests Effectively.* San Francisco, CA: Jossey-Bass Publishers, 1992.

6. Kubiszyn, T. and Borich, G. *Educational Testing and Measurement,* 3rd Edition. New York, NY: Harper-Collins Publishers, 1990.

7. Nadler, L. and Nadler, Z. *Designing Training Programs: The Critical Events Model,* 2nd Edition. Houston, TX: Gulf Publishing Company, 1994.

8. Byham, W. C. "How Assessment Centers Are Used to Evaluate Training's Effectiveness," *Training,* February 1992, p. 32.

CHAPTER 9

Collecting Data: Application and Business Impact Evaluation

Collecting data after the HRD program has been conducted or implemented provides an opportunity to obtain application data (Level 3) and impact data (Level 4). It is the first operational phase of the ROI process, as described in an earlier chapter. This step is usually the most time consuming of all steps and is also the part of the ROI process that can be most disruptive to the organization. Fortunately, a variety of methods are available to capture data at the appropriate time after training. This chapter outlines ten common approaches for collecting post-program data after the sources of data are defined.

Using Follow-Up Questionnaires and Surveys

Probably the most common data-collection method is the follow-up questionnaire. Ranging from brief assessment forms to detailed follow-up tools, questionnaires can be used to obtain subjective information about skill application and to document measurable business results for an ROI analysis. With this versatility and popularity, the questionnaire is the preferred method for capturing Level 3 and 4 data in many organizations.

Surveys represent a specific type of questionnaire with several applications for measuring the success of training and development programs. Surveys are used in situations in which only attitudes, beliefs, and opinions are captured, whereas a questionnaire has much more flexibility and captures data ranging from attitudes to specific improvement statistics. The principles of survey construction and design are similar to questionnaire design.

Although the word questionnaire is used in this section, the development of both types of instruments is covered.[1]

Questionnaire Design Steps

Questionnaire design is a simple and logical process and was covered in the previous chapter. To a certain extent, the following steps repeat some of the issues presented there.

Determine the type of data needed. Anticipated skill and knowledge application or attitudes expected to change on the job are reviewed for potential items for the questionnaire. If Level 4 data is planned for collection, specific business measures are identified for possible inclusion. Also, other issues and factors related to the application of the program are explored for potential inclusion in the questionnaire.

Involve management in the process. Management should be involved in this process to the extent possible, either as a client, sponsor, supporter, or interested party. If possible, managers most familiar with the program or process should provide information on specific issues and concerns that frame the actual questions and data planned on the questionnaire. In some cases, managers want to provide input on specific issues or items. Not only is manager input helpful and useful in the questionnaire design, but it also builds ownership in the measurement and evaluation process.

Select the type(s) of questions appropriate for required information. The first step in questionnaire design is to select the type(s) of questions, presented in the previous chapter, that will be best for the specific data needed. Objective questions are recommended. The planned data analysis and variety of data to be collected should be considered in deciding which type(s) of questions to use.

Develop the appropriate questions. The next step is to develop the questions based on the types of questions planned and the type of data needed. Questions should be simple, objective, and brief. A single question should only address one issue. If multiple issues need to be addressed, the question can be separated into multiple parts or a separate question may be developed for each issue. Terms or expressions unfamiliar to the participant should be avoided.

Check the reading level. To ensure that the questionnaire can be easily understood by the target audience, it is helpful to assess the questionnaire's reading level. Most word processing programs have features that will evaluate the reading difficulty according to grade level. This provides an important check to ensure that the perceived reading level of the target audience matches with questionnaire design.

Test the questions. Proposed questions should be tested for understanding. Ideally, the questions should be tested on a sample group of participants. If this is not feasible, the sample group of employees should be at approximately the same job level as participants. Feedback, critiques, and suggestions from this sample group are sought to improve the questionnaire design.

Address the anonymity issue. Participants should feel free to respond openly to questions without fear of reprisal. The confidentiality of their responses is of the utmost importance, since there is usually a link between anonymity and accuracy. Therefore, questionnaires should be anonymous unless there are specific reasons why individuals have to be identified. In situations in which participants must complete the questionnaire in a captive audience or submit a completed questionnaire directly to an individual, a neutral third party should collect and process the data, ensuring that participants' identities are not revealed. In cases where the actual identity must be known (e.g., to compare output data with the previous data or to verify the data), every effort should be made to protect the respondents' identities from those who may be biased in their actions.

Design for ease of tabulation and analysis. Each potential question should be viewed in terms of data tabulation, data summary, and analysis. If possible, the data analysis process should be outlined and reviewed in mock-up form. This step helps avoid inadequate, cumbersome, and lengthy data analysis caused by improper wording or design.

Develop the completed questionnaire and prepare a data summary. Questions should be integrated to develop an attractive questionnaire with proper instructions so that it can be administered effectively. In addition, a summary sheet should be developed so that data can be tabulated quickly for analysis.[2]

Questionnaire Content Issues

One of the most difficult tasks in developing a questionnaire is determining which specific issues to address. The following items represent a comprehensive list of possibilities for questionnaire content to capture both Level 3 and 4 data. Appendix 5 presents a questionnaire used in a follow-up evaluation of a two-day program on effective meetings. The evaluation was designed to capture the ROI and the primary method of data collection was this follow-up questionnaire. This example will be used to illustrate many of the issues involving potential content items for questionnaire design.

Progress with objectives. Sometimes it is helpful to assess progress with objectives in the follow-up evaluation, as is illustrated by question 1 on Appendix 5. While this issue is usually assessed during the program, it is sometimes helpful to revisit the objectives after the participants have had an opportunity to apply what has been learned.

Action plan implementation. If an action plan is required in the program, the questionnaire should reference the plan and determine the extent to which it has been implemented. If the action plan requirement is very low-key, perhaps only one question would be devoted to the follow-up on the action plan, as illustrated in question 2 in Appendix 5. If the action plan is very comprehensive and contains an abundance of Level 3 and 4 data, then the questionnaire takes a secondary role and most of the data-collection process will focus directly on the status of the action plan.

Relevance of program. Although the relevance of the program is often assessed during the program as Level 1 data, it is sometimes helpful to assess the relevance of various aspects of the program after the skills and knowledge have been applied (or attempted) on the job. This feedback helps program designers know which parts of the program were actually useful on the job, providing lasting value. Question 3 in Appendix 5 shows one approach to this issue.

Use of program materials. If participants are provided with materials to use on the job, then it may be helpful to determine the extent to which those materials have been used. This is particularly helpful when operating manuals, reference books, and job aids have been distributed, explained in the program, and are expected to be used on the job. Question 4 in Appendix 5 focuses on this issue.

Knowledge/skill application. Perhaps one of the most important questions focuses on job applications (Level 3 data). As question 5 in Appendix 5 shows, specific skills and knowledge areas are listed, and the question is framed around the amount of change since the program was conducted. This is the recommended approach when there is no pre-program data. If pre-program data has been collected, it is more appropriate to compare that data with post-program assessments, using the same question.

Skill frequency. As question 6 in Appendix 5 shows, it is sometimes helpful to determine the most frequently used skills directly linked to the program. A more detailed variation of this question lists each skill and asks for an indication of the frequency of use. For many skills, it is important to experience frequent use quickly after the skills are acquired so that they become internalized.

Changes in work unit. Sometimes it is helpful to determine what specific activities or processes have changed in participants' work as a result of the program. As question 7 in Appendix 5 illustrates, the participant explores how the skill applications listed previously have actually changed work habits, processes, and output. Question 8 is a continuation of 7, in which specific numbers or values are provided to reflect how their behavior has changed. (In this case, meeting behavior is the issue.) Question 9 is an opportunity for the participant to indicate the level of confidence in the information provided in question 8. Questions 8 and 9 are unique to this type of situation.

Measurable improvements/accomplishments. Question 10 in Appendix 5 begins a series of four impact questions that are appropriate for most follow-up questionnaires. The first question in the series, question 10, seeks specific accomplishments and improvements directly linked to the program. This question focuses on specific measurable successes that can be easily identified by the participants. Since this question is an open-ended question, it can be helpful to provide examples that indicate the nature and range of responses requested. However, examples can also be constraining in nature and may actually limit the responses.

Monetary impact. Perhaps the most difficult question, number 11 in Appendix 5, asks participants to provide monetary values for the improvements identified in question 10. Only the first-year improvement is sought. Participants are asked to specify net improvements so that the actual monetary values will represent gains from the program. An important part of the question is the basis for the calculation, in which participants specify the steps taken to develop the annual net value and the assumptions made in the analysis. It is very important that this basis be completed with enough detail to understand the process.

Confidence level. To adjust for the uncertainty of the data provided in question 11, question 12 asks participants to offer a level of confidence for the estimation, expressed as a percentage with a range of 0%–100%. This input allows participants to reflect their level of certainty with the process.

Improvements linked with program. The final question in the impact series, question 13, isolates the effects of training. Participants indicate the percent of the improvement that is directly related to the program. As an alternative, participants may be provided with various factors that have influenced the results and asked to allocate appropriate percentages to each factor. Still another variation asks participants to provide a confidence estimate for this particular value, as was the case for the estimate in question 11.

Investment perception. The program's value from the viewpoint of the participant can be useful information. As illustrated in question 14 in Appendix 5, participants are asked if they perceive this program to be a good investment. Another option is to present the actual cost of the program so that participants can respond more accurately from the investment perspective. It may be useful to express the cost as a per participant cost. Also, the question can be divided into two parts; one reflecting the investment of money by the company, and the other reflecting an investment of the participants' time in the program.

Linkage with output measures. It is sometimes helpful to determine the degree to which the program has influenced certain output measures, as shown in question 15 in Appendix 5. In some situations a detailed analysis may reveal specifically which measures have been influenced by this program. However, when this issue is uncertain, it may be helpful to list potential business performance measures influenced by the program and seek input from the participants. The question should be worded so that the frame of reference is for the time period after the program was conducted.

Barriers. A variety of barriers can influence the successful application of the skills and knowledge learned in the training program. Question 16 in Appendix 5 identifies these barriers. As an alternative, the perceived barriers are listed with a box for participants to check all that apply. Still another variation lists barriers with a range of responses indicating the extent to which the barrier inhibited results.

Enablers. Just as important as barriers are the enablers: those issues, events, activities, situations, or aids that have enabled the process to be applied successfully on the job. The same options are available with this question as in the question on barriers.

Management support. Management support is critical to the successful application of newly acquired skills. For most programs, at least one question should be included on the degree of management support provided to participants. Sometimes this question includes various descriptions of management support, and participants check the one that applies to their situation. This information is very helpful in removing or minimizing barriers.

Other solutions. A training program is only one of several potential solutions to a performance problem. If the needs assessment is faulty, or if there are alternative approaches to developing the desired skills or knowledge, other potential solutions may have been more effective or achieved the same success. The participant is asked to identify other solutions that could have been effective in obtaining the same or similar results. This information can be particularly helpful as the training and development function continues to shift to a performance improvement function.

Target audience recommendations. Sometimes it is helpful to solicit input about the most appropriate target audience for this program. In this question, participants are asked to indicate which groups of employees would benefit most from attending this program.

Suggestions for improvement. As a final wrap-up question, participants are asked to provide suggestions for improving any part of the program or process. As illustrated in question 17 in Appendix 5, the open-ended structure is intended to solicit qualitative responses to be used in making improvements.

Improving the Response Rate for Questionnaires and Surveys

The content items listed above represent a wide range of potential issues to explore in a follow-up questionnaire or survey. Obviously, asking all of the questions could cause the response rate to be reduced considerably. This is a critical issue when the questionnaire is the primary data-collection activity and most of the evaluation hinges on the questionnaire results. The following actions can be taken to increase response rate.

Provide advance communication. If appropriate and feasible, participants should receive advance notice of the requirement for a follow-up questionnaire. This minimizes some of the resistance to the process, provides an opportunity to explain the circumstances surrounding the evaluation in more detail, and positions the follow-up evaluation as an integral part of the program—not an add-on activity that someone initiated three months after the program.

Communicate the purpose. Participants should understand the reason for the follow-up questionnaire, including who or what has initiated this specific evaluation. Participants should know if the evaluation is part of a systematic process or a special request for this program.

Have an executive sign the introductory letter. For maximum effectiveness, the letter sent with the questionnaire should be signed by a senior executive responsible for a major area in which the participants work. Employees may be more willing to respond to a senior executive than to a member of the training and development staff.

Explain who will see the data. It is important for participants to know who will see the data and the results of the questionnaire. If the questionnaire is anonymous, that should be clearly communicated along with the steps taken to ensure anonymity. If senior executives will see the combined results of the study, participants should know it.

Describe the data integration process. Participants should understand how the questionnaire results will be combined with other data. Often the questionnaire is only one of the data-collection methods utilized. Participants should know how the data is weighted and integrated to provide the final report.

Use anonymous input. When possible, the questionnaire should not identify the respondent, because anonymous input will be more candid. Also, using anonymous input will increase the response rate.

Keep the questionnaire as simple as possible. A simple questionnaire does not always provide the full scope of data necessary for an ROI analysis. However, the simplified approach should always be kept in mind when questions are developed and the total scope of the questionnaire is finalized. Every effort should be made to keep the questionnaire as simple and brief as possible.

Simplify the response process. The questionnaire should be as easy to respond to as possible. If appropriate, a self-addressed stamped envelope should be included, or perhaps the e-mail system could be used for response. In still other situations, a response box is provided near the work station.

Utilize local manager support. Management involvement at the local level is critical to response rate success. Managers can distribute questionnaires, make reference to them in staff meetings, follow-up to see if they have been completed, and generally show support for completing the questionnaire. This direct supervisor support will cause some participants to respond with usable data.

Let the participants know they are part of the sample. If appropriate, participants should know that they are part of a carefully selected sample and that their input will be used to make decisions regarding a much larger target audience. This action appeals to a sense of responsibility and often encourages participants to provide usable, accurate data for the questionnaire.

Consider incentives. A variety of different types of incentives can be offered, usually falling into one of three categories. In the first, an incentive is provided in exchange for the questionnaire. When participants return the questionnaire they receive a small gift, such as a T-shirt or mug. If identity is an issue, a neutral third party can provide the incentive.

In the second category, the incentive is provided to make participants feel guilty about not responding. Examples are a dollar bill clipped to the questionnaire or a pen enclosed in the envelope. Participants are asked to "take the dollar, buy a cup of coffee and fill out the questionnaire," or "please use this pen to complete the questionnaire."

A third group of incentives is designed to obtain a quick response. This approach is based on the assumption that a quick response will ensure a greater response rate. If an individual puts off completing the questionnaire, the odds of completing it diminish considerably. Therefore, either a more expensive gift is provided for the initial group of respondents or the initial group of respondents will be part of a drawing for an incentive. For example, in one study the first 25 returned questionnaires were placed in a drawing for a $400 gift certificate, leaving 25 to 1 odds of winning. The next 25 were included with the first 25 in the next drawing, leaving 50 to 1 odds of winning. The longer a participant waits, the lower the odds of winning.

Use follow-up reminders. Follow-up reminders should be sent a week after the questionnaire is received and again two weeks later. These times could be adjusted depending on the questionnaire and the situation. In some situations, a third follow-up is recommended. The follow-up could also be sent in different media. For example, a questionnaire may be sent by regular mail whereas the first follow-up reminder is given by the immediate supervisor in a meeting and the second follow-up reminder is sent by e-mail.

Send a copy of the results to the participants. Even if it is an abbreviated form, participants should see the results of the study. More importantly, participants should be told that they will receive a copy of the study when they are asked to provide the data. This promise will often increase the response rate, as some individuals want to see the results of the entire group along with their particular input.

Collectively, these items help boost response rates of follow-up questionnaires and surveys. Using all of these strategies can result in response rates in the 50%–60% range, even with a lengthy questionnaire that might take 30 minutes to complete.

Follow-Up Interviews

Another helpful collection method is the interview, although it is not used as frequently as questionnaires. Interviews can be conducted by the HRD staff, the participant's supervisor, or an outside third party. Interviews can provide data not available in performance records or difficult to obtain through written responses or observations. Also, interviews can uncover success stories that may be useful in communicating evaluation results. Participants may be reluctant to describe their results in a questionnaire but will volunteer the information to a skillful interviewer who uses probing techniques. While the interview process uncovers changes in behavior, reaction, and results, it is primarily used with Level 3 data. A major disadvantage of the interview is that it is time consuming. It also requires training interviewers to ensure that the process is consistent.[3]

Types of Interviews

Interviews usually fall into two basic types: structured and unstructured. A structured interview is much like a questionnaire. Specific questions are asked with little room to deviate from the desired responses. The primary advantages of the structured interview over the questionnaire are that the interview process ensures that the questionnaire is completed and that the interviewer understands the responses supplied by the participant.

The unstructured interview allows for probing for additional information. This type of interview uses a few general questions that can lead into more detailed information as important data are uncovered. The interviewer must be skilled in the probing process. Typical probing questions are:

☐ Can you explain that in more detail?
☐ Can you give me an example of what you are saying?
☐ Can you explain the difficulty that you say you encountered?

Interview Guidelines

The steps for interview design are similar to those for the questionnaire. A brief summary of key interview issues is outlined here.

Determine specific information needed. The topics, skills, issues, barriers, and other needed information is identified.

Develop questions to be asked. Once a decision has been made about the type of interview, specific questions need to be developed. These questions should be brief, precise, and designed for easy response.

Try out the interview. The instrument should be tested on a small number of participants. If possible, the interviews should be conducted as part of the trial run of the HRD program. The responses should be analyzed and the interview revised, if necessary.

Train the interviewers. The interviewer should have appropriate skills, including active listening and the ability to ask probing questions, collect information, and summarize it in a meaningful form.

Give clear instructions to the participant. The participant should understand the purpose of the interview and know what will be done with the information. Expectations, conditions, and rules of the interview should be thoroughly discussed. For example, the participant should know if statements will be kept confidential. If the participant is nervous during an interview and develops signs of anxiety, he or she should be made to feel at ease.

Administer the interviews according to a scheduled plan. As with other evaluation instruments, interviews need to be conducted according to a predetermined plan. The timing of the interview, the person to conduct the interview, and the place of the interview are all issues that become relevant in developing an interview plan. For a large number of participants, a sampling plan may be necessary to save time and reduce the cost of the evaluation.

Follow-Up Focus Groups

An extension of the interview, focus groups are particularly helpful when in-depth feedback is needed for a Level 3 evaluation, although Level 4 data can also be collected with the process. The focus group is a small group discussion conducted by an experienced facilitator. It is designed to solicit qualitative judgments on a planned topic or issue. Group members are all required to provide their input and individual input builds on group input.

When compared with questionnaires, surveys, tests, or interviews, the focus group strategy has several advantages. The basic premise of using focus groups is that when quality judgments are subjective, several individual judgments are better than one. The group process, in which participants often motivate one another, is an effective method for generating new ideas and hypotheses. It is inexpensive and can be quickly planned and conducted. Its flexibility makes it possible to explore a training program's unexpected possible outcomes or applications.[4]

Applications for Evaluation

The focus group is particularly helpful when qualitative information is needed about the success of a training program. For example, the focus group can be used in the following situations:

☐ To evaluate reactions to specific exercises, cases, simulations, or other components of a training program
☐ To assess the overall effectiveness of the program as perceived by the participants immediately following a program
☐ To assess the impact of the program in a follow-up evaluation after the program is completed

Essentially, focus groups are helpful when evaluation information is needed that cannot be collected adequately with simple, quantitative methods.

Guidelines

While there are no set rules on how to use focus groups for evaluation, the following guidelines should be helpful:

Ensure that management supports the focus group process. Because this is a relatively new process for evaluation, it may be unknown to some management groups. Managers need to understand focus groups and their advantages. This should raise their level of confidence in the information obtained from group sessions.

Plan topics, questions, and strategy carefully. As with any evaluation instrument, planning is the key. The specific topics, questions, and issues to be discussed must be carefully planned and sequenced. This enhances the comparison of results from one group to another and ensures that the group process is effective and stays on track.

Keep the group size small. While there is no magic group size, a range of 6–12 seems to be appropriate for most focus group applications. A group has to be large enough to ensure different points of view, but small enough to give every participant a chance to talk freely and exchange comments.

Ensure that there is a representative sample of the target population. It is important that groups be stratified appropriately so that participants represent the target population. The group should be homogeneous in experience, rank, and influence in the organization.

Insist on facilitators with appropriate expertise. The success of a focus group rests with the facilitator, who must be skilled in the focus group process. Facilitators must know how to control aggressive members of the group and diffuse the input from those who want to dominate the group. Also, facilitators must be able to create an environment in which participants feel comfortable offering comments freely and openly. Because of this, some organizations use external facilitators.

In summary, the focus group is an inexpensive and quick way to determine the strengths and weaknesses of training programs, particularly with management and supervisory training. However, for complete evaluation, focus group information should be combined with data from other instruments.

Observing Participants On the Job

Another potentially useful data-collection method is observing participants to record changes in behavior. The observer may be a member of the HRD staff, the participant's supervisor, a member of a peer group, or an outside party. The most common observer, and probably the most practical, is a member of the HRD staff.

Guidelines for Effective Observation

Observation is often misused or misapplied to evaluation situations, leading some to abandon the process. The effectiveness of observation can be improved with the following guidelines:

Observers must be fully prepared. Observers must fully understand what information is needed and what skills are covered in the program. They must be trained for the assignment and provided a chance to practice observation skills.

Observations should be systematic. The observation process must be planned so that it is executed effectively without any surprises. The persons observed should know in advance about the observation and why they are being observed unless the observation is planned to be invisible. The timing of observations should also be a part of the plan. There are right times to observe a participant, and there are wrong times. If a participant is observed when times are not normal (e.g., in a crisis), the data collected may be distorted.

Planning a systematic observation is important. Several steps are necessary to accomplish a successful observation.

☐ Determine what behavior will be observed.
☐ Prepare the forms for the observers to use.

☐ Select the observers.
☐ Prepare a schedule of observations.
☐ Train observers in what to observe and what not to observe.
☐ Inform participants of the planned observations with explanations.
☐ Conduct observations.
☐ Summarize the observation data.

Observers should know how to interpret and report what they see. Observations involve judgment decisions. The observer must analyze which behaviors are being displayed and what actions are being taken by the participants. Observers should know how to summarize behavior and report results in a meaningful manner.

The observers' influence should be minimized. Except for mystery observers and electronic observations, it is impossible to completely isolate the overall effect of an observer. Participants may display the behavior they think is appropriate, and they will usually be at their best. Therefore, the presence of the observer must be minimized. To the extent possible, the observer should blend into the work environment.

Select observers carefully. Observers are usually independent of the participants, typically a member of the HRD staff. The independent observer is usually more skilled at recording behavior and making interpretations of behavior, and is usually unbiased in these interpretations. Using independent observers enables the HRD department to bypass training observers and relieves the line organization of that responsibility. On the other hand, the independent observer has the appearance of an outsider checking the work of others. There may be a tendency for participants to overreact and possibly resent this kind of observer. Sometimes it might be more feasible to recruit observers from outside the organization. This approach has an advantage of neutralizing the prejudicial feelings entering the decisions.

Observation Methods

Five methods of observation are utilized, depending on the circumstances surrounding the type of information needed. Each method is described briefly.

Behavior checklist and codes. A behavior checklist can be useful for recording the presence, absence, frequency, or duration of a participant's behavior as it occurs. A checklist usually will not provide information on the quality, intensity, or possibly the circumstances surrounding the behavior observed. The checklist is useful, since an observer can identify exactly which behaviors should or should not occur. Measuring the duration of a behavior may be more difficult and requires a stopwatch and a place on the form to record the time interval. This factor is usually not so important when compared to whether or not a particular behavior was observed and how often. The number of behaviors listed in the checklist should be small and listed in a logical sequence if that is how they normally occur. A more time-consuming variation of this approach involves coding specific behaviors on a form.

Delayed report method. With a delayed report method the observer does not use any forms or written materials during the observation. The information is either recorded after the observation is completed or at particular time intervals during an observation. The observer tries to reconstruct what has been observed during the observation period. The advantage of this approach is that the observer is not as noticeable. There are no forms being completed or notes being taken during the observation, so the observer can be more a part of the situation and less distracting. An obvious disadvantage is that the information written may not be as accurate and reliable as the information collected at the time it occurred. A variation of this approach is the 360° feedback process in which surveys are completed on other individuals based on observations within a specific time frame.

Video recording. A video camera records behavior in every detail, an obvious advantage. However, this intrusion may be awkward and cumbersome and the participants may be unnecessarily nervous or self-conscious when they are being videotaped. If the camera is concealed, the privacy of the participant may be invaded. Because of this, video recording of on-the-job behavior is infrequently used.

Audio monitoring. Monitoring conversations of participants who are using the skills taught in the training program is an effective observation technique. For example, in a large communication company's telemarketing department, sales representatives are trained to sell equipment by telephone. To determine if employees are using the skills properly, telephone conversations are monitored on a selected and sometimes random basis. While this approach may stir some controversy, it is an effective way to determine if skills are being applied consistently and effectively. For it to work smoothly, it must be fully explained and the rules clearly communicated.

Computer monitoring. For employees who work regularly with a keyboard, computer monitoring is an effective way to "observe" participants as they perform job tasks. The computer monitors times, sequence of steps, errors, and other activities to determine if the participant is performing the work according to what was learned in the training program. As technology continues to be a significant part of jobs, computer monitoring holds promise of monitoring actual applications on the job. This approach is helpful for Level 3 and 4 data.

Monitoring Performance Data

Data are available in every organization to measure performance. Monitoring performance data enables management to measure performance in terms of output, quality, costs, time, and satisfaction. In determining the use of data in the evaluation, the first consideration should be existing databases and reports. In most organizations, performance data suitable for measuring the improvement resulting from an HRD program are available. If not, additional record-keeping systems will have to be developed for measurement and analysis. At this point, as with many other points in the process, the question of economics enters. Is it economical to develop the record-keeping system necessary to evaluate an HRD program? If the costs are greater than the expected return for the entire program, then it is meaningless to develop them.

Using Current Measures

If existing performance measures are available, specific guidelines are recommended to ensure that the measurement system is easily developed.

Identify appropriate measures. Performance measures should be thoroughly researched to identify those that are related to the proposed objectives of the program. Frequently, an organization will have several performance measures related to the same item. For example, the efficiency of a production unit can be measured in a variety of ways.

☐ The number of units produced per hour
☐ The number of on-schedule production units
☐ The percent utilization of the equipment
☐ The percent of equipment downtime
☐ The labor cost per unit of production
☐ The overtime required per piece of production
☐ Total unit cost

Each of these, in its own way, measures the efficiency of the production unit. All related measures should be reviewed to determine those most relevant to the HRD program.

Convert current measures to usable ones. Occasionally, existing performance measures are integrated with other data, and it may be difficult to keep them isolated from unrelated data. In this situation all existing related measures should be extracted and retabulated to be more appropriate for comparison in the evaluation. At times conversion factors may be necessary. For example, the average number of new sales orders per month may be presented regularly in the performance measures for the sales department. In addition, the sales costs per sales representative are also presented. However, in the evaluation of an HRD program, the average cost per new sale is needed. Both existing performance records are required to develop the data necessary for comparison.

Develop a data-collection plan. A data-collection plan defines when data are collected, who will collect it, and where it will be collected. This plan should contain provisions for the evaluator to secure copies of performance reports in a timely manner so that the items can be recorded and available for analysis.

Developing New Measures

In some cases, data are not available for the information needed to measure the effectiveness of an HRD program. The HRD staff must work with the participating organization to develop record-keeping systems if they are economically feasible. In one organization a new employee orientation system was implemented on a company-wide basis. Several measures were planned including early turnover, representing the percentage of employees who left the company in the first six months of their employment. An effective employee orientation program should influence this variable. At the time of the program's inception, this measure was not available. When the program was implemented, the organization began collecting early turnover figures for comparison.

When creating new measures several questions are relevant.

☐ Which department will develop the measurement system?
☐ Who will record and monitor the data?
☐ Where will it be recorded?
☐ Will forms be used?

These questions will usually involve other departments or a management decision that extends beyond the scope of the HRD department. Possibly the administration division, HR department, or information technology section will be instrumental in helping determine if new measures are needed and, if so, how they will be collected.

Action Planning and Follow-Up Assignments

In some cases, follow-up assignments can develop Level 3 and Level 4 data. In a typical follow-up assignment, the participant is instructed to meet a goal or complete a particular task or project by the determined follow-up date. A summary of the results of these completed assignments provides further evidence of the impact of the program.

This section fully describes the action plan, which is the most common type of follow-up assignment. This approach requires that participants develop action plans as part of the program. Action plans contain detailed steps to accomplish specific objectives related to the program, and are typically prepared on a printed form such as the one shown in Appendix 6. The action plan shows what is to be done, by whom, and the date by which the objectives should be accomplished. The action plan approach is a straightforward, easy-to-use method for determining how participants will change their behavior on the job and achieve success with training. The approach produces data that answer such questions as

☐ What on-the-job improvements have been realized since the program was conducted?
☐ Are the improvements linked to the program?
☐ What may have prevented participants from accomplishing specific action items?

With this information, HRD professionals can decide if a program should be modified and in what ways, while managers can assess the findings to evaluate the worth of the program.

Developing the Action Plan

The development of the action plan requires two tasks: determining the areas for action, and writing the action items. Both tasks should be completed during the program. The areas for action should originate from the content of the program and, at the same time, be related to on-the-job activities. A list of potential areas for action can be developed independently by participants or a list may be generated in group discussions. The list may include an area needing improvement or represent an opportunity for increased performance.

After the initial areas are identified, the following questions should be asked when developing action steps:

☐ How much time will this action take?
☐ Are the skills for accomplishing this action item available?

☐ Who has the authority to implement the action plan?
☐ Will this action have an effect on other individuals?
☐ Are there any organizational constraints for accomplishing this action item?

The specific action items are usually more difficult to write than the identification of the action areas. The most important characteristic of an action item is that it is written so that everyone involved will know when it occurs. One way to help achieve this goal is to use specific action verbs. Some examples of action items are:

☐ Learn how to operate the new RC-105 drill press machine in the adjacent department, by (date).
☐ Identify and secure a new customer account, by (date).
☐ Handle every piece of paper only once to improve my personal time management, by (date).
☐ Learn to talk with my employers directly about a problem that arises rather than avoiding a confrontation, by (date).

If appropriate, each action item should have a date for completion and indicate other individuals or resources required for completion. Also, planned behavior changes should be observable. It should be obvious to the participant and others when it happens. Action plans, as used in this context, do not require prior approval or input from the participant's supervisor, although it may be helpful.

Using Action Plans Successfully

The action plan process should be an integral part of the program and not an add-on or optional activity. To gain maximum effectiveness from action plans and to collect data for ROI calculations, the following steps should be implemented:

Communicate the action plan requirement early. One of the most negative reactions to action plans occurs due to the surprise factor in the way in which the process is introduced. When program participants realize that they must develop a detailed action plan, there is often immediate, built-in resistance. Communicating to participants in advance, and showing the process to be an integral part of the program, will often minimize resistance to developing action plans. When participants fully realize the benefits before they attend the first session, they take the process more seriously and usually perform the extra steps to make it more successful.

Describe the action-planning process at the beginning of the program. At the first session, discuss action plan requirements including an outline of the purpose of the process, why it is necessary, and basic requirements during and after the program. Some facilitators furnish a separate notepad for participants to collect ideas and useful techniques for their action plan. This is a productive way to focus more attention and effort on the process.

Teach the action-planning process. An important prerequisite for action plan success is an understanding of how it works and how specific action plans are developed. A portion of the program's agenda can be allocated to teaching participants how to develop plans. In this session, the requirements are outlined, special forms and procedures are discussed, and a positive example is distributed and reviewed. Sometimes an entire program module is allocated to this process so that participants will fully understand and use it. Any available support tools, such as key measures, charts, graphs, suggested topics, and sample calculations should be used in this session to help facilitate the development of the plan.

Allow time to develop the plan. When action plans are used to collect data for an ROI calculation, it is important to allow participants to develop plans during the program. Sometimes it is helpful to have participants work in teams to share ideas as they develop specific plans. In these sessions, facilitators often monitor the progress of individuals or teams to keep the process on track and answer questions. In some management and executive development programs, action plans are developed in an evening session, as a scheduled part of the program.

Have the facilitator approve the action plans. It is essential for the action plan to be related to program objectives and, at the same time, represent an important accomplishment for the organization when it is completed. It is easy for participants to stray from the intent and purposes of action planning and not give it the attention that it deserves. Consequently, it is helpful to have the facilitator actually sign off on the action plan, ensuring that the plan reflects all of the requirements and is appropriate for the program. In some cases a space is provided for the facilitator's signature on the action plan document. If more than one facilitator is involved, the lead or principal facilitator usually approves the plan.

Require participants to assign a monetary value for each improvement. Participants are asked to determine, calculate, or estimate the monetary value for each improvement outlined in the plan. When the actual improvement has occurred, participants will use these values to capture the annual monetary benefits of the plan. For this step to be effective, it may be helpful to provide examples of typical ways in which values can be assigned to the actual data.[5]

Ask participants to isolate the effects of the program. Although the action plan is initiated because of the training program, the actual improvements reported on the action plan may be influenced by other factors. Therefore, the action planning process itself should not take full credit for the improvement. For example, an action plan to reduce employee turnover in a division could take only partial credit for an improvement, because of the other variables that will affect the turnover rate. While there are at least ten ways to isolate the effects of training, participant estimation is usually more appropriate in the action planning process.[6] Consequently, the participants are asked to estimate the percent of the improvement actually related to this particular program. This question can be asked on the action plan form or on a follow-up questionnaire.

Ask participants to provide a confidence level for estimates. Since the process to convert data to monetary values may not be exact and the amount of the improvement actually related to the program may not be precise, participants are asked to indicate their level of confidence in those two values, collectively. On a scale of 0% to 100%, where 0% means the values are completely false to 100% means the estimates represent certainty, this value provides participants with a mechanism to express their certainty of their ability to be exact with the process.

Require action plans to be presented to the group, if possible. There is no better way to secure commitment and ownership of the action-planning process than to have a participant describe his or her action plan in front of a group of fellow participants. Presenting the action plan helps to ensure that the process is thoroughly developed and will be implemented on the job. If the number of participants is too large for individual presentations, perhaps one participant can be selected from each team, if the plans are developed in teams. Under these circumstances, the team will usually select the best action plan for presentation to the group.

Explain the follow-up mechanism. Participants must leave the session with a clear understanding of the timing of the action plan implementation and the planned follow-up. The method in which the data will be collected, analyzed, and reported should be openly discussed. Five options are common:

☐ The group is reconvened to discuss the progress on the plans.
☐ Participants meet with their immediate manager and discuss the success of the plan. A copy is forwarded to the HRD department.

☐ The program evaluator, the participant, and the participant's manager meet to discuss the plan and the information contained in it.

☐ Participants send the plan to the evaluator and discuss it in a conference call.

☐ Participants send the plan directly to the education and training department with no meetings or discussions. This is the most common option.

While there are other ways to collect the data, it is important to select a mechanism that fits the culture and constraints of the organization.

Collect action plans at the predetermined follow-up time. Because it is critical to have an excellent response rate, several steps may be necessary to ensure that action plans are completed and the data returned to the appropriate individual or group for analysis. Some organizations use follow-up reminders by mail or e-mail. Others call participants to check progress. Still others offer assistance in developing the final plan. These steps may require additional resources, which have to be weighed against the importance of having more data. When the action plan process is implemented as outlined in this chapter, the response rates will normally be very high, in the 50%–70% range. Participants will usually see the importance of the process and develop their plans in detail before leaving the program.

Summarize the data and calculate the ROI. If developed properly, each action plan should have annualized monetary values associated with improvements. Also, each individual will have indicated the percent of the improvement that is directly related to the program. Finally, each participant will have provided a confidence percentage to reflect his or her certainty of the process and the subjective nature of some of the data that may be provided. Because this process will involve estimates, it may not appear to be accurate. Several adjustments during the analysis make the process credible and more accurate. Although data analysis is presented in a later chapter, the following adjustments are suggested:

Step 1: For those participants who do not provide data, it is assumed that they had no improvement to report. This is a very conservative assumption.

Step 2: Each value is checked for realism, usability, and feasibility. Extreme values are discarded and omitted from the analysis.

Step 3: Because the improvement is annualized, it is assumed the program had no improvement after the first year. Some programs should add value at years two and three.

Step 4: The usable data items are then adjusted by the percent of the improvement related directly to the program using straight multiplication. This isolates the effects of training.

Step 5: The new values from step 4 are then adjusted for the confidence level, by multiplying it by the confidence percent. The confidence level is actually an error possibility suggested by the participants. For example, a participant indicating 80% confidence with the process is reflecting a 20% error possibility. In a $10,000 estimate with an 80% confidence factor, the participant is suggesting that the value could be in the range of $8,000 to $12,000. To be conservative, use the lower number. Thus, the confidence factor is multiplied times the amount of improvement.

The monetary values determined in these five steps are totaled to arrive at a total program benefit. Since these values are already annualized, the total of these benefits represents the annual benefits for the program. This value is placed in the numerator of the ROI formula to calculate the ROI.

Advantages/Disadvantages

Although there are many advantages, there are at least two concerns with action plans. The process relies on direct input from the participant with no assurance of anonymity, so the information can sometimes be biased and unreliable. Also, action plans can be time consuming for the participant and if his or her supervisor is not involved in the process there may be a tendency for the participant not to complete the assignment.

As this section has illustrated, the action plan approach has many inherent advantages. The plans are simple and easy to administer, and participants can easily understand the approach. Also, they can be used with a wide variety of programs, are appropriate for all types of data (learning, behavior changes, and results), and can be used alone or in conjunction with other evaluation methods. Because of the tremendous flexibility and versatility of the process, and the conservative adjustments that can be made in analysis, action plans have become an important data-collection tool for evaluation and ROI analysis.

Performance Contracts

The performance contract is essentially a slight variation of the action-planning process. Based on the principle of mutual goal setting, a performance contract is a written agreement between a participant and the participant's supervisor. The participant agrees to improve performance in an area of mutual concern related to the subject material in the HRD program. The agreement is in the form of a project to be completed or goal to be accomplished soon after the program is over. The agreement spells out what is to be accomplished, when, and with what results.

Although the steps can vary according to the specific kind of contract and the organization, a common sequence of events is as follows:

1. With supervisor approval, the employee (participant) decides to attend an HRD program.
2. The participant and supervisor mutually agree on a subject for improvement.
3. The participant and supervisor set specific, measurable goals.
4. The participant attends the program at which the contract is discussed, and plans are developed to accomplish the goals.
5. After the program, the participant works on the contract against a specific deadline.
6. The participant reports the results of the effort to his supervisor.
7. The supervisor and participant document the results and forward a copy to the HRD department, along with appropriate comments.

The individuals mutually select the subject or action to be performed or improved prior to the beginning of the program. The process of selecting the area for improvement is similar to that used in the action-planning process. The topic can cover one or more of the following areas:

☐ Routine performance—includes specific improvements in routine performance measures such as production targets, efficiency, and error rates.

☐ Problem solving—focuses on specific problems such as an unexpected increase in accidents, a decrease in efficiency, or a loss of morale.

☐ Innovative or creative applications—includes initiating changes or improvements in work practices, methods, procedures, techniques, and processes.

☐ Personal development—involves learning new information or acquiring a new skill to increase individual effectiveness.

The topic selected should be stated in terms of one or more objectives. The objectives should state what is to be accomplished when the contract is complete. These objectives should be

☐ Written
☐ Understandable (by all involved)
☐ Challenging (requiring an unusual effort to achieve)
☐ Achievable (something that can be achieved)
☐ Largely under the control of the participant
☐ Measurable and dated

The details required to accomplish the objectives of the contract are developed following the guidelines under action plans presented earlier. Also, the methods for analyzing data and reporting progress are essentially the same as with the action-planning process.

Program Follow-Up Session

In some situations, the program is redesigned to allow for a follow-up session in which evaluation is addressed along with additional education and training. For example, an interactive selling-skills program, originally a three-consecutive-day program, was redesigned as a two-day workshop to build skills, followed by a one-day session three weeks later. The follow-up session provided an opportunity for additional training and evaluation. During the first part of the day, Level 3 evaluation data were collected using a focus group process. Also, specific barriers and problems encountered in applying the skills were discussed. The second half of the day was devoted to additional skill building and refinement, along with techniques to overcome particular barriers to using the skills. Thus, in effect, the redesigned program provided a mechanism for follow-up.

Selecting the Appropriate Method

This chapter presented ten methods to capture post-program data for an evaluation. Collectively, they offer a wide range of opportunities to collect data in a variety of situations. Eight specific issues should be considered when deciding which method is appropriate for a situation.

Type of Data

Perhaps the most important issue to consider when selecting a post-program evaluation method is the type of data to be collected. Some methods are more appropriate for Level 4 data while others are best for Level 3. Table 9-1 shows the most appropriate type of data for a specific method. Follow-up surveys, observations, interviews, and focus groups are best suited for Level 3 data. Performance monitoring, action planning, and questionnaires can easily capture Level 4 data.

Participant Time

Another important factor in selecting the data-collection method is the amount of time participants must devote to the data collection and evaluation process. Time requirements should always be minimized and the method

Table 9-1
Appropriate Post-Program Data-Collection Methods
for Specific Types of Data

	Level 3	Level 4
☐ Follow-Up Surveys	√	
☐ Follow-Up Questionnaires	√	√
☐ Observation On the Job	√	
☐ Interviews with Participants	√	
☐ Follow-Up Focus Groups	√	
☐ Program Assignments	√	√
☐ Action Planning	√	√
☐ Performance Contracting	√	√
☐ Program Follow-Up Session	√	√
☐ Performance Monitoring		√

should be positioned so that it is value-added activity (that is, the participants can see that this activity is something they should do). This requirement often means that sampling is used to keep the total participant time to a
reasonable amount. Some methods, such as performance monitoring, require
no participant time, while others, such as interviews and focus groups,
require a significant investment in time.

Supervisor Time

The time that a participant's direct supervisor must devote to data collection is another important issue in the selection of the method. This time
requirement should always be minimized. Some methods, such as performance contracting, may require extensive supervisor involvement both prior
to and after the program. Other methods, such as questionnaires and surveys
administered directly to participants, may not require any supervisor time.

Costs

Costs are always a consideration when selecting the method. Some data-
collection methods are more expensive than others. For example, interviews
and observations are very expensive, while surveys, questionnaires, and performance monitoring are usually inexpensive.

Disruption of Normal Work Activities

One of the most critical issues when selecting the appropriate method, and
perhaps the one that generates the most concern with managers, is the
amount of disruption the data collection will create. Routine work processes

should be disrupted as little as possible. Some data-collection techniques, such as performance monitoring, require very little time and distraction from normal activities. Questionnaires can often be completed in only a few minutes of time, or even after work, and not disrupt the work environment. On the other extreme, items such as observations and interviews may be too disruptive for the work unit.

Accuracy

The accuracy of the technique is another factor when selecting the method. Some data-collection methods are more accurate than others. For example, performance monitoring is usually very accurate, whereas surveys can be distorted and unreliable. If actual on-the-job behavior must be captured, unobtrusive observation is clearly the most accurate process.

Utility

Because there are many different methods to collect data, it is tempting to use too many. Multiple data-collection methods add to the time and cost of the evaluation and may result in very little additional value. Utility refers to the added value of the use of an additional data-collection method. When more than one method is used, this question should always be addressed. Does the value obtained from the additional data warrant the additional time and expense of the method? If the answer is no, the additional method should not be implemented.

Culture/Philosophy

Finally, the culture or philosophy of the organization can dictate which data-collection methods are used. For example, some organizations are accustomed to using questionnaires and find that the process fits well within their culture. Some organizations will not use observation because their culture does not support the potential invasion of privacy associated with it.

Summary

This chapter has provided an overview of the most common approaches to collecting data to be used in evaluation. A variety of options are available that can usually match any budget or situation. Some methods are gaining more acceptance for use with Level 4 data. In addition to performance monitoring, follow-up questionnaires and action plans are regularly used to collect data for an ROI analysis, as described in this chapter. Other methods can be helpful in providing a complete picture of the on-the-job applications and business impact of the program.

Discussion Questions

1. Use examples to illustrate the differences among evaluation instrument design, evaluation design, and data-collection methods.
2. Why are follow-up evaluations important?
3. Design a follow-up questionnaire for a three-day performance management workshop for middle managers. Make any assumptions necessary to complete the assignment.
4. Why is the response rate on questionnaires so critical?
5. How can the questionnaire in question 3 be administered for maximum returns?
6. Do organizations use performance contracts on a routine basis? Explain.
7. What advantages do action plans have over questionnaires?
8. What are the weaknesses of the interview process?
9. When is it appropriate to use the interview as part of the evaluation process? What are the differences in the interview and the focus group process?
10. What are the problems with the focus group process?
11. When is it appropriate to use observations in the evaluation process?
12. What difficulties are encountered when using evaluation information obtained from observers?
13. What performance records are available in your organization (or one with which you are familiar)?
14. Which is the most effective data-collection method? Why?
15. Is it possible to use all data-collection methods in the evaluation of a single program? Explain.
16. In your organization (or one with which you are familiar), which types of data-collection methods are commonly used? Why?

References

1. Rea, L. M. and Parker, R. A. *Designing and Conducting Survey Research.* San Francisco, CA: Jossey-Bass Publishers, 1992.
2. Fink, A. *How to Design Surveys.* Thousand Oaks, CA: Sage Publications, Inc., 1995.
3. Frey, J. H. and Oishi, S. M. *How to Conduct Interviews by Telephone and in Person.* Thousand Oaks, CA: Sage Publications, Inc., 1995.

4. Ellis, C. and Flaherty, M. G. (Eds.) *Investigating Subjectivity: Research on Lived Experience.* Newbury Park, CA: Sage Publications, Inc., 1992.
5. Phillips, J. J. "How Much is the Training Worth?" *Training and Development,* Vol. 50, No. 4, April 1996, pp. 20–24.
6. Phillips, J. J. "Was it the Training?" *Training and Development,* Vol. 50, No. 3, March 1996, pp. 28–32.

CHAPTER 10

Isolating the Effects of Training

When a significant increase in performance is noted after a major training program has been conducted, the two events appear to be linked. While the change in performance may be linked to the training program, other non-training factors usually have contributed to the improvement as well. The challenge is to develop one or more specific strategies to isolate the effects of training. The cause and effect relationship between training and performance can be very confusing and difficult to prove, but this can be accomplished with an acceptable degree of accuracy.

The material presented in this chapter is an extension of the research design issues presented earlier. In essence, the goal of a proper research design is to isolate the effects of the program on performance. The classical designs presented in Chapter 5 are inadequate in most settings within organizations, as it is sometimes difficult to establish control groups and time series designs. Consequently, other approaches must be utilized in an attempt to determine the impact of the program on specific outcome measures. This chapter explores ten useful strategies for isolating the effects of training when collecting Level 3 and 4 data. These strategies have been used by some of the best organizations to evaluate training and development programs and determine the amount of improvement that is directly related to a program. Portions of this chapter were published in another reference for evaluation.[1] To a certain extent, there will be some overlap in the material presented here and in the chapter on research design.

Identifying Other Factors: A First Step

As a first step in isolating training's impact on performance, all key factors that may have contributed to the performance improvement should be identified. This step communicates to interested parties that other factors may have influenced the results, underscoring that the training program is not the sole source of improvement. Consequently, the credit for improvement is shared with several possible variables and sources, an approach that is likely to gain the respect of management.

There are several potential sources to identify major influencing variables. If the program is designed on request, the client organization itself may be able to identify factors that will influence the output variable. The client will usually be aware of other initiatives or programs that may impact the output.

Program participants are usually aware of other influences that may have caused performance improvement. After all, it is the impact of their collective efforts that is being monitored and measured. In many situations, they have witnessed previous movements in performance measures and can pinpoint reasons for change.

Program analysts and developers are another source for identifying variables that have an impact on results. The needs analysis will usually uncover these influencing variables, which program designers analyze while addressing the training transfer issue.

In some situations, participants' supervisors may be able to identify variables that have influenced the performance improvement. This is particularly useful when training program participants are non-exempt employees (operatives) who may not be fully aware of the variables that can influence performance.

Finally, middle and top management may be able to identify other influences based on their own experience and knowledge of the situation. Perhaps they have monitored, examined, and analyzed the variables previously. The authority of these individuals often increases the data's credibility.

Taking time to focus attention on variables that may have influenced performance brings additional accuracy and credibility to the process. It moves beyond presenting results with no mention of other influences, a situation that often destroys the credibility of a report on training impact. It also provides a foundation for some of the strategies described in this chapter by identifying the variables that must be isolated in order to show the effects of training. A word of caution is appropriate here. Halting the process after this step would leave many unknowns about the actual impact of training and might leave a negative impression with management since it may have identified variables that management did not previously consider. Therefore, it is recommended that the HRD staff go beyond this initial step and utilize one or more of the ten strategies to isolate the impact of training—the focus of this chapter.

Use of Control Groups

The most accurate method to isolate the impact of training is the use of control groups in an experimental design process.[2] This approach involves the use of an experimental group that attends training and a control group that does not. The groups' composition should be as identical as possible and, if feasible, participants for each group should be selected randomly. When this is achieved and both groups are subjected to the same environmental influences, the difference in the performance of the two groups can be attributed to the training program. The control group and experimental group do not necessarily have pre-program measurements. Measurements are taken after the program and the difference in the performance of the two groups shows the amount of improvement that is directly related to the training program.

Control group arrangements appear in many settings. A recent review cited a Federal Express ROI analysis using control groups as a good example of the state of the art in measuring ROI.[3] The study focused on 20 employees who went through an intense, redesigned two-week training program soon after being hired to drive company vans. Their performance was compared with a control group of 20 other new hires whose managers were told to do no more or less on-the-job training than they normally would. The two groups' performance was tracked for 90 days in categories such as accidents, injuries, time-card errors, and domestic air-bill errors. The ten performance categories were assigned dollar values by experts from engineering, finance, and other groups. The program demonstrated that the performance of the highly trained employees was superior to that of the group that did not receive the upgraded training, and resulted in a 24% return on investment.

One caution to keep in mind is that the use of control groups may create an image that the HRD staff is creating a laboratory setting, which can cause a problem for some executives. To avoid this stigma, some organizations run a pilot program as the experimental group and do not inform the non-participating control group. Another example will illustrate this approach. An international specialty manufacturing company developed a program for its customer service representatives who sell directly to the public.[4] The program was designed to improve selling skills and produce higher levels of sales. Previously, sales skills acquisition was informal, on-the-job learning by trial and error. The HRD manager was convinced that formal training would significantly increase sales. Management was skeptical and wanted proof, a familiar scenario. The program was pilot tested by teaching the art of selling to sixteen customer service representatives randomly selected from the thirty-two most recently hired. The remaining sixteen served as a control group and did not receive training. Prior to training, performance was measured using average daily sales (sales divided by number of days) for thirty days (or length of service, if shorter) for each of the two groups. After training, the average daily sales were recorded for another thirty days. A significant difference in the sales of the two groups emerged, and because the groups were almost identical and subjected to the same environmental influences, it was concluded that the sales differences were a result of training and not other factors. In this setting, pilot testing allowed the use of a control group without the typical publicity and potential criticism of the use of control groups.

The control group process does have some inherent problems that may make it difficult to apply in practice. The first major problem is the selection of the groups. From a practical perspective it is virtually impossible to have identical control and experimental groups. Dozens of factors can affect employee performance, some of them individual and others contextual. To tackle the issue on a practical basis, it is best to select two or three variables that will have the greatest influence on performance. For example, in an interactive selling-skills program in a retail store chain, three groups were trained and their performance was compared to three similar groups that served as the control groups. The selection of the particular groups was based on three variables store executives thought would influence performance most from one store to another: actual market area, store size, and customer traffic. Although there are other factors that could influence performance, these three variables were considered most important and were used to make the selection.

Another problem is contamination, which can develop when participants in the training program actually teach others who are in the control group. Sometimes the reverse situation occurs when members of the control group model the behavior from the trained group. In either case, the experiment becomes contaminated as the influence of training is passed on to the control group. This can be minimized by ensuring that control groups and experimental groups are at different locations, or have different shifts. When this is not possible, it is sometimes helpful to explain to both groups that one group will receive training now and another will receive training at a later date. Also, it may be helpful to appeal to the sense of responsibility of those being trained and ask them not to share the information with others.

A third problem occurs when various groups function under different environmental influences. This can easily occur, particularly when the groups are in different locations. Sometimes the selection of the groups can help prevent this problem from occurring. Also, using more groups than necessary and discarding those with some environmental differences is another tactic.

A fourth problem with using control groups is that it may appear to be too research oriented for most business organizations. For example, management may not want to take the time to experiment before proceeding with a program or withhold training from a group just to measure the impact of an experimental program. Because of this concern, some HRD practitioners do not entertain using control groups. When the process is used, however, some organizations conduct it with pilot participants as the experimental group and select non-participants to serve as the control group. Under this arrangement, the control group is not informed of their control group status.

Because this is an effective approach for isolating the impact of training, it should be considered when a major ROI impact study is planned. In these situations it is important for the program impact to be isolated to a high level of accuracy; the primary advantage of the control group process is accuracy.[5]

Trend-Line Analysis

Another useful technique for approximating the impact of training is trend-line analysis. With this approach, a trend line is drawn using previous performance as a base and extending the trend into the future. When training is conducted, actual performance is compared to the trend line. Any improvement of performance over what the trend line predicted can then be reasonably attributed to training. While this is not an exact process, it provides a reasonable estimation of the impact of training.

Figure 10-1 shows an example of this trend-line analysis taken from a shipping department of a large distribution company. The percent of schedule shipped reflects the level of actual shipments compared to scheduled shipments. Data is presented before and after a team training program that was conducted in July. As shown in the figure, there was an upward trend on the data prior to conducting the training program. Although the program apparently had a dramatic effect on shipment productivity, the trend line shows that the improvement would have continued anyway, based on the trend that had been previously established. It is tempting to measure the improvement by comparing the average shipments six months prior to the program (87.3%) to the average six months after the program (94.4%),

Shipment Productivity

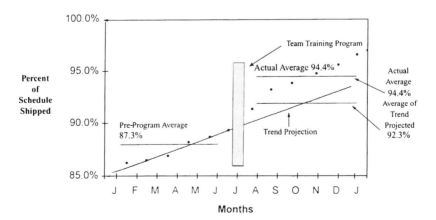

Figure 10-1. Example of trend-line analysis.

yielding a 7.1% difference. However, a more accurate comparison is to use the six-month average after the program compared to the trend-line value at the same point of the trend line (92.3%). In this example, the difference is 2.1%. Using this more modest measure increases the accuracy and credibility of the process.

The trend line as projected directly from the historical data using a straightedge may be acceptable. If additional accuracy is needed, the trend line can be projected with a simple computer program, available in many calculators and software packages.

A primary disadvantage of this trend-line approach is that it is not always accurate. The use of this approach assumes that the events that influenced the performance variable prior to the program are still in place after the program, except for the implementation of the training program. Also, it assumes that no new influences entered the situation at the time training was conducted. This may not always be the case.

The primary advantage of this approach is that it is simple, inexpensive, and takes very little effort. If historical data are available, a trend line can quickly be drawn and differences estimated. While not exact, it does provide a very quick assessment of training's impact.

Forecasting Methods

A more analytical approach to trend-line analysis is to use forecasting methods to predict a change in performance variables. This approach represents a mathematical interpretation of the trend-line analysis discussed above when other variables entered the situation at the time of training. A linear model, in the form of $y = ax + b$, is appropriate when only one other variable influences the output performance and that relationship is characterized by a straight line. Instead of drawing the straight line, a linear equation is developed from which to calculate a value of the anticipated performance improvement.

An example will help explain the application of this process. A large retail store chain implemented a sales-training program for sales associates.[6] The three-day program was designed to enhance sales skills and prospecting techniques. The application of the skills should increase the sales volume for each sales associate. An important measure of the program's success is the sales per employee six months after the program when compared to the same measure prior to the program. The average daily sales per employee prior to training, using a one-month average, was $1,100. Six months after the program, the average daily sales per employee was $1,500. Two related questions must be answered: Is the difference in these two values attributable to the training program? Did other factors influence the actual sales level?

After reviewing potential influencing factors with several store executives only one factor, the level of advertising, appeared to have changed significantly during the period under consideration. When reviewing the previous sales per employee data and the level of advertising, a direct relationship appeared to exist. As expected, when advertising expenditures were increased, the sales per employee increased proportionately.

Using the historical values to develop a simple linear model yielded the following relationship: $y = 140 + 40x$, where y is the daily sales per employee and x is the level of advertising expenditures per week (divided by 1,000). The development of this equation is a process of deriving a mathematical relationship between two variables using the method of least squares. This is a routine option on some calculators and is included in many software packages.

The level of weekly advertising expenditures in the month preceding training was $24,000 and the level of expenditures in the sixth month after training was $30,000. Assuming that the other factors that might influence sales were insignificant, as concluded by the store executives, the impact of the training program is determined by plugging in the new advertising expenditure amount, 30, for x and calculating the daily sales, which yields $1,340.

Thus, the new sales level caused by the increase in advertising is $1,340, as shown in Figure 10-2. Since the new actual value is $1,500, then $160 ($1,500–$1,340) must be attributed to the training program. Figure 10-3 shows graphically the effect of both the training and advertising.

A major disadvantage with this approach occurs when many variables enter the process. The complexity multiplies and the use of sophisticated statistical packages for multiple variable analysis is necessary. Even then, a

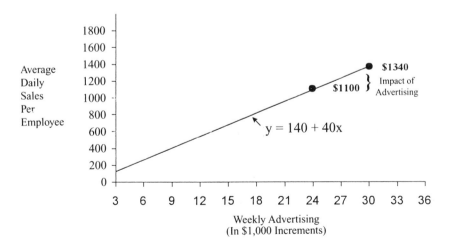

Figure 10-2. Forecasting daily sales based on advertising.

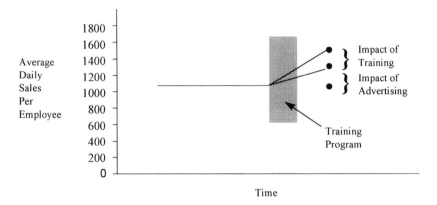

Figure 10-3. Isolating the impact of training.

good fit of the data to the model may not be possible. Unfortunately, some organizations have not developed mathematical relationships for output variables as a function of one or more inputs. Without them, it is difficult to use the forecasting method.

The primary advantage of this process is that it can be an accurate predictor of business performance measures without training, if appropriate data and models are available. The presentation of specific methods is beyond the scope of this book and may be found in other works.[7]

Participant's Estimate of Training's Impact

An easily implemented method to isolate the impact of training is to obtain information directly from program participants. The effectiveness of this approach rests on the assumption that participants are capable of determining or estimating how much of a performance improvement is related to the training program. Because their actions have produced the improvement, participants may have very accurate input on the issue. They should know how much of the change was caused by applying what they have learned in the program. Although an estimate, this value will usually have considerable credibility with management because participants are at the center of the change or improvement. Participant estimates are obtained by asking the following series of questions after describing the improvement:

☐ What percent of this improvement can be attributed to the application of skills/techniques/knowledge gained in the training program?
☐ What is the basis for this estimate?
☐ What confidence do you have in this estimate, expressed as a percent?

☐ What other factors contributed to this improvement in performance?
☐ What other individuals or groups could estimate this percentage or determine the amount?

Table 10-1 illustrates this approach with an example of one participant's estimates.

Participants who are unable or unwilling to provide information should be excluded from the analysis. Also, erroneous or extreme information should be discarded before any analysis is attempted. To be very conservative when using this approach, the confidence percentage can be factored into the values. The confidence percentage is actually a reflection of the error in the estimate. Thus, an 80% confidence level equates to a potential error range of ± 20%. With this approach, the level of confidence is multiplied by the estimate using the lower side of the range. In the example, the participant allocates 50% of the improvement to the training program, but is only 70% confident about this estimate. The confidence percentage is multiplied by the estimate to develop a usable value of 35%. This adjusted percentage is then multiplied by the amount of the improvement to isolate the portion attributed to training. The data are then ready for conversion to monetary values and, ultimately, use in calculating the return on investment.

Perhaps an illustration of this process can reveal its effectiveness and acceptability. A large telecommunications company was assessing the impact of a leadership program for new managers. Because the decision to calculate the training's impact was made after the program had been conducted, the control group arrangement was not feasible as a method to isolate the effects of training. Also, specific Level 4 data linked to the program were not identified before the program was implemented. Consequently, it was difficult to use trend-line analysis. Participants' estimates proved to be the most useful way to estimate the impact. In a detailed follow-up questionnaire, partici-

Table 10-1
Example of a Participant's Estimate

Factor That Influenced Improvement	Percent of Improvement Caused By	Confidence Expressed as a Percent
Training Program	50%	70%
Change in Procedures	10%	80%
Adjustment in Standards	10%	50%
Revision to Incentive Plan	20%	90%
Increased Management Attention	10%	50%
Other _____	___%	___%
Total	100%	

pants were asked a variety of questions regarding the application of what was learned from the program. As part of the program, the individuals were asked to develop and implement action plans, although no specific follow-up plan was needed. The following series of impact questions provided participants estimates on the impact:

☐ How have you and your job changed as a result of attending this program? (Skills and Knowledge Application)

☐ What is the impact of these changes in your work unit? (Specific Measures)

☐ What is the annual value of this change or improvement in your work unit? Although this is difficult, please make every effort to estimate this value.

☐ What is the basis for the estimate provided above? Please indicate the assumptions you made and the specific calculations you performed to arrive at the value.

☐ What confidence do you place in the estimate above? (100% = Certainty, 0% = No Confidence)

☐ Recognizing that many factors influence output results in addition to training, please estimate the percent of the improvement that is directly related to this program. It may be helpful to first identify all the other factors first and then provide an estimate of this factor.

Although this series of questions is challenging, they can be very effective when set up properly and presented to participants in an appropriate way. Table 10-2 shows a sample of the calculations from these questions for this particular program.

Although this is an estimate, this approach does have considerable accuracy and credibility. Five adjustments are effectively utilized with this approach to reflect a conservative approach.

1. The individuals who do not respond to the questionnaire or provide usable data on the questionnaire are assumed to have no improvements. This is probably an overstatement because some individuals will have improvements but not report them on the questionnaire.

2. Extreme data and unrealistic claims are omitted from the analysis, although they may be included in the intangible benefits.

3. Since only annualized values are used, it is assumed that there are no benefits from the program after the first year of implementation. In reality, leadership training should be expected to add value for perhaps several years after training has been conducted.

Table 10-2
Sample of Input from Participants in a Leadership Program for New Managers

Participant	Annual Improvement Value	Basis for Value	Confidence	Contribution Factor	Adjusted Value
11	$36,000	Improvement in efficiency of group. $3,000 per month × 12 (Group Estimate)	85%	50%	$15,300
42	90,000	Turnover Reduction. 2 turnover statistics per year. Base salary × 1.5 = $45,000	90%	40%	32,400
74	24,000	Improvement in customer response time (8 hours to 6 hours). Estimated value: $2,000/month	60%	55%	7,920
55	2,000	5% improvement in my effectiveness ($40,000 × 5%)	75%	50%	750
96	10,000	Absenteeism Reduction (50 absences per year × $200)	85%	75%	6,375
117	8,090	Team project completed 10 days ahead of schedule. Annual salaries $210,500 = $809 per day × 10 days	90%	45%	3,276
118	$159,000	Under budget for the year by this amount.	100%	30%	$47,700

4. The confidence level, expressed as a percent, is multiplied by the improvement value to reduce the amount of the improvement by the potential error.
5. The improvement amount is adjusted by the amount directly related to training, expressed as a percent.

When presented to senior management, the results of this impact study were perceived to be an accurate assessment or understatement of the program's success. The data were considered to be credible and accurate.

As an added enhancement to this method, management may be asked to approve the amounts that have been estimated by participants. For example, in an HRD program involving the performance management skills program for Yellow Freight Systems, a large trucking company, participants estimated the amount of savings that should be attributed to the program.[8] A sample of these estimates are shown in Table 10-3. Managers at the next two levels above participants reviewed and approved the estimates. Thus, the managers actually confirmed participants' estimates.

This process has some disadvantages. It is an estimate and consequently does not have the accuracy desired by some HRD managers. Also, the input data may be unreliable since some participants are unwilling or incapable of providing these types of estimates. They might not be aware of exactly which factors contributed to the results.

Several advantages make this strategy attractive. It is a simple process, easily understood by most participants and others who review evaluation data. It is inexpensive and takes very little time and analysis, thus resulting in an efficient addition to the evaluation process. Estimates originate from a credible source: the individuals who actually produced the improvement.

The advantages seem to offset the disadvantages. Isolating the effects of training will never be precise, but this estimate may be accurate enough for most clients and management groups.

Supervisor's Estimate of Training's Impact

In lieu of, or in addition to, participant estimates, the participant's supervisor may be asked to provide input as to the extent of training's role in producing a performance improvement. In some settings, participants' supervisors may be more familiar with other factors influencing performance. Consequently, they may be better equipped to provide estimates of impact. Recommended questions to ask supervisors, after describing the improvement caused by the participants, are

☐ What percent of the improvement in performance resulted from the training program?

Table 10-3
Sample of Results from Performance Management Skills

Terminal in Division I	Improvement	Percentage of Improvement Attributed to Performance Management Skills	Dollar Value*
A	To reduce high cost per bill due to poor planning on pickup and delivery and low sales, manager installed job models and feedback systems, coached supervisors and drivers, and praised all employees for improved performance. Cost per bill decreased an average of $1.30.	25%	$6,928 (C)
B	In new terminal with cost per bill running high, manager installed job models and used coaching and rewards for supervisory, clerical, and sales staff. Terminal's profits increased from $43,253 to $49,024.	10%	$27,680 (R)
C	Terminal had low bill count and high cost per bill. Manager installed job models and feedback systems, and used interpersonal skills. Cost per bill decreased an average of $1.79 over same period before the program.	5%	$800 (C)
D	Terminal had low bill count, which contributed to a high cost per bill. Manager installed job models and feedback systems, and used rewards and coaching with office staff, supervisors, and sales representatives. Cost per bill decreased an average of $0.92; number of bills increased from 7,765 to 9,405 per month.	25%	$9,856 (C)
E	Terminal had low bill count and high cost per bill. Manager installed job models and had his sales manager and operations manager install job models, also. All managers used rewards, coaching, and interpersonal skills. Cost per bill decreased from $22.49 to $21.00; number of bills increased from 11,716 to 12,974 per month.	50%	$56,060 (C)
F	Terminal had rising cost per bill with a fluctuating bill count. Manager used job models and feedback reports. Cost per bill decreased from $17.13 to $15.46; number of bills rose from 6,160 to 7,357 per month.	10%	$5,754 (C)

(R) indicates a revenue gain; (C) indicates decreased costs.

☐ What is the basis for this estimate?
☐ What is your confidence in this estimate, expressed as a percentage?
☐ What other factors could have contributed to this success?
☐ Please list the factors, with estimates, in the table provided.
☐ What other individuals or groups would know about this improvement and could estimate this percentage?

These questions are essentially the same ones described in the participant's questionnaire, and should be analyzed in the same manner as participant estimates. To be more conservative, actual estimates could be adjusted by the confidence percentage. When participants' estimates have also been collected, the decision of which estimate to use becomes an issue. If there is some compelling reason to think that one estimate is more credible than the other, then that estimate should be used. The most conservative approach is to use the lowest value and include an appropriate explanation. Another potential option is to recognize that each source has its own unique perspective and that an average of the two is appropriate, placing an equal weight on each input. If feasible, it is recommended that input be obtained from both participants and supervisors.

An example will illustrate the process for both participant and supervisor estimates. A restaurant chain implemented a training program on performance management for manager trainees. The program teaches participants how to establish measurable goals for employees, provide performance feedback, measure progress toward goals, and take action to ensure that goals are met. During the program, each manager trainee developed an action plan for improvement, using skills taught in the program. As part of the program, managers learned how to convert measurable improvements into an economic value for the restaurant. The action plan could focus on any improvement area as long as it was accompanied by skills acquired in the program and on the condition that the area be converted to either cost savings or restaurant profits. Some improvement areas were inventory, food spoilage, cash shortages, employee turnover, absenteeism, and productivity.

As part of the follow-up evaluation, each action plan was thoroughly documented showing results in quantitative terms, which were converted to monetary values. Realizing that other factors could have influenced the improvement, manager trainees were asked to estimate the percent of improvement that resulted from the application of the skills acquired in the training program. Each manager trainee was asked to be conservative with the estimates. The annual monetary value for each improvement for each participant was calculated. Independently, restaurant managers (immediate supervisors) were asked to estimate, for each manager trainee, the percent of improvement from the action plan that should be attributed to the training program. Restaurant managers are usually aware of factors that influence costs and profits and know how much of an improvement is traceable to the training program. Also, they were closely involved in the action-planning process for this program. The results are shown in Table 10-4.

The estimate of training's impact can be calculated using the conservative approach of selecting the lower value. As an alternative, the average value of the two can be used. The conservative approach yields an overall improvement of $78,905, whereas the average of the two percentages yields a value of $83,721. Participant 5 did not submit a completed action plan and is discarded from the analysis, although the participant's costs are still included in the ROI calculation.

Another interesting observation emerges from this type of analysis. When the average of the upper 3 participant improvements (listed in order of largest improvement to the smallest) is compared with the average of the lower 3 items, important information is revealed about the potential for return on investment. (In this case, $21,667 compared to $1,947, before adjustments.) If all of the participants focused on high impact improvements, a substantially higher ROI could have been achieved. This can be helpful information for the management group whose support is often critical to the success of programs. While an impressive ROI is refreshing, a potentially much greater ROI is outstanding.

This approach has the same disadvantages as participant estimates. It is subjective and, consequently, may be viewed with skepticism by senior management. Also, supervisors may be reluctant to participate or incapable of providing accurate estimates of this impact. In some cases they may not know about other factors which contributed to the improvement.

The advantages of this approach are also similar to the advantages of participant estimation. It is simple and inexpensive and enjoys an acceptable degree of credibility because it comes directly from the supervisors of those individuals who received the training. When combined with participant estimation, the credibility is enhanced considerably. Also, when factored by the level of confidence, its value further increases.

Management's Estimate of Training's Impact

In some cases, upper management may estimate the percent of improvement which should be attributed to the training program. For example, in Litton Guidance and Control Systems, management adjusted the results from a self-directed team process.[9] After considering additional factors such as technology, procedures, and process changes that could have contributed to the improvement, management then applied a subjective factor, in this case 60%, to represent the portion of the results that should be attributed to the training program. The 60% factor was developed in a meeting with top managers and therefore had the benefit of group ownership. While this process is

Table 10-4
Estimates of Training Impact from Participants and Supervisors

Manager Trainee (Participant)	Improvement (Dollar Value)	Basis	Percent Estimate from Manager Trainees	Percent Estimate from Store Managers	Conservative Integration	Average Value Integration
1	$5,500	Labor Savings	60%	50%	$2,750	$3,025
2	15,000	Turnover	50%	40%	6,000	6,750
3	9,300	Absenteeism	65%	75%	6,045	6,510
4	2,100	Shortages	90%	80%	1,680	1,785
5	0	—	—	—	—	—
6	29,000	Turnover	40%	50%	11,600	13,050
7	2,241	Inventory	70%	100%	1,569	1,905
8	3,621	Procedures	100%	90%	3,259	3,440
9	21,000	Turnover	75%	70%	14,700	15,225
10	1,500	Food Spoilage	100%	100%	1,500	1,500
11	15,000	Labor Savings	80%	70%	10,500	11,250
12	6,310	Accidents	70%	75%	4,417	4,575
13	14,500	Absenteeism	80%	75%	11,600	11,238
14	3,650	Productivity	100%	90%	3,285	3,468
	$97,722				$78,905	$83,721

very subjective, the input is received from the individuals who often provide or approve funding for the program. Sometimes their level of comfort with the process is the most important consideration.

Customer Input

Another helpful approach in some narrowly focused situations is to solicit input on the impact of training directly from customers. In these situations, customers are asked why they chose a particular product or service or to explain how their reaction to the product or service has been influenced by individuals applying skills and abilities learned in a training program. This strategy focuses directly on what the training program is often designed to improve. For example, after a teller training program was conducted following a bank merger, market research data showed that the percentage of customers who were dissatisfied with teller knowledge was reduced by 5% when compared to market survey data before training.[10] Since teller knowledge was increased by training, 5% of the reduction of dissatisfied customers was directly attributable to the training program.

In another example, a large real estate company provided a comprehensive training program for agents, focusing on presentation skills. When customers listed their homes with an agent they received a survey exploring their reasons for deciding to list their home with the company. Among the reasons listed was the agent's presentation skills. Responses on this question and related questions provided evidence of the percentage of new listings attributable to the training program.

Expert Estimate of Training's Impact

External or internal experts can sometimes provide an estimate of the portion of results that can be attributed to training. When using this strategy, experts must be carefully selected based on their knowledge of the process, program, and situation. For example, an expert in quality might be able to provide estimates of how much change in a quality measure can be attributed to training and how much can be attributed to other factors in the implementation of a TQM program.

An example will illustrate this process. Omega Consultants, training providers for the banking industry, has implemented sales training programs in a variety of settings. Using control group arrangements, Omega has determined that one of their programs will generate a 30% increase in sales volume three months after implementation. Given this value, implementation should result in a 30% improvement in another financial institution with a similar target audience. Although the situation can vary considerably, this is an approximate value to use in comparison. If more than 30% was achieved, the additional amount could be due to a factor other than training. Experts, consultants, or researchers are usually available for almost any field. They can bring their experience with similar situations into the analysis.

This approach does have disadvantages. It can be inaccurate unless the program and setting on which the estimate is based are very similar to the program in question. Also, this approach may lose credibility because the estimates come from external sources and may not necessarily involve those who are close to the process.

This process has an advantage in that its credibility often reflects the reputation of the expert or independent consultant. Sometimes top management will place more confidence in external experts than in their own internal staff.

Subordinate Input on Training's Impact

In some situations, the subordinates of the participants being trained can provide input concerning the extent of training's impact. Although they will not usually be able to estimate how much of an improvement can be attributed to the training, they can provide input in terms of what other factors might have contributed to the improvement. This approach is appropriate in programs where leaders, supervisors, and managers are being trained to implement work unit changes or develop new skills for use with employees. Improvements are realized through the application of the skills. The supervisor's employees provide input about changes that have occurred since the training was conducted and help determine the extent to which other factors in addition to supervisor behavior have changed.

Subordinate input is usually obtained through surveys or interviews. When the survey results show significant changes in supervisor behavior after training and no significant change in the general work climate, the improvement in work performance must be attributed to the changes in supervisor behavior.

An example illustrates this process. In a training program designed to improve performance of work units by enhancing supervisory skills, significant results were obtained at CIGNA, a large insurance company.[11] After the training program was conducted, action plans were developed and the supervisors reported significant improvements in the performance of their work units. To isolate the impact of training, pre- and post-survey data were taken with the employees to determine the extent of changes in supervisor behavior and the general climate. The survey consisted of 36 Likert-type, 5-point scale items that were used to create 7 different indices. Six of these indices measured the supervisor's behavior and the seventh measured general organizational climate for which the supervisor is not necessarily responsible. The survey results showed significant differences in supervisor behavior before and after training. It did not, however, show a significant change in the general climate. Therefore, the improvement in work performance must be attributed to the changes in supervisor behavior since other factors appeared to remain constant.

This approach has some disadvantages. Data from subordinates are subjective and may be questionable because of the possibility for biased input. Also, in some cases the subordinates may have difficulty in determining changes in the work climate. This approach does offer a useful way to isolate the impact of training from other sources. In some cases, subordinates are aware of the factors that caused changes in their work unit and can provide input about the magnitude or quantity of these changes. This process has increased credibility when combined with other methods to isolate impact.

Calculating the Impact of Other Factors

Although not appropriate in all cases, there are some situations in which it may be feasible to calculate the impact of factors other than training that influenced improvement, and then conclude that training is credited with the remaining portion. In this approach, training takes credit for improvement that cannot be attributed to other factors.

An example will help explain the approach.[12] In a consumer-lending program for a large commercial bank, consumer loan volume significantly increased after a training program was conducted for consumer loan officers. Part of the increase in volume was attributed to the influence of other factors operating during the same time period and the remaining was due to training. The other factors identified by the evaluator were the improvement of a loan officer's production over time and falling interest rates, causing an increase in consumer volume.

In regard to the first factor, as loan officers make loans their confidence improves. They use consumer-lending policy manuals and gain knowledge and expertise through trial and error. The amount of this factor was estimated by using input from several internal experts in the marketing department.

For the second factor, industry sources were utilized to estimate the relationship between increased consumer loan volume and falling interest rates. These two estimates together accounted for a certain percent of increased consumer loan volume. The remaining improvement was attributed to the training program.

This method is appropriate when other factors are easily identified and the appropriate mechanisms are in place to calculate their impact on the improvement. In some cases it is just as difficult to estimate the impact of other factors as it is to estimate the impact of the training program, leaving this approach less advantageous. This process can be very credible if the method used to isolate the impact of other factors is credible.

Using the Strategies

With ten strategies available to isolate the impact of training, selecting the most appropriate strategies for the specific program can be difficult. Some strategies are simple and inexpensive, while others are more time consuming and costly. When attempting to make the selection decision, several factors should be considered.

☐ Feasibility of the strategy
☐ Accuracy provided by the strategy
☐ Credibility of the strategy with the target audience
☐ Specific cost to implement the strategy
☐ Amount of disruption in normal work activities as the strategy is implemented
☐ Participant, staff, and management time needed with the particular strategy

Multiple strategies or multiple sources for data input should be considered since two sources are usually better than one. When multiple sources are used, a conservative method is recommended to combine the inputs, as a conservative approach builds acceptance. The target audience should always be provided explanations of the process and the various subjective factors involved. Multiple sources allow an organization to experiment with different strategies and build confidence with a particular strategy. For example, if management is concerned about the accuracy of participants' estimates, a combination of a control group arrangement and participants' estimates could be attempted to check the accuracy of the estimation process.

It is not unusual for the ROI in training and development to be extremely large. Even when a portion of the improvement is allocated to other factors, the numbers are often still impressive. The audience should understand that although every effort was made to isolate the impact, it is still a figure that is not precise and may contain error. It represents the best estimate of the impact given the conditions, time, and resources that the organization is willing to commit to the process. Chances are it is more accurate than other types of analyses in the organization.

Summary

This chapter presented a variety of strategies to isolate the effects of training. The strategies used by some of the most progressive organizations represent the most effective approaches to tackle this issue. Too often results are reported and linked with training without any attempt to isolate the portion of results that can be attributed to training. If the training and development function is to continue to improve its professional image as well as to meet its responsibility for obtaining results, this issue must be addressed early in the process.

Discussion Questions

1. It is often said that the most critical issue in ROI is isolating the effects of training. Explain.
2. Why is a control group so difficult to apply in practice?
3. Under what conditions will the trend-line analysis be effective?
4. Do most organizations have relationships between input measures, such as advertising, and output measures, such as sales? Could these relationships be used to forecast results? Explain.
5. What are the advantages of using participants' estimates of the impact of training? Disadvantages?
6. When is it appropriate to collect input from participants' supervisors on the impact of training?
7. Under what conditions should management input be used to isolate the effects of training?
8. Describe a situation in which customer input can be used to isolate the effects of a training program for sales representatives?
9. When is it appropriate to estimate or calculate the effects of other factors, instead of estimating the effects of training?
10. Is it possible to always utilize one of the methods to isolate the effects of training? Explain.

References

1. Phillips, J. J. *Return on Investment in Training and Performance Improvement Programs.* Houston, TX: Gulf Publishing Company, 1997.
2. Pine, J. and Tingley, J. C. "ROI of Soft Skills Training," *Training,* February 1993, pp. 55–66.
3. Hassett, J. "Simplifying ROI," *Training,* September 1992, p. 54.
4. This brief example is taken from a case in which the company preferred not to be identified.
5. Gummesson, E. *Qualitative Methods in Management Research.* Newbury Park, CA: Sage Publications, Inc., 1991.
6. This brief example is taken from a very complicated case. Some of the values have been changed, and it has been simplified to enhance understanding of the process.
7. For additional information, see Makridakis, S. *Forecasting Methods for Management,* 5th ed. New York, NY: Wiley, 1989.

8. Zigon, J. "Performance Management Training," in *In Action: Measuring Return on Investment, Vol. 1*. J. J. Phillips (Ed.), Alexandria, VA: American Society for Training and Development, 1994, pp. 253–270.

9. Graham, M., Bishop, K., and Birdsong, R. "Self-Directed Work Teams," in *In Action: Measuring Return on Investment, Vol. 1*. J. J. Phillips (Ed.), Alexandria, VA: American Society for Training and Development, 1994, pp. 105–122.

10. Rust, R. T., Zahorik, A. J., and Keiningham, T. L. *Return on Quality: Measuring the Financial Impact of Your Company's Quest for Quality.* Chicago, IL: Probus Publishers, 1994.

11. Kirkpatrick, D. L. "The Bottom Line: CIGNA Corporation," in *Evaluating Training Programs.* San Francisco, CA: Berrett Koehler, 1994, pp. 190–206.

12. Phillips, J. J. "Measuring ROI in an Established Program," in *In Action: Measuring Return on Investment, Vol. 1*. J. J. Phillips (Ed.), Alexandria, VA: American Society for Training and Development, 1994, pp. 187–197.

CHAPTER 11

Converting Data to Monetary Benefits

Traditionally, most impact evaluation studies stop with a tabulation of business results, detailing improvements such as quality enhancements, reduced absenteeism, or improved customer satisfaction. While these results are important, it is more meaningful to compare the monetary value of the results to the cost of the program, because some programs cost more than the value of the delivered business results.[1] This ultimate evaluation is the fifth level in the five-level evaluation framework presented earlier. This chapter shows how leading organizations are moving beyond tabulating business results to calculating a return on investment on HRD programs.

Preliminary Issues

Sorting Out Hard and Soft Data

After collecting performance data, many organizations find it helpful to divide data into hard and soft categories as described earlier. Hard data are the traditional measures of organizational performance: objective, easy to measure, and easy to convert to monetary values. Hard data are common measures that achieve high credibility with management and are available in every type of organization: manufacturing, service, non-profit, government, and educational.

Hard data represent the output, quality, cost, and time of work-related processes. Almost every department or unit will have hard data performance measures. For example, a state government office approving applications for new drivers licenses will have these four measures among its overall performance measurement: the number of applications processed (Output), cost per application processed (Cost), the number of errors made processing applications (Quality), and the time it takes to process and approve an application (Time). Ideally, training programs for employees in this unit should be linked to one or more hard data measures.

Because many training programs are designed to develop soft skills, soft data are needed in evaluation. Soft data are behaviorally oriented, usually subjective, sometimes difficult to measure, almost always difficult to convert to monetary values. When compared to hard data, soft data are usually less credible as a performance measure.

Soft data items can be grouped into several categories. Measures such as employee turnover, absenteeism, and grievances are considered soft data items, not because they are difficult to measure, but because it is difficult to accurately convert them to monetary values.

General Steps to Convert Data

Before describing specific strategies to convert either hard or soft data to monetary values, the general steps used to convert data are briefly summarized. These steps should be followed for each data conversion.

Focus on a unit of measure. First, identify a unit of improvement. For output data, a typical unit of measure is an item produced, a service provided, or a confirmed sale. Quality is a common measure and the unit may be an error, reject, defect, or rework item. Time measures are varied and include items such as the time to complete a project, cycle time, or customer response times. The unit is usually expressed as minutes, hours, or days. Soft data measures are varied, and the unit of improvement may include items such as a grievance, an absence, an employee turnover statistic, or a one-point change in the customer satisfaction index.

Determine the value of each unit. Place a monetary value (V) on the unit identified in the first step. For measures of production, quality, cost, and time, the process is relatively easy. Most organizations have records, reports, or standards reflecting the value of items such as one unit of production or the cost of a defect. Soft data are more difficult to convert to a monetary value. For example, the cost of one absence, one grievance, or a one-point change in the job satisfaction survey is often difficult to pinpoint. The ten approaches in this chapter provide an array of techniques to make this conversion. When more than one value is available, the most credible value is used. In the absence of information on credibility of the values, the lowest value should be used.

Calculate the change in performance data. Calculate the change in output data after the effects of training have been isolated from other influences. The change (ΔP) is the performance improvement, measured as hard or soft data, that is directly attributable to the training program. The value may represent the performance improvement for an individual, a team, a total group of participants, or several groups of participants.

Determine an annual amount for the change. Annualize the ∆P value to develop a total change in the performance measure for one year. This procedure has become a standard approach with many organizations to capture the total benefits of a training program. Although the benefits may not be realized at the same level for an entire year, some programs will continue to produce benefits beyond one year. Therefore, using first-year benefits is considered a conservative approach.

Calculate the total value of the improvement. Develop the total value of improvement by multiplying the annual performance change (∆P) by the unit value (V) for the complete group in question. For example, if one group of participants in a program is being evaluated, the total value will include total improvement for all participants in the group. This value for annual program benefits is compared to the cost of the program, usually through a return on investment formula.

The five-step process of converting data to monetary values is described in an example taken from a team-building program at a manufacturing plant. This program was developed and implemented after a needs assessment revealed that a lack of teamwork was causing an excessive number of grievances. The actual number of grievances resolved at Step 2 in the grievance process was selected as an output measure. Table 11-1 shows the steps taken to assign a monetary value to the data arriving at a total program impact of $546,000.

Ten strategies are available to convert data to monetary values.[2] Some strategies are appropriate for a specific type of data or data category, while other strategies can be used with virtually any type of data. The HRD staff's challenge is to select the particular strategy that best matches the type of data and situation. Each strategy is presented next, beginning with the most credible approach.

Converting Output Data to Contribution

When a training program has produced a change in output, the value of the increased output can usually be determined from the organization's accounting or operating records. For organizations operating on a profit basis, this value is usually the marginal profit contribution of an additional unit of production or unit of service provided. For example, a production team in a major appliance manufacturer is able to boost production of small

Table 11-1
An example to illustrate the steps to convert data to monetary value

Setting: Team-building Program in a Manufacturing Plant

Step 1 - **Focus on a Unit of Improvement.**
One grievance reaching Step 2 in the four-step grievance resolution process.

Step 2 - **Determine a Value of Each Unit.**
Using internal experts—the labor relations staff—the cost of an average grievance was estimated to be $6,500, when considering time and direct costs. (V = $6,500)

Step 3 - **Calculate the Change in Performance Data**
Six months after the program was completed, total grievances per month reaching Step 2 declined by ten. Seven of the ten grievance reductions were related to the program as determined by supervisors (Isolating the effects of training).

Step 4 - **Determine an Annual Amount for the Change.**
Using the six-month value, 7 per month, yields an annual improvement of 84 ($\Delta P = 84$)

Step 5 - **Calculate the Annual Value of the Improvement**
Annual Value = ΔP times V
= 84 times $6,500
= $546,000

refrigerators with a series of highly focused training programs. The unit of improvement is the profit margin of one refrigerator. In not-for-profit organizations this value is usually reflected in the savings accumulated when an additional unit of output is realized for the same input requirements. For example, in the visa section of a government office an additional visa application is processed at no additional cost. Thus, an increase in output translates into a cost savings equal to the unit cost of processing a visa.

The formulas and calculations used to measure this contribution depend on the organization and its records. Most organizations have this type of data readily available for performance monitoring and goal setting. Managers often use marginal cost statements and sensitivity analyses to pinpoint values associated with changes in output. If the data are not available, the HRD staff must initiate or coordinate the development of appropriate values.

In one case involving a commercial bank, a sales seminar for consumer loan officers was conducted that resulted in additional consumer loan volume (output).[3] To measure the return on investment in the training program, it was necessary to calculate the value (profit contribution) of one additional consumer loan. This was a relatively easy item to calculate from the bank's records. As shown in Table 11-2, several components went into this calculation.

The first step was to determine the yield, which was available from bank records. Next, the average spread between the cost of funds and the yield received on the loan was calculated. For example, the bank could obtain

Table 11-2
Loan Profitability Analysis

Profit Component	Unit Value
Average loan size	$15,500
Average loan yield	9.75%
Average cost of funds (including branch costs)	5.50%
Direct costs for consumer lending	0.82%
Corporate overhead	1.61%
Net Profit Per Loan	**1.82%**

funds from depositors at 5.5% on average, including the cost of operating the branches. The direct costs of making the loan, such as the salaries of employees directly involved in consumer lending and the advertising costs for consumer loans, had to be subtracted from this difference. Historically, these direct costs amounted to 0.82% of the loan value. To cover overhead costs for other corporate functions, an additional 1.61% was subtracted from the value. The remaining 1.82% of the average loan value represented the profit margin of a loan.

Calculating the Cost of Quality

Quality is a critical issue, and its cost is an important measure in most manufacturing and service firms. Since many training programs are designed to improve quality, the HRD staff must place a value on certain quality measures' improvement. For some of these measures, the task is easy. For example, if quality is measured with a defect rate, the value of the improvement is the cost to repair or replace the product. The most obvious cost of poor quality is the scrap or waste generated by mistakes. Defective products, spoiled raw materials, and discarded paperwork all are the results of poor quality. This scrap and waste translates directly into monetary values. For example, in a production environment the cost of a defective product is the total cost incurred to the point the mistake is identified, minus the salvage value.

Employee mistakes and errors can cause expensive rework. The most costly rework occurs when a product is delivered to a customer and must be returned for correction. The cost of rework includes both labor and direct costs. In some organizations, the cost of rework can be as much as 35% of operating costs.[4]

Perhaps the costliest element of poor quality is customer and client dissatisfaction. In some cases, serious mistakes can result in lost business. Customer dissatisfaction is difficult to quantify, and attempts to arrive at a monetary value may be impossible using direct methods. Usually the judgment and expertise of sales, marketing, or quality managers are the best sources by which to try to measure the impact of dissatisfaction. Some quality experts are now measuring customer and client dissatisfaction with market surveys.[5] However, other strategies discussed in this chapter may be more appropriate to measure the cost of customer dissatisfaction.

Converting Employee Time

Reduction in employee time is a common objective for training programs. In a team environment, a program could enable the team to perform tasks in a shorter time frame or with fewer people. On an individual basis, time management workshops are designed to help professional, sales, supervisory, and managerial employees save time in performing daily tasks. The value of the time saved is an important measure of the program's success, and this conversion to monetary values is a relatively easy process.

The most obvious time savings are from the reduction of labor costs for performing work. The monetary value is found by multiplying the hours saved times the labor cost per hour. For example, after attending a time management training program called Priority Manager, participants estimated an average time savings of 74 minutes per day, worth $31.25 per day or $7,500 per year.[6] This time savings was based on the average salary plus benefits for the typical participant.

The average wage with a percent added for employee benefits will suffice for most calculations. However, employee time may be worth more. For example, additional costs in maintaining an employee such as office space, furniture, telephone, utilities, computers, secretarial support, and other overhead expenses could be included in the average labor cost. Thus, the average wage rate may quickly escalate to a large number. However, the conservative approach is to use the salary plus employee benefits.

In addition to the labor cost per hour, other benefits can result from a time savings. These include improved service, avoidance of penalties for late projects, and the creation of additional opportunities for profit. These values can be estimated using other methods discussed in this chapter.

A word of caution is in order when time savings are developed. Time savings are only realized when the amount of time saved translates into a cost reduction or profit contribution. If a training program results in a savings in manager time, a monetary value is only realized if the manager used the additional time in a productive way. If a team-based program generates a new process that eliminates several hours of work each day, the actual savings will be realized only if there is a cost savings from a reduction in employees or overtime pay. Therefore, an important preliminary step in developing time savings is to determine if a true savings will be realized.

Using Historical Costs

Sometimes the value of a measure will be contained in historical records that reflect the cost (or value) of a unit of improvement. This strategy involves identifying the appropriate records and tabulating the actual cost components for the item in question. For example, a large construction firm implemented a training program to improve safety performance. The program was designed to reduce the number of accidents. Examining the company's records using one year of data enabled the HRD staff to calculate the average cost for an accident, as illustrated in Table 11-3.

Historical data are usually available for most hard data. Unfortunately, this is generally not true for soft data, and other strategies, explained in this chapter, must be employed to convert the data to monetary values.[7]

Using Internal and External Experts

When faced with converting soft data items for which historical records are not available, it might be feasible to consider input from experts on the processes. Using this approach, internal experts are asked to provide the cost (or value) of one unit of improvement. Those individuals who have knowledge of the situation and the respect of the management group are often the best prospects for expert input. These experts must understand the processes and be willing to provide estimates, along with the assumptions used in arriving at the estimate. When requesting input from these individuals, it is

Table 11-3
The Cost of an Accident

☐ Direct Medical Costs Related to Accidents	$114,390.00
☐ Worker Compensation Payments	327,430.00
☐ Insurance Premiums	120,750.00
☐ Legal Expenses	75,600.00
☐ Total Operating Budget for Safety and Health Department (Minus the Above Values) Including Salaries and Benefits of Safety Staff	455,280.00
☐ Management and Supervisory Time Devoted to Accident Prevention and Investigation	105,000.00
☐ Safety Training Costs Not Included in Above Operating Budget	31,000.00
☐ Safety Awareness Materials	23,000.00
☐ Lost Productivity for Safety Training, Safety Meetings, Accident Investigation, and Replacement Staff	95,000.00
Total	**$1,347,450.00**
Total Number of Accidents	**53**
Cost Per Accident	**$25,423.60**

best to explain the full scope of what is needed, providing as many specifics as possible. Most experts have their own methodology to develop this value.

An example will help clarify this approach. In one manufacturing plant, a team-building program was designed to reduce the number of grievances filed at Step 2 (See Table 11-1). This is the step at which the grievance is recorded in writing and becomes a measurable soft data item. Except for the actual cost of settlements and direct external costs, the company had no records of the total costs of grievances (for example, there were no data for the time required to resolve a grievance). Therefore, an estimate was needed from an expert. The manager of labor relations, who had credibility with senior management and thorough knowledge of the grievance process, provided an estimate of the cost. He based his estimate on the average settlement when a grievance was lost; the direct costs related to the grievances (arbitration, legal fees, printing, research); the estimate of the amount of supervisory, staff, and employee time associated with the grievance; and a factor for reduced morale. This internal estimate, although not a precise figure, was appropriate for this analysis and had adequate credibility with management.

When internal experts are not available, external experts are sought. External experts must be selected based on their experience with the unit of measure. Fortunately, many experts are available who work directly with important measures such as employee attitudes, customer satisfaction, turnover, absenteeism, and grievances. They are often willing to provide estimates of the cost (or value) of these items. Because the credibility of the value is directly related to the expert's reputation, his or her reputation is critical.

Using Values from External Databases

For some soft data items, it may be appropriate to use estimates of the cost (or value) of one unit based on the research of others. This strategy taps external databases that contain studies and research projects focusing on the cost of data items. Fortunately, many databases are available that report cost studies of a variety of data items related to training programs.[8] Data are available on the cost of turnover, absenteeism, grievances, accidents, and even customer satisfaction. The challenge lies in finding a database with studies or research efforts for a situation similar to the program under evaluation. Ideally, the data would come from a similar setting in the same industry, but that is not always possible. Sometimes data on all industries or organizations would be sufficient, perhaps with an adjustment to fit the industry under consideration.

An example illustrates the use of this process. An HRD program was designed to reduce turnover of branch managers in a financial services company.[9] To complete the evaluation and calculate the ROI, the cost of turnover was needed. To develop the turnover value internally, several costs would have to be identified, including the costs of recruiting, employment processing, orientation, training new managers, lost productivity while a new manager is trained, quality problems, scheduling difficulties, and customer satisfaction problems. Additional costs include the regional managers' time needed to address turnover issues and, in some cases, exit costs of litigation, severance, and unemployment. Obviously, these costs are significant. Most HRD managers do not have time to calculate the cost of turnover, particularly when it is needed for a one-time event such as evaluating a training program. In this example, turnover cost studies in the same industry placed the value at about one-and-a-half times the average annual salaries of the employees. Most turnover cost studies report the cost of turnover as a multiple of annual base salaries. In this example, management wished to be conservative and adjusted the value downward to equal the average base salary of branch managers.

Using Estimates from Participants

In some situations, program participants estimate the value of a soft data improvement. This strategy is appropriate when participants are capable of providing estimates of the cost (or value) of the unit of measure improved by applying the skills learned in the program. This process makes some participants uneasy because they may be unable to accurately estimate the values, but other participants are willing and capable of providing values.[10] When using this approach, participants should be provided with clear instructions, along with examples of the type of information needed. The advantage of this approach is that individuals closest to the improvement are often capable of providing the most reliable estimates of its value.

An example illustrates this process. A group of supervisors attended an interpersonal-skills training program, "Improving Work Habits," that was designed to lower the absenteeism rate of the employees in their work units. Successful application of the skills learned in the training program was expected to result in a reduction in absenteeism. To calculate the ROI for the program, it was necessary to determine the average value of one absence in the company. As is the case with most organizations, historical records for the cost of absenteeism were not available. Furthermore, experts were not available and external studies were sparse for this particular industry. Consequently, supervisors (program participants) were asked to estimate the cost of an absence. In a group interview format, each participant was asked to recall the last time an employee in his or her work group was unexpectedly absent and describe what was necessary to compensate for the absence. Because the impact of an absence will vary considerably from one employee to another within the same work unit, the group listened to all explanations.

After reflecting on what must be done when an employee is absent, each supervisor was asked to provide an estimate of the average cost of an absence in the company.

Although some supervisors are initially reluctant to provide estimates, with prodding and encouragement they will usually provide a value. The group's values are averaged, and the result is the cost of an absence to be used in evaluating the program. Although this is an estimate, it is probably more accurate than data from external studies, calculations using internal records, or estimates from experts. More importantly, because it comes from supervisors who confront the issue daily, it will usually have credibility with senior management.

Using Estimates from Supervisors

In some situations, participants may be incapable of placing a value on the improvement. Their work may be so far removed from the output of the process that they cannot reliably provide estimates. In these cases, team leaders, supervisors, or managers of participants may be asked to provide a value for a unit of improvement linked to the program. For example, a training program for customer service representatives was designed to reduce customer complaints. Applying the skills and knowledge learned from the program resulted in a reduction in complaints, but the value of a single customer complaint was needed to determine the value of improvement. Although customer service representatives had knowledge of some issues surrounding customer complaints, they could not gauge the full impact, so their supervisors were asked to provide a value.

In other situations, supervisors are asked to review and approve participants' estimates. For example, an HRD program for terminal managers with Yellow Freight Systems involved the implementation of both training and performance appraisal.[11] After the program was completed, participants estimated the value of improvements that were directly related to their participation in the program. Their immediate managers were then asked to review the estimates and the process by which the participants arrived at them. Supervisors could either confirm, adjust, or discard the values provided by the participants.

Using Estimates from Senior Managers

In some situations, senior management provides estimates of the value of data. With this approach, senior managers interested in the process or program are asked to place a value on the improvement based on their perception of its worth. This approach is used in situations in which it is difficult to calculate the data's value, or other sources of estimation are unavailable or unreliable. An example illustrates this strategy. A hospital chain was attempting to improve customer satisfaction with a training program for all employees. The program was designed to improve customer service and, thus, the external customer satisfaction index. To determine the value of the program, a value for a unit of improvement (one point on the index) was needed. Because senior management was interested in improving the index, they were asked to provide input on the value of one unit. In a routine staff meeting of hospital administrators and other senior executives, each senior manager and hospital administrator was asked to describe the benefits to the hospital when the index increases. After some discussion, each individual was asked to provide an estimate of the monetary value gained when the index moves one point. Although initially reluctant to provide the information, with some encouragement, values were furnished and averaged. The result was an estimate of the worth of one unit of improvement, which was used as a basis for calculating the benefit of the program. Although this process is subjective, it does have the benefit of ownership from the same senior executives who approved the program's budget.

Using HRD Staff Estimates

The final strategy for converting data to monetary values is to use HRD staff estimates. Using all available information and experience, the staff members most familiar with the situation provide estimates of the value. For example, an international oil company created a dispatcher training program designed to reduce absenteeism, along with other performance measure problems.[12] The HRD staff estimated the cost of an absence to be $200. This value was then used in calculating the savings gained by the reduction of absenteeism following the dispatchers' customer service training. Although the HRD staff may be capable of providing accurate estimates, this approach may be perceived as being biased and should therefore be used only when other approaches are unavailable.

Selecting the Appropriate Strategy

With so many strategies available, the challenge is to select one or more strategies appropriate to the situation. The following guidelines can help determine proper selection.

Use the strategy appropriate for the type of data. Some strategies are designed specifically for hard data, while others are more appropriate for soft data. Consequently, the type of data available will often dictate the strategy. Hard data, while always preferred, are not always available. Soft data are often required and must be addressed with appropriate strategies.

Move from most accurate to least accurate strategies. The ten strategies are presented in order of accuracy and credibility, beginning with the most credible. Working down the list, each strategy should be considered for its feasibility in the situation. The most accurate strategy feasible for the situation should be used.

Consider availability and convenience when selecting strategy. Sometimes the availability of a particular source of data will drive the selection. In other situations, the convenience of a technique may be an important factor in selecting the strategy.

When estimates are sought from individuals, use the source who has the broadest perspective on the issue. The individual providing the estimate must have knowledge of the processes and issues surrounding the value of the data.

Use multiple strategies when feasible. Sometimes it is helpful to have more than one strategy for obtaining a value for the data. When multiple sources are feasible, more than one source should be used to serve as a comparison or to provide another perspective. When multiple sources are used, the data must be integrated using a convenient decision rule such as the lowest value, which is preferred because of its conservative nature.

Minimize the amount of time required to select and implement the appropriate strategy. As with other processes, it is important to keep the time invested in this phase of the process as low as possible, so that the total time and effort for the ROI does not become excessive. Some strategies can be implemented with less time than others. Too much time at this step can dampen an otherwise enthusiastic attitude about the process.

Accuracy and Credibility of Data

The Credibility Problem

The strategies presented in this chapter assume that each data item collected and linked with training can be converted to a monetary value. Very subjective data, such as a change in employee morale or a reduction in the number of employee conflicts, are difficult to convert to monetary values. Although estimates can be developed using one or more strategies, the process of converting this data to a monetary value may lose credibility with the target audience, who may question its use in analysis. The key question for this determination is: "Could these results be presented to senior management with confidence?" If the process does not meet this credibility test, the data should not be converted to monetary values and instead should be listed as an intangible benefit. Other data could be used in the ROI calculation, leaving the very subjective data as intangible improvements.[13]

Data's accuracy and the credibility of the conversion process are important concerns. HRD professionals sometimes avoid converting data because of these issues. They are more comfortable reporting that a training program resulted in reducing absenteeism from 6% to 4%, without attempting to place a monetary value on the improvement. They assume that each person receiving the information will place a value on the absenteeism reduction. Unfortunately, the target audience may know little about the cost of absenteeism and will usually underestimate the actual value of the improvement. Consequently, there should be some attempt to include this conversion in the ROI analysis.

How the Credibility of Data Is Influenced

When ROI data are presented to selected target audiences, credibility will be an issue. The degree to which the target audience believes the data will be influenced by the following factors:

Reputation of the source of data. The actual source of the data represents the first credibility issue. How credible is the individual or group providing the data? Do they understand the issues? Do they possess knowledge of all the processes? This issue often causes the target audience to place more credibility on data obtained from those employees who are closest to the source of the actual improvement or change.

Reputation of the source of the study. The target audience will scrutinize the reputation of the individual, group, or organization presenting the data. Do they have a history of providing accurate reports? Are they unbiased in their analyses? Are they fair in their presentation? Answers to these and other questions will form an impression about the presenter's reputation.

Motives of the evaluators. Do the individuals conducting the study or presenting the data have an axe to grind? Do they have a personal interest in creating a favorable or unfavorable result? The target audience will examine the motives of those involved in the study.

Methodology of the study. The audience will want to know specifically how the research was conducted. How were the calculations made? What steps were followed? What processes were used? A lack of information about methodology will cause the audience to become wary and suspicious of the results, and they will often insert their own assumptions.

Assumptions made in the analysis. In many ROI studies, assumptions are made on which to base calculations. What are those assumptions? Do they represent generally accepted practices? How do they compare to assumptions from other studies? When assumptions are omitted, the audience will substitute their own assumptions, which are often unfavorable.

Realism of the outcome data. Impressive ROI values could cause problems. When outcomes appear to be excessive, the target audience may have difficulty believing them. Huge claims often fall on deaf ears, causing reports to be discarded before they are examined.

Types of data. The target audience will usually have a preference for hard data in the form of business performance data (output, quality, costs, or time). These measures are usually easy to understand, and are closely related to organizational performance. Conversely, soft data are sometimes viewed suspiciously from the outset, as many senior executives are concerned about their soft nature and limitations on the analysis.

Scope of analysis. The scope of the analysis also influences credibility. Does the evaluation involve just one group, or all employees in the organization? Limiting the study to a small group, or series of groups, of employees makes the process more accurate and the results more believable.

Guidelines for the Study

Collectively, these factors will influence the credibility of an ROI impact study and provide a framework from which to develop the ROI report. Thus, when considering each of the issues, the following key points are suggested for an ROI impact study:

☐ Use the most credible and reliable source for estimates.

☐ Present the material in an unbiased, objective way.

☐ Fully explain the methodology used throughout the process, preferably step by step.

☐ Define the assumptions made in the analysis, and compare them to assumptions made in similar studies.

☐ Consider factoring or adjusting output values when they appear to be unrealistic.

☐ Use hard data whenever possible, combining with soft data if available.

☐ Keep the scope of the analysis very narrow. Conduct the impact study with one or more groups of participants in the program, instead of all participants or all employees.

Making Adjustments

Two potential adjustments should be considered before finalizing the monetary value. In some organizations that use soft data and derive values with imprecise methods, senior management is sometimes offered the opportunity to review and approve the data. Because of the subjective nature of this process, management may factor (reduce) the data so that the final results are more credible. For example, at Litton Industries senior managers adjusted the value for the benefits derived from the implementation of self-directed teams.[14]

The other adjustment concerns the time value of money. Since an investment in a program is made at one time period and the return is realized in a later time period, some organizations adjust the program benefits to reflect the time value of money, using discounted cash flow techniques. The actual monetary benefits of the program are adjusted for this time period. The amount of this adjustment, however, is usually small compared with the typical benefits realized from training and development programs.

Summary

In conclusion, organizations are attempting to be more aggressive when defining training and development's monetary benefits. Progressive HRD managers are no longer satisfied with reporting business results from training. Instead, they are taking additional steps to convert business results data to monetary values, compare them with program costs, and obtain an ultimate level of evaluation, the return on investment. This chapter presented ten strategies to convert business results to monetary values, offering an array of techniques to fit any situation and program.

Discussion Questions

---

1. Identify a common output measurement and convert it to a monetary value. How difficult is this process?
2. Identify a measure taken from the quality field and convert it to a monetary cost savings. Comment on the difficulty of this conversion.
3. Identify a time savings measure and convert it to a monetary value. Why is time savings difficult to calculate?

4. In general, how can experts be located internally and externally to place a value on a measure?
5. When is it appropriate to have participants estimate the value of a measure?
6. Select at least two soft data measurements and convert them to a monetary value of savings.
7. Which of the approaches to converting soft data measurements is most appropriate? Why?
8. An HRD executive was quoted as follows, "The conversion of soft data to a monetary value creates an illusion of a precision that does not exist. As a result, we do not use soft data savings in any of our evaluation projects." Explain the concern that generated this comment.
9. For each of the following, please indicate the most appropriate method to use to convert data to monetary values. Assume the setting is in your organization (or one with which you are familiar):

☐ Accidents
☐ Employee Turnover
☐ Customer Complaints
☐ Project Completion
☐ Grievances
☐ Absenteeism
☐ Tardiness
☐ Customer Response Time

10. When is it appropriate to have management review the process for arriving at the value for a measure?
11. Should management be allowed to make adjustments to the values? If so, when?

References

1. Kaplan, R. S. and Norton, D. P. *Translating Strategy Into Action: The Balanced Scorecard.* Boston, MA: Harvard Business School Press, 1996.
2. Phillips, J. J. "How Much Is the Training Worth?" *Training & Development,* Vol. 50, No. 4, April 1996, pp. 20–24.
3. Phillips, J. J. "Measuring ROI in an Established Program," in *In Action: Measuring Return on Investment, Vol. 1.* J. J. Phillips (Ed.), Alexandria, VA: American Society for Training and Development, 1994, pp. 187–198.
4. Seimke, R. "Cost of Quality: You Can Measure It," *Training,* August 1990, pp. 62–63.

5. Rust, R. T., Zahorik, A. J. and Keiningham, T. L. *Return on Quality: Measuring the Financial Impact of Your Company's Quest for Quality.* Chicago, IL: Probus Publishers, 1994.

6. Stamp, D. *The Workplace of the 21st Century.* Bellevue, WA: Priority Management Systems, 1992.

7. Pine, J. and Tingley, J. "ROI of Soft-Skills Training," *Training,* February 1993, pp. 55–60.

8. Hronec, S. M. *Vital Signs.* New York, NY: American Management Association, 1993.

9. Schoeppel, C. "Turning Down Manager Turnover," in *In Action: Measuring Return on Investment, Vol. 1.* J. J. Phillips (Ed.), Alexandria, VA: American Society for Training and Development, 1994, pp. 213–222.

10. Fitz-enz, J. "Yes . . . You Can Weigh In Training's Value," *Training,* July 1994, pp. 54–58.

11. Zigon, J. "Performance Management Training," in *In Action: Measuring Return on Investment, Vol. 1.* J. J. Phillips (Ed.), Alexandria, VA: American Society for Training and Development, 1994, pp. 253–270.

12. Payne, Rebecca. "Improving Customer Service Skills," in *In Action: Measuring Return on Investment, Vol. 1.* J. J. Phillips (Ed.), Alexandria, VA: American Society for Training and Development, 1994, pp. 169–186.

13. Hassett, J. "Simplifying ROI," *Training,* September 1992, pp. 53–57.

14. Graham, M., Bishop K., and Birdsong, R. "Self-Directed Work Teams," in *In Action: Measuring Return on Investment, Vol. 1.* J.J. Phillips (Ed.), Alexandria, VA: American Society for Training and Development, 1994, pp. 112–122.

CHAPTER 12

Identifying Intangible Measures

HRD program results have both tangible measures and intangible measures, which are defined as benefits directly linked to the program but not converted to monetary values. Although intangible measures may represent Level 3 or Level 4 data, they are usually Level 4 soft data. These measures are often monitored after the program has been conducted and, although not converted to monetary values, are very important in the evaluation process. While the range of measures is almost limitless, this chapter presents twenty intangible measures that represent some of the more common benefits linked with HRD. Table 12-1 lists the measures briefly described in this chapter. It should be emphasized that specific measures selected are unique to the HRD program being evaluated.

Key Issues

Importance

Not all measures can or should be converted to monetary values. By design, some are captured and reported as intangible measures. Although they may not be perceived as being as valuable as the measures converted to monetary values, intangible measures are critical to the overall evaluation process. When combined with monetary benefits, they create a balanced assessment of results.[1] In some programs, such as interpersonal skills training, team development, leadership, communications training, and management development, the intangible or non-monetary benefit measures can be more important than monetary or tangible measures. Some senior executives prefer that data on behavior change and improvements be presented in intangible measures.[2] These measures should be monitored and reported as part of the overall evaluation. In practice, every training program, regardless of its nature, scope,

Table 12-1
Typical Intangible Measures Linked with Training

☐ Attitude Survey Data	☐ Employee Transfers
☐ Organizational Commitment	☐ Customer Satisfaction Survey Data
☐ Climate Survey Data	☐ Customer Complaints
☐ Employee Complaints	☐ Customer Retention and Loyalty
☐ Grievances	☐ Customer Response Time
☐ Discrimination Complaints	☐ Teamwork
☐ Stress Reduction	☐ Cooperation
☐ Employee Turnover	☐ Conflict
☐ Employee Absenteeism	☐ Decisiveness
☐ Employee Tardiness	☐ Communication

and content, will have intangible measures associated with it.[3] The challenge is to identify them efficiently and report them appropriately.

Identification of Measures

Intangible measures can be identified from different sources and at different times in the process, as depicted in Figure 12-1. They can be uncovered early in the process, during the needs assessment, and planned for collection as part of the overall data-collection strategy. For example, a team leader training program has several hard data measures linked to the program. An intangible measure, job satisfaction, is identified and monitored with no plans to convert it to a monetary value. Thus, this measure is destined from the beginning to be a non-monetary benefit reported along with the ROI results.

Intangible measures can also be identified during discussions with clients or sponsors on the impact of training. Clients can often identify intangible measures influenced, or expected to be influenced, by the program. For example, a management development program in a large multinational company was conducted, and an ROI analysis is planned. Program developers,

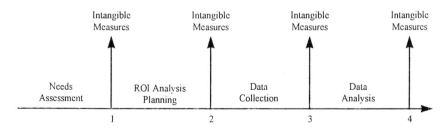

Figure 12-1. Identification of intangible measures: timing and source.

instructors, participants, managers, and senior executives were able to identify potential intangible measures that were perceived to be influenced by the program, including new product ideas, number of development plans initiated, number of employee transfers, number of promotions, and improvement in organizational commitment.

A third opportunity to identify intangible measures presents itself during a follow-up evaluation. Although the measure was not anticipated in the initial design of the program, it may surface on a questionnaire, in an interview, or during a focus group. Questions are often asked about other improvements linked to the training program, and participants usually provide several intangible measures for which there are no plans to assign a value. For example, in the evaluation of a customer service training program, participants were asked what specifically had improved about their work unit and relationship with customers as a result of the application of the skills acquired in the program. The participants provided over a dozen intangible measures perceived to be linked directly to the program, including customer loyalty, customer retention, stress reduction, and job satisfaction.

The fourth opportunity to identify intangible measures is at the data analysis step, during an attempt to convert the data to monetary values. If the process used to convert the data to a monetary value loses credibility, the measure should instead be reported as an intangible benefit. For example, in a selling skills program, customer satisfaction was identified early in the process as a measure of training success. A conversion to monetary values was attempted, but lost accuracy and credibility. Consequently, customer satisfaction was reported as an intangible benefit.

The different opportunities and sources for intangible measures underscore the importance of these measures in the overall evaluation scheme. Intangibles should not be perceived as an add-on part of the evaluation, discovered unintentionally in a follow-up evaluation. The identification, analysis, and use of intangible measures should be fully integrated into the planning, development, and execution of the evaluation.

Analysis

No specific analysis is planned for most intangible data. Although there may have been previous aborted attempts to convert intangible data to monetary units, no further analysis is usually conducted. In some cases there may be attempts to isolate the effects of training using one or more of the methods outlined in Chapter 10. This step is necessary when there is a need to know the specific amount of change in the intangible measure linked to the program. In many cases, however, the intangible data reflect improvement that cannot be clearly identified or linked directly to the training. Since the value of this data is not included in the ROI calculation, it is not normally used to justify additional training or the continuation of existing training. Intangible benefits are viewed as supporting evidence of the program's success, and therefore detailed analysis is not needed.

Employee Satisfaction

Employee satisfaction is one of the most important intangible measures. Almost any training program will improve job satisfaction if it is perceived as successful by the participants and their employees, customers, and peer group members.[4] Some of the most influential employee satisfaction measures are briefly described here.

Attitude Survey Data

Many organizations conducted attitude surveys that reflect the degree to which employees are satisfied with their organization, job, supervisor, coworkers, and a host of other issues. Employee job satisfaction is closely correlated with absenteeism and turnover, both of which are linked with some training programs. Some attitude survey items focus on issues directly related to training programs, such as satisfaction with managers' and supervisors' quality of leadership. When specific issues on the attitude survey are related to training, data are usually linked to training results. For example, in a diversity training program conducted at a television station for all employees, the annual attitude survey contained five questions directly tied to perceptions and attitudes influenced by the training program.

Unfortunately, attitude survey data are usually taken annually and may not be in sync with the timing of the training program. However, some organizations design the survey instrument around issues related to the training program and conduct surveys at a prescribed time frame after training. This approach, often used when job satisfaction is one of the program's objectives, is very expensive.

Organizational Commitment Data

Organizational commitment is perhaps a more important measure to reflect employees' motivational state. Organizational commitment instruments are similar to attitude surveys and reflect the degree to which employees are aligned with company goals, values, philosophy, and practices. High levels of organizational commitment often correlate with high levels of productivity and performance.[6] Some training programs are specifically designed to improve employee performance, and organizational commitment is an important intangible measure of the program's success. The difficulty with using this intangible measure is that it is not routinely measured in organizations.

Climate Survey Data

In some organizations, climate surveys are taken to reflect changes in the work climate on issues such as communication, openness, trust, and quality of feedback. Climate surveys are similar to attitude surveys, but often focus on a broader range of workplace issues and environmental enablers and inhibitors.[7] Climate surveys conducted before and after training may reflect the extent to which it has influenced the work climate. These changes in climate data are rarely converted to monetary benefits and are instead reported as intangible data.

Employee Complaints

Some organizations monitor employee complaints through a formal process of reporting and recording complaints. Because a reduction in the number of employee complaints is sometimes directly related to HRD programs such as team building and empowerment, the level of complaints is reported as an intangible measure and used as a measure of the program's success.[8]

Grievances

Grievances can often reflect the level of dissatisfaction or disenchantment with a variety of factors in both union and non-union organizations. When the number of grievances is considered excessive, HRD programs such as labor management cooperation are sometimes designed to reduce their number.[9] An improvement in the grievance level reflects the success of the program. This measure can be converted to a monetary value or reported as an intangible measure.

Discrimination Complaints

Employee dissatisfaction can appear in a variety of different types of discrimination complaints, ranging from informal complaints to external charges and even litigation. Training programs, such as a sexual harassment prevention workshop, may be designed to prevent complaints or reduce the current level of complaint activity. Figure 12-2 shows a reduction in the number of internal formal complaints of sexual harassment in a large hospital chain[10], using one year of pre-program data and one year of post-program data. The result of the program, in terms of complaint reduction, may not be

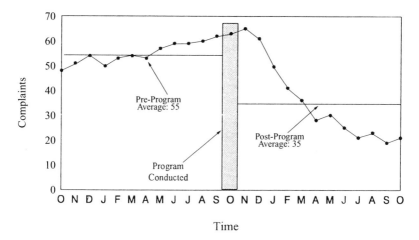

Figure 12-2. Formal internal complaints of sexual harassment.

converted to monetary values because of the various assumptions and estimates involved in the process. When this is the case, these measures are reported as intangible benefits of the program.

Stress Reduction

Occasionally, training programs reduce stress by showing participants a variety of techniques to improve work relationships, accomplish more with time management skills, or relieve tension and anxiety with conflict resolution techniques.[11] A subsequent reduction in stress may be directly linked to the training program and is usually reported as an intangible benefit.

Employee Withdrawal

When employee satisfaction deteriorates to the point that employees withdraw from work or the organization, either permanently or temporarily, the results can be disastrous. Several employee withdrawal measures are monitored, and are often linked to training or performance programs. Additional information on employee withdrawal measures outlined in this section can be found in other resources.[12]

Employee Turnover

Employee turnover is perhaps the most critical employee withdrawal variable. Turnover is an extremely costly variable and, when excessive, it can have devastating consequences for organizations.[13] Many supervisor and team leader training programs are designed to reduce employee turnover in work units. Although turnover is occasionally converted to monetary values using one of the methods described in Chapter 11, the multitude of costs and assumptions involved in developing the value may make the conversion process infeasible. In this case, turnover should be reported as an intangible benefit, reflecting part of the success of the training program.

Employee Absenteeism

Absenteeism is another disruptive and costly variable. Many training programs are designed to reduce absenteeism, and therefore the impact of training on absenteeism can usually be pinpointed.[14] Although absenteeism's cost can be developed, the conversion process is not always credible enough, and absenteeism changes are consequently reported as intangible benefits.

Employee Tardiness

Many organizations monitor tardiness, particularly those that use electronic and computerized time-reporting. Tardiness is an irritating and problematic work habit that can cause inefficiencies and delays. A few training programs are designed to reduce it, but tardiness is very difficult to convert to a monetary value. Consequently, when tardiness is presented as an improvement from a training program it is usually as an intangible benefit.

Employee Transfers

Another way in which employees withdraw is to request a transfer to another section, department, or division of the organization. Requests for transfers often reflect dissatisfaction with a variety of issues including management, policies, and working conditions. Training programs are sometimes designed to reduce or remove these unpleasant environmental influences. Some of these programs monitor and record requests for transfers as an intangible benefit of training, although there is usually no attempt to assign monetary values to them.

Customer Service

Because of the importance of building and improving customer service, a variety of measures are often monitored and reported as a payoff of training. Customer service training programs usually have a direct influence on these measures, but because of the difficulty of placing values on them, the measures are often reported as intangible benefits. Several measures are described here.

Customer Satisfaction Survey Data

The degree to which customers are pleased with products and services is one of the most important measures in survey data. These survey values, reported as absolute data or as an index, represent important data that can be used to judge the success of customer service training. Although techniques are available to convert survey data to monetary values, in most situations the conversion is rarely attempted[15] and improvements are reported as intangible benefits.

Customer Complaints

Most organizations monitor customer complaints, along with the disposition and the time required to resolve the complaint, as well as specific costs associated with the complaint resolution. Training programs are sometimes designed to reduce the number of customer complaints, but because it is difficult to assign the complaint an accurate monetary value, the measure is usually reported as a very important intangible benefit.

Customer Retention and Loyalty

In recent years, there has been more focus on building and retaining loyal customers who will not only remain with the organization, but will also expand their scope of purchase of products and services.[16] This emphasis has led to a variety of training programs designed to enhance customer retention and loyalty. Direct measures from these programs include actual measures of customer retention, defection rates, and customer loyalty. Because of the difficulty of converting these measures to monetary values, they are usually reported as intangible benefits.

Customer Response Time

Providing prompt customer service is a critical issue in most organizations, and the time it takes to respond to specific customer service requests or problems is often recorded and monitored. Although response-time reduction is sometimes a benefit of training programs, the measure is not usually converted to monetary values. Thus, customer response time is presented as an important intangible benefit.

Other Customer Responses

A variety of other types of measures can be tracked such as the creativity of responses to customers, responsiveness to cost and pricing issues, and any other important issues customers may specify or require.[17] Monitoring these measures can provide more evidence of the results of a training program. Because of the difficulty of assigning values to the measures, they are usually reported as intangible benefits.

Team Effectiveness Measures

A variety of measures are often monitored to reflect how well teams are working. Although the output and quality of teams' work are often measured as hard data and converted to monetary values, other interpersonal measures may be monitored and reported separately.[18] A few of these measures are represented here.

Teamwork

The level of teamwork is sometimes measured with a survey of team members before and after training. Several versions of a team effectiveness survey are available to measure teamwork.[19] The monetary value of increased teamwork is rarely developed and, consequently, is usually reported as an intangible benefit.

Cooperation

The success of a team often depends on the cooperative spirit of team members. Some instruments measure the level of cooperation before and after training, but because of the difficulty of converting this measure to a monetary value, it is always reported as an intangible benefit.

Conflict

At the other end of cooperation is conflict. Instruments are available to measure the level of conflict in a team environment. In most situations, a monetary value is not placed on conflict reduction and it is reported as an intangible benefit.

Decisiveness

Teams make decisions, and because the timing of the decision-making process often becomes an issue, decisiveness is sometimes measured in terms of the speed at which decisions are made. Survey measures may reflect perception of this issue or, in some cases, how quickly a decision has actually been made.[20] Some training programs are expected to influence this process, and improvements are usually reported as intangible benefits.

Communication

A variety of communication instruments reflect the quality and quantity of communication within a team.[21] Changes in communications skills, or perceptions of skills, driven by a training program are not usually converted to monetary values and are instead reported as an intangible benefit.

Other Team Measures

While the measures listed above are common, there are many other potential measures available to reflect the performance and function of teams. Table 12-2 shows a report on intangible measures after completion of a team-building program.[22] These measures, obtained as part of a survey process, show the variety of measures used to reflect team success.

Summary

A variety of intangible measures that reflect the success of an HRD program are available. Although they may not be perceived as being as valuable

Table 12-2
A Sample of Intangible Measures of Team Effectiveness

Item	# Of Resp.	Point Range	Total Points	Point Average	Rank (By Avg.)
Clearly states mission/goals	7	4–6	34	4.9	4
Operates creatively	7	3–7	37	5.3	2
Focuses on results	7	4–5	31	4.3	6
Clarifies roles and responsibilities	7	2–6	34	4.9	4
Is well-organized	7	4–6	36	5.1	3
Builds upon individual strengths	7	5–7	41	5.9	1
Supports leadership/each other	7	4–6	37	5.3	2
Develops team climate	5	3–5	21	4.2	7
Resolves disagreements	6	2–5	20	3.3	9
Communicates openly	7	2–4	21	3.0	10
Makes objective decisions	7	3–6	33	4.7	5
Evaluates its own effectiveness	7	2–4	24	3.4	8

Source: Bader, G.E., Bloom, A.E., and Chang, R.Y. Measuring Team Performance. *Irvine, CA: Richard Chang Associates, 1994.*

as specific monetary measures, they are nevertheless an important part of an overall evaluation. Intangible measures should be identified, explored, examined, and monitored for changes linked to the program. Collectively, they add a unique dimension to the overall program results since most, if not all, programs have intangible measures associated with them. While some of the most common intangible measures were covered in this chapter, the coverage was not meant to be complete. The number of intangible measures is almost unlimited, and must be identified and developed for each specific program.

Discussion Questions

1. Why are intangible benefits important?
2. How does the presentation of intangible benefits relate to a balanced view of evaluation?
3. Why is it appropriate to identify/capture intangible benefits at different time frames?
4. Are intangible measures Level 3 or Level 4 data? Explain.
5. What types of intangible benefits might be expected from a three-day training program on negotiating skills for managers? A five-day continuous process improvement program for an intact team?
6. Can job satisfaction be converted to monetary values? Customer satisfaction? Explain.

References

1. Kaplan, R. S. and Norton, D. P. "Putting the Balanced Scorecard to Work," *Harvard Business Review,* September–October 1993, pp. 134–147.
2. Stone, R. D., Steele, D. R., Wallace, D. M., and Spurrier, W. B. "Training's Contribution to a Major Change Initiative," in *In Action: Measuring Return on Investment, Vol. 2.* J. J. Phillips (Ed.), Alexandria, VA: American Society for Training and Development, 1997.
3. Denzin, N. K. and Lincoln, Y. S. (Eds.) *Handbook of Qualitative Research.* Thousand Oaks, CA: Sage Publications, Inc., 1994.
4. Cranny, C. J., Smith, P. C., and Stone, E. F. *Job Satisfaction.* New York, NY: Lexington Books, 1992.
5. Fink, A. *The Survey Handbook.* Thousand Oaks, CA: Sage Publications, Inc., 1995.
6. Bray, D. W. and Associates. *Working with Organizations and Their People: A Guide to Human Resources Practice.* New York, NY: The Guilford Press, 1991.

7. Bridges, W. *Job Shift: How to Prosper in a Workplace Without Jobs.* Reading, MA: Addison-Wesley Publishing Company, 1994.

8. Kayser, T. A. *Building Team Power: How to Unleash the Collaborative Genius of Work Teams.* Burr Ridge, IL: Irwin Professional Publishing, 1994.

9. Carrell, M. R. and Heavrin, C. *Labor Relations and Collective Bargaining,* 4th Edition. Englewood Cliffs, NJ: Prentice Hall, Inc., 1995.

10. Hill, D. and Phillips, J. J. "Healthcare, Inc." in *In Action: Measuring Return on Investment, Vol. 2.* J. J. Phillips, (Ed.), Alexandria, VA: American Society for Training and Development, 1997.

11. Karasek, R. and Theorell, T. *Healthy Work: Stress, Productivity, and the Reconstruction of Working Life.* New York, NY: Basic Books, 1990.

12. Phillips, J. J. *Return on Investment in Training and Performance Improvement Programs.* Houston, TX: Gulf Publishing Company, 1997.

13. Fitz-enz, J. *How to Measure Human Resources Management,* 2nd Edition. New York, NY: McGraw-Hill, Inc., 1995.

14. Hope, T. and Hope J. *Transforming the Bottom Line: Managing Performance with the Real Numbers.* Boston, MA: Harvard Business School Press, 1996.

15. Evans, N. *Using Questionnaires and Surveys to Boost Your Business.* London, U.K.: Pitman Publishing, 1995.

16. Bhote, K. R. *Beyond Customer Satisfaction to Customer Loyalty: The Key to Greater Profitability.* New York, NY: AMA Membership Publications Division, 1996.

17. Naumann, E. and Giel, K. *Customer Satisfaction Measurement and Management Using the Voice of the Customer.* Cincinnati, OH: Thomson Executive Press, 1995.

18. Wellins, R. S., Byham, W. C., and Dixon, G. R. *Inside Teams.* San Francisco, CA: Jossey-Bass Publishers, 1994.

19. Harrington-Mackin, D. *The Team Building Tool Kit.* New York, NY: American Management Association, 1994.

20. Robbins, H. and Finley, M. *Why Teams Don't Work.* Princeton, NJ: Peterson's/Pacesetter Books, 1995.

21. Sanborn, M. *Teambuilt: Making Teamwork Work.* New York, NY: Master Media, 1992.

22. Bader, G. E., Bloom, A. E., and Chang, R. Y. *Measuring Team Performance: A Practical Guide to Tracking Team Success.* London, U.K.: Kogan Page Ltd., 1994.

CHAPTER 13

Determining Program Costs

Importance of Costs

Capturing costs is challenging because they must be accurate, reliable, and realistic. Although most organizations can develop costs with more ease than the economic value of the benefits, the true cost of training is often an elusive figure, even in some of the best organizations. While the total HRD direct budget is usually easily developed, it is more difficult to determine the specific costs of a program, including its indirect costs. To develop a realistic ROI, costs must be accurate and credible. Otherwise, the painstaking attention to benefits will be wasted because of inadequate or inaccurate costs.

The cost of providing HRD in an organization is increasing and, as organizations scramble to fund their budgets, it is imperative that they know how and why the money is spent. This chapter examines the rationale for determining costs and provides specific methods and techniques for classifying, allocating, and reporting those costs. Although the specific methods must be tailored to the organization, a number of fundamental principles and guidelines can be useful for any organization.

Rationale for Developing Cost Data

While the most significant reason to undertake an evaluation is to determine the benefits versus costs of an HRD program, there are many other important reasons to monitor the cost of HRD. Although these reasons are almost the same as the purposes for evaluation, a review should be helpful. All of these reasons may not be applicable for all organizations.

To determine the total expenditures for HRD. Every organization should know approximately how much money is being spent on HRD. A few organizations now calculate this expenditure and make comparisons with other organizations, but such comparisons are difficult because of the different bases for cost calculations.

Some organizations calculate HRD costs as a percent of payroll costs and set targets. For example, Motorola budgets 3.6% of its payroll for employee education.[1] Other organizations calculate HRD costs as a percent of revenue or develop HRD costs on a per-employee basis. Arthur Andersen & Co. spends about 9.5% of revenue on training. Total expenditures may go beyond the overall budget for the HRD department and include additional costs such as participants' salaries, travel expenses, replacement costs, facilities expense, and general overhead. An effective system of cost-data collection enables an organization to calculate the magnitude of the total HRD expenditure. Collecting this information also helps top management answer two important questions:

1. How much do we spend on HRD compared to other organizations?
2. How much should we spend on HRD?

To determine the relative cost of each individual HRD program. The HRD department should know which programs are most cost effective. They also need to know if some programs with strong support and management commitment are carrying other programs that cost more but provide fewer results. Monitoring costs by program allows the HRD staff to evaluate the relative contribution of a program and determine how those costs are changing. If a program's cost has risen, it might be time to reevaluate its impact and overall success.

It may be useful to compare specific components of costs to other programs or organizations. For example, the cost per participant for one program could be compared to the cost per participant for a similar program. Wide differences may signal a problem. It may be helpful, for example, to know why it costs approximately $2,000 more to train a plumber than to train an electrician. Also, costs associated with evaluation, development, or other items could be compared to other programs within the organization and used to develop cost standards.

To predict future program costs. Historical costs provide the best basis for predicting future costs. Sophisticated cost models provide the capability to estimate or predict costs with reasonable accuracy.

To calculate benefits versus costs for a specific program. Perhaps the most significant reason to collect costs is to prepare data to use in a benefits-versus-costs comparison. In this respect, cost data is equally as important as the data that determines the program's economic benefits. The benefits-versus-costs concept approaches HRD expenditures as an investment with a potential return.

To improve the efficiency of the HRD department. Controlling costs is an important management function, to which HRD personnel should pay close attention. Most HRD departments have monthly budgets that project costs by various accounts and, in some cases, by project or program. Cost reports, generated to show how the department is doing, are excellent tools for spotting problem areas and taking corrective action. From a practical management sense, the accumulation of cost data is a necessity.

To evaluate alternatives to a proposed HRD program. Realistic cost data provide management with the cost of a proposed program. The data can then be used to evaluate the cost effectiveness of alternatives to a particular program. For example, the servicing division of a major credit card company decided to computerize its data management systems and relocate to a different area of the country. It was faced with the need to train a large number of employees immediately, and expected its needs for training to continue into the future. These conditions suggested a mix of computer-based instruction and classic classroom training. To compare the two approaches, cost data must be developed for each approach.

To plan and budget for next year's operations. A final reason for tracking HRD costs is in the preparation of next year's operating budget. The operating budget usually includes all of the expenditures within the HRD department, and may also include other costs such as participants' salaries and their associated travel expenses. In recent years the budgeting process has become more scrutinized, and a percentage increase from last year's budget is no longer acceptable for most organizations. An increasing number of organizations have adopted zero-based budgets, in which each activity must be justified and no expenses are carried over from the previous year. An accurate accounting of expenditures enables the HRD manager to defend proposed ideas and programs in a line-item review with management.

To develop a marginal-cost pricing system. HRD expenditure data are important when developing marginal-cost pricing strategies. When management is able to include the cost necessary for employee training when considering a new organizational strategy, it has a better sense of value for pursuing that strategy. Several organizations have developed standard cost data that can easily fit into expansion plans, changes in procedures or policies, or changes in products or services. Standard cost data will allow organizations to quickly factor the investment in human resources.

To integrate data into the human resource information systems. An HRD department should collect training-cost data so that these data can be integrated into existing databases for other human resource functions such as compensation, benefits, and selection information. Aligning training-cost information in these databases provides information on training's relative contribution to profitability. Some sophisticated human resource information systems electronically track and monitor costs, while other systems require cost data to be manually entered into the system.

In conclusion, developing, collecting, and monitoring cost data are crucial aspects of the HRD functions. However, in many organizations this type of data is either inaccurate or unavailable.[2]

General Considerations

Whether developing a cost system or not, there are certain issues surrounding costs that need consideration. This section explores these issues in the form of helpful advice.

Collect costs even if they are not used in evaluation. Cost data should be developed in anticipation of future needs. Too often, an HRD department will neglect to collect and report costs adequately because they are not part of their present evaluation processes. These costs can be very useful management tools and are necessary for an effective organization.

Costs will not be precise. An accurate reflection of all costs associated with a program is almost impossible. There are many hidden costs that make it difficult to get a completely accurate picture, but this lack of precision should not discourage attempts to monitor and collect costs. A reasonably accurate cost estimate is better than no cost estimate. If used in an evaluation, the costs are probably going to be as accurate as the economic value of the benefit of a program.

Use a practical approach in building a system. The HRD department must define the purposes for developing a cost system before it is designed. There will be trade-offs in accuracy versus the feasibility of maintaining the system. The organization should not be burdened with a vast amount of additional paperwork, calculations, and other analyses that can become unproductive and may not add to the precision of cost data. What is needed is a system that is simple yet as accurate as possible. It should be easy to administer and understand, and should be incorporated into the organization's ongoing processes. Some account categories or line-item descriptions will be different, but the manner of collecting, compiling, storing, and reporting the data should be consistent with established practices.

Use caution when reporting cost data. Cost data may be used for a number of purposes. Taken out of context, without proper explanations, cost data might be frightening to top management and other interested observers.

The effort to set up a cost system is considerable. In most organizations there is a formal cost-accounting system designed to accumulate cost by department, section, product line, and other categories. This type of system is usually adequate for collecting much of the cost data necessary to develop HRD program costs. However, the effort to set up such a system may require a modification of the current system, which will usually involve input from the finance and accounting sections of the organization.

Cost Classification Systems

HRD costs can be classified in two basic ways. One is by a description of the expenditure such as labor, materials, supplies, travel, etc. These are expense account classifications. The other is by categories in the HRD process or function such as program development, delivery, and evaluation. An effective system will monitor costs by expense account categories, but also include a method for accumulating costs by the HRD process/functional category. While the first grouping is sufficient to give the total cost of the program, it does not allow for a useful comparison with other programs or indicate areas where costs might be excessive by relative comparisons. Therefore, two basic classifications are recommended to develop a complete costing system.

Developing a Classification System

When developing an HRD classification system, the following steps can help ensure that the system provides the information needed:

Define which costs will be collected. A system of cost classification may be subject to several interpretations, so all relevant costs must be identified. Cost accounts should be clearly defined to reduce possible classification errors, leaving little room for doubt as to how an item should be charged (e.g., office supplies or duplication). Also, the various process/functional categories need to be clearly defined so that items can be properly grouped in those accounts.

Assign responsibility for developing the system. Because the implementation of a costing system involves input from many people, each individual's or department's responsibilities should be detailed and a consensus reached to reduce delays in implementation and errors in the final product.

Determine the HRD process/functional categories. Cost categories, such as administrative and development costs, should be determined early.

Determine the expense account classification descriptions. Each of the account categories should be developed to be consistent with the organization's current chart of accounts and in a manner that will ease the application and use of the system. The classifications should be practical and describe the types of costs that make up each account.

Use standard cost data when appropriate. There are many situations in which standard cost data can be useful. Usually developed internally, standard costs can save time and improve the accuracy of total cost calculations. An example of standard cost data is the percent of payroll for employee benefits when calculating the total compensation of participants. Another example is the average per diem for participants when attending an out-of-town HRD program.

Carefully select data sources. A valid data source is critical to the costing system. The source must be readily available, ideally from an existing system, and it should be consistent with other reports of the same data. Typical data sources are payroll records, budget reports, standard cost reports, travel expense records, purchase orders, and petty cash vouchers.

Consider a separate computerized system. Although the cost-accounting system may be capable of tracking costs, it may be appropriate to use a separate system using a PC-based arrangement. With the local area network's (LAN) capability and low costs, this approach is feasible.

Addressing these issues appropriately makes the development of a costing system easier, and helps ensure that the system is implemented on schedule.

Process/Functional Classifications

Table 13-1 shows the process/functional categories for costs in four different ways. In Column A there are only two categories: operating costs, and support costs. Operating costs include all expenses involved in conducting the HRD program; support costs include all administrative, overhead, development, analysis, or any other expenditures not directly related to conducting the program. While it is simple to separate the two, it does not provide enough detail to analyze costs on a functional basis. Column B adds a third category and provides a little more detail, but does not provide information on program development costs, a useful item to have. Column C provides for development costs as a separate item, but it still falls short of an ideal situation. There is no way to track evaluation costs, which are becoming a

Table 13-1
Process/Functional Categories for Cost

A	B
Operating Costs Support Costs17	Administrative Costs Participant Compensation and Facility Costs Classroom Costs

C	D
Program Development Costs Administrative Costs Classroom Costs Participant Costs	Analysis Costs Development Costs Delivery Costs Evaluation Costs

more significant part of the total HRD process. Column D represents an appropriate HRD process cost breakdown: analysis, development, delivery, and evaluation. The administrative costs are allocated to one of these areas.

Analysis cost will usually be in the range of 15%–20% of the HRD budget. Development costs will run in the 30%–35% range while delivery is 40%–45% of the budget. Evaluation is usually less than 5%.[3] The actual breakdown of costs will depend on how costs are accumulated in the organization and will vary considerably with each program, particularly in the development and delivery components. If a program is developed from one already in operation, development costs should be low. Similarly, in a lengthy program involving a large amount of participant time, delivery costs may be much higher.

Expense Account Classifications

The most time-consuming step in developing an HRD cost system is defining and classifying the various HRD expenses. Many of the expense accounts, such as office supplies and travel expenses, are already a part of the existing accounting system. However, there are expenses unique to the HRD department that must be added to the system. The system design will depend on the organization, the type of programs developed and conducted, and the limits imposed on the current cost-accounting system, if any. Also, to a certain extent, the expense account classifications will depend on how the HRD process/functional categories have been developed, as discussed in the previous section. Figure 13-1 illustrates the expense account system in one organization with more than 8,000 employees. Each account is assigned an account number and is clearly defined. Additional accounts could make the system more precise and avoid misallocation of expenses but, from a practical standpoint, this classification seems to be adequate for most HRD cost analyses.

00—*Salaries and Benefits—HRD Personnel*
This account includes the salaries and employee benefit costs for HRD personnel, both supervisory and non-supervisory.

01—*Salaries and Benefits—Other Company Personnel*
This account includes the salaries and employee benefit costs for other company personnel, both supervisory and non-supervisory.

02—*Salaries and Benefits—Participants*
This account includes the salaries and employee benefit costs for participants, both supervisory and non-supervisory.

03—*Meals, Travel, and Incidental Expenses—HRD Personnel*
This account includes meals, travel, and incidental expenses of Corporate HRD Department employees.

04—*Meals, Travel, and Accommodations—Participants*
This account includes meals, travel accommodations, and incidental expenses for participants attending HRD programs.

05—*Office Supplies and Expenses*
This account includes expenses incurred for items such as stationery, office supplies and services, subscriptions, postage, telephone and telegraph service.

06—*Program Materials and Supplies*
This account includes the cost of materials and supplies purchased for specific programs and includes such items as films, binders, hand-out materials, and purchased programs.

07—*Printing and Reproduction*
This account includes expenses incurred for printing and reproduction of all material.

08—*Outside Services*
This account includes the costs incurred for fees and expenses of outside corporations, firms, institutions, or individuals other than company personnel who perform special services, such as management consultants and professional instructors.

09—*Equipment Expense Allocation*
This account includes that portion of original equipment cost allocated to specific HRD programs, including computers.

10—*Equipment—Rental*
This account includes rental payments for equipment used in administrative work and HRD programs.

11—*Equipment—Maintenance*
This account includes expenses incurred in repairing and servicing company-owned equipment and furniture.

12—*Registration Fees*
This account includes employee registration fees and tuition for seminars and conferences paid for by the company. Membership dues and fees in trade, technical, and professional associations paid by the company for employees are also included in this account.

13—*Facilities Expense Allocation*
This account includes an expense allocation for use of a company-owned facility for conducting an HRD program.

14—*Facilities Rental*
This account includes rental payments for facilities used in connection with an HRD program.

15—*General Overhead Allocation*
This account includes general overhead expenses prorated to each HRD program.

16—*Other Miscellaneous Expenses*
This account includes miscellaneous expenses not provided for elsewhere.

Figure 13-1. Human Resource Development costs—expense account classifications.

Cost Accumulation and Estimation

Cost Classification Matrix

The previous section presented two ways of classifying costs. Costs will be accumulated under both classifications, as the two are related. A final step in the process is to define which kinds of costs in the account classification system normally apply to the process/functional categories. Table 13-2 presents a matrix for the categories necessary to accumulate all HRD-related costs in the organization. Those costs, which are usually part of a process/functional category, are checked in the matrix. Each member of the HRD staff should know how to charge expenses properly. For example, equipment is rented to use in the development and delivery of a program. Should the cost be charged to development? Or to delivery? More than likely, the cost will be allocated in proportion to the extent the item was used for each category.

Table 13-2
Cost Classification Matrix

Expense Account Classification	Process/Functional Categories			
	Analysis	Development	Delivery	Evaluation
00 Salaries and Benefits— HRD Personnel	X	X	X	X
01 Salaries and Benefits— Other Company Personnel		X	X	
02 Salaries and Benefits— Participants			X	X
03 Meals, Travel, and Incidental Expenses—HRD Personnel	X	X	X	X
04 Meals, Travel, and Accommodations—Participants			X	
05 Office Supplies and Expenses	X	X		X
06 Program Materials and Supplies		X	X	
07 Printing and Reproduction	X	X	X	X
08 Outside Services	X	X	X	X
09 Equipment Expense Allocation	X	X	X	X
10 Equipment – Rental		X	X	
11 Equipment – Maintenance			X	
12 Registration Fees	X			
13 Facility Expense Allocation			X	
14 Facility Rental			X	
15 General Overhead Allocation	X	X	X	X
16 Other Miscellaneous Expenses	X	X	X	X

Cost Accumulation

With expense account classifications clearly defined and process/functional categories determined, it is an easy task to track costs on individual programs. This can be accomplished through the use of special account numbers and project numbers. An example illustrates the use of these numbers.

A project number is a three-digit number representing a specific HRD program. For example:

New employee orientation	112
Team leader training program	215
Valuing Diversity workshop	418
Interviewing skills workshop	791

Numbers are also assigned to the process/functional breakdowns. Using the example presented earlier, the following numbers are assigned:

Analysis   1
Development   2
Delivery   3
Evaluation   4

Using the two-digit numbers assigned to the expense account classifications, an accounting system is complete unless there are other requirements from the existing system. For example, if participant workbooks are reproduced for the Valuing Diversity workshop, the appropriate charge number for printing the workbooks is 07-3-432. The first two digits denote the account classification, the next digit the process/functional category, and the last three digits the project number. This system enhances accumulation and monitoring of HRD costs. Total costs can be presented

☐ By HRD program (Valuing Diversity workshop)
☐ By process/functional categories (delivery)
☐ By expense account classification (printing and reproduction)

Cost Estimation

The previous sections covered procedures to classify and monitor costs related to HRD programs. This is important to compare ongoing costs with the budget or projected costs. Another significant reason for tracking costs is to predict the cost of future programs. This is usually accomplished through a formal method of cost estimation unique to the organization.

Some organizations use cost-estimating worksheets to arrive at the total cost for a proposed program. Figure 13-2 shows an example of cost-estimating worksheets used to calculate costs for analysis, development, delivery, and evaluation. The worksheets contain a few formulas that make it easier to estimate the cost. In addition to these worksheets, current charge rates for services, supplies, and salaries are available. Because these data become quickly outdated, they are usually prepared periodically as a supplement.

The most appropriate basis for predicting costs is to analyze actual costs incurred in all phases of a previous program, from analysis to evaluation. Historical data reveal how much is being spent in the different categories and programs. Until adequate cost data are available, it is necessary to use the detailed analysis in the worksheets for cost estimation.

Analysis Costs

Salaries & Employee Benefits—HRD Staff (No. of
  People × Average Salary × Employee Benefits
  Factor × No. of Hours on Project) _____
Meals, Travel, and Incidental Expenses _____
Office Supplies and Expenses _____
Printing and Reproduction _____
Outside Services _____
Equipment Expenses _____
Registration Fees _____
General Overhead Allocation _____
Other Miscellaneous Expenses _____
  Total Analysis Cost =======

Development Costs

Salaries & Employee Benefits (No. of People ×
  Avg. Salary × Employee Benefits Factor ×
  No. of Hours on Project) _____
Meals, Travel, and Incidental Expenses _____
Office Supplies and Expenses _____
Program Materials and Supplies _____
  Film _____
  Videotape _____
  Audiotapes _____
  35mm Slides _____
  Overhead Transparencies _____
  Artwork _____
  Manuals and Materials _____
  Other _____
Printing and Reproduction _____
Outside Services _____
Equipment Expense _____
General Overhead Allocation _____
Other Miscellaneous Expenses _____
  Total Development Costs =======

(*continued on next page*)

Delivery Costs

Participant Costs   _____
Salaries & Employee Benefits (No. of Participants
    × Avg. Salary × Employee Benefits Factor ×
    Hrs. or Days of Training Time)   _____
Meals, Travel, & Accommodations (No. of
    Participants × Avg. Daily Expenses × Days of Training)   _____
Program Materials and Supplies   _____
Participant Replacement Costs (if applicable)   _____
Lost Production (Explain Basis)   _____
Instructor Costs   _____
    Salaries & Benefits   _____
    Meals, Travel, & Incidental Expenses   _____
    Outside Services   _____
Facility Costs   _____
Facility Rental   _____
Facility Expense Allocation   _____
Equipment Expenses   _____
General Overhead Allocation   _____
Other Miscellaneous Expenses   _____
    Total Delivery Costs   _____

Evaluation Costs

Salaries & Employee Benefits—HRD Staff (No. of People
    × Avg. Salary × Employee Benefits Factor × No. of Hours
    on Project)
Meals, Travel and Incidental Expenses   _____
Participant Costs   _____
Office Supplies and Expenses   _____
Printing and Reproduction   _____
Outside Services   _____
Equipment Expenses   _____
General Overhead Allocation   _____
Other Miscellaneous Expenses   _____

    Total Evaluation Costs   _____

TOTAL PROGRAM COSTS   ══════

Figure 13-2. Cost estimating worksheet.

Cost Strategies

Pressure to Disclose All Costs

Today there is more pressure than ever before to report all costs of training, or what is referred to as fully-loaded costs.[4] This takes the cost profile beyond the direct cost of training and includes the time that participants are involved in training, including their benefits and other overhead. For years, management has realized that there are many indirect costs of training, and now they are asking for an accounting of those costs. Perhaps this point is best illustrated by a situation that recently developed in state government. The management controls of a large state agency were audited, with a portion of the audit focusing on training costs. The following comments are taken from the auditor's report:

Costs tracked at the program level focus on direct or "hard" costs and largely ignore the cost of time spent participating in or supporting training. The costs of participant time to prepare for and attend training are not tracked. For one series of programs, including such costs raised the total training cost dramatically. The agency stated that total two-year costs for the specific program were $608,834. This figure generally includes only direct costs and, as such, is substantially below the costs of the time spent by staff in preparing for and attending the program. When accounting for prework and attendance, the figure comes to a total of $1.39 million. If the statewide average of 45.5% for fringe benefits is considered, the total indirect cost of staff time to prepare for and attend the program becomes $2,032,543. Finally, if the agency's direct costs of $608,834 are added to the $2.03 million total indirect cost just noted, the total becomes $2,641,377. Among other factors that would drive actual total costs higher still are

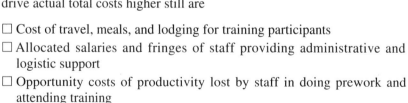 Cost of travel, meals, and lodging for training participants
☐ Allocated salaries and fringes of staff providing administrative and logistic support
☐ Opportunity costs of productivity lost by staff in doing prework and attending training

Failure to fully consider indirect or "soft" costs may expose the agency to non-compliance with the Fair Labor Standards Act (FLSA), particularly as training spreads through rank-and-file staff. Since FLSA requires that such staff be directly compensated for overtime, it will no longer be appropriate for the agency to ask employees to complete training prework on their own time. Continuing to handle such overtime work this way may also encourage false overtime reporting, skew overtime data, and/or increase the amount of uncompensated overtime.

Numerous barriers exist to agency efforts at determining "How much does training cost?"

☐ Cost systems tend to hide administrative, support, internal, and other indirect or "soft" costs

☐ Costs generally are monitored at the division level rather than at the level of individual programs or activities

☐ Cost information required by activity-based cost systems is not being generated

As this case vividly demonstrates, the cost of training is much more than direct expenditures, and training and development departments are expected to report fully-loaded costs in their reports.

Fully-Loaded Costs

It is recommended that training costs be fully-loaded when calculating the ROI. With this conservative approach, all costs that can be identified and linked to a particular program are included. The philosophy is simple: If it is questionable as to whether or not a cost should be included, it is recommended that it be included, even if the cost guidelines for the organization do not require it. The ROI process should withstand even the closest scrutiny of its accuracy and credibility. The only way to meet this test is to ensure that all costs are included. Of course, from a realistic viewpoint, if the controller or Chief Financial Officer insists on not using certain costs, then it is best to leave them out.

The Danger of Costs Without Benefits

It is dangerous to communicate the costs of training without presenting benefits but, unfortunately, many organizations have fallen into this trap for years. Because costs can easily be collected, they are presented to management in all types of ingenious ways, such as cost of the program, cost per employee, and cost per development hour. While these may be helpful for efficiency comparisons, it can be troublesome to present them without benefits.[5] When most executives review training costs, a logical question comes to mind: What benefit was received from the program? This is a typical management reaction, particularly when costs are perceived to be very high. For example, in one organization, all costs associated with executive leadership programs were tabulated and reported to senior management. The total figure exceeded the estimates from the executive group, and they immediately requested a summary of the program's benefits. This reaction caused a review of the programs, with the ultimate conclusion that they offered few, if any, economic benefits. Consequently, the programs were drastically reduced. While this may be an extreme example, it shows the danger of presenting only half of the equation. Some organizations have developed a policy of not communicating training cost data unless the benefits can be captured and presented along with the costs. The benefit data is included with the cost data even if it is subjective and intangible, thereby helping to keep balance in the two issues.

Cost Monitoring and Reporting Issues

The most important task is to define which specific costs are included in a tabulation of program costs. This task involves decisions that are made by the HRD staff and usually approved by management. If appropriate, the Finance and Accounting staff may also need to approve the list. Table 13-3 shows the recommended cost categories to report for a fully-loaded, conservative approach to estimating costs. These issues and categories go beyond the basic process/functional categories described earlier. Each category is described below.

Prorated versus Direct Costs

All costs related to a program are usually captured and expensed to that program. However, three categories are usually prorated over several sessions

Table 13-3
Training Program Cost Categories

Cost Item	Prorated	Expensed
Needs Assessment	√	
Design and Development	√	
Acquisition	√	
Delivery		√
• Salaries/Benefits—Facilitators		√
• Salaries/Benefits—Coordination		√
• Program Materials and Fees		√
• Travel/Lodging/Meals		√
• Facilities		√
• Salaries/Benefits–Participants		√
• Contact Time		√
• Travel Time		√
• Preparation Time		√
Evaluation	√	
Overhead/Training and Development	√	

of the same program. Needs assessment, design and development, and acquisition are all significant costs that should be prorated over the shelf life of the program. Some organizations will conservatively estimate one year of operation for the program, while others may estimate two or three years. If there is some question about the time period, the Finance and Accounting staff should be consulted for the specific amount of time to use in the proration formula.

A brief example will illustrate the proration of development costs. A large telecommunications company developed a computer-based training program at a cost of $98,000. It was anticipated that it would have a three-year life cycle before it would have to be updated at a cost of about one-half of the original development costs, or $49,000. The program would be conducted with 25 groups in a three-year period, and an ROI calculation is planned for one specific group. Since the program will have one-half of its residual value at the end of three years, one-half of the cost should be written off for this three-year period. The $49,000 representing half of the development costs would be spread over the 25 groups as a prorated development cost. Thus, an ROI on one group would include a development cost of $2,000 in the cost profile.

Benefits Factor

When presenting the salaries of participants and staff associated with programs, a benefits factor should be included. This number is usually well-known in the organization and is used in other costing formulas. It represents the cost of all employee benefits expressed as a percent of base salaries. In some organizations this value is as high as 50%–60%, while others may be as low as 25%–30%. The average in the U.S.A. is 38%.[6]

Needs Assessment

Perhaps one of the often overlooked items is the cost of conducting a needs assessment. In some programs this cost is zero because the program is conducted without a needs assessment. However, as more organizations focus increased attention on needs assessment, this item will become a more significant cost. All costs associated with the needs assessment should be captured to the fullest extent possible, including the time of staff members conducting the assessment, direct fees and expenses for external consultants, and internal services and supplies used in the analysis. The total costs are usually prorated over the life of the program. Depending on the type and nature of the program, the shelf life should be kept to a very reasonable number in the one-to-two-year time frame. Of course, very expensive programs are an exception as they are not expected to change significantly for several years.

Design and Development Costs

One of the more significant items is the cost of designing and developing the program. These costs include internal staff time in both design and development, the use of consultants, and the purchase of supplies, videos, CD ROMs, and other materials directly related to the program. Design and development costs are usually prorated, perhaps using the same time frame as the needs assessment. One to two years is recommended unless the program is not expected to change for many years.

Acquisition Costs

In lieu of development costs, many organizations purchase packaged programs to use directly or in a modified format. Acquisition costs include the purchase price for instructor materials, train-the-trainer sessions, licensing agreements, and other costs associated with the right to deliver the program. These acquisition costs should be prorated using the same rationale as above; one to two years should be sufficient. If the program requires modification or additional development, these costs should be included as development costs. In practice, many programs have both acquisition and development costs.

Delivery Costs

The largest segment of training costs usually comprises those costs associated with delivery.[7] Five major categories are included.

Facilitators' and Coordinators' Salaries. The salaries of facilitators or program coordinators should be included. If a coordinator is involved in more than one program, the time should be allocated to the specific program under review. If external facilitators are used, all charges should be included for the session. The important issue is to capture all of the direct time of internal employees or external consultants who work directly with the program. The benefits factor should be included each time direct labor costs are involved. This factor is usually a widely accepted value generated by the finance and accounting staff, and is often in the range of 30%–40%.

Program Materials and Fees. Specific program materials such as notebooks, textbooks, case studies, exercises, and participant workbooks should be included in the delivery costs, along with user fees and royalty payments. Pens, paper, certificates, and calculators are also included in this category.

Travel, Lodging, and Meals. Direct travel costs for participants, facilitators, or coordinators are included. Lodging, meals, and refreshments are included for participants during travel, as well as during the stay for the program.

Facilities. The direct cost of facilities for the training should be included. For external programs, this is the direct charge from the conference center, hotel, or motel. If the program is conducted in-house, the cost of the conference room should be estimated and included even if it is not standard practice to include facilities' costs in other reports.

Participants' Salaries and Benefits. Participants' salaries and employee benefits for the time involved in the program represent an expense that should be included. If the program has already been conducted, these costs can be estimated using average or midpoint values for salaries in typical job classifications. When a program is targeted for an ROI calculation, participants can provide their salaries directly, in a confidential manner.

Evaluation

To compute the fully-loaded cost of a program, the total cost of the evaluation should be included. ROI costs include developing the evaluation strategy, designing instruments, collecting data, analysis of data, and report preparation and distribution. Cost categories include time, materials, purchased instruments, or surveys. A case can be made to prorate the evaluation costs over several programs instead of charging the total amount as an expense. For example, 25 sessions of a program are conducted in a three-year period and one group is selected for an ROI calculation. The ROI costs could logically be prorated over the 25 sessions, because the results of the ROI analysis should reflect the other programs' success and will perhaps result in changes that will influence the other programs as well.

Overhead

A final charge is the cost of overhead, the additional costs in the training function not directly related to a particular program. The overhead category represents any training department cost not considered in the above calculations. Typical items include the cost of clerical support, departmental office expenses, salaries of training managers, and other fixed costs. In some organizations, the total is divided by the number of program participant days for the year to obtain an estimate for allocation. This becomes a standard value to use in calculations.

Summary

Costs are important and should be fully loaded in the ROI calculation. From a practical standpoint, including some costs may be optional based on the organization's guidelines and philosophy. However, because of the scrutiny involved in ROI calculations, it is recommended that all costs be included.

This chapter presented the information necessary to develop a cost system to accumulate, monitor, and report the costs of HRD programs. Information collected for evaluation can then be used in analysis as explained in Chapter 10.

Discussion Questions

1. Discuss the importance of monitoring HRD costs in an organization.
2. How do an organization's HRD costs compare to other human resources functions such as recruiting, compensation, benefits, and labor relations?
3. For what reasons does your organization collect costs?
4. How much should an organization spend on HRD? Please explain.
5. Why are HRD practitioners reluctant to monitor costs and report them to management on a program-by-program basis?
6. Compare the expense account classification system in your organization (or one with which you are familiar) to the one presented in this chapter.
7. Which process/functional cost classification system is appropriate for your organization (or one with which you are familiar)? Explain.
8. Are all costs accounted for in the classification system presented here? Explain.
9. What are the advantages of using the cost classification matrix as presented in this chapter?
10. Why are fully-loaded costs necessary in an ROI calculation?
11. An HRD manager stated, "There is no way you can ever accurately assess costs of training in an organization." Is this true? Explain.
12. The American Society for Training and Development estimates that employers spend, collectively, $210 billion on training annually. How is this figure calculated, and how reliable is it?

References

1. Henkoff, R. "Companies That Train Best," *Fortune,* March 22, 1993, pp. 62–75.
2. Barrow, T. "A New Wave in Training Funding," *Training & Development,* August 1996, pp. 28–33.

3. Kimmerling, G. "Gathering Best Practices," *Training & Development,* September 1993, pp. 28–36.

4. Kaufman, R. and Watkins, R. "Cost-Consequences Analysis," *Human Resource Development Quarterly,* Vol. 7, No. 1, Spring 1996, pp. 87–100.

5. Marrelli, A. F. "Cost Analysis for Training," *Technical & Skills Training,* October 1993, pp. 35–40.

6. Annual Employee Benefits Report, *Nations Business,* January 1996, p. 28.

7. Reynolds, A. "The Basics: Cost-Benefit Analysis," *Technical & Skills Training,* August/September 1993, pp. 13–14.

CHAPTER 14

Data Analysis

Data-collection methods yield numerical data that must be analyzed and interpreted to be meaningful. The type of analysis necessary is usually determined when the evaluation is planned. This chapter presents the basic methods of data analysis, with an emphasis on statistical techniques appropriate for evaluation data developed from HRD programs. Data analysis is a complex but important subject. Armed with this information, the HRD program evaluator should have adequate tools to analyze most evaluation issues.

Guidelines for Analyzing Data

Before approaching the use of statistics, a review of a few general guidelines for analyzing evaluation data should be helpful.[1]

Review for consistency and accuracy. While this may be obvious, additional checks are necessary to ensure the accuracy and consistency of the data. Incorrect, insufficient, or extreme data items should be eliminated. Also, accuracy is of the utmost importance, because the analysis and interpretation will only be as reliable as the data itself. If caution is not exercised to ensure accurate data, the remaining steps in the process are meaningless.

Use all relevant data. In most evaluations improvement is desired by the person conducting the evaluation, which may provide a built-in bias. Improvement is not always possible, and some data will be both positive and negative. It may be tempting to eliminate data that does not support the desired outcome, but all relevant data should be used. If data is not used, there should be an explanation as to why it was deleted.

Treat individual data confidentially. Data collected will usually be the result of individual performances. When analyzing and interpreting data and reporting results, the confidentiality of the sources should be an important concern unless there are conditions that warrant their exposure. The same atmosphere of confidentiality used in collecting data should be used in the analysis and reporting phases. Also, the specifics of this issue should be clearly communicated to participants before the evaluation begins.

Use the simplest statistics possible. There are many ways to analyze data, and a variety of statistical techniques are available to compare performance variations. The analysis should be as simple as possible and limited to what is necessary to draw the required conclusions from the data. Additional analyses that serve no benefit should be avoided.

As a simple example, suppose the average number of sales calls is a performance improvement measure for an HRD program on time and territory management for salespersons. There are three measures of the average: mean, median, and mode. The mean value is needed in the analysis. While the data for the median and the mode are available and easily computed, it would not add additional meaning to the analysis to include them.

Use of Statistics

Statistics should be considered for inclusion in reporting the results of HRD evaluations because they provide a concrete means by which results can be reviewed. A basic understanding of data analysis makes it possible for even the novice HRD practitioner to compute and present results in a simple, understandable form.

This chapter is not intended to build significant skills. Many other books serve that purpose.[2] The material that follows covers a few very basic concepts and provides enough insight so that elementary analyses can be performed. The simplest and most useful statistical methods are presented first, followed by more sophisticated techniques.

Caution: The presentation of one part of the subject of statistics often leads to other possibilities. Many variables can influence the statistical techniques that should be used and the type of analysis to pursue. Any analysis involving all of the concepts in this chapter should be reviewed by someone familiar with statistical methods.

The use of statistics in evaluation has three primary purposes.[3] Briefly, they are:

1. **Statistics enable large amounts of information to be summarized.** Probably the most practical use of statistics is in summarizing information. Under this category there are two basic measures. One is the measure of central tendency, or average, which is the mean, median, and mode. This measure presents, in a single number, a summary of the

characteristics of an entire group, such as the average absenteeism rate for a group of employees.

The other category is dispersion, or variance. The most useful measure of dispersion is the standard deviation. This reveals how much the individual items in the group are dispersed. For example, a large standard deviation for an average attendance means that there is a wide variation among the absenteeism records for the group of employees.

2. **Statistics allow for the determination of the relationship between two or more items.** In analyzing data, the relationship between one or more items may be important. The term used for this relationship is "correlation," which represents the degree to which the items are related and is expressed in terms of a coefficient. A positive correlation between two items means that as one item increases, the other increases. For example, a high achievement score on a knowledge examination in an HRD program might correlate with a high level of performance on the job. There also can be a negative correlation between items in which as one item increases, the other item decreases. In this case the correlation coefficient is negative.

3. **Statistics show how to compare the differences in performance between two groups.** When performance improves after an HRD program, a likely question is: Did the improvement occur because of the program, or could it have occurred by chance? In other words, without the HRD program, would the same results have been achieved? And, how accurately can the conclusions be drawn? Statistical analyses enable a confidence level to be placed on conclusions about differences in groups of data. Normally, conclusions are based on a 95% confidence level.

Frequency Distributions

Before reviewing the basic calculations involved in statistics, it is best to review frequency distribution, a useful way to present raw data. For example, Table 14-1 represents pre-program and post-program measurements of performance for a group of 15 employees.

One way to present the post-training data is to group it into small ranges, called class intervals, as shown in Table 14-2.

These groupings can be plotted on a diagram to yield a frequency histogram, as shown in Figure 14-1. This graphic presentation of the data reveals that after training more employees had a unit hour rating in the range of 60–64 than any other range. The graphic presentation of data can be useful to show the central tendency, where most of the items are grouped, and also the dispersion, the extent to which the data is scattered.

Table 14-1
Pre-Program and Post-Program Measurements

Employee Number	Production Rates (Unit Hours) Before Training	After Training
1	43	47
2	45	59
3	61	79
4	59	69
5	66	63
6	54	55
7	49	51
8	52	58
9	55	72
10	60	63
11	50	61
12	55	60
13	58	65
14	56	63
15	63	67
Total	826	932

Table 14-2
Class Intervals

Unit Hours by Class Intervals	Employees in Each Class
45–49	1
50–54	1
55–59	3
60–64	5
65–69	3
70–74	1
75–79	1
Total	15

Statistical Measures

Measures of Central Tendency

As mentioned earlier, the most common measures of central tendency are the mean, median, and mode. The mean is the arithmetic average for a group of numbers. It is calculated by adding all of the values and dividing by the total number.

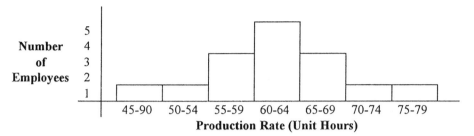

Figure 14-1. A frequency histogram.

The formula is:

$$\overline{X} = \frac{\Sigma X_i}{n}$$

where   i = subscript used to identify an individual employee.

X_i = performance level of employee i.

Σ = summation sign, which means that the items following the sign should be added. Therefore, ΣX_i is the sum of all the x values.

n = sample size.

$\overline{X}$ = average value or mean for the sample.

To illustrate the calculation, refer to the data in Table 14-1. The post-training measurements yield a mean value of:

$$\overline{X} = \frac{\Sigma X_i}{n} = \frac{932}{15} = 62.13$$

This figure represents the mean level of performance of the 15 employees after the HRD program. The mean is the number that best represents the set of data, and it is the most useful statistic to show performance after completing an HRD program.

Another measure of central tendency is the median, or middle value. When the numbers are arranged in order of magnitude, there are an equal number of values above and below the median. In the case of an even number of data items, the median is the average of the two middle values. The post-training data originally presented in Table 14-1 can be rearranged in order of magnitude, as shown in Table 14-3.

The median is 63, the eighth number in the list of 15. The median can serve as a useful shortcut to show the estimate of the whole group when the mean is not readily available or required.

The final measure of central tendency is the mode, or the value which occurs with the greatest frequency. In the previous example, 63 is the mode because it occurs three times in the list. The mode has limited application

Table 14-3
Median of Program Data

Employee	Unit Hour	
7	47	
7	51	
6	55	
8	58	
2	59	
12	60	
11	61	
5	63	Median
10	63	
14	63	
13	65	
15	67	
4	69	
9	72	
3	79	

and may not exist at all in some data. For instance, if all of the employees had different levels of performance, there would not be a mode for the distribution.

In summary, for the post-training data, the three measures of central tendency are

Mean = 62.13
Median = 63
Mode = 63

This agrees with the conclusion about the frequency distribution shown in Figure 14-1 (that is, the majority of employees have a unit hour rating in the range of 60–64). When the three measures are almost equal, the distribution is called normal or bell-shaped.

Measures of Dispersion

The degree to which data varies from the average, or mean, is called dispersion. The most common measures of dispersion are the range, variance, and standard deviation. The range is the simplest measure of dispersion. It is the difference between the largest and smallest of a set of numbers. In the example of post-training values, the range is 79 minus 47, or 32. This value gives a simple picture of how much the data varies from one extreme point to the other. A larger range reflects more dispersion.

The variance is the average value of the squares of the deviations from the mean. It is calculated by the following formula:

$$s^2 = \frac{\Sigma\,(X_i - \overline{X})^2}{n}$$

The mean value, $\overline{X}$, is subtracted from each item, X_i, and squared. These squared values are all added and divided by the sample size, n. The variance, denoted by s^2, reflects the degree to which the numbers vary from the mean.

By itself, the variance is not very useful, since it represents squared values. A more useful value is the standard deviation, s. It is calculated by taking the square root of the variance:

$$s = \sqrt{s^2} = \frac{\sqrt{\Sigma\,(X_i - \overline{X})^2}}{n}$$

As its name implies, standard deviation represents how much the data deviates from the mean value for the group. If the standard deviation is low, then the data are grouped together very closely to the mean value. If the standard deviation is large, the data are spread throughout the range.

Using the post-training data from Table 14-1, the standard deviation is:

$$s = \frac{\sqrt{\Sigma\,(X_i - \overline{X})^2}}{n} = \frac{899.78}{15} = 7.75$$

Table 14-4 shows some of the detailed calculations.

In a frequency histogram (Figure 14-1) the data graphically simulates a bell-shaped curve if the center points of each of the rectangles are connected. If there were many items with smaller intervals, the histogram would form a bell-shaped curve as shown in Figure 14-2. For this kind of distribution, which is called a normal distribution, approximately 95% of the values are within two standard deviations of the mean as the figure illustrates. In other words, two standard deviations on each side of the mean, for a total of four, account for approximately 95% of the total of the values. Therefore, for normal distributions the range will equal approximately four standard deviations. In our example of post-training measurements, the standard deviation was 7.75. Four times this standard deviation is 31, close to the actual range of 32. This represents a shortcut to calculating an approximation of the standard deviation.[4]

Table 14-4
Calculating the Standard Deviation

Post-Training Value X_i	$X_i - \overline{X}$	$(X_i - \overline{X})^2$
47	15.13*	228.92
59	3.13	9.80
79	16.87	284.60
69	6.87	47.20
63	0.87	0.76
55	7.13	50.84
51	11.13	123.88
58	4.13	17.06
72	9.87	97.42
63	0.87	0.76
61	1.13	1.28
60	2.13	4.54
65	2.87	8.24
63	0.87	0.76
67	4.87	23.72
	Total	899.78

* Sample calculation:
$\overline{X} = 62.13$, $X_i = 47$
$X_i - \overline{X} = 47 - 62.13 = -15.13$
(No need to use the minus sign, because the values are squared to get the next column.)

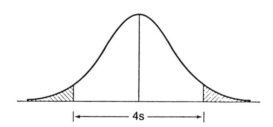

Figure 14-2. The normal distribution or bell-shaped curve.

Measures of Association

In evaluation, there is an occasional need to know if a relationship exists between two or more groups of data, or variables. This relationship is useful in predicting performance based on program results or prerequisite criteria. The following examples will help illustrate this point.

Example 1. A large manufacturer is evaluating its cooperative education program. Among other aspects, the employer wants to know if the participants' grade point average (GPA) in the program is related to their rates of promotion and salary increases after program completion. This analysis answers the question: Do co-op students with higher grades experience more job success?

Example 2. An electronics manufacturer employs electronic circuit board testers. Employees selected for this job must complete an initial training program. At the end of the program, a test is administered, covering all the procedures necessary to perform electronic circuit board testing effectively. The test scores at the end of the program are compared to both the production efficiency and quality of their work after training. The efficiency relates to the number of circuit board tests completed, and quality represents the percentage of the circuit boards tested improperly. If there is a direct relationship between end-of-the-program scores and after-the-program performance, this will assist in the validation of the test and provide a predictor of performance without the expense of a follow-up. Table 14-5 shows the program scores (listed in random order) and production efficiency for this example.

The previous examples illustrate the need to determine if a relationship exists between two variables and, if so, the extent of that relationship. The relationship is called correlation, and the degree of that relationship is measured by a correlation coefficient.

A basic approach to examining data for a possible relationship is to plot the two variables on a diagram and visually determine the likelihood of the correlation. Figure 14-3 shows a plot, called a scatter diagram, of the two variables from Table 14-5. End-of-program test scores are plotted on the horizontal, or "x," axis. The efficiency of circuit board test rates is plotted on

Table 14-5
Performance of Electronic Circuit Board Testers

Program Test Scores (%)	Production Efficiency (%)
75	105
68	95
88	116
92	119
78	111
82	113
74	100
90	120
95	125
100% = Perfect Score	100% = Standard Score

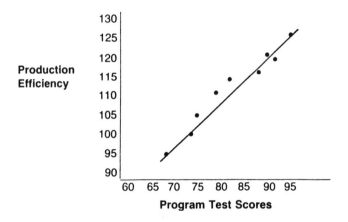

Figure 14-3. Scatter diagram of two variables.

the vertical, or "y," axis. The diagram shows that the higher the test score, the higher the efficiency rate of the employee, revealing a good possibility that there is a correlation between the two.

A relationship between two variables can be expressed in the form of an algebraic equation. The process of determining the relationship or the equation for the relationship between variables is known as curve fitting. In the example in Figure 14-3, a straight line approximates the relationship. This is called a linear relationship, and the line through the data is called a trend line. This trend line can be drawn as shown in Figure 14-3 and extended to show approximately where data will be located past the data points on the graph.

The method of determining the equation of a relationship is called the method of least squares. When the equation of the relationship is known, test scores can be plugged into the equation, and the corresponding values for production efficiency can be calculated. The specific formulas for determining the equations are beyond the scope of this book, but there are many resources, including several of those listed at the end of this chapter, appropriate for providing information on these calculations.[5]

There are several different types of correlation coefficients. The particular coefficient to use depends on the type of data, how the data are arranged, and the relationship between the two variables. Most of the data used in evaluation will be numerical from test scores and performance measurements. For this type of data, the correlation coefficient used is the Pearson's Product-Moment Correlation Coefficient. This coefficient applies only when there is a linear relationship, a straight-line relationship with no curve in the trend line of the graphic plot of the data. Fortunately, in many cases there is a linear relationship, particularly with performance data. This coefficient will be used in the remainder of this chapter. Consult the additional references for further information on other correlation coefficients and when they should be used.

The correlation coefficient varies between −1 and +1: the minus denotes negative correlation, and the plus denotes positive correlation. When there is a perfect negative correlation, the coefficient is −1; when there is no correlation between the two variables, the coefficient is 0; when there is perfect positive correlation, the coefficient is +1. Figure 14-4 illustrates these extreme situations graphically.

The range between these two extreme values represents the degree of correlation. As a rough guide, Table 14-6 shows ranges of possible correlations and their rough interpretations. These are only approximate, and the actual interpretation of a specific correlation value depends on the confidence placed on that value.[6]

The formula for calculating the correlation coefficient, r, is

$$r = \frac{n\Sigma X_i Y_i - (\Sigma X_i)(\Sigma Y_i)}{\sqrt{\left\{ n\left(\Sigma X_i^2\right) - (\Sigma X_i)^2 \right\}\left\{ n\Sigma y_i^2 - (\Sigma Y_i)^2 \right\}}}$$

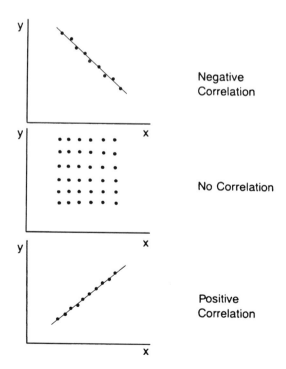

Figure 14-4. Extreme examples of correlation coefficients.

Table 14-6
Ranges of Correlation Coefficients and Their Approximate Interpretations

Correlation Value	General Description
−1.0	Perfect negative correlation
−.8 to −1.0	Very high degree of negative correlation
−.6 to −.8	High degree of negative correlation
−.4 to −.6	Medium degree of negative correlation
−.2 to −.4	Low degree of negative correlation
+.2 to −.2	Probably no correlation
+.2 to +.4	Low degree of positive correlation
+.4 to +.6	Medium degree of positive correlation
+.6 to +.8	High degree of positive correlation
+.8 to +1.0	Very high degree of positive correlation
+1.0	Perfect positive correlation

where

n = sample size.
X_i = values on the x axis.
Y_i = values on the y axis.

Most scientific calculators have this formula pre-programmed on function keys, and it is standard on many software packages. It may be helpful to illustrate the calculation, as shown in Table 14-5, using the two variables of program test scores and efficiency. Table 14-7 shows the calculations in detail. Plugging data into the formula, the coefficient is

$$r = \frac{9(83,490) - (742)(1,004)}{\sqrt{\left\{9(61,866) - (742)^2\right\}\left\{9(112,782) - (1,004)^2\right\}}} = \frac{6,442}{\sqrt{(6,230)(7,022)}} = .97$$

This coefficient represents almost perfect positive correlation. However, a word of caution is in order about correlation. The determination of a relationship between two variables does not mean that one necessarily caused the other. Outside factors could have influenced the changes. Therefore, as with many areas of statistics, this process provides additional useful information but does not provide the exact answer to the data's relationship.

Statistical Inference

Some HRD program evaluations state a hypothesis, although it is not necessary. A hypothesis is a proposed explanation of the relationship between two or more variables such as performance and training. An example is: "production employees' performance will improve as a result of the training

Table 14-7
Data for Calculating the Correlation Coefficient

Item Number	(X_i) Program Test Score	(Y_i) Production Efficiency	X_i^2	Y_i^2	X_iY_i
1	758	105	5,625*	11,025†	7,875‡
2	68	95	4,624	9,025	6,460
3	88	116	7,744	13,456	10,208
4	92	119	8,464	14,161	10,948
5	78	111	6,084	12,321	8,658
6	82	113	6,724	12,769	9,266
7	74	100	5,476	10,000	7,400
8	90	120	8,100	14,400	10,800
9	95	125	9,025	15,625	11,875
Total	742	1,004	61,866	112,782	83,490

Sample calculations:
$*X_i^2 = 75 \times 75 = 5,625$
$†Y_i^2 = 15 \times 105 = 11,025$
$‡X_iY_i = 75 \times 105 = 7,875$

program." The statement is either accepted or rejected based on the evaluation data, the results of the statistical analysis, and a statistical test. Some individuals prefer to use the terminology "fail to reject" or "not rejected" rather than "accept." The rationale is that, in some situations, failing to reject the hypothesis on the basis of a single test may not be sufficient to accept the hypothesis.[7] The development of hypotheses, statistical analyses, statistical testing, and types of errors are presented in Appendix 7. An example is included to illustrate the process.

Statistical Deception

No chapter on data analysis and interpretation would be complete without a few words warning that statistics might deceive the reader and result in erroneous conclusions from data gathered in an HRD program. Almost anything can be proved using statistics. Benjamin Disraeli, the British statesman, once said there are three kinds of lies: lies, damned lies, and statistics. The following cautions are presented to show some common ways in which statistics can deceive the casual observer, often unintentionally.[8]

Unsupported Results

A common deception is presenting conclusions from data without proper statistical analysis. This chapter discussed the necessity of conducting thorough analyses. If data are properly used in a conclusion, they should be expressed with some level of reliability or confidence. Without support, data are subject to distortion and may be useless.

Biased Sampling

Appendix 3 presents sampling procedures. An improperly selected sample used in an experimental versus control group comparison may yield inconclusive results. If the experimental group comprises high achievers and the control group represents the general population, the improvement in the experimental group, from a statistical point of view, may be conclusive. However, because of the bias in the sample selection, the actual results are distorted. Random sampling and proper sample sizes usually can overcome biases in the selection.

Improper Use of Percentages and Averages

Another error involves the use of different bases for comparisons. For example, an HRD program in quality improvement has resulted in the error rate being reduced from 20 units per 1,000 down to 15 units per 1,000. There are two ways to show that improvement. Normally, it can be expressed as a 25% reduction, a change in 5 divided by 20. However, another way to express the result is that the new error rate is 33% less than the old rate. In this case 5 is divided by 15 to give 33%. Obviously, there is a big difference in the two numbers.

Another deception relates to the use of averages. It is not unusual for a set of data to have a different value for the three types of averages: mean, median, and mode. An evaluator can improperly select the one that best suits the situation, depending on what message is needed, and disguise it under the term "average."

Graphic Distortions

Visual presentation of data in the form of graphs and charts can distort true comparisons of data. For example, examine the two charts shown in Figure 14-5. The same data are presented in two different charts, but the scale of the vertical axis is changed. The one on the right shows a very small amount of increase; the one on the left shows a large increase in proportion to the horizontal axis. This difference can easily account for a distorted picture of what has happened.

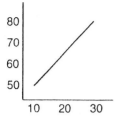
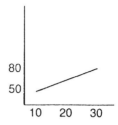

Figure 14-5. Two presentations of the same data.

Consider another example. The change in output of a steel mill's melting department resulting from an HRD program is presented visually. The output is in tons of production per employee, and a drawing of a blast furnace is used to show the visual differences in the outputs. Figure 14-6 shows that there was a 50% improvement. The blast furnace on the left shows the output before the program; the one on the right shows output after the program. The one on the right is 50% taller than the one on the left. The basis of comparison is a vertical axis only. However, the taller blast furnace has a wider base. Therefore, a 50% improvement looks like at least a 100% improvement.

Drawing Erroneous Conclusions

Much caution needs to be exercised when data from a single program, particularly on a pilot or experimental basis, are used to make inferences

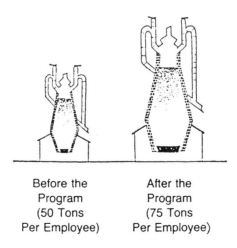

Before the
Program
(50 Tons
Per Employee)

After the
Program
(75 Tons
Per Employee)

Figure 14-6. Distortion in visual presentation.

about the entire population. If care is taken to select a random sample and the proper statistical analysis is conducted, the predictions for the remaining population will usually be accurate. However, without the proper care, distortions can easily come into play.

Consider this extreme example. Following a pilot HRD program on work simplification, one participant suggested a way to simplify a procedure, which saved the company $10,000 annually. In the report, one of the conclusions read this way:

If every employee could save $10,000, then, with an employment level of 450, the resulting savings would be $4,500,000. And since the program cost is only $50,000, a 9000% return on investment would be realized.

That is an erroneous conclusion. Only one employee had a savings of $10,000. The average savings were closer to $200. Using one statistic to make inferences about the entire population suggested a far better and vastly distorted conclusion.

Another example involves correlation. A correlation does not necessarily show a cause-and-effect relationship. Suppose the production output for a group of employees correlates with age. The older the employee, the greater the output. Using this correlation to draw a conclusion, the best recruiting strategy might be to hire employees in their sixties. Further analysis of the data reveals that the employees in the sample were in their early twenties to mid-thirties. No employees in their forties or fifties were in the sample.

The previous examples illustrate common methods of statistical deception. They represent traps the HRD program evaluator should avoid when analyzing, interpreting, and presenting data.[9]

Summary

Data analysis is important, but it may not be appropriate for every evaluation. When used, it should be kept as simple as possible. If there are problems with data analysis, seek additional resources or help from someone familiar with statistical methods.

Discussion Questions

1. How important are statistics in the evaluation process?
2. How important is data analysis to the overall evaluation process?
3. It is often said that data analysis is the most confusing, misunderstood, and feared part of evaluation. Why?
4. Why is it important to know about the dispersion of data?
5. What represents a good correlation coefficient? Why?
6. How have computers changed the data analysis process? Please elaborate.
7. How is statistical inference used in the evaluation process?
8. In your organization (or one with which you are familiar), indicate specific examples of the use of statistics in the evaluation process. Include examples of measures of central tendency, measures of dispersion, measures of association, and statistical inference.
9. Cite examples of statistical distortion in data analysis and presentation. Are they intentional or unintentional?
10. What can be done to take the fear and mystery out of data analysis?

References

1. Fink, A. *How to Analyze Survey Data.* Thousand Oaks, CA: Sage Publications, Inc., 1995.
2. Anderson, D. R., Sweeney, D. J. and Williams, T. A. *Introduction to Statistics Concepts and Applications,* 2nd Edition. St. Paul, MN: West Publishing Company, 1986.
3. Swanson, R.A. "Backyard Research in Human Resource Development," in *The ASTD Training & Development Handbook,* 4th Edition. R. L. Craig (Ed.), New York, NY: McGraw-Hill, 1996, pp. 357–369.
4. Hildebrand, D. K. and Ott, L. *Statistical Thinking for Managers,* 3rd Edition. Boston, MA: PWS-Kent Publishing Company, 1991.
5. Bobko, P. *Correlation and Regression: Principles and Applications for Industrial/Organizational Psychology and Management.* New York, NY: McGraw-Hill, Inc., 1995.
6. Daniel, W. W. and Terrell, J. C. *Business Statistics for Management and Economics,* 7th Edition. Boston, MA: Houghton Mifflin Company, 1989.
7. Fay, C. H. and Wallace, M. J. Jr. *Research-Based Decisions,* New York, NY: Random House, Inc., 1987.

8. Dewdney, A. K. *200% of Nothing.* New York, NY: John Wiley & Sons, Inc., 1993.

9. Crossen, C. *Tainted Truth: The Manipulation of Fact in America.* New York, NY: Simon & Schuster, 1994.

10. Phillips, J. J. *Return on Investment in Training and Performance Improvement Programs,* Houston, TX: Gulf Publishing Company, 1997.

CHAPTER 15

Calculating the Return on Investment

The monetary values for program benefits, developed in Chapter 11, are combined with program cost data, developed in Chapter 13, to calculate the return on investment. This chapter explores several approaches to developing the return on investment, describing various techniques, processes, and issues involved. Before presenting the formulas for calculating the ROI, a few basic issues are described. An adequate understanding of these issues is necessary to complete this major step in the ROI process.

Key ROI Issues

The Basic Concept of ROI

The term "return on investment" is often misused in HRD, sometimes intentionally. In some situations a very broad definition of ROI is used to include any benefit from the program. In these situations, ROI is a vague concept and even subjective data linked to a program are included in the concept of the return.[1] In this book, the return on investment is more precise and is meant to represent an actual value developed by comparing program cost to benefits. The two most common measures are the cost/benefit ratio and the ROI formula. Both are presented here, along with other approaches to calculating the return.

For many years, training and development practitioners and researchers have sought to calculate the actual return on the investment for training. If employee training is considered an investment—not an expense—then it is appropriate to place the training and development investment in the same funding mechanism as other investments, such as those in equipment and facilities. Although these other investments are quite different, they are often viewed by management in the same way. Thus, it is critical to the success of the training and development field that specific values that reflect the return on the investment are developed.

Annualized Values

All of the formulas presented in this chapter use annualized values to develop the first-year impact of the investment in a program. Using annual values is becoming a generally accepted practice for developing the ROI in many organizations. This approach is a conservative way to develop the ROI since many short-term training programs have added value in the second or third year. For long-term training programs, annualized values are inappropriate and longer time frames need to be used. For example, in an ROI analysis on a program to send employees to the U.S.A. to obtain an MBA degree, a Singapore-based company used a seven-year time frame. The program itself required two years, and a five-year impact with post-program data was used to develop the ROI. However, for most programs of one-day to one-month duration, first-year values are appropriate.

Communication is Critical

When selecting an approach to measure ROI, it is important to communicate to the target audience the formula used and the assumptions made to arrive at the decision to use it. This action can avoid misunderstandings and confusion surrounding how the ROI value was actually developed. Although several approaches are described in this chapter, two stand out as the preferred methods, the cost/benefit ratio and the basic ROI formula. These two approaches are described next, with only brief coverage of the other approaches.

Cost/Benefit Ratio

One of the earliest methods for evaluating training investments is the cost/benefit ratio.[2] This method compares the program's benefits to its costs. In formula form, the ratio is:

$$CBR = \frac{Program\ Benefits}{Program\ Costs}$$

In simple terms, the cost/benefit ratio compares the annual economic benefits of the program to the cost of the program. A cost/benefit ratio of one means that the benefits equal the costs. A cost/benefit ratio of two, usually written as 2:1, indicates that for each dollar spent on the program, two dollars were returned as benefits.

The following example will illustrate the use of the cost/benefit ratio. An applied behavior management program, designed for managers and supervisors, was implemented at an electric and gas utility company.[3] In a follow-up evaluation, action planning and business performance monitoring were used to capture benefits. The first-year payoff for the program was $1,077,750, while the total fully-loaded implementation costs were $215,500. Thus, the cost/benefit ratio was:

$$CBR = \frac{\$1,077,750}{\$215,500} = 5:1$$

For every one dollar invested in this program, five dollars in benefits were returned.

The principal advantage of using this approach is that it avoids traditional financial measures, so there is no confusion when comparing training investments with other company investments. For example, investments in plants, equipment, or subsidiaries are not usually evaluated with the cost/benefit method. Some training and development executives prefer not to use the same method to compare the return on training investments as is used with the return on other investments. The ROI for training investments stands alone as a unique type of evaluation.

Unfortunately, there are no standards as to what constitutes an acceptable cost/benefit ratio. A standard should be established within an organization, perhaps even for a specific type of program. However, a 1:1 ratio is unacceptable for most programs since it represents a break-even situation. In some organizations a 1.25:1 ratio is required, where 1.25 times the cost of the program is sought as a benefit.

ROI Formula

The most appropriate formula to evaluate training investments uses net program benefits divided by cost. The ratio is usually expressed as a percent. In formula form, the ROI becomes:

$$ROI\ (\%) = \frac{\text{Net Program Benefits}}{\text{Program Costs}} \times 100$$

Net benefits are program benefits minus program costs. The ROI value is related to the CBR by a factor of one. For example, a CBR of 2.45 is the same as an ROI value of 145%. This formula is essentially the same as ROI in other types of investments. For example, when a firm builds a new plant, the ROI is annual earnings divided by investment. The annual earnings is comparable to net benefits (annual benefits minus the cost), and the investment is comparable to program costs, which represent the investment in the program.

An ROI on a training investment of 50% means that the costs are fully recovered and an additional 50% of the costs are reported as "earnings." A training investment of 150% indicates that the costs have been recovered and an additional 1.5 times the costs are captured as "earnings". An example will illustrate the ROI calculation. An eighteen-week literacy program was conducted for entry-level electrical and mechanical assemblers at Magnavox Electronics Systems Company.[4] The results of the program were impressive. Productivity and quality alone yielded an annual value of $321,600, while the total fully-loaded costs for the program were only $38,233. Thus, the return on investment becomes:

$$\text{ROI}\ (\%) = \frac{\$321,600 - \$38,233}{\$38,233} \times 100 = 741\%$$

For each dollar invested, Magnavox received $7.4 dollars over the cost of the program.

The ROI formula essentially places training investments on a level playing field with other investments by using the same formula and similar concepts. The ROI calculation is easily understood by key management and financial executives who regularly use ROI with other investments.

While there are no generally accepted standards, some organizations establish a minimum requirement or hurdle rate for an ROI in a training program, such as 25%. This target value is usually above the percentage required for other types of investments. The rationale: the ROI process for training is still a relatively new concept and often involves subjective input, including estimations. Because of that, a higher standard is suggested or required.

Case Application for CBR and ROI

Background Information

Retail Merchandise Company (RMC), a large national chain located in most major American markets, attempted to boost sales with an interactive selling-skills program for sales associates. The program, developed and delivered by an outside vendor, was responding to a clearly defined need to increase the level of interaction between sales associates and customers. The program consisted of two days of skills training, one day of follow-up and additional training, and three weeks of on-the-job application of the skills. Three groups, from electronics departments in three stores, were initially trained as a pilot implementation. The program had a total of forty-eight participants.

ROI Analysis

Post-program data collection was accomplished using three methods. First, the average weekly sales of each associate were monitored (business performance monitoring of output data). Second, a follow-up questionnaire was distributed three months after the training's completion to determine Level 3 success (actual application of the skills on the job). Third, by design, the third day of the program served as a follow-up session during which Level 3 data were solicited. In this session, participants disclosed their success (or lack thereof) with the application of new skills. They also discussed techniques to overcome the barriers to program implementation.

The method used to isolate the effects of training was a control group arrangement. Three store locations were identified (control group) to compare with the three groups in the pilot training (experimental group). Store size, store location, and customer traffic levels were used to match the two groups so that they could be as identical as possible. The method used to convert data to monetary values is a direct profit contribution of the increased output. The actual profit obtained from an additional one dollar of sales was readily available and used in the calculation.

CBR and ROI Calculations

Although the program was evaluated at all five levels, the emphasis was on the Level 5 calculation. Level 1, 2 and 3 data either met or exceeded expectations. Table 15-1 shows the Level 4 data, which was the average weekly sales of both groups after the training. For convenience and at the

Table 15-1
Level 4 Data: Average Weekly Sales

| Weeks After Training | Post-Training Data | |
	Trained Groups	Control Groups
1	$9,723	$9,698
2	9,978	9,720
3	10,424	9,812
13	13,690	11,572
14	11,491	9,683
15	11,044	10,092
Average for weeks 13, 14, 15	$12,075	$10,449

request of management, a three-month follow-up period was used. Management wanted to implement the program at other locations if it appeared to be successful in this first three months of operation. Although three months may be premature to determine the total impact of the program, it often is a convenient time period for evaluation. Table 15-1 shows data for the first three weeks after training, as well as for the last three weeks of the evaluation period (weeks 13, 14, and 15). The data shows what appears to be a significant difference in the two values.

Two steps are required to move from Level 4 data to Level 5: Level 4 data must be converted to monetary values, and the cost of the program must be tabulated. Table 15-2 shows the annualized program benefits. Because only forty-six participants were still in their job after 3 months, the other two participants' potential improvement was removed from the calculation. The profit contribution at the store level, obtained directly from the accounting department, was 2%, meaning that for every one dollar of additional sales attributed to the program, two cents would be considered to be the added value. At the corporate level, the number was even smaller, about 1.2%. First-year annualized values are used to reflect the total impact of the program. Ideally, if new skills are acquired as indicated in the Level 3 evaluation, there should be some value for the use of those skills in year two or perhaps even year three. However, for short-term training programs, only the first-year values are used, thus requiring the investment to have an acceptable return in a one-year time period. The total benefit of this training program was $71,760.

Table 15-3 shows the cost summary for this three-course program. Costs are fully-loaded, including data for all forty-eight participants. Since the program is conducted by a vendor, there are no direct development costs. The facilitation fee covers the pro-rated development costs as well as the delivery costs. The participants' salaries plus a 35% factor for employee benefits were included. Facilities costs were included although the company does not normally capture the costs when internal facilities are used, as was the case

Table 15-2
Annualized Program Benefits

Average Weekly Sales Trained Groups	$12,075
Average Weekly Sales Untrained Groups	$10,449
Increase	$ 1,626
Profit Contribution 2%	$ 32.50
Total Weekly Improvement ($\times$ 46*)	$ 1,495
Total Annual Benefits ($\times$ 48 weeks)	**$71,760**

* Forty-six participants were still in job after 3 months

Table 15-3
Cost Summary

Facilitation Fees: 3 courses @ $3,750	$11,250
Program Materials: 48 @ $35/participant	1,680
Meals/Refreshments: 3 days @ $28/participant/day	4,032
Facilities: 9 days @ $120	1,080
Participant Salaries Plus Benefits (35%)	12,442
Coordination/Evaluation	2,500
Total Costs	**$32,984**

with this program. The estimated costs for the coordination and evaluation were also included, for a total program cost of $32,984. Thus, the cost/benefit ratio becomes:

$$CBR = \frac{\$71,760}{\$32,984} = 2.2 : 1$$

and the return on investment becomes:

$$ROI\ (\%) = \frac{\$71,760 - \$32,984}{\$32,984} \times 100 = 118\%$$

Thus, the program has an excellent return on investment in its initial trial run after three months of on-the-job application of skills.

Other ROI Measures

In addition to the traditional ROI formula described above, several other measures are occasionally used under the general term of return on investment. These measures are designed primarily for evaluating other types of financial measures, but sometimes work their way into training evaluations.

Payback Period

The payback period is a common method for evaluating capital expenditures. With this approach, the annual cash proceeds (savings) produced by an investment are equated to the original cash outlay required by the investment to arrive at some multiple of cash proceeds equal to the original investment. Measurement is usually in terms of years and months. For example, if the cost savings generated from an HRD program are constant each year, the payback period is determined by dividing the total original cash investment (development costs, outside program purchases, etc.) by the amount of the expected annual or actual savings. The savings represent the net savings after the program expenses are subtracted. To illustrate this calculation, assume that an initial program's costs are $100,000 with a three-year useful life. The annual net savings from the program are expected to be $40,000. Then:

$$\text{Payback period} = \frac{\text{Total Investment}}{\text{Net Annual Savings}} = \frac{100,000}{40,000} = 2.5 \text{ years}$$

The program will "pay back" the original investment in 2.5 years.

The payback period is simple to use, but has the limitation of ignoring the time value of money. It has not enjoyed widespread use in evaluating training investments.

Discounted Cash Flow

Discounted cash flow is a method of evaluating investment opportunities that assigns certain values to the timing of the proceeds from the investment. The assumption, based on interest rates, is that a dollar earned today is more valuable than a dollar earned a year from now.

There are several ways of using the discounted cash-flow concept to evaluate capital expenditures such as a large investment in an HRD program. The most popular one is probably the net present value of an investment. This approach compares the savings, year by year, with the outflow of cash required by the investment. The expected savings received each year is discounted by selected interest rates. The outflow of cash is discounted by the same interest rate. If the present value of the savings should exceed the present value of the outlays after discounting at a common interest rate, the investment is usually acceptable in the eyes of management. The discounted cash-flow method has the advantage of ranking investments, but it becomes difficult to calculate and may be too confusing for most training and development professionals.

Internal Rate of Return

The internal rate of return (IRR) method determines the interest rate required to make the present value of the cash flow equal to zero. It represents the maximum rate of interest that could be paid if all project funds were borrowed and the organization had to break even on the projects. The IRR considers the time value of money and is not affected by the scale of the project. It can be used to rank alternatives, and can be used to make accept/reject decisions when a minimum rate of return is specified. A major weakness of the IRR method is that it assumes that all returns are reinvested at the same internal rate of return. This can make an investment alternative with a high rate of return look even better than it really is and a project with a low rate of return look even worse. In practice, the IRR is rarely used to evaluate training investments.

Utility Analysis

Another interesting approach for developing training's payoff is utility analysis. Utility is a function of the duration of a training program's effect on employees, the number of employees trained, the validity of the training program, the value of the job for which training was provided, and the total cost of the program.[5]

Utility analysis measures the economic contribution of a program according to how effective the program was in identifying and modifying behavior, and hence the future service contribution of employees. Schmidt, Hunter, and Pearlman derived the following formula for assessing the dollar value of a training program:[5]

$$\Delta U = T \times N \times dt \times Sdy - N \times C$$

where

ΔU = dollar value of the training program.

T = duration, in number of years, of a training program's effect on performance.

N = number of employees trained.

dt = true difference in job performance between the average trained and the average untrained employees in units of standard deviation.

Sdy = standard deviation of job performance of the untrained group in dollars.

C = cost of training per employee.

Of all the factors in this formula, the true difference in job performance and the value of the target job are the most difficult to develop. The validity is determined by noting the performance differences between trained and untrained employees. The simplest method for obtaining this information is to have supervisors rate the performance of each group. The value of the target job, Sdy, is estimated by supervisors and experts in the organization.

Utility analysis is based totally on estimations. Because of the subjective nature of this approach, it has not achieved widespread acceptance by training and development professionals as a practical tool for evaluating the return on training investments.

Consequences of Not Training

For some training situations, the consequences of not training can be very serious. A company's inability to perform adequately might mean that it is unable to take on additional business or that it may lose existing business because of an untrained work force. Also, training can help avoid serious operational problems such as accidents or non-compliance issues. This method of calculating the return on training has received recent attention and involves the following steps:

1. Establish that there is a potential problem, loss, or opportunity.
2. Develop an estimate of the potential value of the problem, loss, or opportunity.
3. Isolate the factors involved in lack of performance that may create problems, such as non-compliance, loss of business, or an inability to take on additional business.
4. If other factors are involved, determine the impact of each factor on the loss of income.
5. Estimate the total cost of training using the techniques outlined in Chapter 13.
6. Compare costs with benefits.[6]

This approach has some disadvantages. The potential loss of income can be highly subjective and difficult to measure. Also, it may be difficult to isolate the factors involved and determine their weight relative to lost income. Because of these concerns, this approach to evaluating the return on training investments is limited to certain types of programs and situations.

ROI Issues

ROI Complexity

Developing the return on investment in training and development is a complex issue. This book takes the process and breaks it down into small steps in an attempt to simplify the process and make it understandable to a variety of audiences. Figure 15-1 illustrates the complexity of this process.

This book presented the ten most common ways to collect post-program data, ten ways to isolate the effects of training on business performance measures, and ten ways to convert data into monetary values. In essence, there are 1,000 possible ways to evaluate a training program, as shown in Figure 15-1. This alone is often enough to cause some individuals to avoid the ROI process. However, when each step is taken separately, the decisions are

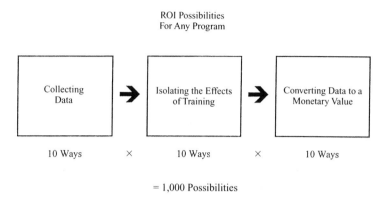

Figure 15-1. ROI complexity.

made incrementally all the way through the process. This reduces a complex process to a more simplified and manageable effort. Figure 15-1 underscores an important advantage of the ROI process: with so many different ways to tackle these three critical issues, the process can be applied to almost any type of program in any setting.

Cautions When Using ROI

Because of the complexity and sensitivity of the ROI process, caution is needed when developing, calculating, and communicating the return on investment. The implementation of the ROI process is a very important issue that is a goal of many training and development departments.[7] A few issues, described below, should be addressed to keep the process from going astray.

The ROI process should be developed for programs for which a needs assessment has been conducted. Because evaluation problems can develop when there is not a clear needs assessment, it is recommended that the ROI be conducted only with programs for which there has been a comprehensive needs assessment, preferably with Level 3 and Level 4 data. However, practical considerations and management requests may prohibit this suggested requirement.

The ROI analysis should always include one or more strategies for isolating the effects of training. This step in the process must not be ignored due to the importance of accounting for the influence of other factors. Too often, an excellent study from what appears to be a very successful training effort is perceived to be worthless because there was no attempt to account for other factors. Omission of this step seriously diminishes the value of the study.

When making estimates, use the most reliable and credible sources. Because estimates are critical to any type of analysis, they will often be an important part of the ROI process. When they are used, they should be developed properly and obtained from reliable and credible sources who understand the overall situation and can provide the most accurate estimation.

Take a conservative approach to developing both benefits and costs. Conservatism in ROI analysis builds accuracy and credibility. What matters most is how the target audience perceives the value of the data, so a conservative approach is always recommended for both the numerator of the ROI formula (benefits) and the denominator (program costs).

Use caution when comparing the ROI in training and development with other financial returns. There are many ways to calculate the return on funds invested or assets employed to produce earnings. The ROI is just one of them. Although the calculation for ROI in training and development uses the same basic formula as in other investment evaluations, it may not be fully understood by the target group. Its method of calculation and meaning should be clearly communicated. More importantly, it should be an item accepted by management as an appropriate measure for training program evaluation.

Involve management in developing the return. Management ultimately makes the decision as to whether or not an ROI value is acceptable. Therefore, management should be involved in setting the parameters for calculations and establishing targets by which programs are judged acceptable within the organization.[8]

Approach sensitive and controversial issues with caution. Occasionally, sensitive and controversial issues will be generated when discussing an ROI value. It is best to avoid debates over what is measurable and what is not measurable unless there is clear evidence of the issue in the specific program under discussion. Also, some programs are so fundamental to the survival of the organization that any attempt to measure it is unnecessary. For example, a program designed to improve customer service in a customer-focused company may escape the scrutiny of an ROI evaluation on the assumption that if the program is well designed, it will improve customer service.

Teach others the methods for calculating the return. Each time an ROI is calculated, the training and development manager should use the opportunity to educate other managers and colleagues in the organization. Even if it is not in their area of responsibility, these individuals will be able to see the value of this approach to training and development evaluation. Also, when possible, each project should serve as a case study to educate the HRD staff on specific techniques and methods.

Do not boast about a high return. It is not unusual to generate what appears to be a very high return on investment for an HRD program.[9] Several examples in this book have illustrated the possibilities. An HRD manager boasting about a high rate of return will be open to potential criticism from others, including the finance and accounting staff, unless there are indisputable facts on which the calculation is based.

Do not try to use ROI on every program. Some programs are difficult to quantify and an ROI calculation may not be feasible. Other methods of presenting the benefits may be more appropriate. HRD executives are encouraged to set targets for the percentage of programs for which ROIs are developed. Also, specific criteria should be established to use in selecting programs for this type of analysis.

Converting to a Profit Center

Another approach to measuring the return on investment on HRD is to convert the department to a profit-center concept. The concept involves a conversion from a budget-based center to one that either breaks even or generates a profit. The revenue is generated from sales of products, programs, or services delivered to the user departments. A profit-center approach can replace or be used in conjunction with individual ROI calculations. Although the concept is in the embryonic stage, many organizations have at least planned for the conversion.[10]

One company was forced to embrace this concept during restructuring.[11] The education division of IBM, once a much-admired training entity that spent $2 billion on worldwide training each year, has refashioned itself into a very different kind of training field.

In brief, the company has

☐ Spun off its vaunted education division into two separate IBM subsidiaries—Skill Dynamics and Workforce Solutions—that are expected to keep balance sheets and report profit-and-loss statements to IBM corporate headquarters, as do other IBM operating units.

☐ Told those two entities that they must sink or swim. In other words, if Workforce Solutions and Skill Dynamics can't persuade anyone inside or outside the parent company to buy training products and services from them, they'll go out of business. IBM headquarters provides no subsidy.

☐ Freed its education subsidiaries to sell training products and services, including custom-designed training, to any outside company that will pay for it. During 1993, Skill Dynamics took in an estimated $130 million from sales to outside firms.

By undertaking such significant change in the way the company delivers training, IBM officials are tacitly acknowledging that their old approach to education and development was, if not wrong, at least unsuited to the kind of organization IBM wants to become.

Rationale for Conversion

No department wants to be a burden on others. Yet many HRD departments are considered staff overhead. The HRD staff is referred to as excess, overhead, a burden, or an administrative expense. Those references create frustrating conditions for many professional HRD personnel. One way to move to a self-sufficient posture is to convert the HRD department to a profit center.[12]

The profit-center concept lessens the need to calculate the ROI for individual programs, because the profit generated from revenues is used to calculate an overall return for the department. Unprofitable programs will either be subsidized by profitable ones or disappear. However, there is still a need for evaluation because of all the purposes other than cost/benefit comparisons.[13]

Some professionals perceive the HRD profit-center concept as being the same as an independent HRD/consulting firm. Hundreds of firms provide consulting services and HRD programs as their sole source of revenue. They develop and customize in-house programs to meet their clients' needs. They have survived and make a profit; many of them are very successful. The internal HRD department should be able to provide the same programs or services, also at a profit.[14]

If the profit-center concept is effective, the HRD department must negotiate or establish fees and prices for parts or all of their efforts. There are several types of profit-center concepts, and many issues must be considered before making this conversion. The remainder of this chapter will be devoted to these issues and an initial discussion of the true profit center.

Sources of Revenue

A typical HRD department has several sources of revenue. These are usually divided into the following categories:

Professional services. Departments pay for services, including professional staff time devoted to assisting an organization in conflict resolution, problem solving, needs analysis, or other activities aimed at developing employees in the organization. Service fees may be collected on the development work necessary to produce an HRD program.

Program fees. Internal clients pay fees for seminars, workshops, or HRD programs. Fees cover the costs of delivering an HRD program as well as overhead, analysis, development, and evaluation.

Products. Product sales include the self-contained packaged programs for departments or divisions within the organization. For example, a self-sufficient computer-based instruction course that does not necessarily need support from the HRD staff is sold at a fixed price.

Administrative services. Departments are charged fees for routine services provided by the HRD staff. Examples include processing tuition refund requests, coordinating outside seminar participation, or maintaining a human resources planning system.

A few organizations also have outside income from sales of services and programs to other organizations. DuPont, General Motors, Xerox, and Westinghouse are only a few of the many organizations now selling their programs to the public.

Fee/Price Determination

The determination of fees, charges, or prices for revenue items is critical to the success of a conversion. Prices must be high enough for the department to generate the desired profit, yet low enough to be competitively priced. Three basic approaches are available for setting fees.

Fee negotiation. The HRD staff and the client organization, whether a department, division, or section, can negotiate a fair and equitable fee for the services offered. This approach is particularly useful when determining the fee to charge for professional assistance. Some consideration might be given to using a rate similar to those set by external HRD consulting firms providing the same or similar service.

Competitive pricing. Another possibility is to price the program or service equal to or less than the market price for the same or similar items. This is probably the best approach when pricing a product such as a packaged HRD program or a workshop similar to one offered publicly. The prices must compete with those that are commercially available and, ideally, should be lower than those the organization can obtain externally. Of course, the enhanced quality and custom tailoring should be a definite plus. This approach is difficult when a program is needed, and no programs are commercially available for comparison. In this situation, programs similar in terms of length, content, and difficulty may be used for comparison purposes.

Administrative service charges. A third approach is to establish a service charge for providing a service to the organization. This charge, determined internally with input from finance and accounting personnel, should be fair and equitable. An example is a 10% service charge for processing all tuition refund applications.

Variations of the Profit-Center Concept

The concept just described is a true profit center. With fixed or negotiated fees and prices, revenue offsets expenses, and additional funds represent profit generated by the HRD department. The ROI is the department earnings divided by the investment in resources to deliver those products and services. While this concept may seem to represent utopia, it is in the distant future for most organizations. Other variations short of the true profit center may be appropriate for some organizations on an interim basis.

Protected profit center. A profit center that is subsidized to ensure the availability of resources is called a protected profit center. This approach involves pricing some services and products and subsidizing other programs and essential services. This approach assumes that it is difficult to establish prices for some necessary services. Other departments and sections may not use the HRD department to supply those services, and the result may cause inefficiencies. For example, if a department was unwilling to pay a 10% administrative service charge for the tuition refund program and insisted on processing its own tuition refunds, it could jeopardize the program's standards. An easy way to avoid this problem is to subsidize the department to provide funds necessary to administer those programs.

Cost center. Another approach involves estimating the cost of various services and products delivered and charging the client for those costs. All department costs are allocated in some way to user departments. This approach requires detailed and accurate cost forecasts and cost accumulation. Also, when parts of the organization refuse to use a program or service, the cost for providing that service to other parts of the organization may increase. For example, suppose ten departments share the cost of an HRD program and two departments decide not to participate. All costs, including prorated development and delivery costs, must be spread over eight departments instead of ten, raising the overall cost of those departments. This approach provides little incentive for HRD departments to minimize costs, and there is no opportunity for a profit.

Break-even center. This variation is similar to the cost-center concept, except that fees and prices are established to enable the department to reach a break-even point at the year's end. Higher prices are established for popular or frequently offered programs to offset losses on programs or services that are difficult to price or represent a loss. With this approach, users may pay more for some programs and less for others, when they should cost approximately the same. One problem is the lack of opportunity to profit in the HRD department.

Considerations for Conversion

Several critical factors should be considered when converting from present operation to a version of the profit-center concept. The strength or weakness of these factors may determine if such a move is feasible.

Gradual change. A conversion from an expense-based department to a profit center requires a gradual change. Management may have concerns about the concept of paying for these services. One organization approached the conversion with the following ten steps:

1. Establish HRD accounts in each department.
2. Allocate all costs of outside programs/seminars to user departments.
3. Allocate the costs of special, non-routine HRD programs.
4. Charge each user department for tuition refunds of their employees.
5. Charge a fee for participation in major programs.
6. Set prices for all formal HRD programs.
7. Charge all management trainee salaries to the sponsoring department.
8. Negotiate fees for new program development.
9. Negotiate fees for consulting work.
10. Charge an administration fee for all regular support services.

This organization took approximately five years to move from a centralized budget-based department to a self-sufficient profit center.

Effective products and services. Products and services provided by the organization must be effective and perceived as a worthwhile investment. The HRD department must have an excellent reputation and be known for success with previous programs; otherwise, such a conversion could be disastrous.

Management commitment and support. A successful conversion requires good management support and commitment at all levels. Management must see the need for effective HRD and be willing to pay for it, investing today for a return tomorrow. Also, managers must be willing to let employees participate in programs and become more involved in the development and implementation of new programs.

HRD staff commitment. Another consideration is the commitment of the full HRD staff. Too often, a major change is implemented at the initiation of a single key individual in the HRD department. A successful conversion requires the commitment and involvement of the entire staff. Otherwise, the function could cease to exist.

Competitive fees/prices. Revenue items must be competitively priced. Charging more than the competition on the premise of providing a better product may not influence profit-minded executives. Operating department managers are seeking results, and they must be convinced that they will be receiving a superior product at a fair price.

Method of charges. Simple and equitable methods for charging departments must be devised. One problem that may surface is double charges. In many organizations, the HRD department is funded through direct charges or allocations to all operating departments, regardless of their participation in these programs. If a department is charged an additional fee for employee participation in an HRD program then, in effect, there is a double charge. This perception has caused some conversion efforts to fail.

A more realistic approach is to credit a predetermined amount to those departments and charge only if the fees or prices of the products and services used become greater than the allocated amount. This approach encourages use of the products and services of the HRD department. For example, suppose a department has a $15,000 cost allocation for the HRD department. When the department sends a participant to a program or otherwise uses a department service, the predetermined fee or price is credited to the fictitious department account. If the department uses more than $15,000, the excess amount is charged against the department. A manager interested in HRD will certainly use the total allocation for the department, assuring that $15,000 worth of HRD products and services are used.

Profit-center impact. A final factor should be considered before pursuing the conversion. The impact of the profit-center concept on the organization should be assessed thoroughly. This impact analysis includes the types of courses delivered, services provided, the reaction of the management group, and the reaction of the HRD staff.

Some courses, particularly those perceived as unnecessary, will die a natural death because no one will pay for them. This may be cause for concern. For example, suppose all team leaders, supervisors, and managers have been required to participate in a valuing diversity workshop. The company feels that it is necessary for all leaders to understand various laws and the company's commitment to diversity. Some managers may be reluctant to send participants to the program if it is not perceived as essential. These issues must be addressed before conversion.

Some insight into potential impact may be gained by surveying the management group to determine to what extent they will use the department's services if they must pay directly for them. The results of this survey can help determine if the process is feasible. Negative attitudes could signal problems ahead or pinpoint areas where attention is needed before implementing a conversion plan.

Caution. It is important to examine the philosophy and structure of the organization when implementing this concept. The profit-center concept is not as effective if training is decentralized to the lowest level in the organization, because it is difficult to pinpoint precise costs to be charged to the user organization. In essence, a highly centralized approach moves the cost of training nearest to the user organization and this action is a step toward the concept of paying for services provided.

Overall, the profit-center approach is a legitimate, viable alternative for many organizations.[15] It should only be tackled if human resource development is respected and already considered a contributing force in the organization. A conversion that succeeds can be very rewarding to the HRD department. A failure can be disastrous.

Summary

After program benefits are collected and converted to monetary values, and program costs are developed in a fully-loaded profile, the ROI calculation becomes very easy. It is just a matter of plugging in the appropriate formula to develop the value. This chapter has presented the two basic approaches to calculating the return: the ROI formula, and the cost/benefit ratio. Each has its own advantages and disadvantages. Other approaches were briefly discussed as alternatives to an ROI development. Several examples were presented along with key issues that must be addressed in ROI calculations. Profit center is an extension of ROI and may represent a feasible approach for some organizations. When approached methodically and gradually a profit center can dramatically change an HRD department.

Discussion Questions

1. What are the advantages and disadvantages of using annualized values in the ROI formula? When would this approach not be appropriate?
2. In what type of projects would the calculation of a return on investment be most appropriate? What type would be least appropriate?
3. The ROI values reported in literature are often quite large—in the 100–500% range. How do you account for these large values?
4. It is often reported that supervisory training, management training, and sales training are high-impact training programs. Explain.
5. What are some advantages of return on investment over other types of quantitative evaluations?
6. What are the advantages of using the cost/benefit ratio over other financial measures?
7. Search the literature for an example in which a return on investment has been calculated. Critique the approach and the results.
8. What are the advantages of utility analysis? Disadvantages?
9. What important precautions should be taken when monetary values are reported in program evaluations?
10. Why has the profit center concept been slow to develop?
11. Develop a plan to convert the HRD department in your organization (or one with which you are familiar) from an expense-based to a profit center concept.
12. What are some natural barriers to the use of the profit center concept?
13. Under what conditions should a profit center approach be considered?

References

1. Lyau, N. M. and Pucel, D. J. "Economic Return on Training Investment at the Organization Level," *Performance Improvement Quarterly,* 8 (3), 1995, pp. 68–79.
2. Marrelli, A. F. "Determining Training Costs, Benefits, and Results," *Technical & Skills Training,* November/December 1993, pp. 8–14.
3. Westcott, R. "Applied Behavior Management Training," in *In Action: Measuring Return on Investment,* Vol. 1. J. Phillips (Ed.), Alexandria, VA: American Society for Training and Development, 1994, pp. 235–252.
4. Ford, D. "Three Rs in the Workplace," in *In Action: Measuring Return on Investment,* Vol. 1. J. Phillips (Ed.), Alexandria, VA: American Society for Training and Development, 1994, pp. 85–104.
5. Schmidt, F. L., Hunter, J. E. and Pearlman, K. "Assessing the Economic Impact of Personnel Programs on Workforce Productivity," *Personnel Psychology,* Vol. 35, p. 333–347, 1982.

6. Johnson, D. A. "Cost-Effectiveness Evaluation of Decentralized International Technical Training," *Human Resource Development Quarterly,* Vol. 4, No. 3, Fall 1993, pp. 265–275.

7. Fitz-enz, J. "Yes . . . You Can Weigh In Training's Value," *Training,* July 1994, pp. 54–58.

8. Parry, S. B. "Measuring Training's ROI," *Training & Development,* May 1996, pp. 72–77.

9. Davidove, E.A. "Evaluating the Return on Investment of Training," *Performance & Instruction,* January 1993, pp. 1–8.

10. Chaddock, P. "Building Value with Training," *Training & Development,* July 1995, pp. 22–26.

11. Geber, B. "A Clean Break for Education at IBM," *Training,* February 1994, pp. 33–36.

12. Smith, P. A. "Reinventing SunU," *Training & Development,* July 1994, pp. 23–27.

13. Filipczak, B. "The Business of Training at NCR," *Training,* February 1992, pp. 55–59.

14. Smith, E. "Continuous Learning Arthur Andersen Style," *Corporate University Review,* July/August 1996, pp. 14–19.

15. Noonan, J. V. "How to Escape Corporate America's Basement," *Training,* December 1993, pp. 39–42.

CHAPTER 16

ROI at Multiple Levels

Sometimes there is confusion about when it is appropriate to develop the ROI, including the types of data to collect and the level of evaluation that is appropriate for an ROI calculation. The traditional, and recommended, approach is to base ROI calculations strictly on business results from the program. Business performance measures (Level 4 data) are converted to a monetary value to include in the ROI calculation. Sometimes these measures are not available and it is assumed that an ROI calculation is out of the question. This chapter shows how ROI calculations are possible at all levels of evaluation.

ROI at Level 1: Reaction

When a Level 1 evaluation includes planned applications of training, important data can be collected that can ultimately be used in an ROI calculation. By including a series of questions that ask how participants plan to apply what they have learned and the results that they expect to achieve, higher-level evaluation information can be developed. Figure 16-1 presents questions that illustrate how this type of data is collected with an end-of-program questionnaire for a supervisory training program. Participants are asked to state specifically how they plan to use the program material and the results they expect to achieve. They are then asked to convert their accomplishments to an annual monetary value and show the basis for developing those values. Participants can moderate their responses by indicating their level of confidence with the process, making the data more credible.

In the tabulation of data, the confidence level is multiplied by the annual monetary value to develop a conservative estimate to use in the data analysis. For example, if a participant estimated that the monetary impact of the program would be $10,000, but was only 50% confident, a $5,000 value is used in the calculations.

Several steps are taken to develop a summary of expected benefits. First, any data that are incomplete, unusable, extreme, or unrealistic are discarded. Next, an adjustment is made for the confidence estimate, as described above. Individual data items are then totaled. Finally, as an optional exercise, the

---

Planned Improvements

■ What do you estimate to be the increase in your personal effectiveness as a result of this program, expressed as a percent?

■ Please indicate what you will do differently on the job as a result of this program. (Please be specific.)

1. _____

2. _____

3. _____

4. _____

5. _____

■ Please estimate (in monetary values) the annual benefits to your organization (for example, reduced absenteeism, reduced employee complaints, better teamwork, increased personal effectiveness, etc.) as a result of any change in your thinking, new ideas, or planned actions.

_____

_____

■ What is the basis of this estimate?

_____

_____

■ What confidence, expressed as a percentage, can you put in your estimate? (0% = No Confidence; 100% = Certainty) _____%

Figure 16-1. Important questions to ask on feedback questionnaires.

total value is adjusted again by a factor that reflects the subjectivity of the process and the possibility that participants will not achieve the results they anticipate. This figure can be developed with input from management or established by the training and development staff. Some organizations divide the benefits by two to develop a number to use in the equation. Finally, the ROI is calculated using the net program benefits divided by the program costs. This value, in essence, becomes the expected return on investment.

This process can be best described using an actual case. M&H Engineering and Construction Company designs and constructs large commercial projects such as plants, paper mills, and municipal water systems. Safety is a critical issue at M&H and commands much management attention. To improve the current level of safety performance, a two-day safety awareness program was developed for project engineers and construction superintendents. The program focused on safety leadership, safety planning, safety training, safety meetings, accident investigation, safety policy and procedures, safety standards, and worker compensation. A dozen safety performance measures used in the company were also presented and discussed. After completing the training program, participants were expected to improve the safety performance of their specific construction projects. At the end of the two-day program, participants completed a comprehensive Level 1 reaction questionnaire that probed into specific action items and their monetary value, planned as a result of this program. In addition, participants were asked to explain the basis for their estimates and place a confidence level on them.

Table 16-1 presents data provided by the first group of participants. Only 18 of the 24 participants supplied usable data. (Our experience has shown that approximately 50–70% of participants will provide usable data on this series of questions.) The total cost of the program, including participant salaries, was $29,000. Prorated development costs were included in this figure.

The monetary value of the planned improvements is extremely high, reflecting the optimism and enthusiasm of participants at the end of a very effective program. As a first step in the analysis, extreme data items are omitted. Data such as millions, unlimited, and $4,000,000 are discarded, and each remaining value is multiplied by the confidence value and totaled. The resulting tabulations yielded a total improvement of $655,125. Because of the subjectivity of the process, the values were adjusted by a factor of two, an arbitrary number suggested by the HRD manager and supported by the management group. This "adjusted" value is $327,563, or $328,000 with

Table 16-1
Level 1 Data for ROI Calculations

Participant No.	Estimated Value	Basis	Confidence Level
1	$ 80,000	Reduction in Accidents	90%
2	$ 90,000	OSHA Reportable Injuries	80%
3	$ 50,000	Accident Reduction	100%
4	$ 10,000	First Aid Visits/Visits to Doctor	100%
5	$ 50,000	Reduction in Lost-Time Injuries	95%
6	$ Millions	Total Accident Cost	100%
7	$ 75,000	Worker Compensation	80%
8	$ 7,500	OSHA Citations	75%
9	$ 50,000	Reduction in Accidents	100%
10	$ 30,000	Worker Compensation	80%
11	$ 150,000	Reduction in Total Accident Costs	90%
12	$ 20,000	OSHA Fines/Citations	70%
13	$ 40,000	Accident Reductions	100%
14	$ 4,000,000	Total Cost of Safety	95%
15	$ 65,000	Total Worker Compensation	50%
16	$ Unlimited	Accidents	100%
17	$ 45,000	Injuries	90%
18	$ 2,000	Visits to Doctor	100%

rounding. The projected ROI based on the end-of-program questionnaire is as follows:

$$ROI = \frac{328,000 - 29,000}{29,000} \times 100 = 1,031\%$$

These projected values should be communicated with caution, although the value was twice adjusted downward. It should be emphasized that the forecasted results, while subjective, were generated by participants in the program who should be aware of what they can accomplish. The communication should also mention that a follow-up is planned to determine if the results were actually delivered by the group.

A further word of caution is in order when using Level 1 ROI data. These calculations are highly subjective and may not reflect the extent to which participants will apply what they have learned and achieve results. A variety of influences in the work environment can enhance or inhibit participants' attainment of performance goals, and high expectations at the end of a program are no guarantee that those expectations will be met. Disappointments are documented regularly in programs throughout the world and are reported in research findings.[1]

While this process is subjective and possibly unreliable, it is somewhat useful. First, if evaluation must stop at this level, this approach provides more insight into the value of the program than data from typical reaction questionnaires. (Managers will usually find this data more useful than a report stating, for example, "80% of participants rated the program above average.") Unfortunately, there is evidence that a high percentage of evaluations stop at this first level of evaluation.[2] The majority of HRD programs do not enjoy rigorous evaluations at Levels 3 and 4, and reporting Level 1 ROI data is still a more useful indication of the program's potential impact than simply reporting attitudes and feelings about the program and instructor.

Second, this data can form a basis for comparison of different presentations of the same program. If one program forecasts an ROI of 300% whereas another projects 30%, then it appears that one program may be more effective than the other. The participants in the first program have more confidence in the planned application of the program material.

Third, collecting this type of data causes increased attention to program outcomes. Participants leave the program with an understanding that specific behavior change is expected, which produces results for the organization. This issue becomes clear to participants as they anticipate results and convert them to monetary values. Even if this projected improvement does not materialize, the exercise sends an important message to participants.

Fourth, if a follow-up is planned to pinpoint post-program results, the data collected in the Level 1 evaluation can be very helpful for comparison. This end-of-program data collection helps participants plan the implementation of what they have learned. (Incidentally, when a follow-up is planned, participants are more conservative with these estimates.)

The use of Level 1 ROI is increasing and some organizations have based all of their ROI calculations on Level 1 data.[3] Although it may be very subjective, it does add value, particularly when it is included as part of a comprehensive evaluation system.

ROI at Level 2: Testing

Testing for changes in skills and knowledge is a common technique for Level 2 evaluation. In many situations, participants are required to demonstrate their knowledge or skills at the end of the program and their performance is expressed as a numerical value. When this type of test is developed, it must be reliable and valid. A reliable test is one that has consistent results over time. A valid test is one that measures what it purports to measure. Since a test should reflect the content of the HRD program, successful mastery of program content should be related to improved job performance. Consequently, there should be a relationship between test scores and subsequent on-the-job performance. Figure 16-2 illustrates this relationship between test scores and job performance in a perfect correlation. This relationship, expressed as a correlation coefficient, is a measure of the test's validity.

This testing situation provides an excellent opportunity for an ROI calculation using test results (Level 2 data). When there is a statistically significant relationship between test scores and on-the-job performance, and the performance can be converted to monetary units, then it is possible to use test scores to estimate the ROI from the program, using the following steps:

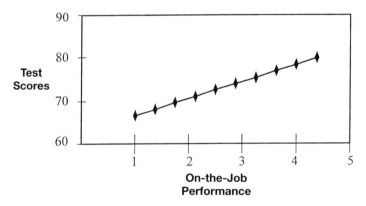

Figure 16-2. Relationship between test scores and performance.

1. Ensure that the program content reflects desired on-the-job performance.
2. Develop an end-of-program test that reflects program content.
3. Establish a statistical relationship between participants' test data and output performance.
4. Predict each participant's performance levels with given test scores.
5. Convert performance data to monetary value.
6. Compare total predicted value of program with program costs.

An example illustrates this approach. Consumer Products Marketing (CPM) is the marketing division of a large consumer products company. Sales representatives for CPM make frequent sales calls on large retail food and drug companies with the objective of increasing sales and market share of CPM products. Sales representatives must ensure that retailers understand the advantages of CPM products, provide adequate space for their products, and assist in promotional and advertising efforts.

CPM has developed a strong sales culture and recruits highly capable individuals for sales representative assignments. Newly recruited sales representatives rotate through different divisions of the company in a two-month assignment to learn where and how the products are made, their features and benefits, and specific product marketing strategies. This initial assignment culminates in an intensive one-week Professional Marketing Training Program that focuses on sales techniques, marketing strategies, and customer service skills. At the end of the one-week program, participants complete a comprehensive exam that reflects the knowledge and skills taught in the program. As part of the exam, participants analyze specific customer service and sales situations and decide on specific actions. The test also covers product features, policies, and marketing practices.

To validate the test, CPM developed correlations between test scores and actual on-the-job performance as measured by sales volumes, sales growth, and market share for sales representatives. The correlations were statistically significant with each variable. As a quick way of calculating the expected ROI for a program, CPM estimates output levels for each item using the test scores, converts them to monetary values, and calculates the ROI.

As with the previous ROI estimate using end-of-program questionnaires, some cautions are in order. This is a forecast of the ROI, not the actual value. Having acquired skills and knowledge from the program is no guarantee that participants will apply the techniques and processes successfully and that the desired results will be achieved. This process assumes that the current group of participants has the same relationship to output performance as previous groups, thereby ignoring a variety of environmental influences that can alter the situation. Finally, the process required to calculate the initial correlation coefficient may be difficult to develop for most tests.

Although this approach, based on historical relationships, is an estimate, it has several advantages and can be useful in a comprehensive evaluation strategy. First, if post-program evaluations (Level 4) are not planned, this process yields more information about the program's projected value than do raw test scores. It represents an expected return on investment based on the historical relationships involved. Second, developing individual ROI measurements and communicating them to participants has reinforcement potential. It communicates to participants that increased sales and market share are expected through the application of what was learned in the program. Third, this process often has considerable credibility with management and can preclude expensive follow-ups and post-program monitoring. If these relationships are statistically sound, the estimate should have credibility with the target group.

ROI at Level 3: Skills and Competencies

In almost every HRD program, participants are expected to change their on-the-job behavior through the application of the program materials. On-the-job applications are critical to program success. Although use of the skills on the job is no guarantee, most programs assume that if knowledge and skills are applied, then results will follow. Some prestigious training organizations, such as Motorola University, base their ultimate evaluation on this assumption.[4] A few organizations attempt to take this process a step further and measure the value of on-the-job behavior change and calculate the ROI. In these situations, estimates are taken from individual participants, their supervisors, the management group, or experts in the field. The following steps are used to develop the ROI:

1. Develop competencies for the target job.
2. Indicate percentage of job success that is covered in the training program.
3. Determine monetary value of competencies, using participants' salaries and employee benefits.
4. Compute the worth of pre- and post-program skill levels.
5. Subtract post-program values from pre-program values.
6. Compare the total added benefits with the program costs.

Perhaps an example will illustrate one technique to measure the value of on-the-job applications. The United States Government redesigned its Introduction to Supervision course, a five-day training program for newly appointed supervisors.[5] The program focuses on eight competencies:

1. Role and responsibilities of the supervisor
2. Communications

3. Planning, assigning, controlling, and evaluating work
4. Ethics
5. Leadership and motivation
6. Analyzing performance problems
7. Customer service
8. Managing diversity

The new supervisors' immediate managers indicated that the above competencies accounted for 81% of the first-level supervisor's job. For the target group being evaluated, the average annual salary plus benefits was $42,202. Multiplying this figure by the amount of job success accounted for by the competencies (81%), yielded a dollar value of $34,184 per participant. If a person was performing successfully in these eight competencies for one year, the value to the agency would be $34,184. Of course, this assumes that employees are paid an amount equal to their contribution.

Managers rated the new supervisors' skills for each of the competencies before the program was conducted using a scale of 0–9. The average level of skills required to be successful in the job was determined to be 6.44. The skill rating prior to the job was 4.96, which represented 77% of the 6.44 (that is, participants were performing at 77% of the skill level needed to be successful in the competencies.) After the program the skill rating was 5.59, representing 87% of the skill level needed to be successful.

Monetary values were assigned based on the participants' salaries. Performance at the required level was worth $34,184. At a 77% proficiency level, the new supervisors were performing at a contribution value of $26,322. After training, this value had reached 87%, representing a contribution value of $29,740. The difference in these values, $3,418, represents the gain per participant attributable to training. The program cost $1,368 per participant. Thus, the ROI is:

$$\text{ROI} = \frac{\$3,418 - \$1,368}{\$1,368} = \frac{2,050}{1,368} = 150\%$$

As with other estimates, a word of caution is in order. These results are subjective, and may not necessarily be an accurate assessment of the program's value. Also, because training is usually implemented to help the organization achieve its objectives, some managers insist on tangible changes in hard data such as quantity, quality, cost, or time. For them, Level 3 evaluation is not always a good substitute for Level 4 data.

Although this process is subjective, it does have several advantages. First, if there are no plans to track the actual impact of the program in terms of specific measurable business results (Level 4), then this approach represents a credible substitute. In many programs, and particularly with skill-building programs for supervisors, it is difficult to identify tangible on-the-job changes. Therefore, alternate approaches to determine the worth of a program are needed. Second, this data is usually credible with the management group if they understand the assumptions behind it and how it is developed. An important point to make is that the data on the changes in competence level came from the managers. In this specific project, the numbers were large enough to make the process statistically significant.

ROI at Level 4: Business Results

For most programs for which an ROI calculation has been developed, the focus is on business results (Level 4 data) that have been influenced by the HRD program. These output variables are usually expressed in terms of cost reduction, productivity increases, improved quality, increased customer service, or reduced response times. It is relatively easy to convert these terms to monetary values. Earlier chapters focused on this type of data for ROI calculations. A brief explanation is presented here to contrast with ROI at other levels.

There are two critical issues involved in Level 4 ROI development. The first issue involves isolating the effects of training. When a program has been conducted and output measures have changed, the first step is to determine the extent to which the training program changed the output variables. As presented in Chapter 10, at least ten strategies can be used to isolate these variables. Each of these strategies vary in terms of their ability to provide reliable estimates of the program's influence. The second challenge is to convert business results to a monetary unit using one or more of the strategies covered in Chapter 11. This step involves converting output data such as a reduction in error rates, improvement in customer service, or a decrease in response times to actual monetary units so that a monetary value can be developed. In some situations, this is a relatively easy task. For example, cost reductions usually can be moved directly to the benefit side of the equation without a conversion. Productivity measures can be converted to units of profit from the additional productivity. It is more difficult to assign a monetary value to quality improvements, response times, and customer satisfaction levels. There are at least ten strategies to make this conversion, each of which provides a reliable process for developing the value.

An example will illustrate the process. The Magnavox Electronic Systems Company was experiencing a lack of basic skills with mechanical and electrical assemblers.[6] On a trial basis, the company implemented a workplace basic skills (literacy) training program to improve verbal and mathematical skills. The program was evaluated at all four levels. The Level 4 evaluation showed a reduction in scrap rates and rework costs, and improvements in productivity. Management estimated the amounts of these variables that were attributable to the program and converted the resulting values to monetary units. Overall, the program netted annualized improvements of $321,600. When compared to the program cost of $38,233, this yields an ROI value of 741%.

ROI calculations on business results are credible and reliable if appropriate processes have been used to isolate the effects of training and the conversion of results to monetary units is accurate. When ROI data are needed, this level of evaluation should always be sought if at all possible. ROI with Level 4 thus becomes the fifth level of evaluation, the ultimate level of accountability.

Summary

This chapter illustrated how ROI calculations can be developed at different levels of evaluation, although most practitioners and researchers focus only on Level 3 and 4 data for ROI calculations. While post-program data is desired, there are situations in which Level 3 and Level 4 data are not available or evaluations at those levels are not attempted or planned. ROI estimates developed at Levels 1 and 2 can be very useful to management and the HRD staff, while at the same time focusing program participants' attention on the economic impact of their training. Bear in mind, however, that using ROI estimates at Levels 1 and 2 may give a false sense of accuracy. Figure 16-3 shows the relationship of ROI at the different levels. As would be expected, ROI calculations with Level 1 data are the lowest in credibility and accuracy, but have the advantage of being inexpensive and relatively easy to conduct. ROIs using Level 4 data are high in credibility and accuracy, but are very expensive and difficult to develop.

Although ROI calculations at Level 4 are preferred, ROIs at other levels are an important part of a comprehensive and systematic evaluation process.

ROI with:	Data–Collection Timing (Relative to Program)	Credibility	Accuracy	Cost to Develop	Difficulty
Pre-Program Forecast	Before				
Level 1 Data	During				
Level 2 Data	During				
Level 3 Data	After				
Level 4 Data	After				

Figure 16-3. ROI at different levels.

Table 16-2
Targets for ROI Calculations

Level of Evaluation	Evaluated at this Level	Target Percent of ROI
1. Reaction/Planned Action	90%	15%
2. Learning	50%	10%
3. Job Application	25%	10%
4. Business Results	10%	5%
5. ROI	5%	N/A

This usually means that targets for evaluation should be established as illustrated in Table 16-2.

The first set of targets is the percentage of courses evaluated at a particular level. Level 1 is usually very high, in the 90–100% range, whereas Level 5 is extremely low, usually in the 5% range. The next target is the percentage of courses in which ROI is developed at that level. The ROIs at Level 1 would usually have the highest percent, whereas ROI at Level 4 is much lower. These targets are very specific to the organization and reflect the staff's desire to develop ROI calculations and the resources available to pursue them.

Discussion Questions

1. Why is it important to consider ROI at different time frames?
2. How would you use Level 1 ROI data? How would you communicate these forecasts to senior managers?
3. Why is Level 2 ROI data impractical in most organizations?
4. What are the advantages of Level 3 ROI data? Disadvantages?
5. Explain how Level 2 ROI data are more accurate and credible than Level 1 ROI data.
6. Explain how Level 3 ROI data are more accurate and credible than Level 2 ROI data.
7. Explain how Level 4 ROI data are more accurate and credible than Level 3 ROI data.
8. Could the ROI be developed prior to implementation of the program? Explain.
9. For your organization (or one with which you are familiar), develop a profile of ROI usage at different levels.

References

1. Dixon, N. M. "The Relationship Between Trainee Responses on Participant Reaction Forms and Post-Test Scores," *Human Resource Development Quarterly,* 1(2), Summer 1990, pp. 129–137.
2. Industry Report, *Training,* 33(10), 1996, pp. 36–79.
3. Phillips, J. "Return on Investment—Beyond the Four Levels," in *Academy of HRD 1995 Conference Proceedings.* E. Holton (Ed.), 1995.
4. Geber, B. "Does Training Make a Difference? Prove It!" *Training,* March 1995, pp. 27–34.
5. Broad, M. "Built-in Evaluation," in *In Action: Measuring Return on Investment,* Vol. 1. J. Phillips (Ed.), Alexandria, VA: American Society for Training and Development, 1994, pp. 55–70.
6. Ford, D. "Three Rs in the Workplace," in *In Action: Measuring Return on Investment,* Vol. 1. J. Phillips (Ed.), Alexandria, VA: American Society for Training and Development, 1994, pp. 85–104.

CHAPTER 17

Evaluating
Outside Resources

Of the $59.8 billion that U.S. employers spend annually on training and development, 22%, or $13 billion, goes to outside providers in a supplier network of consultants, colleges, vocational schools, government agencies, professional associations, trade unions, conference providers, packaged training suppliers, and other organizations.[1] Collectively, they represent an important tool for cost-effective training and development. The link between internal training and development departments and training suppliers is strong because few in-house HRD departments can meet their corporate training needs. Employers usually contract with outside providers when internal training functions lack the expertise, time, facilities, or staff to create necessary training services. Outside services range from needs analysis and instructional design guidance to off-the-shelf or customized packaged programs.

Additionally, corporations are shifting paradigms to embrace principle-centered leadership, total quality management, and other revolving business philosophies so quickly that it is difficult for internal HRD departments to become primed, much less competent, in teaching them.

This chapter explores four common types of outside resources that HRD departments use.

1. Seminars
2. Packaged training programs
3. HRD consultants
4. External facilities

Each of these services brings unique evaluation challenges. With outside seminars, the organization is interested in maximizing the benefits derived from employee participation. Steps must be taken to ensure that the right seminar is selected, and that seminar material is properly used. Just as evaluating the results of a packaged training program is no different from evaluating those of an internally produced program, the programs external consultants develop or conduct should follow regular evaluation procedures. The most critical activity is evaluating their capabilities prior to contracting for services. Finally, as part of an organization's philosophy toward training delivery, a decision must be made concerning the use of external facilities. Each of these unique evaluation opportunities will be explored in this chapter.

Evaluating Outside Seminars

The Problem

The seminar business is a big business. Each year nearly one million managers and executives attend some type of seminar, workshop, or conference. Seminar fees alone approach $3.7 billion per year.[1] Every employer is flooded with flyers promising programs that will instill or revive professional or managerial skills. With all this activity, people who go to seminars sometimes learn, more than anything else, the importance of picking the seminars carefully.

An HRD manager in one organization received this memo from the employment manager:

The course in New Orleans was the worst that I have ever attended. The instructor did not follow the outline presented to us and was unprepared to discuss the subject matter. He would start talking about a subject, forget where he was, and then ask the class to tell him what he was talking about.

The next instructor was a substitute. The day was a complete waste of time. He read from a book most of the time, and the class got up and left before it was over.

Approximately a week after the course was over, I received a letter from the first instructor boasting about the high ratings he received from the class. He mentioned that his book was sold out of its last printing and said he was available as a consultant if we needed him.

This situation frustrates even the most understanding HRD professionals, yet it is not uncommon. Too many organizations develop and present poorly designed and ineffective seminars.

A common objection to seminars is the content. Many participants complain that the information is too general and offers few solutions to real problems. Speakers are another area of complaint. Occasionally, speakers are ill-prepared, lack the necessary expertise, and sometimes have less experience than those in the audience. Others complain that knowledgeable speakers hold back during seminars because they do not want to give away their secrets, and want to hold out for consulting fees after the program is conducted.

Too little attention is paid to the quality of seminars. In the past, companies relied on participants to provide the necessary quality control. The participants' ratings at the end of the program provided input to program designers and speakers. Too often these ratings were ignored as long as new participants enrolled. Some companies have registered formal complaints with the seminar sponsors, with little or no success.

To provide quality control, two actions are needed. First, the seminar must be prescreened, obtaining the information necessary to avoid a disaster. Second, each organization must evaluate the program and ensure that the information is put to effective use in the organization.

Concern for Evaluation

Employees attend seminars for a variety of reasons. Because some of these are the wrong reasons, there may be general apathy toward evaluation of outside seminars.

One reason participants attend seminars is to get out of the office. The seminar is a reward for performance or represents a change of pace in their regular work routine. These participants are more concerned with the location and dates of the seminar than the content or quality of the program. If participants attend a seminar for other than its original purpose, it is difficult to evaluate the seminar objectively. It is also more difficult to implement information collected in the program. Fortunately, tight budgets and an emphasis on accountability have forced some organizations to spend less money on unnecessary seminars.

There is another reason for lack of concern about evaluation. Some argue that, regardless of the seminar's effectiveness, an energetic and enthusiastic employee will be able to collect some new ideas from the program and apply them to the job. This is questionable thinking. Consider the cost involved in a typical one-week program. The seminar fee will be between $1,500 and $2,000. The attendee's salary, including benefits, averages more than $800. Travel expenses could easily add another $1,000. Together, this represents an investment of $3,300–$3,800 for an employee to attend a one-week training program.

Now for the important question: Would an organization spend $3,800 on equipment without some prior evaluation or comparison of the different brands, models, and specifications? In all likelihood the answer would be no. What can a company do to get the best seminar for its money?

Collecting Additional Information on Seminars

The answer to the previous question lies in getting the proper information early so that the seminar can be evaluated prior to attendance.[2] The following six guidelines are recommended to get a complete profile of the seminar. Not all of the information may be necessary for a given seminar or a specific situation in the organization.

Beware of the brochure. Never judge a seminar on its brochure. Professional organizations that conduct seminars produce very compelling brochures that often have flashy headlines and are expensively printed. It is difficult to distinguish between a sales pitch and real information. A good brochure will list all of the information needed to make a decision.

☐ Ample information about seminar leaders
☐ A complete and detailed agenda
☐ A detailed explanation of the costs
☐ The method(s) of instruction and other items to enhance the learning environment
☐ Evaluation data, if any is available
☐ The target audience

Of course, necessary information about the location, registration cutoff, refund policy, and other administrative details are standard items to be included in any brochure. Ideally, the brochure should contain enough information to answer initial questions, stimulate interest, and provide input to help decide whether to attend or seek additional information.

Collect additional details. When additional information is needed, the seminar sponsor should be contacted for a more detailed outline and other information defining its target audience and explaining how the program will be conducted. Additional information might also be needed about the sponsoring organization. Some are well-known and have very good reputations, while others new to the business may not present a quality program. Typical questions to ask are

☐ How will the program be conducted?
☐ How many participants have attended?
☐ Who designed the program?
☐ How long has the current instructor conducted the program?

Answers to these questions give additional insight into the overall program content, its purpose, and its method of instruction.

Check out the speakers. Most outside seminars are only as good as the speaker. If different instructors teach the same program, there may not be any similarity between them. Ask about specific speakers for the program in question. Check them out. See what experience they have had not only in conducting seminars but in practicing the topic at hand. Questions to ask are

☐ Do they have a track record in accomplishing what they will be discussing?
☐ Do they have any experience in the field?
☐ What have been their ratings in the past?
☐ Why are they conducting this program?

That last question deserves an additional comment. Most seminar leaders are either consultants or college professors, because their work schedules are usually flexible enough to allow them to conduct seminars. Generally, practitioners who are successfully applying many of the techniques discussed in seminars are too busy plying their trades to conduct seminars for others. This is unfortunate, not because of poor quality of instruction from professors or consultants, but because many seminar participants do not have the opportunity to interface with individuals who have a track record in the field.

One organization recently challenged a university in its selection of a speaker. The seminar title was "How to Manage the Training and Development Department". It was conducted by a professor at the university who had never been a manager of a training department, nor had he ever worked as a member of a training staff. Regardless of the professor's ability, it is difficult to build the credibility needed for the seminar topic without some relevant experience.

Check with previous participants. A list of previous participants is an excellent source of unbiased information. If this can be secured, contact as many previous participants as feasible in your organization's field with job titles similar to the prospective participants. Typical questions to ask are

☐ Why did you attend the program?
☐ What was your overall reaction to the program?
☐ Did it meet the program objectives?
☐ What results have you achieved because of this program?
☐ Was the speaker effective?
☐ Was the program material up to date?

If an organization refuses to give you a list of participants, ask them why. If they do not have a good reason, they possibly could have many dissatisfied past participants. Obviously, there are no past participants for first-time presentations of a seminar. In that case, it might be wise to wait until it is offered again.

Investigate the learning environment. The program and the environment in which a seminar is conducted should be designed for maximum learning. The method of instruction is usually one area that reveals much information about the learning environment. If the method is a lecture-only type program, it may result in very little learning. On the other hand, discussion with active participation and involvement from the participants increases the chances that they will learn more.

The facility can also enhance the learning environment. Programs conducted at a conference center, as opposed to a local hotel, usually have a better learning environment, especially if the center is designed for conferences only.

A final note about the learning environment involves the use of hand-out materials. This material can support the information presented in the program and provide for additional analysis and follow-up when the participant is back on the job. Ideally, hand-out material should be used in class as the subject is presented and have space for notes.

Secure additional evaluation data. Occasionally, the sponsors of successful seminars have collected additional information on their effectiveness. This information may be in the form of dollar savings as a result of the program, testimonial letters from participants, or analysis of changes that have taken place on the job as a result of the program. Such evaluation data are usually contained in the program announcement; however, it may be too detailed to present, or it could have been collected after the brochure was printed. In any case, the information should be obtained if it is available. If the organization does not collect such information, or does not consider it important, then perhaps the effectiveness of the seminar should be questioned. Also, an organization reluctant to provide additional information about their programs may have reason for their actions. It's analogous to developing a product but being unwilling to indicate how it is to be used. When faced with this situation, the best approach is to ignore the sponsoring organization completely.

Pre-Program Planning

An internal seminar's success involves a combination of company policy, management support, and careful planning by the HRD department. The HRD department should be the central agency for coordinating, processing, and approving participants' attendance in outside seminars. Otherwise, it is difficult to know what activity is taking place, and it is difficult to gather the necessary base of information to give advice and help select the right seminars. The term "advice" needs some amplification. The HRD department should know which frequently offered programs are effective. The department can be a very helpful resource to the organization in identifying appropriate seminars and providing evaluation data.

Management support is necessary for obtaining maximum effectiveness from an outside seminar. Support must represent the organization's general philosophy and attitude toward expenditures for an outside HRD program. Helping select the appropriate program is another area in which support is needed. Finally, requiring improvement or the implementation of the material presented after attendance is the most significant area of support.

Pre-program planning can help ensure the success of an off-site venture. This is where the HRD department can have a significant impact. After the program is selected and the decision is made to send a participant, the HRD department should get in touch with the participant and his or her supervisor. This communication has three general purposes.

1. To give the necessary administrative details about the seminar (location, travel arrangements, payment of fees)
2. To provide attendees a copy of the evaluation form, which must be completed after attendance
3. To require the participant and his supervisor to discuss the program prior to attending

An internal evaluation form should be given to participants prior to the program. The evaluation should provide clear instructions on what is required in the evaluation process. The form, shown as Figure 17-1, provides a section to evaluate the program as well as space for indicating what action will take place as a result of attending the program. It also asks for an estimate of the dollar savings over a period of one year. The dollar-savings information, if appropriate, can be useful in summarizing the effectiveness of outside programs.

Communication between participants and their supervisors prior to attendance is important. Unfortunately, many attendees leave for the seminar with no discussion about what is expected when they return. Ideally, they should discuss the following areas:

☐ Program content
☐ Important areas of the seminar
☐ Areas in which additional information is needed
☐ Potential on-the-job applications of the material

Prior discussion can stimulate the participant's involvement in the program, increase eagerness to attend, and help ensure that the material is put to

INSTRUCTIONS: Please complete this form immediately after attending your seminar, training program, or conference, and return to your supervisor within one week of program completion. Your information will be valuable to others in evaluating this program for future participation. Important: After you complete this form, your supervisor and department manager should review it and forward it to the Training & Development Department.

Name _____

Department _____

Course _____

Date attended _____ Cost $ _____

Location of Program _____ Length _____

Sponsoring Organization _____

Instructor _____

Briefly describe the content of the program _____

_____

What specific knowledge, techniques, or ideas were learned, and how do you plan to apply them on your job? Use an example.

Planning of work	*I will plan and organize my time to increase my productivity a*
Example	*minimum of ten percent (10%) within the next month.*
1 _____	_____
	_____
2 _____	_____
	_____

As the result of this course, please estimate (in dollars) the amount of money that will be saved (e.g., increased productivity, improved methods, reduced costs) over a period of one year. $_____ Please explain.

_____

_____

Please put a (√) check in the column that best answers the following questions:

	Ratings				
	1.	2.	3.	4.	5.
				More than	Out-
	Inadequate	Marginal	Adequate	Adequate	standing
GENERAL					
How would you rate this course overall?	_____	_____	_____	_____	_____
How well did this course meet its announced goals and contents?	_____	_____	_____	_____	_____
General interest of course material to you personally	_____	_____	_____	_____	_____
How applicable was this course material to your job?	_____	_____	_____	_____	_____

	Ratings			
1.	2.	3.	4.	5.
			More than	Out-
Inadequate	Marginal	Adequate	Adequate	standing

CONTENT

How would you rate the difficulty or
technical level of the material?

How up-to-date, factual, and reliable
was the information?

How practical was the material presented?

INSTRUCTION

Effort and preparation made by instructor

Competence of instructor in material
presented

Instructors ability to effectively
communicate material covered

Instructors ability to handle questions

Your satisifaction with amount and type
of discussion allowed in class

OUT-OF-CLASS STUDY

The amount and difficulty of homework
or self-study expected of you

Relationship of homework assignments
to material covered in course

Degree to which homework is helpful

Value of textbooks, notes, or handouts
provided by the instructor

Signed _____ Date _____

Supervisor _____ Manager _____ Received _____
      Initial   Initial   T&D

Figure 17-1. Outside development program evaluation.

use on the job. In addition, these discussions can enhance follow-up evaluation efforts that may be planned by the HRD department. As a side benefit, discussion improves the supervisor-subordinate relationship.

Participants frequently have questions about attending a seminar. They want to know why they were selected and what is expected when they return. If attendance is not considered a reward, attendees may be concerned that something is wrong with their performance.

Post-Program Activities

After the participant attends the program, a critical part of the process begins. The participant's supervisor should sign the form to ensure that there has been a post-program discussion. A memo from the HRD department, with a copy to the participant's supervisor, should serve as a reminder to return the evaluation by the pre-established deadline.

Once the evaluation form is returned, it should be reviewed by the HRD department. Two areas need particular attention: (1) the actions planned by the participant, and (2) the monetary savings (with appropriate explanations). If these are left blank, the form should be returned to the participant with an explanation of the importance of the information. It is not unusual to get an adverse reaction when asked about dollar savings for attending the outside program. Savings are difficult to quantify, and even the best estimate can be unrealistic. The HRD department should insist on this information if it is feasible for the program. One such approach is to formally answer adverse comments about the information. Figure 17-2 shows a memo to a frustrated marketing manager explaining why dollar savings are required on the evaluation form. This approach, if handled diplomatically, can increase support in the evaluation of outside seminars and internal HRD programs.

Building a Database

The HRD department should function as a central agency for all employees attending outside seminars. This enables the department to build a database that represents current information on program effectiveness. Seminar participants should be required to keep the HRD department informed about the effectiveness of training and development programs. Candid evaluations of outside courses can steer future participants away from ineffective programs. Some independent firms attempt to perform this function as a service to other organizations.[3] Although this service can provide information on various programs, it can be unreliable because it is collected on a voluntary basis.

Another reason for establishing a database is to keep track of the costs of attending outside programs. External training represents a significant expenditure; cost summaries of expenses should be developed and reported.

A final reason for establishing a database is to evaluate the overall impact of outside program attendance. In addition to evaluating the impact of an individual program, management may want to know if the ROI for this total expenditure is acceptable. This can be accomplished with the proper completion of evaluation forms and supervisor/subordinate follow-up. This information enables the HRD department to calculate an approximate ROI for the expenditure.

XYZ CORP. MEMO

To: Marketing Manager
From: Jack Phillips
President, PRO
Date: May 8, 1997
Re: Outside Program Evaluation

Thank you for your evaluation of the course you attended on industrial product management. On the evaluation form, you commented that estimating the dollar savings is an exercise in nonsense. I'd like to challenge that statement. It is true that applications of ideas and techniques gained in some seminars and external courses are difficult to measure in terms of overall benefit to the company. While this appears to be the case with your course, we should not forget the purpose of attending external training programs.

Whenever a supervisor or manager attends a program, the value to the company depends on the knowledge and skills gained in the program and the subsequent on-the-job impact, however difficult it is to estimate. The mere presence of the question relating to monetary savings causes some employees to think more precisely in terms of saving money, reducing waste or increasing profits.

For too long, training and development staff members believed it was impossible to tie training programs to monetary savings. While often difficult to calculate, new evaluation processes make it possible to determine the return on investment. We will continue to pursue the financial effects of training and development on the company at every opportunity and to request the cooperation of each course attendee. We look forward to the day when this generates an idea that will help XYZ Corp. save money.

Thanks for your comments and for completing the evaluation.

JJP:tdb

Figure 17-2. Sample memo to marketing manager regarding outside program evaluation.

Follow-Up

At a predetermined period of time, usually three–six months after the seminar, the HRD department should conduct a follow-up with the participant to ensure the successful application of information. The purpose is to determine what changes have taken place as a result of the program. Formal follow-ups are usually limited to programs of at least a week in duration. Behavioral changes and specific activities planned at the end of the program are audited to see if they were carried out. Additional data on improvement directly attributed to the program are collected.

The HRD department should send a follow-up, usually a questionnaire, to the participant with a copy to the participant's supervisor. To make this process effective, the participants must

☐ Know in advance that the follow-up will be conducted.
☐ Have the full support, cooperation, and commitment of their superior to put into practice the items agreed to at the end of the program.
☐ See the need for supplying this information to the HRD department.

This follow-up should not be time consuming, but should contain enough detail to provide a complete evaluation. Most follow-up techniques for internally conducted HRD programs apply to the follow-up of an outside program.

A few organizations conducting seminars provide their own follow-up to see what impact the seminar has had on the participant. Others follow-up on a random basis. This represents an encouraging trend and provides invaluable marketing information that can lead to program improvements.[4]

Evaluating Packaged Programs

Today, more commercially packaged training programs are available than ever before. This deluge of programs may confuse the HRD specialist responsible for the decision to build or buy a program. If a purchase is planned, further confusion may arise over the choice of which one to buy. A recent survey revealed that the use of external suppliers represents 22% of American employers' total human resource development expenditures, and $13.0 billion overall.[1] The survey also revealed that HRD executives expect their use of external suppliers to increase in the future. This section outlines a recommended approach to address this question.

Evaluation Questions

The decision to make or buy a program is extremely difficult for HRD specialists, particularly in larger organizations. There are usually three major objections to outside purchases.

1. The belief that a program must be developed in-house to be effective and accepted
2. The belief that no other organization has the same training needs
3. The fear that parts of the program may conflict with practices or philosophies within the organization

These objections are often invalid. Employees are willing to accept programs developed by external suppliers. The "not-invented-here" syndrome does not seem to affect most program participants. Second, commonly required skills are generally similar from one organization to another. An organization's specific training needs, however, may be unique. In response to this concern, commercially available programs can be tailored to the organization's needs. Finally, to ease any fears of conflict with the organization's practices, questionable portions can be eliminated.

Before making the decision to purchase programs from external vendors, it is first necessary to determine the training needs. The steps in the results-based HRD model in Chapter 4 are appropriate for both outside programs and those developed internally. Outside programs should be evaluated to see if they meet the proposed internal requirements.

A list of questions can be developed to assist in the evaluation. Figure 17-3 shows an example of yes/no evaluation questions. The list is very thorough

YES	NO	
_____	_____	1. Are the program's learning objectives consistent with internal objectives?
_____	_____	2. Is the recommended length of the program consistent with internal plans?
_____	_____	3. Are evaluation procedures designed into the program?
_____	_____	4. Does the content match the requirements from the needs analysis?
_____	_____	5. Is the method of presentation compatible with existing practices?
_____	_____	6. Does the program design require participants to be actively involved in the learning process?
_____	_____	7. Are the program materials suitable for the target audience?
_____	_____	8. Are there procedures/methods to ensure the transfer of training to the job?
_____	_____	9. Can the program be used without modification?
_____	_____	10. Does the program allow for skill practices?
_____	_____	11. Are supporting materials available for the participant's supervisor?
_____	_____	12. Is the program attractively packaged?
_____	_____	13. Are the audio-visual requirements compatible with existing hardware?
_____	_____	14. Is instructor training for internal personnel available?
_____	_____	15. Is the program available on a trial basis?
_____	_____	16. Are examples of program success available?
_____	_____	17. Are the costs for the program competitive?

Figure 17-3. Evaluation questions.

and compares the organizational requirements to the specifications of commercially available programs. It will eliminate programs that will not fulfill specific needs.

Ranking of Proposed Programs

After potentially suitable commercial programs have been identified, the next consideration involves cost effectiveness. Is it more cost effective to develop or purchase the program? It is a relatively simple process to estimate the development costs versus the costs of the purchase. If a program is available that will meet the organization's needs, it is usually more cost effective to purchase the program, since the development costs have been spread over a number of organizations. To duplicate the effort may be cost prohibitive. In very large organizations in which internal program development costs can be allocated over many participants, an internal program may have an economic edge over an external program.

After the decision to purchase an existing program has been made, the final step is to select the best one. There are a number of reasons for selecting one program over another.

The relationship with the supplier, the reputation of the supplier, and the unique advantages of a particular program are all factors in selecting a particular program. If there has been no experience with the supplier and the reputation of the program is not a strong factor, the internal decision makers must objectively compare the programs. A comparison ranking is a simple yet effective procedure to select the best program. This involves listing the most important criteria used to select the program. First, assign a weight to each criterion. Next, compare each program, and rate how it best fits the criteria. A three represents the best fit, two the second best, and a one the third best fit for each criterion. These rankings are multiplied by the weight to give an overall value for each program by criteria. They are then added to give a total weighted ranking for each program. The program with the highest number represents the best program. Table 17-1 illustrates this procedure, as used for the selection of an HRD program for supervisors. Three programs are among the finalists that met the basic requirements as outlined in the previous section. The criteria for selection are shown in the left column of the figure. The relative importance (or weight) of each criterion is listed next. The rankings (one, two, or three) are forced rankings in that each of the three programs are compared and a choice of a three, two, or one is required. The rankings for each program are multiplied by the importance factor to obtain a value for each criterion. When the totals are calculated, Program B has the highest number and should therefore be selected, assuming there are no other factors available for making that determination.

Table 17-1
Selection Chart for an HRD Program for Supervisors

Selection Criteria	Relative Importance	Program A Rank	Value	Program B Rank	Value	Program C Rank	Value
Course content	30	2	60	3	90	1	30
Cost	25	3	75	2	50	1	25
Instruction method	10	2	20	1	10	3	30
Supplier reputation	10	1	10	3	30	2	20
Ability to customize	15	3	45	2	30	1	15
Media compatibility	10	2	20	1	10	3	30
Ease of implementation	20	2	40	3	60	1	20
Results orientation	20	1	20	3	60	2	40
Total ranking:			**290**		**340**		**210**

Selecting who should perform the ranking is very important. Key HRD department staff members and managers from the user organizations make an unbeatable team. For a supervisory program, the HRD manager and the management development manager are recommended. Two operating managers who will have participants in the program could round out the team ranking the programs. Together they should reach a consensus on relative rankings for each program.

Test Before Purchase

Another approach to evaluate a packaged program is to test it before the program is actually purchased. There is a tendency to select an attractively packaged program with a successful track record. To save time and implement a program quickly, an HRD professional may prematurely purchase a program before it is thoroughly evaluated. A pilot test can provide two very important pieces of information.

1. The program can be evaluated to see what results are obtained within the organization.
2. The participants' reaction and the adaptability of the program to the organization's personnel can be judged before purchase.

These factors must be considered before the program is purchased and implemented. Otherwise, the program could flop after the purchase. A pilot test period can give the HRD professional more time to familiarize himself with the supplier and to reflect over the initial decision. If the results are there and the program wears well with the participants, then the decision is obviously a good one.[5]

Guaranteed Results

One final area concerning the evaluation of packaged programs is securing guaranteed results from the supplier. Until recently, few if any HRD program suppliers offered a written guarantee. Now these guarantees are beginning to appear in brochures and advertisements. One organization makes this promise: "If you and we agree up front on the desired results, and if you agree to install the courses via our ten-step model, if you aren't satisfied with the results, we will refund the entire cost of the course materials."[6] The concept may appear to be a sales gimmick. However, a guarantee may be a consideration when selecting programs that represent large expenditures. A supplier with an effective and proven program should be willing to guarantee results.

HRD professionals should use caution when dealing with guarantees, since the results of any program will depend to a large measure on how it is implemented in the organization. Before suppliers will offer guarantees, they will certainly ask for some assurances that the program is implemented by their own staff. Nevertheless, the question of guaranteeing results and the response from the supplier might provide additional insight into the effectiveness of the program.

Evaluating External Consultants

The third area of outside resources involves the use of consultants or instructors. The term "consultant" will be used to refer to any individual who assists in internal HRD efforts but is not a regular employee of the organization. The work of the consultant may not be confined to conducting a program but may include determining training needs, developing programs, or solving performance problems.

Concern for Evaluation

The use of external consultants is increasing. Their work can interface with any HRD department's plan of activities. Before contracting for their services, however, consultants should be thoroughly evaluated for at least three major reasons.

Program results. One of the key reasons for prior evaluation is to try to determine the results that may be achieved by the consultant. The HRD department will be held accountable for those results whether the program is conducted internally or by an outside consultant. An HRD department should expect no less from an outsider than they expect from internal professionals.

Cost effectiveness. Consultants are expensive and their costs must be justified. The HRD department must be convinced that their time is cost effective when compared to other alternatives. An effective prior evaluation can help ensure this.

Problem avoidance. An ineffective consultant will reflect unfavorably on the HRD department. Since the consultant will be identified as part of the HRD department's efforts, failure can be embarrassing and affect the success of future programs. An up-front evaluation can possibly prevent this from happening.

Areas of Initial Evaluation

There are many approaches to evaluating consultants.[7] The following areas represent a comprehensive evaluation process that can lead to a more effective consultant/client relationship and help ensure that the desired results are obtained.

Related work experience. The consultant should have related work experience. The organization is seeking expertise for a project, and the consultant should be a specialist in that area. Similar consulting projects, programs conducted in the same field, and other past experiences may be necessary. Published articles or books and public seminar presentations can be evidence of successful previous experiences, and they can easily be reviewed for applicability to the organization's needs. Beware of consultants who specialize in everything and tackle projects regardless of the problem.

References. Consultants should be asked for references, or possibly a complete client list. Several of these clients should be contacted, because too often the client list is an exaggerated document that contains only the best clients and does not show the extent of previous assignments. Specific questions about clients can reveal factual information. If the consultant is a frequent seminar leader, attending one of the seminars can give some additional insight into his capabilities.

Beware of the package containing letters of recommendation. They are usually developed at the request of the consultant and may represent only a minority opinion of the consultant's effectiveness. Check the clients who have not written letters.

Successful projects. Effective consultants will usually have a long list of successful projects that produced measurable improvements. The consultant should be asked to supply information about those successes along with client contacts to verify them. A few consultants develop and update a summary of major projects. The summary shows the results achieved in measurable terms on each major project undertaken.

Even the most effective consultant may not have success with every project. Some efforts will not produce results, and other organizations may not require any type of measurement to see if results were achieved. Responses to these situations should be carefully analyzed, as they may reveal more insight into the consultant's effectiveness.

Consultant demand. Effective consultants are busy and will have several clients with many projects in various stages of completion. Ideally, there should be a good balance between the consultant who is not busy and one who is too busy. If they are not busy, this may be an indication that no one wants to use them. If they are too busy, then they may not be able to spend the required time on a proposed project and will sometimes send a substitute. This is usually true with top-rated consultants. They may be involved in the initial meeting to land a client account, but quickly disappear when the work begins. An organization may have no problem using one of the consultant's associates, but the consultant must make the organization aware that a representative of the firm will be teaching the course. This should be clearly communicated at the beginning of contractual discussions.

Cost. Cost is definitely a factor in evaluating consultants, although it may not be the primary item for consideration. In employing consultants, clients usually get what they pay for. Fees vary considerably and, obviously, more effective, results-oriented consultants demand higher fees. Compare the consultant's costs with the projected benefits from his work. Then compare his costs to those of similar consultants for the same project or similar projects. Beware of a consultant who is vague or gives a wide range of possible costs for his services.

Personality. The meshing of personalities in selecting consultants is far more important than most people realize. The consultant must fit into the organization. He must be able to gain the respect and confidence of the management group and be able to influence key individuals. The consultant's sensitivity to people is a key indicator of his ability. One who listens attentively will get not only the information needed, but also the cooperation necessary to complete the project.

Professionalism. A final consideration involves professionalism. Many individuals who operate as consultants are not professional consultants. Usually, individuals become consultants because they are specialists in their fields and want to help others, or they become so skillful that their services are in great demand. These consultants are usually professional in their approach.

Other individuals are consultants because they cannot do anything else and consequently are very ineffective.

The professional consultant will exhibit excellent communication in all phases of the contact. He will exhibit good business conduct, have excellent follow-up, and present a detailed plan of what will happen at what time with various responsibilities assigned. A professional consultant will give favorable responses to the questions contained in Figure 17-4.

Does the Consultant . . .

1. Listen to determine the client's needs, or is there an attempt to fit textbook solutions or predetermined techniques or products to the client's problems?
2. Use the "first team" or the "top brass" to sell the service, then hand the job over to less experienced people who are often inadequately supervised?
3. Overcommit and make promises beyond their ability to deliver within the agreed-upon time frame?
4. Misrepresent areas of strength and expertise, or is there openness in stating what they are and are not good at?
5. Write out in clear, measurable terms what work will be done and with what results?
6. Refer to other client organizations or divulge names or confidential information obtained while working for another organization?
7. Share with upper management information that was given in confidence during employee interviews or survey research?
8. Criticize management (collectively or by name) when talking with employees, or vice versa?
9. Use the client's name without permission in inferring a testimonial or an endorsement?
10. Bill the client for services that could have been done as well and less expensively by the client?
11. Use materials or technology from other organizations without acknowledging the source or the commission (retainer, finder's fee, etc.) they may be receiving?
12. Violate copyrights by reproducing protected material or modifying it slightly and claiming it as original?

Questions for the Professional Consultant (Reproduced with permission of Training House, Box 3090, Princeton, N.J. 08540.)

Figure 17-4. Questions for the professional consultant.

Selecting the Right Consultant

Using the previous eight areas of evaluation, it is possible to develop a simple ranking form that will enable the organization to select the best consultant, assuming that more than one is available in the area of expertise desired. This process, illustrated in Table 17-2, is very similar to the ranking of the packaged program presented earlier.

Each of the eight previously mentioned areas are listed on the form. Others can be added as appropriate to the evaluation. A relative weight is assigned to each area. For example, a weight of ten is given for the item considered most important, and a one for the item considered least important. There could be several tens or ones, depending on the relative importance of each area. Next, each consultant is rated in the areas of evaluation. These ratings are multiplied by the relative importance to generate an overall value for each area of evaluation. The numbers are added, and the consultant with the highest number represents the best fit for the assignment. A word of caution: assigning numerical values to subjective ratings might show a more precise evaluation than is actually the case.

Evaluating External Facilities

In the last two decades, major organizations heavily involved in the HRD process have developed specially designed training facilities. These conference centers, built in response to a corporate trend toward smaller, regional meetings, provide a distraction-free environment ideal for training, customer presentations, board meetings, and sales and marketing reviews. Twenty years ago there were only a handful of such centers, but today there are more than 300 facilities that generate almost $5 billion in annual revenues.[8]

Table 17-2
Selection Chart for an HRD Program for Supervisors

Area of Evaluation	Weight	Consultant #1 Rating	Consultant #1 Value	Consultant #2 Rating	Consultant #2 Value	Consultant #3 Rating	Consultant #3 Value
Related work experience	10	2	20	2	20	4	40
References	8	3	24	4	32	1	8
Successful projects	10	4	40	4	40	1	10
Consultant demand	5	1	5	2	10	1	5
Costs	7	4	28	3	21	2	14
Personality	4	4	16	3	12	3	12
Professionalism	8	3	24	4	32	1	8
Total rating:			**157**		**167**		**97**

Internal versus External

To a certain degree, the use of external facilities is influenced by the philosophy of the organization. Some organizations want all education and training conducted in their own facilities. Others do not want to invest in buildings and equipment and rely extensively on external facilities. Several factors influence the extent of external facility use.

Costs. For many organizations, it is more economical to use external facilities unless there is a heavy and consistent demand for the facilities' use. State-of-the-art conference centers are expensive to build and maintain. Unless it will be used 70–80% of the time, an organization may be unwise to construct separate training facilities. In addition to routine maintenance, corporate training centers require support staff such as coordinators, specialists, and technicians. Because of this commitment, some organizations use external facilities as a more cost-effective approach to training and development. External facilities are a way for organizations to pool resources and deliver training and development in specially designed conference facilities.

Convenience. Convenience sometimes forces organizations to use external facilities. Training needs may vary and it may be more appropriate to conduct training programs in different geographical areas of the country. It may be impossible for the organization to have adequate training facilities in all areas. Therefore, contracting for the use of a facility in a particular geographic region provides convenience to the HRD staff and program participants. Specially designed conference centers are located in virtually every major metropolitan area.

Recreational interface. For HRD programs that last a week or more, there is a need to integrate recreational activities with training. Although specially designed conference centers were created to give HRD professionals and meeting planners an alternative to crowded resort areas, they are often located in areas where recreation can be integrated into the program. It is not always possible for an organization to have recreational facilities at or near its own training facilities. When they do, it is usually restricted to one geographic region at division or corporate headquarters. In the winter, it may be desirable to meet in warm climate areas, and in the summer it might be more appropriate to use mountain resorts. Many commercially available training facilities are located near recreational centers or resorts.

State-of-the-art technology. Although it has become increasingly important for organizations to use the latest technology for training, it is also becoming increasingly cost prohibitive to upgrade that equipment. Most commercial facilities are committed to making changes as technology advances, and their meeting rooms typically offer ample electronic hookups for computers and access to data, video and audio lines. Some meeting centers are equipped with audio/visual control rooms and have provisions for front and/or rear screen projections, personal computers, interactive video, and other new media technology.

Training demand. The final area for consideration is the actual demand for training. Although closely related to costs, it brings into focus other factors. For example, during periods of corporate expansion, which relate to increases in training and development requirements, existing facilities may not be able to meet requirements on a readily available basis. External facilities may be required just to meet the volume of short-term activity. In this case, the organization has little choice but to go to an external facility. Specially designed conference centers are usually available on shorter notice than high-demand resort facilities.

These factors must be carefully weighed before determining the extent to which organizations should use external facilities. In many organizations, it will be a blend of both. Routine programs are conducted in existing facilities, and other programs, such as executive conferences, are conducted in external facilities.

Selecting the Appropriate Facility

After the decision to use external facilities has been made, several important questions must be addressed in the selection.

Location and convenience. Location plays a key role in the decision to use external facilities, as well as which facility to use. It is important that the facility be easily accessible to most of the participants and convenient to major transportation arteries and airports. The purpose of the event may dictate whether it is best to be near a metropolitan area or in a secluded, quiet location. The selection depends on the type of training needed, as well as the time required for participants to travel to and from the facility.

Facility design. The design of the facility is an important consideration. Successful conference centers designed with the learner in mind have built ergonomic facilities with attention to physical comfort, heating and ventilation, color, acoustics, wall coverings, windows, lighting and furniture, and overall architectural design. Every detail is planned with the objective of maximizing comfort and learning. The first conference centers were developed by large corporations as isolated, off-premise facilities for corporate retreats. These early centers emphasized seclusion and minimal distraction.

The focus on learning as well as ease in presentation make using these newer facilities an enjoyable and meaningful experience.

Support services. The support staff can be a critical issue in deciding which conference center to use. The support staff's availability, capability, and quality are extremely important to program success. Facility owners go to extremes to provide excellent customer service. They have specially trained personnel such as

☐ Conference planners or coordinators to assist meeting planners in all phases of the conference planning and operation, from designing the program to conducting the post-conference evaluation.
☐ Conference concierges to provide support services such as typing, transcribing, photocopying, and mailing.
☐ Security personnel to protect valuable audio/visual inventory, secure the confidentiality of meetings and ensure attendees' safety.
☐ Technical support personnel to ensure equipment works properly.

Availability. The facility must be available when needed by an organization. Some reputable facilities may not be available unless reserved more than a year in advance. This is sometimes beyond the scope of organizations in which training may be required with little or no lead time. Marketplace changes may dictate a swift reaction with a corresponding heavy training schedule or make it necessary to use hotels or vacation resort centers.

Cost. Cost must be a factor in selecting a facility. Specially designed conference centers are not inexpensive; the user will pay for the services provided. The cost can be significant and varies from one facility to another. Cost comparisons must consider available support staff, conveniences, location, and other items that affect cost. Sometimes cost can be negotiated or reduced through contractual arrangements for a fixed amount of use per year.

Reputation. References from current and former clients are helpful when selecting the facility. A complete list of clients should be obtained. Some organizations, such as the International Association of Conference Centers, provide information on the quality of conference centers. To qualify for membership, facilities must be dedicated to meetings and meeting-related activities and fulfill a variety of criteria. For example, a facility may be required to provide comfortable, high-quality meeting rooms as well as audio/visual equipment and knowledgeable operators. Another requirement may be that the facility derive 60% of its business from meeting-related activities.

Collectively, these factors can help an organization select the external facility that best meets its HRD needs. The result will be a facility that is within budgetary constraints, and in which the learning process is enhanced.

Summary

This chapter presented ways to evaluate the use of outside resources: external seminars, packaged programs, consultants, and off-site facilities. The typical HRD department will use all four resources. The evaluation of these resources is critical to the success of the overall effort and can help the organization accomplish its expected benefits. The impact of packaged programs and external consultants is evaluated using the methods presented for internal evaluation. The concepts in this chapter focused on techniques to evaluate the packaged program before purchase or the consultant before contracting for services. This is a necessary and important part of evaluation.

Discussion Questions

1. Most books and articles on evaluation omit reference to evaluating outside resources, yet 22% of HRD expenditures are placed with outside resources. Explain this situation.
2. Why do so few organizations attempt to evaluate the results achieved by employees participating in outside seminars?
3. Critique an outside seminar you recently attended. Would the procedures outlined in this chapter be helpful in evaluating the seminar? Explain.
4. The American Management Association (AMA) is the largest provider of outside seminars. AMA has been the subject of criticism in the content and quality of their programs, yet AMA's seminar business continues to increase. Explain this situation.
5. What techniques are helpful to get seminar participants to estimate a dollar savings as a result of attending the external program?
6. What are the advantages and disadvantages of using external off-the-shelf programs?
7. Apply the list of evaluation questions to an off-the-shelf program. How many negative answers result from this brief analysis?
8. How useful is the selection procedure outlined in Table 17-1? Explain.
9. Review the supplier brochures for off-the-shelf packaged programs. To what extent do they guarantee that results can be achieved with the program?
10. When should an organization buy a training program?

11. Why is it important to carefully evaluate consultants before engaging their services?
12. What approaches are typically used to evaluate consultants in an organization? Explain.
13. Consider one or more consultants in your organization (or one with which you are familiar). Apply the proposed ranking system to evaluate those consultants. Is the process helpful? Explain.
14. How can an organization hold a consultant accountable for the results achieved?
15. What is the appropriate blend of the use of internal versus external consultants?
16. Why has the use of external facilities increased in recent years?
17. What factors has your organization (or one with which you are familiar) used in selecting outside facilities? Explain.
18. Apply the evaluation criteria outlined in this chapter to compare several conference facilities. Comment on the outcome.
19. What is the appropriate blend of the use of external versus internal facilities? Explain.

References

1. Industry Report, *Training,* 33(10), 1996, pp. 36–79.
2. Noonan, J. V. "How to Escape Corporate America's Basement," *Training,* December 1993, pp. 39–42.
3. Chaddock, P. "Building Value with Training," *Training & Development,* July 1995, pp. 22–26.
4. Smith, E. "Continuous Learning Arthur Andersen Style," *Corporate University Review,* July/August 1996, pp. 14–20.
5. Maul, J. P. and Krauss, J. D. "Outsourcing in Training and Education," in *The ASTD Training & Development Handbook.* R.L. Craig (Ed.), New York, NY: McGraw-Hill, 1996, pp. 1,008–1,030.
6. Taken from an ad, "Can Trainers Guarantee Results?" Training House, Princeton, N.J.
7. Parry, S. B. "Consultants," in *The ASTD Training & Development Handbook.* R.L. Craig (Ed.), New York, NY: McGraw-Hill, 1996, pp. 1,031–1,045.
8. Finkel, C. L. "Meeting Facilities," in *The ASTD Training & Development Handbook.* R.L. Craig (Ed.), New York, NY: McGraw-Hill, 1996, pp. 978–989.

CHAPTER 18

Management Influence on HRD Program Results

Management's actions and attitude have a significant effect on the impact and success of an organization's training and development programs. This chapter explores this influence and the environment outside program development and delivery. Although the HRD staff may have no direct control over these factors, they can exert a tremendous amount of influence on them.

Several terms used in this chapter need additional explanation: management commitment, management support, management involvement, reinforcement, maintenance of behavior, and transfer of training. First, management commitment refers to top management and includes their pledge or promise to allocate resources and support to the HRD effort. Management support refers to the support of the entire management group, with emphasis on middle and first-line management. This can have a tremendous impact on the success of HRD programs. Management involvement refers to the extent to which management and other professionals outside the HRD department are actively engaged in the HRD process, in addition to participating in programs. Since management commitment, support, and involvement have similar meanings, they are used interchangeably in current HRD literature.

Reinforcement, maintenance of behavior, and transfer of training also have similar meanings. Reinforcement refers to actions designed to reward or encourage a desired behavior. The goal is to increase the probability of the behavior occurring after a participant attends an HRD program. Maintenance of behavior refers to the organization's actions to maintain a change in behavior on the job after the program is completed. Transfer of training refers to the extent to which the learned behavior from the HRD program is used on the job. These three terms will be presented together in one section on reinforcement.

This chapter underscores the assumption that the responsibility for program results rests primarily with the management group. The HRD function serves as the coordinating agency or facilitator. Managers are ultimately responsible for HRD through their commitment, support, reinforcement, and involvement; the extent of this influence ultimately determines the success of any effort.[1]

Top-Management Commitment

Without strong support and endorsement from top executives and administrators, HRD programs will fall short of their potential. Developing a supportive relationship with top executives is a critical challenge.

A Commitment Check

In principle, the chief executive officer (CEO) has some degree of commitment to HRD. The extent, however, varies with personal style, attitude, and philosophy. A heavy commitment to HRD usually correlates with a successful organization. As a first step in exploring ways to improve top-management commitment, it is helpful to review the current extent of commitment in the organization. Figure 18-1 is a self-test for the chief executive. The interpretation of the number of yes responses will vary with the organization.

Respond to the following checklist:

YES **NO**

☐   ☐   1. Do you have a corporate policy or mission statement for the HRD function?

☐   ☐   2. Do you hold managers accountable for the training, education, and development of their subordinates?

☐   ☐   3. Does your organization set goals for employee participation in formal HRD programs?

☐   ☐   4. Is your involvement in HRD more than written statements, opening comments, or wrap-up sessions?

☐   ☐   5. Did you attend an outside development program in the past year?

☐   ☐   6. Do you require your immediate staff to attend outside development programs each year?

☐   ☐   7. Do you occasionally audit an internal HRD program conducted for other managers?

☐ ☐ 8. Do you require your managers to be involved in the HRD process?

☐ ☐ 9. Do you require your managers to develop a successor?

☐ ☐ 10. Do you encourage line managers to help conduct HRD programs?

☐ ☐ 11. Do you require your management to support and reinforce HRD programs?

☐ ☐ 12. Do you require your top managers to have self-development plans?

☐ ☐ 13. Is your HRD manager's job an attractive and respected executive position?

☐ ☐ 14. Does the top HRD manager report directly to you?

☐ ☐ 15. Does the HRD manager have regular access to you?

☐ ☐ 16. Do you frequently meet with the HRD manager to review HRD problems and progress?

☐ ☐ 17. Do you meet with the HRD manager to review HRD programs at least annually?

☐ ☐ 18. Do you require a proposal for a major new HRD program?

☐ ☐ 19. When business declines, do you resist cutting the HRD budget?

☐ ☐ 20. Do you frequently speak out in support of HRD?

☐ ☐ 21. Do you often suggest that HRD staff help solve performance problems?

☐ ☐ 22. Do you require the HRD department to have a budget and cost-control system?

☐ ☐ 23. Is the HRD department required to evaluate each HRD program?

☐ ☐ 24. Do you ask to see the results of at least the major HRD programs?

☐ ☐ 25. Do you encourage a cost/benefit evaluation for major HRD programs?

Number of Yes Responses	Explanation
More than 20	Excellent top-management commitment, usually tied to a very successful organization.
More than 15	Top-management commitment is good, but there is room for additional emphasis.
More than 10	Poor top-management commitment, much improvement is necessary for the HRD department to be effective.
Less than 10	Almost no top-management commitment; HRD barely exists in the organization, if at all.

Figure 18-1. CEO commitment checklist.

It is recommended that this test be taken by the chief executive in the organization. It can be a revealing exercise that may have a favorable impact, particularly if the HRD manager has made little effort to secure additional commitment for the function.

Areas of Commitment

The self-test for the CEO reveals many places where commitment is needed. These can be grouped into ten general areas of emphasis that show strong top-management commitment, as shown in Figure 18-2. These ten areas need little additional explanation and are necessary for a successful HRD effort. Many of these items have been discussed previously as requirements for a results-oriented HRD philosophy in the organization.

Increasing Commitment

Now for the big question. How can top-management commitment be increased? Quite often the extent of commitment is fixed in the organization before the HRD manager becomes involved with the function. The amount of commitment varies with the size or nature of the organization. It usually depends on how the function evolved, the top-management group's attitude and philosophy toward HRD, and how the HRD function is administered. The key to the question of increasing commitment lies in how the HRD

For strong top-management HRD commitment, the chief executive officer should

1. Develop or approve a mission for the HRD function.
2. Allocate the necessary funds for successful HRD programs.
3. Allow employees time to participate in HRD programs.
4. Get actively involved in HRD programs and require others to do the same.
5. Support the HRD effort and ask other managers to do the same.
6. Position the HRD function in a visible and high-level place on the organization chart.
7. Require that each HRD program be evaluated in some way.
8. Insist that HRD programs be cost effective and require supporting data.
9. Set an example for self-development.
10. Create an atmosphere of open communication with the HRD manager.

Figure 18-2. The ten commitments.

effort is administered. The HRD staff can have a significant effect on future top-management commitment for the department and the function. The following six areas represent items that can help to increase commitment to HRD in an organization.

Results. Top-management commitment will usually increase when HRD programs obtain desired results. This is a vicious cycle, because commitment is necessary to build effective programs with which results can be obtained. And when results are obtained, commitment is increased. Nothing is more convincing to a group of top executives than HRD programs that produce measurable results they can understand and see as valuable to the organization. When a program is proposed, additional funding is usually based solely on the results the program is expected to produce.

Management involvement. Commitment is increased when there is extensive involvement in the HRD process at all levels of management. This involvement, which can occur in almost every phase of the HRD process, shows a strong cooperative effort toward developing employee potential within the organization. Chief executives want their managers to make a concerted effort to increase their staffs' and departments' skills and knowledge. Specific techniques for increasing involvement are covered later in the chapter.

Professionalism. A highly professional HRD unit can help influence the commitment from the top management. Achieving excellence is the goal of many professional groups and should be the mandate of the HRD department. The department must be perceived as professional in all actions, including welcoming criticism, adjusting to the changing needs of the organization, maintaining productive relationships with other staff, setting examples throughout the company, and practicing what is taught in the program. Professionalism will show up in attention to detail in every HRD program—detail that is often overlooked by nonprofessionals.

Communicating needs. The HRD department must be able to communicate development needs to top management and make them realize that HRD is an integral part of the organization. This communication may be in the form of proposals or review sessions with the top management group. When chief executives accept the need, they will respond through additional commitment.

Resourcefulness. The HRD department should not be a narrowly focused function. Too often the department is regarded as capable in technical training, audio-visual support, or management development, but not in problem-solving. When the department is viewed as versatile, flexible, and resourceful, it is used to help solve organizational performance problems and not confined just to formal development activity. The result: additional commitment on the part of management.

Practical approach. The HRD department must be oriented toward the practical. A department that focuses too much on theories and philosophical efforts may be regarded as a non-contributor in the organization. While there is a place for theoretical processes, HRD efforts within the organization should be oriented toward practical application. Programs should be how-to in nature and must be taught by experienced people who understand the program content as well as the business. This practical approach will help ensure additional commitment.[2]

Management Support

Ideal Management Support

Support from middle and first-line management is important to overall program success. Before discussing the techniques involved in improving the support for, and reinforcement of, HRD programs, it is appropriate to present the concept of ideal management support. Ideal support occurs when a participant's supervisor reacts in the following ways to the participant's involvement in an HRD program:

☐ Encourages participants to be involved in HRD programs
☐ Volunteers personal services or resources to assist in the HRD effort
☐ Makes a commitment with the participant prior to attending the program that outlines what changes should take place or what tasks should be accomplished after the program has been completed
☐ Reinforces the behavior change resulting from the program; this reinforcement may be demonstrated in a variety of ways
☐ Conducts a follow-up of the results achieved from the program
☐ Rewards participants who have outstanding accomplishments as a result of attending the HRD program

This kind of support for an HRD program represents utopia for the HRD profession. The remainder of this section explores ways to approach this ideal supportive environment.

Pre-Program Support

Support is necessary before and after the program is conducted. Effective actions prior to an HRD program can have a significant impact on what takes place in the program and what happens back on the job.

Agreements and commitment. An important technique is to execute pre-program agreements or commitments. One type of agreement is between the HRD department and the participant's supervisor. This agreement spells out what the supervisor agrees to do and, in turn, what the HRD department will do. Figures 18-3 shows an example of this type of agreement.

This contract briefly describes the HRD program and the various requirements of each party, and is usually obtained in a meeting with the supervisors of the participants prior to the beginning of the HRD program. Other types of agreements involve commitments between the participant and the participant's supervisor. These may be in the form of the action plans or performance contracts discussed earlier.

Defining responsibilities. Another area of pre-program activity involves defining and distributing the responsibilities of both the participants and their supervisors. Some organizations develop policy statements, brochures, or other documents that outline each party's specific duties. Table 18-1 shows the responsibilities of participants and their managers for a large global company. Participants' responsibilities are sometimes defined prior to, or at the beginning of, an HRD program. This way, participants are fully aware of expectations, particularly those related to getting the desired results.

Instructions to participants. Communicating with participants prior to an HRD program is very important. Employees may wonder if they are being rewarded for good performance or punished for doing something wrong. They may be curious about the program, its purpose, and the target audience. Much of this pre-program anxiety can be eliminated if the participants have straightforward information on the following:

☐ The basis for their selection
☐ The purpose of the program, including a brief review of the program content
☐ The administrative details of the program (time, place, dates, etc.)
☐ Typical results achieved by others attending the same or similar programs
☐ Instructions about pre-program assignments, if any
☐ The specific topics or areas discussed that are most important to the participant's job

This prior information can put the participant at ease and enhance what will be learned in the program. It will help ensure that results are achieved and strengthen the relationship between the participant and his or her supervisor. In addition, participants will have a clearer picture of why they need to attend the HRD program.

Between the Training Department and _____ of the _____. I would like to enroll _____, who reports to me, to attend the Challenge of Management course being held on the following dates: _____. We have discussed the course objectives and content, and agree to make the following commitments so that the training will have maximum impact:

1. The participant named above will attend _____ meetings, one per week, lasting seven hours each. We will work together to arrange work flow and deal with "crash projects" and crises in such a way as to keep them from interrupting the course.
2. The participant will spend 2–3 hours in preparation for each class meeting, going through the pre-workshop assignments and self-assessments. I agree that these exercises require analysis and discussion by both of us, and will make the time available to work together (average time: 20–30 minutes per week).
3. During the week following each class meeting, I will meet with the participant to review the action plan that spells out how the concepts and skills covered in the workshop might best be applied back on the job. We will agree on how and when the plan might best be implemented (average time: 30 minutes per week).
4. I will meet with the participant subsequently, as needed, to provide help in carrying out the action plan. I will plan to attend the executive briefing to be held 6–8 weeks after the course is over, at which time my participant and the other participants will each report on the composite results of their action plans as carried out to date.
5. If the participant misses a class meeting or weekly review meeting with me for reasons beyond our control, we will reschedule and make up the loss (e.g., in another cycle of the course or a special meeting with the instructor). If we miss two such meetings in a row, we understand that the participant will be disenrolled and rescheduled, if we so desire, in a subsequent cycle.

The Training Department agrees to meet the following responsibilities:

☐ To deliver a high-impact program that emphasizes skills development and hands-on learning.
☐ To provide a forum in which participants can learn from one another as well as from the instructor.
☐ To avoid embarrassing any individual or department in class.
☐ To maintain the confidentiality of any sensitive information that might be brought up in class.
☐ To serve as liaison between the group and top management on organizational issues.
☐ To make the learning experience enjoyable as well as beneficial.

Participant's supervisor: _____ Date: _____

Participant: _____ Date: _____

For Training Dept.: _____ Date: _____

Reproduced with permission of Training House, Box 3090, Princeton, N.J. 08540.

Figure 18-3. Agreement between HRD department and participant's supervisor.

Table 18-1
Responsibilities of Participants and Their Managers

Participants in learning solutions have important responsibilities. They must

☐ Participate fully in learning solutions to learn as much as possible.
☐ Explore ways in which learning can be applied on the job.
☐ Partner with their manager to choose learning solutions that can best improve business performance.
☐ Enter into the learning solution with an open mind and be willing to learn new concepts and develop new skills.
☐ Take responsibility for the success of the application of the learning solution.
☐ When requested, provide information and feedback on the success of the learning solution and barriers to implementation.
☐ Partner with manager to identify and remove barriers to the application of learning solutions.
☐ Have the determination to achieve success with the learning solution in the face of many obstacles to application and improvement.

The **participants' managers** have the responsibility to

☐ Partner with their employees in enrolling in learning solutions intended to improve business performance.
☐ When appropriate, discuss the learning solution with the participant prior to attendance/involvement to determine expected outcomes.
☐ Conduct a personal follow-up for the solution results.
☐ Reinforce behavior after the solution has been implemented and provide positive feedback and rewards for successful application of the learning solution.
☐ Assist in the planned formal follow-up activities of the learning solution.
☐ Be proactive in identifying and removing barriers to the application of learning solutions.

Management attendance. For many HRD programs, it is important that participants' supervisors attend the program first. This will help defuse the typical comment too often heard in programs: "My boss should be here for this!" Management attendance, if feasible, enables the manager to review the course material and experience the program in the same way as his or her staff. Managers usually attend separate sessions but cover essentially the same material. A scaled-down version is more appropriate in some situations.

There seems to be much resistance to managers' attendance at HRD programs designed for their subordinates. Sometimes, depending on the nature of the position, there is a feeling that the manager does not need full exposure to the program. Some suggest that the program description or a brief outline, along with an explanation of supervisors' responsibilities, is enough to ensure that proper results are achieved. This approach usually falls short of an optimum situation, because it is difficult for a manager to have a clear understanding of the program unless he experiences it. As an additional benefit, quite often managers are more effective after attending the program. Without this insight, many programs will be doomed to failure because of the lack of management's interest and support.

Timing. The timing of an HRD program is critical. Participants should attend the program when they actually need the skills or knowledge. This may seem trivial, but too often participants attend programs and acquire knowledge or develop skills before they are allowed to use them. A significant gap between the time the knowledge or skills are acquired and when they are put into use can diminish the transfer of training. Therefore, the timing of HRD programs deserves serious attention.

Post-Program Support

In many HRD programs, participants are expected to do something differently after the program is completed. These expectations may be in the form of follow-up assignments, action plans developed in the program, or fulfillment of the pre-program agreement between the participant and the participant's supervisor. These planned actions must be monitored to assess what change has taken place. Follow-up activity must be of real use and integral to the actual job and program, not just an exercise or make-work task.[3]

For most of these follow-up activities, the participant's supervisor is the key person to be involved, whether or not the design of the follow-up assignment necessarily includes the supervisor. The supervisor needs to see the results achieved and understand the importance of the improvement. Some follow-up assignments require the participant to funnel the accomplishments through the supervisor, who adds comments about the significance of the improvement and provides assistance to help produce results.

Closely monitoring these actions can often reveal a success story. The success stories, in turn, can help build support for the HRD department if they are communicated effectively to the management group. Specific methods for this type of communication are discussed in the next chapter.

Reinforcement

The Need for Reinforcement

In results-based HRD, there must be a strong partnership between the facilitator, the participant, and the participant's supervisor. This partnership can be viewed as part of a three-legged stool representing the major components of results-based HRD. One leg of the stool is the discussion leader, who conducts the program. The next leg is the participant, who experiences the program. The third leg is the participant's supervisor, who reinforces what is being taught. If any leg is missing, results-based HRD collapses.

The importance of getting the participant's supervisor involved as an integral part of the HRD process cannot be understated. Too often, participants return from an HRD program and find roadblocks to successfully applying what they have learned. Faced with these obstacles, even some of the best participants revert to old habits and forget most of what was learned in the program. In fact, regardless of how well the skill training is conducted in the classroom, unless it is reinforced on the job, most of the effectiveness is lost.[4]

The reason for this painful finding lies in the nature of learning. In learning a skill participants go through a frustrating period when the skill does not feel natural and is not producing the desired results. This period represents a results decline and is difficult for most participants. However, those who persist gain the expected reward from the new behavior. If the participant continues the new behavior or skill, it eventually feels more natural and performance improves. However, without proper reinforcement, particularly during the results decline, participants may not maintain the acquired skills. They may revert to the familiar old way of behavior with no change.

Sources of Reinforcement

Management reinforcement. Participants' supervisors are the primary focus for reinforcement. They can exert significant influence on the participants' post-program behavior by providing reinforcement in the following ways:

☐ Help participants diagnose problems to determine if new skills are needed.
☐ Discuss possible alternatives for handling specific situations. Act as a coach to help the participants apply the skills.
☐ Encourage participants to use the skills frequently.
☐ Serve as a role model for proper use of the skills.
☐ Give positive rewards to participants when the skills are successfully used.

Each of these activities will reinforce what has been taught and can have a tremendous impact on participants.

Management reinforcement workshops. A management reinforcement workshop is an effective technique. Conducted for supervisors of participants in an HRD program, the primary focus of the workshop is to teach them how to reinforce the behavior taught in an HRD program. Supervisors typically are exposed to the same material the participants will experience, but emphasis is placed on applications of management-reinforcement techniques.

Self-reinforcement. Reinforcement can come from sources other than the supervisor. When participants practice skills and achieve success with those skills, this provides reinforcement to use them again. This self-reinforcement causes some participants to do well in HRD programs in spite of job obstacles that may hinder success. Participants may try new skills if they feel an obligation to use them or if they are curious to see if the new skills will actually work in a realistic setting. Regardless of the reason, if they are successful the impact of that success provides reinforcement.

Peer reinforcement. The peer group is often overlooked as a source of reinforcement. This group includes participants' coworkers at the same level who are engaged in the same or similar kinds of activities. When some participants successfully apply new skills, this can encourage others. Also, it can spawn intergroup coaching among the peer group. In a cooperative environment participants who are most successful will show others how to use skills to get the desired results. Some HRD departments establish support groups to provide this reinforcement.[5]

Improving Supportive Relationships with Managers

Degrees of Support

A key area of support involves post-program activities. In this context the terms "support" and "reinforcement" are almost synonymous, because when support is exhibited, it helps reinforce what the participants have learned. Before pursuing specific techniques for improving post-program support and reinforcement, it is useful to classify managers into four different types according to their degree of support. The term "manager" is primarily used to represent the supervisor of a participant in an HRD program. The same analysis can apply to other managers above that level. A label has been attached to each type of manager that best describes their attitude and actions toward HRD programs and the HRD department.

Supportive. This manager is a strong, active supporter of all HRD efforts who wants to be involved in programs and wants his or her subordinates to take advantage of every appropriate opportunity. He or she vigorously reinforces the material presented in programs and requires participants to apply it successfully. He or she will publicly voice approval for the HRD efforts, give positive feedback to the HRD department, and frequently call on the department for assistance, advice, and counsel. This manager is a friend to the department and a valuable asset.

Responsive. This manager supports HRD programs, but not so strongly as the supportive manager. He or she allows subordinates to participate in HRD programs and encourages them to get the most out of HRD activities. This manager usually voices support for programs, realizing that it is part of his or her responsibility, but will not usually go out of his way to aggressively promote the HRD department or its activities. This manager will reinforce the material presented in the program, probably at the prodding of the HRD staff.

Non-supportive. This manager will privately voice displeasure with formal HRD. He or she reluctantly sends participants to programs, doing so only because everyone else does or because it is required. This manager thinks the organization spends too much time in HRD efforts and does not hesitate to mention how he or she achieved success without formal training. When participants return from a program, there is very little, if any, reinforcement from this manager. This manager's actions may destroy the value of the program. A typical comment after a program will be, "Now that the program is out of the way, let's get back to work."

Unresponsive. This manager works actively to keep participants from attending HRD programs. He or she tries to destroy the HRD effort and openly criticizes the HRD department and its programs. This manager believes that all training and development should be accomplished on the job. When participants return from a program there is usually negative reinforcement, with typical comments such as, "Forget what was discussed in that program and get back to work." Fortunately, this type of manager is rare in today's setting; however, there may be enough of these individuals to cause some concern for the HRD staff.

Improving the Relationship

The degree to which management supports HRD programs is based on the value they place on HRD, its function and role and, in some cases, the actions of members of the HRD staff. To improve management support, the HRD department should carefully analyze each situation and work to improve relationships with individual managers or the management group. This requires a series of critical steps, outlined here.

1. Identify key managers whose support is necessary. They may be the decision makers, the entire middle-management group, or all of senior management. Individuals selected should be strong leaders, either formally or informally.

2. Analyze and classify the degree of support, following the descriptions in the previous section. Input from the entire HRD staff may be helpful to classify all key managers.

3. Analyze reasons for support or non-support. Managers will usually show support (or non-support) of HRD programs based on a series of facts, beliefs, and values related to HRD. A fact is something that is indisputable and can be proven without doubt. A belief is an interpretation of the meaning of past or present experiences and is used to predict what will happen in the future. A value is the worth assigned to a particular belief. An example of a fact is a statement such as, "Each of my employees has spent at least two weeks in training this year already." An example of a belief is, "Supervisory training has not improved any of my supervisors." An example of a value is, "All training should occur on the job." The various degrees of support outlined previously are usually based on the facts, beliefs, or values assigned to the HRD effort by individual managers. The key emphasis of this step is to try to analyze the basis for the manager's support. Which facts, beliefs, or value systems caused an individual's behavior? Once these are established, an approach can be developed to improve the supportive relationship with an individual manager.

4. Select the best approach. The strategy for improving a relationship with a particular manager depends on his or her degree of support. Supportive managers are a welcome sight to the HRD department and it is important to show appreciation for their support. Possibly they should be involved in HRD programs in the capacities described in the next section. This involvement will encourage them to continue to support the department in the future.

Responsive managers need to be sold on the results of HRD programs so they will remain supporters. They view this as a responsibility and look for a return on their investment, whether their investment is in dollars allocated to HRD or in participants' time.

The next two types of managers represent challenges to the HRD department. Primary attention should be focused on non-supportive managers, as they can represent a significant number of managers in the organization. Analyzing the reasons for this lack of support—either facts, beliefs, or values—provides the basis for the non-support. Depending on the basis, the problem can be tackled by providing additional information, getting the managers involved in the HRD effort, showing them the results of HRD programs, or showing the extent of top-management commitment to HRD.

Unresponsive managers are a threat to the HRD department and they cannot be ignored unless they represent a very small minority of managers. If these managers are regarded as leaders in the organization, the HRD department can expect trouble. Dealing with these managers may require confrontations and possibly a few sessions with the manager's immediate superior. Unresponsive managers must be reminded of top management's commitment to the HRD effort. This approach can possibly stop the manager from working against the HRD department; otherwise, efforts to show results or get them involved in the program will be fruitless.

5. Adjust the approach if necessary. Managers are individuals, and what works for one may not work for another. If an attempt to change a manager's behavior does not work, possibly another approach can be successful. If a manager's action is perceived to be based on a belief but instead is based on a value, then an adjustment in approach is necessary. The key point is that each manager responds differently. The HRD staff should analyze the effects of their efforts and make adjustments in the strategy to improve it. The primary concern is to move managers from the non-supportive to the responsive or supportive categories.

Specific actions used to increase support and ensure the transfer of training vary widely, and will involve the efforts of executives, managers, supervisors, facilitators, and participants. The payoff can be tremendous.[6]

Management Involvement

Management involvement in the HRD process is not a new process. Organizations have practiced it successfully for many years.[7] Although there are almost as many opportunities for management's involvement in the HRD process as there are steps in the results-based HRD model presented earlier, management input and active participation will generally only occur in the most significant ones. Line management should be involved in most of the key decisions of the HRD department. The primary vehicles for obtaining or soliciting management involvement are presented here.

Program Leaders

The key to involving management and professional personnel is to use them as course leaders or instructors.[8] This presents some unique challenges to the HRD department. Not everyone has a flair for leading discussions in a development program. Discussion leaders should be carefully chosen based on the following criteria:

☐ Knowledge and expertise in the subject area
☐ Presentation skills
☐ Reputation in the organization
☐ Availability

The knowledge and expertise requirement is usually the largest single reason for soliciting outside assistance. HRD personnel cannot be experts in the majority of programs conducted.

Good presentation skills are very important. Even the most well-respected and knowledgeable manager will fall flat if he or she cannot make an effective presentation. Although it may be possible to assist a manager in developing presentation skills, it may not be feasible because of time constraints.

A good reputation in the organization is another important factor. Managers who are respected because of their ability or position will add credibility to the program. Similarly, managers who are considered to be substandard performers or an improper role model will have a negative impact on the program.

Availability is also important. Effective managers are usually extremely busy individuals. They may not have the time to assist in conducting programs. However, equally effective managers, because of unusual factors, may not be using all of their skills. They are likely candidates for an assignment as a course leader. Sometimes top management will insist that even the busiest line managers are involved in the HRD effort. This attitude makes HRD a high priority and can have a favorable impact on the program.

After outside course leaders are selected, the next major task is to prepare them for their assignment. This is a time-consuming process if it is done correctly. In some cases the actual time involved in preparing others to conduct a program will be greater than the time required for the HRD staff to prepare for the program. Detailed lesson plans, course objectives, a prepared script, visual aids, handouts, and other items should be developed for each course leader. If feasible, course leaders should have a chance to practice a session before presenting it to a group of participants. The HRD staff should critique the session and offer constructive suggestions. At a minimum, an HRD staff member should monitor the first presentation and provide feedback to the leader. This is important to the quality of the program.

The extent to which non-HRD staff are involved in HRD programs can vary considerably. In some efforts the entire program is conducted by the HRD staff. At the other extreme, some programs are conducted entirely by line management. The right combination depends on the following factors:

☐ The professional ability of the HRD staff
☐ The capability of line management and other professional personnel

☐ The value placed on having line management and other professional personnel identified with the program
☐ The size and budget of the HRD staff
☐ The physical location of the program as compared to the location of line management personnel

There may be other factors for the specific organization. In one company the right combination for a two-week supervisory program is shown in Figure 18-4. Outside involvement was high in this example, with the HRD staff conducting only slightly more than 21% of the program.

The use of non-HRD staff personnel in HRD programs creates a strong atmosphere of teamwork. One organization in which management involvement in a program was high held periodic "faculty" meetings and an occasional faculty appreciation luncheon. In these meetings, the results of the program were presented along with proposed changes and general information about the program's future. This created high team spirit and, at the same time, reminded managers that their contribution was appreciated and necessary to make the program effective.[9]

Advisory Committees

Many organizations have developed committees to enhance line-management involvement in the HRD process. These committees, which may have other names such as councils or people development boards, act in an advisory capacity to the HRD department. As shown in Table 18-2, committees

Figure 18-4. Management involvement in conducting 80-hour supervisory program.

can be developed for individual programs, specific functions, or for multiple functions. They can be one-time committees or standing committees, depending on the duration of the program. Committees can be used in many stages of the HRD process, from needs analysis to communicating program results. The HRD staff benefits from management input and from its commitment as well, once the committee buys into a particular program. It is difficult for managers to criticize something of which they are a part. Typical duties of a committee are to

☐ Review the results of a needs analysis
☐ Approve the proposed design of the program
☐ Review the methods of presentation
☐ Recommend potential discussion leaders for the program
☐ Review the program results

Committees can meet periodically or on an as-needed basis. Usually, the purpose of a meeting is to review specific activities in the program to secure input, support, and endorsement for that activity. The business of the committee should be conducted in a professional manner, including detailed agendas. Meetings must consume very little of the members' time; otherwise, they may lose interest and not attend.

Selection of individual committee members is very important. Committee members should be key managers and influential executives who can make things happen, are knowledgeable, and are respected within the organization. A committee comprising ineffective managers who command little respect in

Table 18-2
Types of HRD Committees

Responsible for:	Examples:
*Individual Program	New Supervisors' Development Program Committee
	Account Executives' Training Program Committee
	Product Knowledge Course Committee
	Apprenticeship Training Committee
*Specific Function	Sales Training Committee
	Nurse Development Committee
	Quality Control Training Committee
	Underwriting Training Committee
*Multi-Functions	Management Development Committee
	Faculty Development Committee
	Skills Training Committee
	Government Compliance Training Committee

the organization could get bogged down in irrelevant matters and lose the clout and credibility that it could otherwise have.

Before deciding whether or not a committee is appropriate, the HRD department should determine if the potential benefits outweigh the time that must be taken to work with the committee. Some organizations have a committee for every HRD program, while others manage to survive without them.[10]

HRD Task Forces

Another potential area for management involvement is through the use of an HRD task force. The task force consists of a group of employees, usually management, who are charged with the responsibility for developing an HRD program. Task forces are particularly useful for programs beyond the scope of HRD staff capability. Also, a task force can help considerably reduce the time required to develop a program.

A major difference in the function of a task force and committee is that the task force is required to produce something. They must devote a considerable amount of time to developing the program. The time required may vary from a two-week assignment to a six-month, full-time project. The time span, of course, depends on the nature of the program being developed and the availability of assistance for the task force.

The selection of members for the task force is more critical than it is for committees. A typical task force may include members of management or non-management with the expertise needed for the project. Including management on the task force can add credibility and influence that might be needed to make the program a success. The disadvantage of using management is that they may not be available to contribute the time necessary to complete the project. Individuals' backgrounds are extremely important, and should represent a variety of experiences necessary for the program development and implementation. For example, in a training program with a major insurance company, a task force was assembled to develop a program for a complex word processing system. Four participants were selected who represented each of four main segments: Eastern, Midwestern, Southern, and Western. Each was experienced and had a thorough technical knowledge of the subject matter. In addition, each brought a specialist's insight into a different aspect of the course content. In another example, a maintenance training program was developed using the task-force approach. The task force was made up of an engineer who designed the equipment to be maintained, a local plant engineer, a maintenance manager who had participated in the original start-up of the equipment, and a training manager familiar with performance-based training.

The task-force approach is very economical. It relieves the HRD staff of time-consuming program development that may be an impossibility in a subject unfamiliar to the staff. It is not only the proper way to go, but in some cases necessary to achieve the desired results. And, additional involvement on the part of management and professional personnel can help improve the HRD program's credibility and enhance the results.

Managers as Participants

Managerial participation can range from attending the full program to auditing a portion to examine its content. However, participation may not be feasible for all types of HRD programs, such as specialized courses designed for only a few individuals. It works best when one or more of these conditions exist:

☐ A high percentage of the manager's subordinates will attend the program. In this case, it is important for the manager to know program content and observe the dynamics of the learning process. This will help the manager understand why most of his or her subordinates must attend.

☐ Support and reinforcement from the manager are essential to the program's success. In this case, the manager must know what role he or she must take to support the program and reinforce skills that are taught. The success or failure of many training programs depends on the reinforcement participants receive when they return to their jobs. The manager's role is critical in this instance.

☐ It is essential that the manager have the same knowledge or skills that the subordinates will get from program attendance. Although the program may not be intended for the management group, it may be important that they receive all or part of the information that their subordinates receive. For example, in a new products-application course designed for sales representatives, it may be important for sales managers to attend the program so that they will have a thorough understanding of the new information. Although it may not be essential to them in performing their jobs, it is helpful in keeping them up to date on product developments.

Involving Managers in Training Evaluation

A final major area in which managers can be involved in the HRD process is in the evaluation of HRD programs. Although management is involved to a certain extent in assessing the ultimate outcome of training programs, this process focuses directly on evaluation through a team or committee approach. One approach requires managers to examine collectively the application and business impact of training. Six steps are used.

1. Invite clients to participate in focus groups.
2. Ask clients to collect data on the training's application and impact.
3. Ask participants to share positive results of training.
4. Ask participants to share negative or unachieved results.
5. Reconvene the entire group to share overall results.
6. Consolidate lists and agree on actions.

In addition, by involving managers and executives and showing them how evaluation can work, increased commitment and support for HRD programs should follow.

New Roles for Managers

The approaches described above are primary ways to involve managers in the HRD process when the focus is on achieving results. However, there are many other ways in which managers can be involved. In essence, these types of management involvement define new training roles for managers in an organization.[11] These roles are:

☐ Managers coordinating/organizing training
☐ Managers participating in needs assessment
☐ Managers training employees
☐ Managers serving as subject-matter experts
☐ Managers reinforcing training
☐ Managers evaluating training application and impact

It is imperative that managers assume these key roles, and the HRD staff must communicate frequently about the program's results. Collectively, this process will increase support and commitment as well as enhance input from each training role.

Benefits of Management Involvement

In summary, there are six major benefits from using management and professional personnel in the HRD process.

1. It adds more credibility to the program than it might otherwise have.
2. The program belongs to the management group, since they have been involved in the process of developing, conducting, or evaluating it.
3. Program participants and HRD staff have more interaction with other management, which makes for a stronger working relationship.
4. It enhances the skills of those managers involved in the process.

5. It is more economical to use other managers and professional personnel than to add staff to the HRD department.
6. It rewards good managers for their contributions to the HRD effort.

All of these advantages should encourage more organizations to use the skills and expertise of management personnel in the HRD process. The HRD department cannot afford to ignore the influence of the management group—in particular, key operating and support managers. Otherwise the HRD programs may not achieve desired results.

Summary

This chapter explored the management group's influence on HRD program results. The HRD department cannot afford to ignore this group's influence because their actions and attitudes can have a significant impact on the success of the entire HRD effort. Management commitment, support, reinforcement, and involvement were each discussed along with specific approaches to obtain improvement. Although the HRD department has no direct control over these factors, it can exert a tremendous amount of influence on them. The next chapter presents useful techniques for communicating program results.

Discussion Questions

1. Administer the CEO commitment survey to the CEO in your organization (or one with which you are familiar). Interpret the results.
2. What represents an adequate score on the Commitment Survey? Explain.
3. An HRD consultant was quoted as saying, "Training is too serious a business to be left in the hands of trainers. It requires the full and active participation of top management." Explain.
4. Explain, with practical examples, the difference in management commitment, management support, management involvement, management reinforcement, maintenance of behavior, and transfer of training.
5. To what extent can management commitment be increased in an organization? Why?
6. Assess the degree of management support in your organization (or one with which you are familiar). How does it compare with the ideal management support outlined in this chapter?
7. An HRD consultant was quoted as saying, "If we believe the manager plays a role in most everything a subordinate does, why is the manager suddenly exempted when it comes to the training process?" Explain.

8. Classify the key managers in your organization (or one with which you are familiar) according to the four types of managers as outlined in this chapter. Develop a strategy to improve support from each manager.
9. If reinforcement is so important to training success, then why do so few programs emphasize specific techniques of reinforcement?
10. One HRD executive was quoted as saying, "Without reinforcement, soft-skills training will never take." Please comment.
11. Detail specific actions that are critical to the reinforcement of training.
12. Identify the specific ways in which managers can be involved in the training programs. Which are most effective? Which are least effective?
13. What is the optimum balance of the degree of involvement of managers versus HRD staff members?
14. What can be done to ensure that managers are effective discussion leaders?
15. How are managers involved in HRD in your organization (or one with which you are familiar)?
16. Describe how peer support groups can enhance the transfer of training.
17. What are the advantages of advisory committees in HRD? What types of committees would be appropriate in your organization (or one with which you are familiar)?
18. What are the differences between advisory committees and task forces? Cite examples of each.
19. Why are managers reluctant to attend programs designed for subordinates? What are the advantages of their attendance in these programs?
20. Identify benefits of management involvement in addition to those listed in this chapter.

References

1. Veech, A. M. "Who's on First: Management's Responsibility to the Bottom Line," *P&I,* Vol. 33, No. 7, August 1994, pp. 9–13.
2. Sloman, M. "Coming in from the Cold: A New Role for Trainers," *Personnel Management,* January 1994, pp. 24–27.
3. Parry, S. B. "Using Action Plans to Measure Return on Investment," in *In Action: Measuring Return on Investment, Vol. 1.* J. J. Phillips (Ed.), Alexandria, VA: American Society for Training and Development, 1994, pp. 157–167.
4. Broad, M. L. and Newstrom, J. W. *Transfer of Training.* Reading, MA: Addison-Wesley, 1992.
5. Bell, C. R. "The Heart of HRD Partnerships," *Training & Development,* January 1995, pp. 26–29.

6. Swanson, R. A. "Business Partner: An HRD Mandate," *Human Resource Development Quarterly,* Vol. 4, No. 2, Summer 1993, pp. 121–123.

7. Sujansky, J. G. *The Power of Partnering.* San Diego, CA: Pfeiffer & Company, 1991.

8. Montagu-Pollock, M. "Look Within for Expertise," *Asian Business,* January 1995, pp. 34–36.

9. Carlisle, K. E. and Henrie, D. "Are You Doing High-Impact HR?" *Training & Development,* August 1993, pp. 47–53.

10. Smith, P. A. "Reinventing SunU," *Training & Development,* July 1994, pp. 23–27.

11. Nadler, L. and Nadler, Z. *Designing Training Programs,* 2nd Edition, Houston, TX: Gulf Publishing Company, 1994.

CHAPTER 19

Communicating Program Results

With results in hand, what next? Should they be used to modify programs, justify new programs, gain additional support, or build good will? How should they be presented? Communicating results is as important as achieving results. Achieving results without communicating them is like planting seeds and failing to fertilize and cultivate the seedlings.[1] The yield will just not be as great. This chapter provides useful information to help present evaluation data to various audiences. It covers both oral and written reporting methods.

Communicating Results

General Principles

The skills required to communicate results effectively are almost as delicate and sophisticated as those required to obtain results.[2] Regardless of the message, the audience, or the media, a few general principles apply.

The communication must be timely. Usually, program results should be communicated as soon as they are known. From a practical standpoint, it may be best to delay the communication to a convenient time such as the next edition of the newsletter or general management meeting. Questions about the timing must be considered. Is the audience ready for the results in view of other events that may have happened? Are they expecting them? When is the best time to produce the maximum effect on the audience?

The communication should be targeted to specific audiences. The communication will be more efficient when it is designed for a particular group. The message should be specifically tailored to the interests, needs, and expectations of the target audience.

The media should be carefully selected. For particular groups, some media may be more effective than others. Face-to-face meetings may be better than special bulletins. A memo to top management may be more effective than the company newspaper. The proper method of communication can help improve the effectiveness of the process.

The communication should be unbiased and modest. It is important to separate facts from fiction and accurate statements from opinions. Various audiences may greet communication from the HRD department with skepticism, anticipating biased opinions. Boastful statements sometimes turn off recipients, and most of the content is lost. Observable, believable facts carry more weight than extreme or sensational claims. Although extreme claims may get audience attention, they often detract from the importance of the results themselves.

The communication must be consistent. The timing and the content of the communication should be consistent with past practices. A special communication at an unusual time may provoke suspicion. Also, if a particular group, such as top management, regularly receives communications regarding major program outcomes, they should receive them even if the results are not positive. If some results are omitted, it might leave the impression that only positive results are reported.

Testimonials are more effective if they are from individuals the audience respects. Opinions are strongly influenced by others, particularly by those who are respected and trusted. Testimonials about HRD program results, when solicited from individuals respected by others in the organization, can have a strong impact on the effectiveness of the message. This respect may be related to leadership ability, position, special skills, or knowledge. A testimonial from an individual who commands little respect and is regarded as a sub-standard performer can have a negative impact on the message.

The audience's opinion of the HRD department will affect communication strategy. Opinions are difficult to change. A negative opinion of the HRD department may not be changed by the mere presentation of facts. However, the presentation of facts may strengthen the opinion of those who already agree with the department. It helps reinforce their position and provides a defense in discussion with others. An HRD department with high levels of credibility and respect in the organization may have a relatively easy task communicating results. However, because low credibility may create a problem when trying to be persuasive, the assessment of the department's credibility is an important consideration in developing overall strategy. Communicating program results, assuming the results are significant, should have a positive effect on the department's credibility.

These general principles are important to the overall success of the communication effort. They should serve as a checklist for the HRD professional when disseminating program results.

A Communications Model

The process of communicating program results must be systematic, timely, and well-planned, as illustrated in the model in Figure 19-1. The model represents six components of the communication process, which normally should occur in the sequence shown.[3]

The first step, one of the most important, consists of an analysis of the need to communicate HRD program results. Possibly a lack of support for the HRD effort has been identified, or there is a need to justify a new program or continue funding for a project. Perhaps there is a need to restore confidence or build credibility for the HRD department. Regardless of the triggering event, an important first step is to outline the specific reasons for communicating the results of the program.

The second step involves selecting target audiences for the communication. Audiences may range from top management to past participants, each with their own special communication needs. All groups should be considered in the communications strategy. An artfully crafted, targeted communication may be necessary to win the approval of a specific group.

The third step is concerned with developing written material to explain program results. Written material can come in a wide variety of forms, varying from a brief summary of the results to a detailed research report on the evaluation effort. Usually, a complete report is developed, and selected portions or summaries are used for different media.

Selecting the media is the fourth step. Some groups respond more favorably to certain methods of communication. A variety of approaches, both oral and written, are available to the HRD professional.

Information is presented in the fifth step. The product is delivered with the utmost care, confidence, and professionalism.

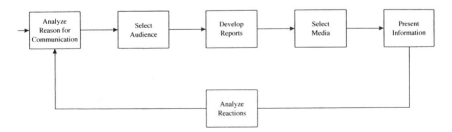

Figure 19-1. A communications model.

340 Handbook of Training Evaluation and Measurement Methods

The last step is the process of analyzing reactions to the communications. Positive reactions, negative reactions, and lack of comments are all indicators of how the information was received and understood. An informal and unscientific analysis may be appropriate for many situations. For instance, tuning in to the reaction of a specific group will suffice. For an extensive communications effort, a formal and structured feedback process may be necessary. Reactions could trigger an adjustment to communications on the same program results or provide input to make adjustments for future communications.

This communications model is not intended to make the process complicated. More than one audience usually receives the results of an HRD program, and each audience has its unique needs. All components of the model should be given consideration, even on an informal basis, before the communication strategy is developed. Otherwise, the full impact of the effort may be diminished. The remainder of this chapter amplifies the different steps of the model.

Reasons for Communications

The reasons for communicating program results depend on the specific program, the setting, and unique needs.[4] The most common reasons are

☐ To secure approval for HRD programs and allocate resources of time and money
☐ To gain support for the HRD department and its mission
☐ To build credibility for the HRD department's strategies, approaches, techniques, and finished products
☐ To obtain a commitment for a participant to attend an HRD program
☐ To create a desire to attend a specific program
☐ To enhance reinforcement of the HRD process
☐ To show the importance of measuring HRD programs' results
☐ To stimulate interest in the HRD department's products and services

Because there may be other reasons for communicating results, the list should be tailored to the organization.

Target Audiences

General Principles

When approaching a particular audience, the following questions should be asked about each potential group:

□ Are they interested in the subject?
□ Do they really want to receive the information?
□ Is the timing right for this audience?
□ Are they familiar with the HRD department's products and services?
□ How do they prefer to have results communicated?
□ Are they likely to find the results threatening?
□ Which medium will be most convincing to this group?

For each target audience, three actions are needed.

Understanding the audience. To the greatest extent possible, the HRD department should know the target audience.

Find out what information is needed and why. Each group will have its own needs relative to the information desired. Some want detailed information while others want only a brief summary. Rely on the input of others to determine audience needs.

Try to understand audience bias. Each member of an audience will have a particular bias or opinion. Some will quickly support the results, while others may be against them or neutral. The staff should be empathetic and try to understand differing views. With this understanding, communications can be tailored to each group. This is especially critical when the potential exists for the audience to react negatively to the results.

Selecting the Audience

Potential target audiences are varied in terms of job levels and responsibilities. Determining which groups will receive information on HRD program results deserves careful thought. Problems can arise when a particular group receives inappropriate information or when another is omitted altogether. A sound basis for proper audience selection is the reason for communication, as discussed in each previous section. Table 19-1 shows common target audiences and the basis for selecting each audience.

Probably the most important target audience is the top-management group. They are responsible for allocating resources for the HRD department and need information to justify expenditures and gauge the effectiveness of the function.

Selected groups of managers (or all managers) are important target audiences. Management's support and involvement in the HRD process and the department's credibility are important to success. Effectively communicating program results to management can increase both support and credibility.

Table 19-1
Common Target Audiences

Audience	Reason for Communication
Top management	Secure approval
All management	Gain support/build credibility
Participants' superiors	Obtain commitment/build credibility
Potential participants	Create desire
Current participants	Enhance reinforcement
HRD staff	Show importance
All employees	Stimulate interest
Stockholders	Secure endorsement

Communicating with the participants' team leaders, supervisors, or managers is essential. In many cases they must allow participants to attend programs. An appropriate return on investment improves their commitment to HRD, in addition to the department's credibility.

Occasionally, results are communicated to encourage participation in a program. This is especially true for those programs offered on a volunteer basis or to a general audience. These potential participants are an important target for communicating results.

Participants need feedback on the overall success of the effort. Some individuals may not have been as successful as others in achieving the desired results. Communicating the results adds additional peer pressure to practice what was taught and improve results for the future. For those achieving good results, the communication will serve as a reinforcement of the HRD process. Communicating results to program participants is often overlooked under the assumption that since the program is over, they do not need to be informed of its success.

The HRD staff must receive information about program results. For small staffs, the individual conducting the evaluation may be external. For larger departments, evaluation may be a separate function. In either case, the program designer, developer, and facilitators must be given information on the program's effectiveness. Evaluation information is necessary so that adjustments can be made if the program is not so effective as it could be.

All employees of the company and its stockholders may be less likely targets. General interest news stories may increase employee respect. Good will and positive attitudes toward the organization may also be a by-product of the communication of program-results. Stockholders, on the other hand, are more interested in the return on their investment.

While Table 19-1 shows the eight most common target audiences, there can be others in a particular organization. For instance, all management or all employees could be subdivided into different departments, divisions, or even subsidiaries of the organization. The number of audiences can be large in a complex organization. At a minimum, four target audiences are always recommended; a senior management group, the participants' immediate managers, the participants, and the HRD staff.

Communicating with Top Management

When it comes to communicating program results, no group is more important than top management. Improving communications with this group requires developing an overall strategy, which may include all or part of the following actions:

Strengthen the relationship with the CEO. An informal and productive relationship should be established between the individual responsible for HRD and the chief executive officer of the organization. Each should feel comfortable discussing HRD needs and program results. One approach is to establish frequent, informal meetings with the chief executive to review problems with current programs, training needs, and performance deficiencies in the organization. Frank and open conversations can provide the CEO insight unavailable from any other source. Also, it can be very helpful to the HRD manager in determining the direction of the HRD effort.[6]

Show how HRD programs have helped solve major problems. While hard results of specific programs are comforting to an executive, solutions to immediate problems may be more convincing.

Distribute memos on program results. When an HRD program has achieved significant results, make appropriate top executives aware of them. This can easily be done with a brief memo outlining what the program was supposed to accomplish, when it was conducted, who attended, and the results achieved. As shown in Figure 19-2, this memo should be presented in a for-your-information format that consists of facts rather than opinion.

All significant communications on HRD programs, plans, activities, and results should include the top executive group. Frequent information from the HRD department, as long as it is not boastful, can reinforce the department's existence and accomplishments.

Appoint top executives to HRD committees. An effective way to enhance commitment from top executives is to ask them to serve on an HRD committee. Committees provide input and advice to the HRD staff on a variety of issues including training needs, problems with current programs, and pro-

---

MEMO

To: Top Executive Group
From: Jack Phillips
Date: 3/27/97
Subject: Explorations in Managing

On February 25–27, twenty-eight middle managers attended "Explorations in Managing." The purpose of the program was to develop managerial skills and improve the manager's relationships with his or her subordinates.

The managers were asked to complete a detailed evaluation questionnaire at the end of this program. A portion of the questionnaire sought information on improvements in personal effectiveness and estimated savings from the application of the skills and knowledge learned in the program. A summary is presented below.

Twenty-six managers indicated an increase in personal effectiveness averaging 22.7% (the range was from 5% to 50%). Twenty managers provided estimates of annual dollar savings to the company as a result of this program. The estimates ranged from $1,200 to $360,000, with a total of $862,000. Nineteen managers provided a confidence level on their dollar estimates. The average confidence level was 48%, ranging from 20% to 100%. The formulas used to arrive at the dollar estimates varied considerably. The most common were based on improvements in personal performance, improvement in productivity of subordinates, reduction in operating costs, reduction in scrap, increases in output, reduction in project completion dates, and a reduction in turnover.

If the total dollar estimates are reduced by the average confidence level, the total savings are reduced to $454,500. As you can see, these estimates are quite high. Even if the total is divided by a factor of five, the savings are still significant compared with the cost of the program (which was approximately $35,000, with salaries of participants included).

Because these questionnaires were administered on the last day of the program, they reflect an enthusiastic feeling toward the whole social experience. We expect a less optimistic report six months after the program and plan to follow up at that time to determine actual savings. If you have any specific questions about this program, please give me a call.

Figure 19-2. Sample informational memo.

gram evaluation.[7] These committees can let each executive know what the programs are achieving.

One effective example involved the appointment of several executives to a committee for a management trainee program. This program was designed for entry-level college graduates who were being developed for management positions. The executives met frequently to review the program, monitor its results, and correct problem areas. The results of this program were in the form of successes on the job and the reduction of turnover of new college graduates. The executives knew the results of the program on a continuous basis. This top executive involvement was crucial to the success of the program.

Conduct an HRD review. An HRD review meeting is a very effective way to communicate HRD program results to top executives.[8] While this review can be conducted more frequently, an annual basis is common. The primary purpose is to show top management what has been accomplished and what is planned for the future. It can last from two hours to two days, depending on the scope of the meeting and the amount of HRD program activity. A typical agenda for this review meeting is shown in Table 19-2.

This meeting may be the single most important event on the HRD department calendar during the year. It must be timely, carefully planned, well-executed, and controlled to accomplish its purpose. This approach has been used in many organizations, and the reaction has been extremely favorable. Top management wants to know what the department is accomplishing, what results have been achieved and, most of all, wants to have input into the decisions for new programs.

Table 19-2
Annual HRD Review Agenda

Annual Human Resource Development Review Meeting

Time	Topic
8:00	Review of HRD programs for the past year.
10:30	Methods of evaluation for each program and the results achieved.
11:30	Significant deviations from the expected results (both good and bad).
12:00	Lunch.
1:00	Basis for determining training and development needs for the next year.
1:45	Planned programs for the coming year (secure support and approval).
3:15	Proposed methods of evaluation and potential payoffs.
4:00	Problem areas in the HRD process (lack of support, where management involvement is needed, or other potential problems that can be corrected by top management).
4:30	Concerns from top management.
5:00	Adjourn.

Developing an Evaluation Report

The type of formal evaluation report depends on the extent of detailed information presented to various target audiences. Brief summaries of program results with appropriate charts may be sufficient for some communication efforts. For other situations, particularly with significant programs requiring extensive funding, the amount of detail in the evaluation report is more crucial. A full evaluation report may be necessary. This report then can be used as the basis for the information for the specific audiences and various media. The report may contain the following sections.

Management/Executive Summary

The management summary is a brief overview of the entire report, explaining the basis for the evaluation and significant conclusions and recommendations. It is designed for individuals who are too busy to read a detailed report. It is usually written last but appears first in the report for easy access.

Background Information

The background information provides a general description of the program. If applicable, the needs assessment that led to the implementation of the program is summarized. The program objectives are presented as well as information on the program content, duration, course materials, facilitators, location, and other specific items necessary to provide a full description of the program. The extent of the detailed information depends on the amount of information the audience needs.

Evaluation Strategy/Methodology

The evaluation strategy outlines all the components that make up the total evaluation process. Several components of the results-based HRD model presented in Chapter 4 and the ROI process model presented in Chapter 5 are discussed in this section. The specific purposes of evaluation are outlined, and evaluation design and methodology are explained. The instruments used in data collection are also described and presented as exhibits. Any unusual issues in evaluation design are discussed. Finally, other useful information related to the design, timing, and execution of the evaluation is included.

Data Collection and Analysis

This section explains the methods used to collect data as outlined in earlier chapters. The data collected are usually presented in the report in summary formats. Next, the methods used to analyze data are presented with interpretations.

Program Costs

Program costs are presented in this section. A summary of the costs, by cost category, is included. Analysis, development, delivery, and evaluation costs are recommended categories for cost presentation. The assumptions made in developing and classifying costs are discussed in this section.

Program Results (Levels 3, 4, and 5)

The program results section presents a summary of the results with charts, diagrams, tables, and other visual aids. The following results are presented:

☐ Level 3 - Application on the job (behavioral data)
☐ Level 4 - Business impact (hard and soft data)
☐ Level 5 - ROI
☐ Intangible benefits-usually Level 4 soft data not converted to monetary benefits

All four types of results provide a complete picture of the evaluation.

Conclusions and Recommendations

This section presents conclusions based on all results. If appropriate, brief explanations are presented on how each conclusion was derived. A list of recommendations or changes in the program, if appropriate, is provided with brief explanations for each recommendation. It is important that the conclusions and recommendations be consistent with one another and with the findings described in the previous section.

These components make up the major parts of a complete evaluation report. It can be scaled down as necessary.[9]

Monitoring Progress

A final part of the implementation process is to monitor overall progress. The initial schedule for implementation provides a variety of key events or milestones. Routine progress reports need to be developed to present the status and progress of these events or milestones, usually at six-month intervals. Two target audiences, the training and development staff and senior managers, are critical for progress reporting. The entire training and development staff should be kept informed on the progress and senior managers need to know the extent to which evaluation is being used and how it is working in the organization. Figure 19-3 shows the table of contents from a typical evaluation report for an ROI evaluation. This specific study was conducted for a large financial institution and involved an ROI analysis on relationship-selling and financial-consulting skills. The report provides background information, explains the processes used and, most importantly, presents the results. Recognizing the importance of on-the-job behavior change, Level 3 results are presented first. Business impact results are pre-

---

■ General Information
  • Background
  • Objectives of Study
■ Methodology for Impact Study
  • Levels of Evaluation
  • ROI Process
  • Collecting Data
  • Isolating the Effects of Training
  • Converting Data to Monetary Values
  • Costs
■ Results: General Information
  • Response Profile
  • Success with Objectives
  • Relevance of Materials
■ Results: Use of Skills/Knowledge
■ Results: Business Impact
  • General Comments
  • Linkage with Business Measures
  • ROI Calculation
■ Barriers and Participants' Recommendations
  • Barriers
  • Positive Comments
  • Suggestions from Participants
■ Conclusions and Recommendations
  • Conclusions
  • Recommendations
■ Exhibits

Figure 19-3. Format of impact study report.

sented next, which include the actual ROI calculation. Finally, other issues are covered along with the intangible benefits.

While this report is an effective and professional way to present ROI data, several cautions need to be addressed. Since this document is reporting the success of a training and development program involving a group of employees outside of the training function, complete credit for all of the success and results must go to the participants and their immediate supervisors. Their performance has generated the success. Also, another important caution is to avoid boasting about the results. Although the ROI process may be accurate and credible, it still may have some subjective issues. Claims of huge success can quickly turn off an audience and interfere with the delivery of the desired message.

A final caution concerns the structure of the report. The methodology should be clearly explained along with the assumptions made in the analysis. The reader should readily see how the values were developed and the specific steps followed to make the process more conservative, credible, and accurate. Detailed statistical analyses should be placed in the appendix.

Communication Media

There are many options available to communicate program results. The most frequently used media are management meetings, HRD newsletters, the organization publication, and case studies.

Management Meetings

Management meetings are fertile ground for communicating program results, if used properly. All organizations have a variety of meetings and, in the proper context, HRD results can be an important part of each kind. A few examples illustrate the variety of meetings.

Staff meetings. Throughout the chain of command, staff meetings are held to review progress, discuss current problems, and distribute information. These meetings can be an excellent forum in which to discuss the results achieved in an HRD program if the program is related to the group's activities. Program results can be sent to executives to use in staff meetings, or a member of the HRD staff can attend the meeting to make the presentation.

Supervisory meetings. Regular meetings with the first-line supervisory group are quite common. Typically, items are discussed that will possibly help supervisors be more effective in their work. A discussion of an HRD program and its results can be integrated into the regular meeting format. In one example, a new safety-training program was announced in a routine supervisory meeting. After the training, the results were discussed at subsequent supervisory meetings until the end of the year.

Panel discussions. Although not common in all organizations, panel discussions can be very helpful to show how a problem was solved. A typical panel might include two or more supervisors discussing their approach to solving a problem common to other supervisors. A successful discussion based on the results of a recent HRD program can provide convincing data to other supervisors and to top management.

Management associations. Management clubs, leadership associations, and local company chapters of the National Management Association are becoming increasingly popular. These organizations usually open their membership to all professional, technical, and managerial employees. Regular meetings are a major part of their activities, with the majority of them featuring management-related topics. HRD program results can be an appropriate topic in these meetings. In one company, a monthly meeting featured a member of the HRD staff discussing the results of an assessment center. In a spotlight presentation, the HRD staff member outlined the program's statistics since its inception and the specific results achieved. This presentation was helpful in showing management that the program was successful in acquiring additional support.

Annual "State of the Company" meetings. A few organizations have initiated an annual meeting for all members of management in which the CEO reviews progress and discusses plans for the coming year. Highlights of major HRD program results integrated into the CEO's speech can have a positive effect on the HRD department, showing top executive interest, commitment, and support. Program results are mentioned along with operating profit, new facilities and equipment, new company acquisitions, and next year's sales forecast.

Whenever a management group convenes in significant numbers, evaluate the appropriateness of communicating an HRD program announcement or program result.

HRD Newsletter

Although usually limited to large HRD departments, a highly visible way to communicate program results is through HRD newsletters. Published or disseminated via computer intranet on a periodic basis, newsletters usually have a twofold purpose.

☐ To inform management about the activities of the HRD department
☐ To communicate the results achieved by the HRD programs

A more subtle reason for a newsletter is to gain additional support and commitment from the management group. The newsletter is produced by the HRD staff and distributed to all managers or a select group of managers in the organization. Format and scope vary considerably. Common topics are presented here.

Schedule of courses. A schedule of planned courses should be an integral part of this newsletter. In addition to registration information, a brief description should be presented that includes

- ☐ Method of presentation
- ☐ Who should attend
- ☐ Prerequisites (if any)
- ☐ Expected outcomes

Plans for new programs. An ongoing training-needs analysis or an update on a program in the development stage might be appropriate for the newsletter. This could generate interest in a program before it is developed and stimulate comments about proposed program content, scheduling, and facilitators.

Reactions from participants. A brief summary of Level 1 evaluations may be appropriate to report initial success. Also, brief interviews with participants after a program might be of interest.

Program results. A key focus of this newsletter should be reports about the results achieved from HRD programs. A headline such as "Productivity Improvement Course Nets Cost Savings of $150,000" will draw the attention of a profit-minded manager. Significant results that can be documented should be presented in an easily understood format. The method(s) of evaluation should be briefly outlined, along with the measurement of the impact or ROI in the program. This might be a regular feature, possibly with a catchy title such as "Focus on Results."

HRD philosophy and policy statements. Comments from a top executive about the organization's philosophies or policies regarding the development of employees can sometimes be used to refine a formal philosophy. In one company, the HRD manager developed what he thought would be the ideal HRD philosophy and discussed it with the CEO. After a few modifications, it became the published philosophy of the company in regard to developing human resources.

Manager's spotlight. A section that features a key supportive manager can be very useful. Emphasis is placed on the manager's efforts and involvement in HRD activity. Statements or interview comments on the following topics may be useful:

☐ Management's support for HRD
☐ Management involvement in various phases of HRD
☐ Expectations of participants
☐ The need for program results
☐ The need for self-improvement

Facilitator's spotlight. A section that highlights a member of the HRD staff can focus additional attention on results. This is an opportunity to recognize outstanding individuals who obtain excellent results with their HRD programs, and bring attention to unusual achievements or accomplishments.

While the previous list may not be suited for every newsletter, it represents topics that should be presented to the management group. When produced in a professional manner, the newsletter can improve management's support and commitment to the HRD effort. A word of caution is in order. The newsletter should not be too boastful, or it might turn off even the best of managers. Facts should be presented, leaving out most of the HRD staff's opinions. Facts are hard to dispute, and opinions and comments from executives outside the HRD department will be respected.

The Organization Publication

HRD professionals can use in-house publications to reach a wide audience in their communication efforts. Whether in a newsletter, magazine, newspaper or electronic (via company intranet) format, this publication usually reaches all employees. The material can be effective if information is carefully selected. It should be limited to general interest articles, announcements, and interviews.

Program results. Results communicated through this media must be significant to arouse general interest. For example, a story with the headline "Safety Training Program Helps Produce One Million Hours Without a Lost-Time Accident" will catch the attention of many people who may have participated in the program and can appreciate the significance of the results. Reports on a group of participants' accomplishments may not create interest unless the audience relates to those accomplishments.

For many HRD programs, results are achieved weeks or even months after the program is completed. Results are not something that occur overnight. Participants need reinforcement from many sources to use what they have been taught. This is particularly true for skills-oriented training. If a program is communicated to a general audience, including the participant's subordinates or peers, there is additional pressure on the participant to put their newly acquired knowledge into practice.

In one program, supervisors were taught to use specific discussion skills with their employees to improve performance and work habits, administer disciplinary action, etc. When an article in the company newspaper described the skills, the supervisors who had attended the program used the skills with more frequency. Furthermore, the participants' subordinates knew to expect changes after reading about the program in the company newspaper.

Building interest. Stories about participants involved in an HRD activity and the results they achieve create a favorable image. Employees are made aware that the company is investing time and money to improve their performance and prepare them for future assignments.

This type of story provides information about programs that employees otherwise may not have known about and sometimes creates a desire for them to participate. This communication strategy may be used to obtain quality applicants and may motivate self-development among employees, particularly if programs are offered after hours.

One organization had a program for potential supervisors. Although it was not publicized as a presupervisory program, it was understood that the participants were being groomed for supervisory positions. It was a highly visible program that involved visiting various departments as well as classroom training. Information about the participants was published in the company's monthly newspaper and resulted in a long list of employees who expressed interest in future programs.

Participant recognition. General audience communication can bring recognition to participants in a training program, particularly those who excel in some aspect of the program. When participants are selected for a prestigious and sought-after slot in a training program, public recognition can enhance their self-esteem.

Human interest stories. Many human interest stories can be developed as a result of HRD activities. A rigorous program with difficult selection requirements can provide the basis for an interesting story on participants who complete the undertaking.

In one organization, the editor of the company newspaper attended a demanding HRD program and wrote a stimulating article about what it was like to participate. The article gave the reader a tour of the whole course, including what was covered, how it was presented, and its effectiveness in terms of the results achieved. It was an interesting and effective way to communicate about a difficult development activity.

The benefits are many and the opportunities endless for HRD departments to utilize in-house publications and company-wide computer intranets to let others know what is happening in HRD.

Other Materials

In addition to memos, reports, and newsletters, other forms of written communication can be effective in getting the message out about HRD program results. Brochures, booklets, and pamphlets have proven to be effective in a variety of applications. Following are five examples:

E-mail and new media. Internal and external web pages on the Internet, company-wide intranets, and e-mail are excellent vehicles to release results, promote ideas, and inform employees and other target groups of HRD program results. E-mail, in particular, provides a virtually instantaneous means by which to communicate with and solicit responses from large numbers of people.

Program brochures. A program brochure might be appropriate for programs conducted on a continuing basis in which participants are selected from many potential applicants. A typical brochure is printed on standard-size paper and folded twice. It should be attractive and present a complete description of the program, with a major section devoted to results obtained with previous participants, if available. Measurable results and reactions from participants, or even direct quotes from individuals, could add spice to an otherwise dull brochure.

Program catalogs. A program catalog can be distributed to the management group, particularly in large organizations. This catalog describes the programs for the coming month, quarter, or year. Some necessary items to include are descriptions of the programs, their schedule and duration, the instructor, and most important, the results expected. If the program has been offered in the past, presenting evaluation data can have an impact on those making the decision whether or not to attend. The catalog should be attractively packaged and reflect the concept of getting results.

Recruiting brochures. For some programs, candidates are recruited from outside the organization. Brochures are developed to help bring individuals into programs for management trainees, nurses, account executives, salespersons, and other entry-level professional jobs. These brochures, while attractive, usually devote little attention to the results obtained from the program. Most brochures aim to describe the program and the entrance requirements. The programs should include information on success or potential effectiveness and quotes or testimonials from past participants.

Special achievement. Occasionally, the HRD department may have an opportunity to publicize a success story—an achievement linked to an HRD program. A pamphlet on this story, developed and distributed to the management group in general management meetings or staff meetings, can be beneficial if there is a direct tie with an HRD program. The brochure should be aimed at reducing costs, improving productivity, or other tangible measures, and should show what an employee, a group of employees, or a department has achieved. It should detail what was done, how it was done, and what was achieved, with subtle tie-ins to HRD programs. If developed and presented in a professional manner, these brochures, booklets, and pamphlets are effective and inexpensive vehicles to let others know about HRD programs and the results they have achieved.

Case Studies

Case studies are an effective way to communicate the results from a significant evaluation study. It is recommended that a few projects be developed in a case-study format. A typical case study will describe the situation, provide appropriate background information including the events that led to the program, present the techniques and strategies used to develop the study, and highlight the key issues in the project. Cases tell an interesting story of how the evaluation was developed and the problems and concerns identified along the way.

Case studies have many useful applications in an organization. First, they can be used in group discussions so that interested individuals can react to the material, offer different perspectives, and draw conclusions about approaches or techniques. Second, the case study can serve as a self-teaching guide as individuals try to understand how evaluation is developed and used in the organization. Finally, case studies provide appropriate recognition for those who were involved in the actual case. More importantly, it recognizes the participants who achieved the results, and the managers of participants who allowed them to attend the program. The case-study format has become one of the most effective ways to learn about evaluation.

A Case Example

These various methods for communicating HRD program results can be creatively combined to fit any situation. Here is an effective example utilizing three approaches: a case study, management meetings, and a pamphlet.

A production unit had achieved outstanding results through the efforts of a team of two supervisors. These results were in the form of key bottom-line measures such as absenteeism, turnover, lost-time accidents, grievances, scrap rate, and unit hour. The unit hour was a basic measure of individual productivity.

These results were achieved through the efforts of the supervisors applying the basic skills taught in a supervisor training program. This fact was discreetly mentioned in the beginning of a presentation made by the supervisors. In a panel discussion format with a moderator, the two supervisors outlined how they achieved results. It was presented in a question-and-answer session at a monthly meeting for all supervisors. They mentioned that many of the skills were acquired in the training program.

The comments were published in a pamphlet and distributed to all supervisors through their department managers. The title of the publication was *Getting Results: A Success Story.* On the inside cover, specific results were detailed, along with additional information on the supervisors. A close-up photograph of each supervisor taken during the panel discussion was included on this page. The next two pages presented a summary of the techniques used to secure the results. The pamphlet was used in staff meetings as a discussion guide to cover the points from the panel discussion. Top executives were also sent copies. In addition, the discussion was video-taped and used in subsequent training programs as a model of application of skills. The pamphlet served as a handout.

The communications effort worked. Favorable responses were received from all levels of management. Top executives asked the HRD department to prepare and conduct similar meetings. Other supervisors began to use more of the skills and techniques presented by the two supervisors.

Analyzing the Reaction to Communication

Commitment and support from the management group are the best measurements of the effectiveness of communicating program results. The allocation of resources when requested and strong top-management commitment are tangible evidence of management's perception of HRD program results. In addition to this overall measurement, there are a few techniques the HRD department can use to measure the effectiveness of its communication efforts.

Whenever results are communicated, the reaction of the target audiences can be monitored. These reactions may include non-verbal gestures, oral remarks, written comments, or indirect actions, that reveal how the communication was received. Usually, when results are presented in a meeting, the presenter will have some indication of how the results were received by the group. The interest and attitudes of the audience can usually be quickly evaluated.[10]

During the presentation, questions may be asked, or in some cases, the information challenged. In addition, a tabulation of these challenges and questions can be useful in evaluating the type of information to include in future communication. Positive comments about the results are desirable and when they are made, whether formally or informally, they should also be noted and tabulated.

HRD department staff meetings are an excellent arena for discussing reactions to communicating program results. Comments can come from many sources, depending on the particular target audiences. Input from different members of the staff can be summarized to help judge overall effectiveness.

When major program results are communicated, a feedback questionnaire may be used on an entire audience or a sample of the audience. The purpose of this questionnaire is to determine the extent to which the audience understood and believed the information presented. This is practical only when the effectiveness of the communication has a significant impact on the future actions of the HRD department.

Another approach is to survey the management group to determine the perception of the HRD programs' results. Specific questions should be asked about program results: What does the management group know about the results? How believable are the results? What additional information is desired about the HRD program? This type of survey can help provide the HRD department guidance, not only in communicating the results but in altering the direction of the department.

The overall purpose of analyzing reactions is to make adjustments in the communication process—if adjustments are necessary. Although the reactions may involve intuitive assessments, a more sophisticated analysis will provide more accurate information to make these adjustments. The net result should be a more effective communication process.

Summary

This chapter presented the final step in the results-based HRD model introduced in Chapter 4. Communicating program results is a crucial step in the overall evaluation process; if it is not taken seriously, the full impact of the program results will not be realized. The chapter began with the general principles of communicating program results. A communications model was presented that can serve as a guide for any significant communications effort. Various target audiences were discussed and, because of its importance, emphasis was placed on the top management group. A suggested format for a detailed evaluation report was provided. Much of the remainder of the chapter included a detailed presentation of the most commonly used media for communicating program results, including meetings, periodic publications, other written materials, and new electronic media. Numerous examples were included to illustrate the concepts.

Discussion Questions

---

1. Why is communication the often-neglected phase of the results-based process?
2. An HRD executive was quoted as saying, ". . . We don't see a need to communicate program results to a wide variety of audiences. The individuals who achieve the results know what they have done and that is what is important to us." What is wrong with this philosophy?
3. Consider a recent evaluation project in your organization (or one with which you are familiar). What communication of results was planned and executed? What specific reasons for communication were addressed?
4. In the evaluation project identified in question 3, who were the target audiences for communication? Why?
5. Why is it important to communicate to program participants the results that were achieved by all participants?
6. Which of the target audiences are most important? Why?
7. Should an evaluation report be prepared for each evaluation project? Explain.
8. In your organization (or one with which you are familiar), develop an HRD review-meeting agenda indicating the topics and emphasis of the meeting.
9. In your organization (or one with which you are familiar), which types of management meetings would be appropriate for communicating program results?
10. Under what conditions would an HRD newsletter be appropriate?
11. What are the disadvantages of using the organizational publication to communicate program results?
12. Why are organizations reluctant to include program results in HRD catalogs and brochures?
13. Identify a success story in your organization (or one with which you are familiar) that relates to the results achieved from training. Write the success story in a format to present to top management.
14. What are the strengths and weaknesses of the case-study approach to communicating program results?
15. What precautions are important when communicating results from HRD programs?

References

1. Connors, R., Smith, T., and Hickman, C. *The OZ Principle.* Englewood Cliffs, NJ: Prentice Hall, 1994.
2. Reeves, M. *Evaluation of Training.* London, U.K.: The Industrial Society, 1993.
3. Kraut, A. I. *Organizational Surveys.* San Francisco, CA: Jossey-Bass Publishers, 1996.
4. Bleech, J. M. and Mutchler, D. G. *Let's Get Results Not Excuses!* Hollywood, FL: Lifetime Books, Inc., 1995.
5. Sujansky, J. G. *The Power of Partnering.* San Diego, CA: Pfeiffer & Company, 1991.
6. Bowsher, J. "Making the Call on the CEO," *Training & Development,* May 1990, pp. 64–66.
7. Dixon, J. R., Nanni, A. J., and Vollmann, T. E. *The New Performance Challenge.* Homewood, IL: Dow Jones-Irwin, 1990.
8. Shandler, D. *Reengineering the Training Function.* Delray Beach, FL: St. Lucie Press, 1996.
9. Basarab, D. J. and Root, D. K. *The Training Evaluation Process.* Boston, MA: Kluwer Academic Publishers, 1992.
10. Fink, A. "How to Report on Surveys," in *The Survey Kit.* Thousand Oaks, CA: Sage Publications, Inc., 1995.

CHAPTER 20

Implementation Issues

The best-designed process model or technique will be worthless unless it is integrated efficiently and effectively into the organization. Although the models presented in this book are step-by-step, methodical, and simplistic procedures, they will fail even in the best organizations if they are not properly implemented, fully accepted, and supported by those who can make the process work in the organization. This chapter focuses on the critical issues involved in implementing a comprehensive measurement and evaluation process in the organization.

Planning the Implementation

Few initiatives will be effective without proper planning, and measurement and evaluation are no exception. Planning is synonymous with success. Several issues are presented below to show how the organization should plan for and position evaluation as an essential element of the training and development process.

Identifying a Champion

As a first step, one or more individuals should be designated as the internal leader for measurement and evaluation. As in most change efforts, someone must take the responsibility for ensuring that the process is implemented successfully. This leader is usually the one who understands the process best and sees the vast potential for the contribution of the process. More importantly, this leader is willing to teach others.

The measurement and evaluation leader is usually a member of the training staff who has this responsibility full-time in larger organizations or part-time in smaller organizations. The typical job title for a full-time leader is Manager of Measurement and Evaluation. Some organizations assign this responsibility to a team and empower them to lead the effort. For example, Nortel, a global telecommunications company, selected five individuals to lead this effort as a team. All five received certification in the ROI process.

Developing the Leader

In preparation for this assignment, individuals usually obtain special training to build specific skills and knowledge for measurement and evaluation. The role of the implementation leader is very broad and serves a variety of specialized duties. In some organizations, the implementation leader can take on as many as 14 roles, as indicated below.

☐ Technical Expert
☐ Consultant
☐ Problem Solver
☐ Initiator
☐ Designer
☐ Developer
☐ Coordinator
☐ Cheerleader
☐ Communicator
☐ Process Monitor
☐ Planner
☐ Analyst
☐ Interpreter
☐ Teacher

It is a difficult and challenging assignment that will need special training and skill building. In the past there have been only a few programs available to help build these skills. Now there are several available and some are quite comprehensive. For example, one program is designed to certify individuals who are assuming a leadership role in the implementation of ROI.[1] This certification is built around ten specific skill sets identified with the success of an ROI implementation. These are

☐ Planning for evaluation
☐ Collecting evaluation data
☐ Isolating the effects of training
☐ Converting data to monetary values
☐ Monitoring program costs
☐ Analyzing data, including calculating the ROI
☐ Presenting evaluation data
☐ Implementing the measurement and evaluation process
☐ Providing internal consulting on evaluation
☐ Teaching evaluation to others

This process is quite comprehensive, but may be necessary to build the appropriate skills to tackle this challenging assignment.

Assigning Responsibilities

Determining specific responsibilities is a critical issue because there can be confusion when individuals are unclear as to their specific assignments in the ROI process. Responsibilities apply to two groups. The first is the measurement and evaluation responsibility for the entire training and development staff. It is important for all of those involved in developing and delivering programs to have some responsibility for measurement and evaluation. These responsibilities include providing input on the design of instruments, planning a specific evaluation, analyzing data, and interpreting the results. Typical responsibilities include

☐ Ensuring that the needs assessment includes specific business impact measures.
☐ Developing application objectives (Level 3) and business impact objectives (Level 4) for each program.
☐ Focusing the content of the program on the objectives of business performance improvement; ensuring that exercises, case studies, and skill practices relate to the desired objectives.
☐ Keeping participants focused on application and impact.
☐ Communicating rationale and reasons for evaluation.
☐ Assisting in follow-up activities to capture business impact data.
☐ Providing technical assistance for data collection, data analysis, and reporting.
☐ Designing instruments and procedures for data collection and analysis.
☐ Presenting evaluation data to a variety of groups.

While it may be inappropriate to have each member of the staff involved in all of these activities, each individual should have one or more responsibilities as part of their regular job duties. This assignment of responsibility keeps evaluation from being disjointed and separate from major training and development activities. More importantly, it brings accountability to those who develop and deliver the programs.

The second issue involves the technical support function. Depending on the size of the training and development staff, it may be helpful to establish a group of technical experts who provide assistance with measurement and evaluation. When this group is established, it must be clear that the experts are not there to relieve others of evaluation responsibilities, but to supplement technical expertise. Some firms have found this approach to be effective. For example, Andersen Consulting has a measurement and evaluation staff of thirty-two individuals who provide technical support for the education and training function.[2] When this type of activity is developed, their responsibilities revolve around six key areas.

1. Designing data-collection instruments
2. Providing assistance for developing an evaluation strategy
3. Analyzing data, including specialized statistical analyses
4. Interpreting results and making specific recommendations
5. Developing an evaluation report or case study to communicate overall results
6. Providing technical support in any phase of measurement and evaluation.

The assignment of responsibilities for evaluation is also an issue that needs attention throughout the evaluation process. Although the training and development staff must have specific responsibilities during an evaluation, it is not unusual to require others in support functions to have responsibilities for data collection. These responsibilities are defined when an evaluation plan is developed and approved.

Setting Targets

As presented earlier, developing specific targets for evaluation levels is an important way to monitor progress with measurement and evaluation. Targets enable the staff to focus on the improvements needed with specific evaluation levels. In this process, the percentage of courses planned for evaluation at each level is developed. The first step is to assess the present situation. The number of all courses, including repeated sections of a course, is tabulated along with the corresponding level(s) of evaluation presently conducted for each course. Next, the percentage of courses using Level 1 reaction questionnaires is calculated. The process is repeated for each level of the evaluation.

After defining the current situation, the next step is to determine a realistic target within a specific time frame. Many organizations set annual targets for changes. This process should involve the input of the full HRD staff to ensure that the targets are realistic and the staff is committed to the process. The training and development staff must develop ownership for the targets; otherwise they will not be met. The improvement targets must be achievable, while at the same time challenging and motivating. Table 20-1 shows the targets established for Andersen Consulting for four levels.[2] Andersen indicates that many of the Level 4 evaluations are taken to ROI. In some organizations, half of the Level 4 calculations are taken to Level 5 while in others, every one of them is taken. Table 20-2 shows current percentages and targets for five years in another organization, a large multinational company. This table shows the gradual improvement of increasing evaluation activity at Levels 3, 4, and 5. In this table, year 0 is the current status.

Table 20-1
Evaluation Targets in Arthur Andersen & Co.

Level	Target
Level 1, Reaction	100%
Level 2, Learning	50%
Level 3, Job Application	≈30%
Level 4, Business Results	10%

Table 20-2
Percentages and Targets for Five Years in a Large Multinational Company

Percentage of Courses Evaluated at Each Level

	Year 0	Year 1	Year 2	Year 3	Year 4	Year 5
☐ Reaction and Planned Action	85%	90%	95%	100%	100%	100%
☐ Learning	30%	35%	40%	45%	50%	60%
☐ Job Application	5%	10%	15%	20%	25%	30%
☐ Business Results	2%	4%	5%	9%	12%	15%
☐ ROI	0%	2%	4%	6%	8%	10%

Target setting is a critical implementation issue. It should be completed early in the process with the full support of the entire HRD staff. Also, if practical and feasible, the targets should have the approval of the key management staff, particularly the senior management team.

Developing a Project Plan for Implementation

An important part of the planning process is to establish timetables for the complete implementation process. This document becomes a master plan for the completion of the different elements presented in this chapter, beginning with assigning responsibilities and concluding with meeting the targets described above. From a practical basis, this schedule is a project plan for transition from the present condition to the desired future state. The items on the schedule include, but are not limited to, developing specific evaluation projects, building staff skills, developing policy, teaching managers the process, analyzing evaluation data, and communicating results. The more detailed the document, the more useful it will become. The project plan is a living long-range document that should be reviewed frequently and adjusted as necessary. More importantly, the training staff should always be familiar with the plan. Figure 20-1 shows an implementation project plan for a large petroleum company.

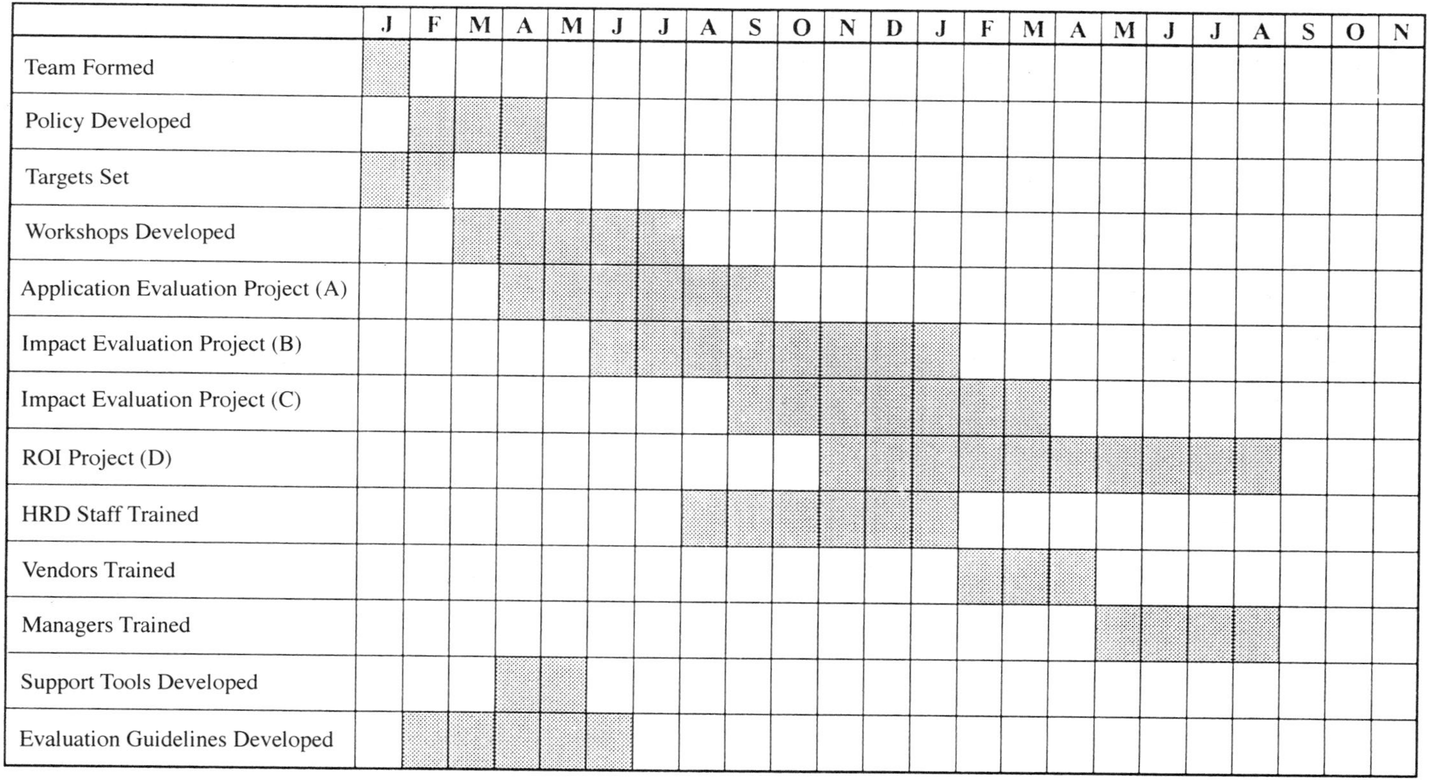

Figure 20-1. Measurement and evaluation implementation project plan for a large petroleum company.

Revising/Developing Policies and Procedures

Another key element of planning is revising (or developing) the organization's policy and procedures concerning measurement and evaluation, which is often a part of policy. Although these items were briefly covered in Chapter 3, they are presented here because of their importance in implementation. The policy statement contains information developed specifically for the measurement and evaluation process. It is frequently developed with the input of the HRD staff and key managers or clients. Sometimes policy issues are addressed during internal workshops designed to build skills with measurement and evaluation. The policy statement addresses critical issues that will influence the effectiveness of the measurement and evaluation process. Typical topics include adopting the five-level model presented in this book, requiring Level 3 and 4 objectives in some or all programs, and defining responsibilities for training and development. Figure 20-2 shows the topics in the measurement and evaluation policy for a large firm in South Africa.

Policy statements are very important because they provide guidance and direction for the staff and others who work closely with the process. It keeps the process clearly in focus and enables the group to establish goals for evaluation. Policy statements also provide an opportunity to communicate basic requirements and fundamental issues regarding performance and accountability. More than anything else, it serves as a learning tool to teach others, but must be developed in a collaborative and collective way. If policy statements are developed in isolation and do not have the endorsement and ownership of the staff and management, they will not be effective.

In some organizations, detailed guidelines for measurement and evaluation are developed. Overall, guidelines show how to utilize tools and techniques, guide the design process, provide consistency in evaluation, ensure that appropriate methods are used, and place the proper emphasis on each part of evaluation. Guidelines are more technical than policy statements and often contain detailed procedures showing how the process is actually undertaken and developed. They often include specific forms, instruments, and tools necessary to facilitate the process. Appendix 2 shows a condensed table of contents of evaluation guidelines for a multinational company. As this table of contents reveals, the guidelines are comprehensive and include significant emphasis on accountability.

Assessing the Climate

A final element in planning implementation is to assess the current climate for achieving results. Two groups are targeted for this effort: the internal training or HRD staff, and the management group. One useful tool for the staff, presented in Chapter 3, is a results-based instrument designed for this

1. Purpose
2. Mission
3. Evaluate all programs that will include the following levels:
   a. Participant satisfaction (100%)
   b. Learning (no less than 70%)
   c. Job applications (50%)
   d. Results (usually through sampling) (10%) (highly visible, expensive)
4. Evaluation support group (corporate) will provide assistance and advice in measurement and evaluation, instrument design, data analysis and evaluation strategy.
5. New programs are developed following logical steps beginning with needs analysis and ending with communicating results.
6. Evaluation instruments must be designed or selected to collect data for evaluation. They must be valid, reliable, economical and subject to audit by the evaluation support group.
7. Responsibility for HRD program results rests with trainers, participants and supervisors of participants.
8. An adequate system for collecting and monitoring HRD costs must be in place. All direct costs should be included.
9. At least annually the management board will review the status and results of HRD. The review will include HRD plans, strategies, results, costs, priorities, and concerns.
10. Line management shares in the responsibility for HRD programs, including evaluation through follow-up, pre-program commitment, and overall support.
11. Managers/supervisors must declare competence achieved through training and packaged programs. When not applicable, HRD staff should evaluate.
12. External HRD consultants must be selected based on previous evaluation. Central data/resource base must exist. All external HRD programs of over one day in duration will be subjected to evaluation procedures. In addition, the quality of external programs will be assessed by participants.
13. HRD program results must be communicated to the appropriate target audience. As a minimum, this includes management (participants' supervisors), participants, and all HRD staff.
14. HRD staff should be qualified to do effective needs analysis and evaluation.
15. Central database will be created for program development to prevent duplication and serve as program resource.
16. Union involvement in total training and development plan.

Figure 20-2. Results-based internal HRD (excerpts from actual policy for a large firm in South Africa).

purpose. This instrument, or some version of it, can serve as an initial assessment of how the training and development staff perceives training and HRD results. This instrument, which is provided with a more detailed analysis in other publications, is an excellent tool to examine important issues and concerns.[4] A gap analysis can reveal specific areas for improvement and goal setting. In addition, some organizations take annual assessments to measure progress.

Because of the importance of support from the management group, it is helpful to assess managers' perceptions of the effectiveness of training and HRD. In these organizations, an instrument designed specifically for management input is used, presented in Appendix 8. An interpretation of scores is presented along with the instrument. An assessment process provides an excellent opportunity to discuss current status and concerns. Then the organization can plan for significant changes, pinpointing particular issues that need support as measurement and evaluation is enhanced. A more detailed analysis is contained in other references.[4]

Preparing the HRD Staff

One group that will often resist a comprehensive evaluation process is the staff who must design, develop, and deliver training and HRD programs. These staff members often see evaluation as an unnecessary intrusion into their responsibilities, absorbing precious time and stifling their freedom to be creative. The cartoon character Pogo perhaps characterized it best when he said, "We have met the enemy and he is us." This section outlines some important issues that must be addressed when preparing the staff for the implementation of a comprehensive measurement and evaluation process.

Involving the Staff

The staff should be involved in the process for each key issue or major decision. As policy statements are prepared and evaluation guidelines are developed, staff input is absolutely essential. It is difficult for the staff to be critical of a process they helped design, develop, and deliver. Consequently, their involvement becomes a critical issue during implementation. Using meetings, brainstorming sessions, and task forces, combined with routine input, the staff can be involved in every phase of developing the framework and supporting the documents for evaluation.

Using Evaluation Data as a Learning Tool

One reason the HRD staff may resist evaluation is that the effectiveness of their programs will be fully exposed, possibly affecting their reputation.

They may have a fear of failure. To overcome this, evaluation should clearly be positioned as a tool for learning, not a vehicle to evaluate staff performance, at least during its early years of implementation. HRD staff members will not be interested in developing a process that may be used against them.

Staff members can learn as much from failures as successes. If the program is not effective, it is best to find out quickly and understand the issues first hand—not from others. If a program is ineffective and not producing the desired results, it will eventually be known to clients and/or the management group, if they don't know it already. Unchecked, this situation will cause managers to become less supportive of training. If the weaknesses and problems are identified early and adjustments are made quickly, not only will effective programs be developed, but credibility and respect for the function will be enhanced.

Removing Obstacles

Several obstacles to the implementation of a comprehensive evaluation process will usually be encountered. Some are realistic barriers, while others are often based on misunderstandings. Each should be explored and addressed. The most common are:

Evaluation is a complex process. Many of the HRD staff will perceive Level 4 and 5 evaluations as too complex to implement. To counter this, the staff must understand that it can be simplified by breaking the process down into individual components and steps.

Staff members often feel they do not have time for evaluation. Staff members need to understand that evaluation efforts can save more time in the future. A comprehensive evaluation may reveal that the program should be changed, modified, or even eliminated. Also, up-front planning of evaluation strategy can save additional follow-up time for the overall evaluation.

The staff must be motivated to pursue evaluation, even when senior executives are not requiring it. Most staff members will know when top managers are pushing the accountability issue. If they do not see that push, they are reluctant to take the time to make it work. They must see the benefits of pursuing higher levels of evaluation even if not required or encouraged by top management.

The staff may be concerned that evaluation results will lead to criticism. Many staff members will be concerned about the use of evaluation information. If the results are used to criticize the performance of program designers or facilitators, there will be a reluctance to embrace the concept.

These and other obstacles can inhibit an otherwise successful implementation. Each must be removed or reduced to a manageable level.

Teaching the Staff

The training and HRD staff will usually have inadequate skills in measurement and evaluation and thus will need to develop some expertise in the process. Measurement and evaluation is not always a formal part of their preparation to become a trainer or instructional designer. Consequently, each staff member must be provided training on evaluation to learn how the overall process works, step-by-step. In addition, staff members must know how to develop an evaluation strategy and specific plan, collect and analyze data from the evaluation, and interpret results from data analysis. Sometimes a one-to-two day workshop is needed to build adequate skills and knowledge to understand the process, appreciate what it can accomplish for the organization, see the necessity for it, and participate in a successful implementation.

Developing Planning Documents

Perhaps the two most useful evaluation planning documents are the data-collection plan and the ROI analysis plan, discussed in an earlier chapter. These plans show what data will be collected, at what time, by whom, and how specific analyses will be conducted, including isolating the effects of training and converting data to monetary values. Each staff member should know how to develop, explain, and use these plans.

Initiating ROI Projects

Important tangible evidence of a comprehensive evaluation is the initiation of the first project in which the ROI is calculated. This section outlines some of the key issues involved in identifying projects and keeping them on track.

Selecting Initial Programs

Selecting a program for ROI analysis is an important and critical issue. Only specific types of programs should be selected for a comprehensive, detailed analysis. Typical criteria for identifying programs for analysis are to select programs that

☐ Involve large target audiences.
☐ Are expected to be viable for a long time.
☐ Are important to overall strategic objectives.

☐ Are expensive.
☐ Have high visibility.
☐ Have a comprehensive needs assessment.

Using these or similar criteria, the staff must select the appropriate program to consider for an ROI project. Ideally, management should concur with or approve the criteria.

The next major step is to determine how many projects to undertake initially and in which particular areas. A small number of initial projects are recommended for two or three programs. The programs may represent the functional areas of the business such as operations, sales, finance, engineering, and information systems. Another approach is to select programs representing functional areas of training such as management and supervisor training, computer-based training, and technical training. It is important to select a manageable number so that the process will be implemented.

Reporting Progress

As the projects are developed and the ROI implementation is under way, status meetings should be conducted to report progress and discuss critical issues with appropriate team members. For example, if a supervisory training program for operations is selected as one of the ROI projects, all of the key staff involved in the program (design, development, and delivery) should meet regularly to discuss the status of the project. This keeps the project team focused on critical issues, generates the best ideas to tackle problems and barriers, and builds a knowledge base to implement evaluation in future programs. Sometimes this group is facilitated by an external consultant with expertise in the ROI process. In other cases, the internal ROI leader may facilitate the group.

These meetings serve three major purposes: reporting progress, learning new skills, and planning additional evaluation steps. The meeting usually begins with a status report on each ROI project, describing what has been accomplished since the previous meeting. Next, specific barriers to success and problems encountered are identified. The group discusses how to remove barriers to success and focuses on suggestions and recommendations, including developing specific plans. During the discussions, new issues are interjected in terms of possible tactics, techniques, or tools.

Establish Discussion Groups

Because the ROI process is considered to be difficult to understand and apply, it is sometimes helpful to establish discussion groups to learn the process. These groups may supplement formal workshops and other training programs and are often very flexible in format. Groups are usually facilitated by an external ROI consultant or the internal ROI leader. In each session, a new topic is presented and discussed thoroughly. Concerns about the topic and specific issues are discussed, including how ROI is applied in the organization. Discussion groups can be very flexible and adjusted to the needs of the group. Ideally, participants in group discussions should have an opportunity to apply, explore, or research topics and issues between sessions. Assignments involving analysis of cases and reading articles are also appropriate between sessions to continue to build knowledge and skills with the process.

Training the Management Team

Perhaps no group is more important to follow-up evaluation than the management team, who must allocate resources for training and development and support the programs. In addition, they often provide input and assistance for evaluation. Specific actions to train and develop the management team should be carefully planned and executed.

A critical issue that must be addressed before training the managers is the relationship between the training and development staff and key managers in the organization. A productive partnership is needed, one that requires each party to understand the concerns, problems, and opportunities of the other. Developing this type of relationship is a long-term process that must be deliberately planned and initiated by HRD managers. The decision to commit resources to, and support for, training is often based on the effectiveness of this relationship.

Needed: A Special Workshop for Managers

One effective approach to prepare managers for a comprehensive measurement and evaluation process is to conduct a workshop for managers, "Training for Non-Training Managers." Varying in duration from one-half to two days, this practical workshop shapes critical skills and changes perceptions to enhance support for evaluation. Managers leave the workshop with an improved perception of the impact of training and a clearer understanding of their roles in the training and development process. More importantly, they often have a renewed commitment to make training work in their organization.

Due to the critical need for the topic, this workshop should be required for all managers unless they have previously demonstrated strong support for the training function. Because of this requirement, it is essential for top executives to be supportive of this workshop and, in some cases, take an active role in conducting it. To tailor the program to specific organizational needs, a brief needs assessment may be necessary to determine the specific focus and areas of emphasis for the program.

Target Audiences. The target audience for this program is usually middle-level managers, but the target group may vary. In some organizations, the target may be first-level managers and in others, the target may begin with second-level managers. Three important questions help determine the proper audience.

1. Which group has the most direct influence on the training and development function?
2. Which management group is causing serious problems with lack of support?
3. Which group has the need to understand follow-up evaluation so they can influence training transfer?

The answer to all of these questions is often middle-level managers.

Timing. This workshop should be conducted early in the management development process, before non-supportive habits are delivered. When this program is implemented throughout the organization, it is best to start with higher-level managers and work down the organization. If possible, a version of the program should be part of a traditional management training program provided to supervisors when they are promoted into managerial positions.

Selling Top Management. Because convincing top management to require this program may be a difficult task, three approaches should be considered.

1. Discuss and illustrate the consequences of inadequate management support for training. The statistics are staggering in terms of wasted time and money.
2. Show how current support is lacking. An evaluation of an internal training program within the organization will often reveal the barriers to successful application of training. Lack of management support is often the main reason, which brings the issue close to home.
3. Demonstrate how savings can be generated and results can be achieved with evaluation.

The endorsement of the top management group is very important. In some organizations, top managers actually attend the program to explore first-hand what is involved and what they must do to make the process work. At a minimum, top management should support the program by signing memos describing the program or by approving policy statements. They should also ask penetrating questions in their staff meetings from time to time. This will not happen by chance. The HRD manager must tactfully coach top executives.

Workshop Content

The workshop will usually cover the topics outlined below. The time allotted for each topic and specific focus will depend on the organization, the experience of the managers, the needs of the managers, and the preparation of the management group. The program can be developed in separate modules, and managers can be exempt from certain modules based on their previous knowledge or experience with the topic. This module concept is recommended and emphasized below.

The Importance of Training. Managers need to be convinced that training and development is a mainstream responsibility that is gaining importance and influence in the organization. They need to understand the results-based approach of today's progressive training and development function. After completing this module, managers should perceive training as a critical process in their organization and be able to describe how the process contributes to strategic and operational objectives. Data from the organization are presented to show the full scope of training. Tangible evidence of top-management commitment in the form of memos, directives, and policies signed by the CEO or another appropriate top executive should be presented. In some organizations, the invitation to attend the program comes from the CEO, a gesture that shows strong top management commitment. Also, external data should be included to illustrate the growth of training budgets and the increasing importance of training and development. Perhaps a case showing the link between HRD and strategy would be helpful.

The Impact of Training. Too often, managers are unsure about the success of training. After completing this module, they will be able to identify steps to measure the impact of training on important output variables. Reports and studies should be presented showing the impact of training using measures such as productivity, quality, cost, response times, and customer satisfaction. Internal evaluation reports, if available, are presented to managers, showing convincing evidence that training is making a significant difference in the organization. If internal reports are not available, success stories or case studies from other organizations can be used. To meet this need, The American Society for Training and Development has published a casebook on measuring the return on investment in training and development.[5] Managers need to be convinced that training is a successful, results-based tool, not only to help with change, but to meet critical organizational goals and objectives.

The Training and Development Process. Managers usually will not support activities or processes that they do not fully understand. After completing this module, managers should be able to describe how the training process works in their organization and understand each critical step from needs assessment to follow-up evaluation. Managers need to be aware of the effort that goes into developing a training program and their role in each step of the process. A short case, illustrating all the steps, is helpful in this module. This discussion also reveals various areas of the potential impact of training and development.

Responsibility for Training. Defining who is responsible for training is important to the success of training. After completing this module, managers should be able to list their specific responsibilities for training and development. Managers must see how they can influence training and the degree of responsibility they must assume in the future. Multiple responsibilities for training are advocated, including managers, participants, participant supervisors, and trainers (developers and instructors). Case studies are appropriate in this module to illustrate the consequences when responsibilities are neglected or when there is failure to follow-up by managers. One specific case is available that was designed for this purpose.[6] In some organizations, job descriptions are revised to reflect training responsibility. In other organizations, major job-related goals are established to highlight management responsibility for training. Overall, this session leaves participants with a clear understanding of how their responsibility is linked to the success of training and development.

Active Involvement. One of the most important ways to enhance manager support for training and development is to get them actively involved in the process. After completing this module, managers will actually commit to one or more ways of active involvement in the future. Table 20-3 shows twelve areas of manager involvement identified for one organization. The information in the table was presented to managers in the workshop with a request that they commit to at least one area of involvement. After these areas are fully explained and discussed, each manager is asked to select one or more ways in which he or she will be involved in training and

Table 20-3
Management Involvement in Training and Education

The following are areas for present and future involvement in the training and education process at this division. Please check your areas of planned involvement.

	In Your Area	Outside Your Area
☐ Attend a Program Designed for Your Staff	☐	☐
☐ Provide Input on a Training Needs Analysis	☐	☐
☐ Serve on a Training Advisory Committee	☐	☐
☐ Provide Input on a Training Program Design	☐	☐
☐ Serve as a Subject Matter Expert	☐	☐
☐ Serve on a Task Force to Develop a Program	☐	☐
☐ Volunteer to Evaluate an External T&E Program	☐	☐
☐ Assist in the selection of a Vendor-Supplied T&E Program	☐	☐
☐ Provide Reinforcement to Your Employees After They Attend Training	☐	☐
☐ Coordinate a Training Program	☐	☐
☐ Assist in Program Evaluation or Follow-Up	☐	☐
☐ Conduct a Portion of the Program as a Facilitator	☐	☐

development in the future. A commitment to sign up for at least one involvement role is required.

If used properly, these commitments are a rich source of input and assistance from the management group. There will be many offers for involvement, and the training and development department must follow through with the offers. A quick follow-up on all offers is recommended.

Summary

The implementation of comprehensive measurement and evaluation is a critical element of the process. If not approached in a systematic, logical, and planned way, evaluation will not become an integral part of training and development and consequently, the accountability of the programs will be lacking. This final chapter presented different elements that must be considered and issues that must be addressed to ensure that implementation is smooth and uneventful. The result would be a complete integration of evaluation as a mainstream activity in the HRD process.

Discussion Questions

1. In your organization (or one with which you are familiar), identify the individual or team who should implement the ROI process. Explain.

2. It is often said, "The time to implement the ROI process is when you don't have to implement it." Relate this comment to the implementation process described in this chapter.
3. Name five barriers to the successful implementation of the ROI process in your organization (or one with which you are familiar). How can they be removed or their effects be minimized?
4. Who should be responsible for training program evaluation? Training results?
5. Establish the evaluation targets for your organization (or one with which you are familiar).
6. One implementation step taken by many organizations is to require Level 3 and 4 objectives for new programs. These same organizations report that this action had a significant impact on the effectiveness of programs. Explain.
7. Training and HRD staff members often resist evaluation. Why? How can this resistance be minimized?
8. What types of projects should be selected for initial ROI studies? Explain.
9. Managers will usually resist formal training on the ROI process even when there is a strong need for it. How can the HRD manager get them to attend? Explain the pros and cons to such an approach.
10. Develop an appropriate ROI implementation process for your organization (or one with which you are familiar). Explain why you have selected each element of your plan.

References

1. *Certification Process for Measuring the Return on Investment in Training and Development Workshop* brochure, 1996, Performance Resources Organization, P.O. Box 380637, Birmingham, AL 35238-0637.
2. Geber, B. "Does Training Make a Difference? Prove It!" *Training,* March 1995, pp. 27–36.
3. Phillips, J. J. "How Results-Based Are Your Training and Development Programs?" in *The 1997 McGraw-Hill Training & Performance Sourcebook.* M. Silberman (Ed.), New York, NY: McGraw-Hill, 1997, pp. 97–109.
4. Silberman, M. (Ed.) *The 1997 McGraw-Hill Training & Performance Sourcebook.* New York, NY: McGraw-Hill, 1997.
5. Phillips, J. J. (Ed.) *In Action: Measuring Return on Investment.* Alexandria, VA: American Society for Training and Development, 1994.
6. Phillips, J. J. *International Electric.* Birmingham, AL: Performance Resources Organization, 1994.

Fear and Loathing on the Evaluation Trail

by **Bernadine Eve Bednarz**
University of Wisconsin—Extension

Last spring, after leading a successful training program, I asked participants for an evaluation of the presenters. Thirty out of 65 participants submitted written evaluations.

I passed the results on to the presenters. Jack, one of the trainers involved in the program, called to tell me he was surprised that I had included this comment about one of the presenters: "She is intelligent, yet has not found her own style—having become a poor carbon copy of the famous person who led the workshop." Jack thought it was a cruel, insensitive remark and felt I could have translated it into kinder terms. He said that he too had struggled with being compared to famous people.

Last week I passed out evaluations for another program. A comment about one of the presenters was: "Due to Justine's zero personality, I find it hard to concentrate on the information she has to offer in her apparently very effective program."

The next day I had three phone calls and one letter from members of the planning committee who felt that the remark was "impolite" and "deadly." They suggested that I should have changed "zero personality" to "retiring personality."

In light of these responses I devised the following list of suggestions for participants evaluating training programs:

1. Make your language acceptable and gentle. If not, I will change it for you.
2. Never call anyone a sexist, racist, ageist, male chauvinist pig, fascist, moderate, conservative, Communist, Socialist, Democrat, Republican, or Whig.
3. Do not tell presenters to improve anything. They do not need it.
4. If you say something hurtful, I will make it palatable.
5. Never mention your disappointment if objectives have not been met. Conceal vigorously.
6. Do not use phrases like "Could you," "Have you thought about," "Is there any chance you would change. . ."
7. Do not take this evaluation too seriously because we won't.
8. Please wear a hood over your face so you will not be recognized when handing in your comments.
9. Sign the name of another participant so we can unjustly blame them.
10. Write out two evaluations with contradictory statements to create confusion: "the room was too hot/the room was too cold"; "he was the best trainer in this area/this man was vastly incompetent."
11. Focus on the insignificant and unimportant parts of the workshop: the dust on the floor, naked light bulbs, no chairs to sit on.
12. Never be specific. Just say, "I never liked John and like his presentation less."
13. Do not challenge sacred cows. They are the leaders in this field, and you are not.
14. Write illegibly; use arcane language.
15. Trainers are fragile; tread carefully.

Reports on how this worked will follow.

(Reproduced with the permission of Bernadine Eve Bednarz, University of Wisconsin—Extension.)

APPENDIX 2

Evaluation Guidelines for a Multinational Company

Section 1: Policy
1.1   The Need for Accountability
1.2   The Bottom Line: Linking Training with Business Needs
1.3   Results-Based Approach
1.4   Implications
1.5   Communication
1.6   Payoff

Section 2: Responsibilities
2.1   Training Group Responsibilities: Overall
2.2   Training Group Responsibilities: Specifics for Selected Groups
2.3   The Business Unit Responsibilities
2.4   Participant Manager Responsibilities
2.5   Participant Responsibilities

Section 3: Evaluation Framework
3.1   Purpose of Evaluation
3.2   Levels of Evaluation
3.3   Process Steps for Training Implementation
3.4   Evaluation Model

Section 4: Level 1 Guidelines
4.1   Purpose and Scope
4.2   Areas of Coverage—Standard Form
4.3   Optional Areas of Coverage
4.4   Administrative Issues
4.5   How to Use Level 1 Data

Section 5: Level 2 Guidelines
5.1 Purpose and Scope
5.2 Learning Measurement Issues
5.3 Techniques for Measuring Learning
5.4 Administration
5.5 Using Level 2 Data

Section 6: Level 3 Guidelines
6.1 Purpose and Scope
6.2 Follow-Up Issues
6.3 Types of Follow-Up Techniques
6.4 Administrative Issues
6.5 Using Level 3 Evaluation

Section 7: Level 4 and 5 Guidelines
7.1 Purpose and Scope
7.2 Business Results and ROI Issues
7.3 Monitoring Performance Data
7.4 Extracting Data from Follow-Up Evaluations
7.5 Isolating the Effects of the Learning Solution
7.6 Converting Data to Monetary Values
7.7 Developing Costs
7.8 Calculating the ROI
7.9 Identifying Intangible Benefits
7.10 Administrative Issues
7.11 Using Business Impact and ROI Data

Sample Selection

When the evaluation involves the use of a sample group of participants, the selection of the sample becomes an important issue. There are two major concerns: the make up of the sample (sample selection), and the size of the sample. Sample selection can be accomplished in relatively easy steps.

Simple Random Sampling

With simple random sampling, participants are selected on a random basis. This eliminates prejudice or unevenness in the selection of those who will participate in an HRD program, and ensures that the validity of the evaluation cannot be questioned.

The most common process for random selection from a relatively small population is through the use of random number tables. A random number table is a computer-generated table of random numbers, as shown in Table A3-1. An example illustrates the use of this table:

Ten production supervisors are to be trained on an experimental basis from a group of 100 production supervisors. The selection is made on a random basis. The supervisors are numbered beginning with 00 up through 99. The numbers in the table are grouped in pairs, since only 2 digits are needed. From the table, the first 10 2-digit random numbers are 51, 77, 27, 46, 40, 33, 12, 90, and 44. The supervisors corresponding to those numbers are selected for the program.

This process is simple, easy to follow, removes selection bias, and adds more credibility to the sample.

Stratified Random Sampling

Sometimes a simple random sampling method will not give the kind of representative sampling desired. In the previous example, suppose that the 100 supervisors were in three departments with one department containing 40 supervisors and the other two containing 30. There is a requirement that the sample be distributed in proportion to the number of supervisors in each

Table A3-1
Random Number Table

51772	74640	42331	29044	46621	62898	93582	04186	19640	87056
24033	23491	83587	06568	21960	21387	76105	10863	97453	90581
45939	60173	52078	25424	11645	55870	56974	37428	93507	94271
30586	02133	75797	45406	31041	86707	12973	17169	88116	42187
03585	79353	81938	82322	96799	85659	36081	50884	14070	74950
64937	03355	95863	20790	65304	55189	00745	65253	11822	15804
15630	64759	51135	98527	62586	41889	25439	88036	24034	67283
09448	56301	57683	30277	94623	85418	68829	06652	41982	49159
21631	91157	77331	60710	52290	16835	48653	71590	16159	14676
91097	17480	29414	06829	87843	28195	27279	47152	35683	47280
50532	25496	95652	42457	73547	76552	50020	24819	52984	76168
07136	40876	79971	54195	25708	51817	36732	72484	94923	75936
27989	64728	10744	08396	56242	90985	28868	99431	50995	20507
85184	73949	36601	46253	00477	25234	09908	36574	72139	70185
54398	21154	97810	36764	32869	11785	55261	59009	38714	38723
65544	34371	09591	07839	58892	92843	72828	91341	84821	63886
08263	65952	85762	64235	39238	18776	84303	99247	46149	03229
39817	67906	48236	16057	81812	15815	63700	85915	19219	45943
62257	04077	79443	95203	02479	30763	92486	54083	23631	05825
53298	90276	62545	21944	16530	03878	07516	95715	02526	33537

Source: Spiegel, M. R., Theory and Problems of Statistics, *Schaum's Outline Series, McGraw-Hill Book Co., New York, 1961, p. 349.*

department. Four supervisors must be selected from the large department, and three each from the other two to yield a sample size of ten. Through the simple random sampling procedure, this random selection may not occur. Stratified random sampling will assure the desired make up. The population of 100 supervisors can be stratified into the three groups, and then simple random sampling can be applied to each of the three groups. In this example the supervisors in the large department are numbered 00 through 40. In the other two departments the supervisors are numbered 00 through 30. The same tables are used to select four from the first department and three each from the other two departments. The digits are selected in pairs, as before. When a number is selected that exceeds the numbers attached to a supervisor, it is tossed out. For instance, 27 would be the first number used since 51 and 77 are larger than 40. The same procedure is repeated for the next two departments until a total of 10 supervisors is chosen.

In this example the population was stratified according to the departmental units, but there are other useful ways for the population to be stratified. Examples are age, sex, work location, output, sales volume, or geographic location. Overall, stratification provides a basis for a sample to be more representative of the true population.

Systematic Random Sampling

The two previous methods for selecting random samples are useful for simple selection when the population is relatively small, which is the case in most HRD evaluation efforts. However, occasionally the population may be large. For instance, suppose a telephone company has 1,000 telephone repairers to be trained. In an experimental training effort a group is selected to participate in the program. Using the two previous methods to select the sample group, all telephone repairers are listed, assigned numbers, and selected using the table of random numbers. With a group this large, this process can become cumbersome and lengthy.

A more useful procedure is to use what is called systematic sampling. This procedure involves selecting employees on some systematic basis, such as every tenth person. In the previous example, assume a sample size of 25 repairers is needed for the experimental group. The list of all repairers is divided into groups of 40 (1,000 ÷ 25). Using simple random sampling, a selection is made from the first group of 40. Suppose this selection yields the twenty-first name. From each of the remaining 24 groups, the twenty-first name is selected. This process will give a precision that is approximately equivalent to that obtained by the simple random sampling when the population is randomly ordered.

Systematic sampling has several advantages. One, of course, is the ease in drawing the sample. Much time and effort are saved. Another advantage is that the process is efficient. The sample is usually spread out more evenly over the population and is thus more representative of the population. As a result, the information per unit cost is greater. However, this spread could depend on a particular characteristic of the population and may not apply in every case. Because of these advantages, systematic sampling is widely used when the population is large.

Simple Cluster Sampling

The final sampling method presented is cluster sampling. This method is another time-saving procedure used when a sample is selected from a fairly large population—one that is grouped into clusters. In the previous example of 1,000 telephone repairers, suppose the telephone repairers are in 10 operating units scattered among 3 states with 100 repairers in each unit. The time involved in using random sampling, coupled with the administrative cost involved in selecting participants from all 10 operating units, may prohibit the use of one of the earlier techniques. These two problems can be overcome if it is recognized that the telephone repairers are actually grouped into clusters of 10 operating units at random and then select 5 repairers at random in each of the 5 units. The samples are confined to operating units, eliminating the need to involve the other 5 operating units. This assumes, of course, that the characteristics in those other 5 units were approximately the same as the 5 selected. This technique can be useful anytime the population under consideration can be divided into a number of similar clusters. The ultimate savings is in preparation, cost, and administration of the sampling process.

The previous four methods are fairly straightforward and simple. They are purposely presented this way in order not to confuse the reader. The subject of statistics, particularly in the sampling theory, is no simple process. Those who desire more precision, especially when the parameters and characteristics of the sampling process are more complex, should seek additional information.[1]

Sample Size Determination

The question of sample size is now addressed. An example will illustrate the importance of sample size:

A large insurance firm has 200 employees who process claims. The average time to process a claim is a closely monitored factor. An HRD program is proposed that will improve the time to process claims. Initially, the program will be conducted with a small pilot group, and their performance will be compared to that of the entire population of claims processors in the organization. How large a group should be chosen? A more general question is, "How many people must participate in the program, on a pilot basis, before we can make general statements about all the people who will complete the program?" If the size is too small, the conclusion from the pilot group may be invalid. An unnecessarily large sample can add additional expense.

While the question of sample size seems to be simple, the answer is complex. From a statistical basis, there are four significant factors that affect the sample size.

The size of the population from which the sample is drawn has an influence. If the population is small, then certainly the sample size should be larger in proportion to the total. If the population consists of 10 claims processors, a sample size of 10 (i.e., the entire population) is probably needed to make an accurate judgment about that population. As the population increases, the required sample size in proportion to the population is smaller.

The sample size also depends on the variation of the data being observed. In the previous example it is the time to process a claim. The greater the variance, the larger the sample size needed. The measure for this variance is called standard deviation.

Through the sample, an estimate of a new average time to process claims is determined. Therefore, the sample is used to predict a value. The precision of the estimate is another factor that determines the sample size. The term "precision" refers to the accuracy desired for the prediction. Should the estimate be within 2 hours of the actual new average time if everyone completes the program? The less precision, the larger the sample size.

In statistical estimation there is the possibility of an error. When a value is predicted based on a sample, there will be a possibility that the sample does not accurately predict the real value. This refers to the reliability of the estimate and is sometimes expressed in a confidence value. If an evaluator wants to be 95% confident that the estimate is indeed a true predictor, then the reliability of the sample should be 95%. The higher the reliability, the larger the sample size required.

To summarize briefly, the actual sample size selected to make an estimate depends on four factors:

1. The actual size of the population of prospective participants.
2. The variation in the quantity to be predicted.
3. The precision of the sample estimator.
4. The reliability of the precision.

These factors can be related to formulas to select the sample size. For large and small populations, the formulas will be slightly different. One fairly simple formula for sample size when the population is more than 30 is:

$$n = \frac{(z\sigma)^2}{d^2}$$

where n is the sample size, z is the reliability coefficient that denotes the reliability, σ represents standard deviation, and d represents the precision. An example will illustrate sample size calculation:

A sequence of operations on an assembly line takes a predetermined amount of time to complete, on the average. A large number of employees perform this assembly sequence. A proposed HRD program will possibly reduce this assembly time. A pilot group will be trained, and their new times for completing the assembly sequence will be calculated. It is anticipated that the average times will be reduced significantly with this training. It is assumed that the variation (standard deviation) in time for participants who complete the program will be approximately equal to the variation in times for all the assemblers. The present average time has been 30 minutes and the standard deviation has been 2. It is desired that the estimate of the new average time to complete the assembly be correct to within 1 minute and that the reliability of this precision be 95% (i.e., being 95% confident that the estimate will be correct within one minute). How many employees should be involved in the pilot program?

Solution: The 95% reliability translates into a reliability coefficient of 1.96 or approximately 2. For our purposes, this translation should be accepted on faith. A detailed analysis can be found in almost any standard text on statistics. The standard deviation is 2. The precision is 1. Plugging this information into the formula, we have the following:

$$n = \frac{(z\sigma)^2}{d^2} = \frac{(2 \times 2)^2}{1^2} = 16$$

The sample size needed is 16. If 16 employees are used in the experiment, the new average time to complete the assembly can be estimated with the desired reliability and precision.

An analysis of the formula reinforces the previous conclusions about the relationship between the various factors and the sample size. A larger sample size is needed when

☐ The bound on precision is smaller.
☐ The standard deviation is larger.
☐ A greater reliability is desired.

From a logical point of view, tighter precision and reliability necessitates a larger sample size. A more precise and reliable estimation requires a sample size closer to the actual size of the population.

There is a non-statistical factor that influences the sample size: comfort level. Decision makers for a proposed program should consider (based on their perceptions) what sample size is desired for an experiment. What size makes them comfortable? This factor may be just as important as the statistical basis for determining the sample size.

There have been many attempts at creating tables to select a sample size based on predetermined characteristics. While these may be helpful when the conditions change very little, they might not be helpful for a variety of applications in the HRD development area.

In summary, the information about sample size selection can be a complex question. It is recommended that a sample as large as possible be used—one that is convincing to the decision makers for the program. If detailed statistical verification is needed to support your sample size selection, more detailed references on statistics may be necessary.[1]

References

1. Yamane, T., *Elementary Sampling Theory,* Prentice Hall, Englewood Cliffs, NJ, 1967, pp. 48–236.

New Supervisors' Development Program Evaluation Questionnaire

Take a few minutes to think about the entire program and give us your answers to the following questions. This information will be very helpful to us in planning future sessions.

General Evaluation

1. The following objectives were stated for the program. To what extent did the program achieve these objectives?

	Completely Successful	Generally Successful	Limited Success	Failed
A. To improve your understanding of the nature, requirements and responsibilities of the supervisor's job	☐	☐	☐	☐
B. To increase your knowledge of basic supervisory principles	☐	☐	☐	☐
C. To develop skills to successfully conduct the most common supervisor/subordinate discussions	☐	☐	☐	☐
D. To increase your effectiveness as a leader through a better understanding of human behavior	☐	☐	☐	☐
E. To improve your knowledge of policies within which you must work	☐	☐	☐	☐
F. To enhance your knowledge of how the company functions and the services available to the supervisor	☐	☐	☐	☐

2. If you wish to explain any of the above ratings, please do so.

_____

_____

_____

3. What was your overall reaction to this program?
   Excellent   ☐
   Better than expected   ☐
   Satisfactory   ☐
   Below average   ☐
4. Did you feel that the program met your needs as a supervisor?
   Yes   ☐
   Uncertain   ☐
   No (Please explain)   ☐

_____

_____

_____

5. Do you feel that you appreciate more the importance of your job as a supervisor having completed this course?
   Yes   ☐
   Uncertain   ☐
   No   ☐
6. Do you feel that you will be better able to do your job after attending this program?
   Yes   ☐
   Uncertain   ☐
   No   ☐
7. Do you have a better attitude about your job now that you have completed this program?
   Yes   ☐
   Uncertain   ☐
   No   ☐
8. Would you recommend that other new supervisors attend this program?
   Yes   ☐
   Uncertain   ☐
   No   ☐
9. Did you think the number of students in the class was:
   Just right   ☐
   Too few   ☐
   Too many   ☐
10. When and how did you first learn that you had been selected to attend this program?

_____

_____

_____

Instructor Evaluation

11. Although you rated each instructor at the end of his or her presentation, please provide the following overall evaluation on the effectiveness of the instructors as a group:

	Very Effective	Better Than Expected	Somewhat Effective	Not Effective
A. Knowledge of subject	☐	☐	☐	☐
B. Organization and preparation	☐	☐	☐	☐
C. Style and delivery	☐	☐	☐	☐
D. Responsiveness to participants	☐	☐	☐	☐
E. Creating appropriate learning climate	☐	☐	☐	☐

12. Comments about the instructors

_____

_____

_____

Method of Presentation

13. Do you think too many instructors were involved in this program?
    Just right   ☐
    Too few   ☐
    Too many   ☐

14. How do you rate the balance of lectures, group discussions, and group exercises?
    Too much lecture   ☐
    Too much discussion   ☐
    Too many exercises   ☐
    Good balance   ☐

15. How helpful were the group exercises?
    Very helpful   ☐
    Helpful   ☐
    Not helpful   ☐

16. How did you feel about the pacing of the program?
    Too fast   ☐
    Just right   ☐
    Too slow   ☐

17. Did you have enough skill practice time?
    Yes   ☐
    Uncertain   ☐
    No   ☐

Program Content

Please refer to the list of modules for the entire program while answering these questions.

18. What did you like best about the program?

_____

_____

_____

19. What did you like least about the program?

_____

_____

_____

20. If any of your attitudes about supervising have changed, please indicate what has changed and what part of the program had the most significant impact on bringing about that change.

_____

_____

No change   ☐

21. Which module will be most useful to you on your job?

_____

_____

_____

22. What do you think should be added to the program?

_____

_____

_____

23. What do you think should be dropped from the program?

_____

_____

_____

24. Do you rate the program length
    Just right   ☐
    Too short   ☐
    Too long   ☐

25. Was the program content logically sequenced?
    Very well sequenced   ☐
    Suitable   ☐
    Poorly sequenced   ☐

26. How valuable was the program content to your current job?
    Very valuable   ☐
    Some value   ☐
    No real value   ☐

27. How much did the program duplicate what you had learned some-
where else?
Much duplication ☐
Some duplication ☐
Very little duplication ☐
28. How do you rate the balance of theoretical and practical material in
the program?
Too theoretical ☐
Good balance ☐
Too practical ☐
29. Which term below do you feel best describes the teaching level of this
program?
Very difficult ☐
Difficult ☐
Suitable ☐
Easy ☐
Too easy ☐
30. Comments about the program content _____
_____
_____

Instructional Materials

31. Did you think enough audio-visual aids were used?
Just right ☐
Too few ☐
Too many ☐
32. How do you rate the quality of the audio-visual aids?
High quality ☐
OK ☐
Below expectations ☐
33. In your opinion, were the number of handouts you received during the
program sufficient?
Just right ☐
Too few ☐
Too many ☐
34. How do you rate the quality of the handout material?
High quality ☐
Fair ☐
Below expectations ☐
35. Was the handout material relevant to the course content?
Yes ☐
Uncertain ☐
No ☐

Out-of-Class Assignments

36. What did you think of the pre-program assignment?
Very valuable ☐
Some value ☐
No real value ☐
37. What did you think of the evening assignments?
Very valuable ☐
Some value ☐
No real value ☐
38. How do you rate the difficulty of the assignments?
Very difficult ☐
Suitable ☐
Easy ☐
39. How do you rate the relevancy of the assignments to the course material?
Very relevant ☐
Suitable ☐
Not relevant ☐

Facilities

40. Did you like the seating arrangement of the classroom?
Yes ☐
Uncertain ☐
No ☐
41. Did you think your chair was comfortable?
Yes ☐
Uncertain ☐
No ☐
42. How do you rate the service (breaks, lunch, etc.)?
Excellent ☐
Better than expected ☐
Satisfactory ☐
Below average ☐
43. How do you rate the physical classroom environment (temperature, lighting, noise, etc.)?
Excellent ☐
Better than expected ☐
Satisfactory ☐
Below average ☐
44. How do you rate the housing accommodations (if applicable)?
Excellent ☐
Better than expected ☐
Satisfactory ☐
Below average ☐

Planned Improvements

45. As a result of this program, what do you estimate to be the increase in your personal effectiveness, expressed as a percent?
    _____%

46. Please indicate what you will do differently on the job as a result of this program (please be specific):
    1. _____
    2. _____
    3. _____
    4. _____

47. As a result of any change in your thinking or new ideas about supervising which you have learned, please estimate (in dollars) the amount of money that you will save the company (i.e., reduced absenteeism and turnover, reduced employee complaints, better teamwork, increase in personal effectiveness, etc.) over a period of one year:
    $_____

48. What is the basis of this estimate?
    _____
    _____

49. What confidence, expressed as a percentage, can you put in your estimate? (0% = No confidence; 100% = Certainty)
    _____%

50. To what degree will your on-the-job environment encourage you to use the skills and concepts presented in this program?
    To a great degree   ☐
    To some degree   ☐
    No encouragement   ☐
    It will discourage their use   ☐

Effective Meetings

Follow-Up Impact Questionnaire

Are you currently in a people management role/capacity? Yes ☐   No ☐

1. Listed below are the objectives of the Effective Meetings program. After reflecting on this program, please indicate the degree of success in meeting the objectives:

As a result of this program, participants will have:	Failed	Limited Success	Generally Successful	Completely Successful
a. the tools and techniques to prepare for, conduct, and follow up on meetings,	☐	☐	☐	☐
b. the ability to facilitate the human dynamics of meetings,	☐	☐	☐	☐
c. the strategies to participate in and chair meetings more effectively.	☐	☐	☐	☐

2. Did you develop and implement an on-the-job action plan for Effective Meetings? Yes ☐   No ☐

If yes, please describe the nature and outcome of the plan. If not, explain why. _____

_____

_____

_____

_____

3. Please rate, on a scale of 1–5, the relevance of each of the program elements to your job, with (1) indicating no relevance, and (5) indicating very relevant.

	1	2	3	4	5
Interactive Activities	☐	☐	☐	☐	☐
Group Discussions	☐	☐	☐	☐	☐
Networking Opportunities	☐	☐	☐	☐	☐
Reading Materials/Video	☐	☐	☐	☐	☐
Program Content	☐	☐	☐	☐	☐

4. Have you used the materials since you participated in the program?
    Yes ☐   No ☐
    Please explain._____
    _____
    _____
    _____
    _____

5. Please indicate the degree to which your knowledge of, or skills with, the following items were enhanced as a result of your participation in Effective Meetings:

	No Change	Little Change	Some Change	Signifi-cant Change	Much Change	No Opportunity To Use Skill
a. Participating Effectively in Meetings	☐	☐	☐	☐	☐	☐
b. Avoiding Meetings Unless They Are Necessary	☐	☐	☐	☐	☐	☐
c. Minimizing the Number of Participants Attending Meetings	☐	☐	☐	☐	☐	☐
d. Setting Objectives for Meetings	☐	☐	☐	☐	☐	☐
e. Developing an Agenda for Each Meeting	☐	☐	☐	☐	☐	☐
f. Controlling Time of Meetings	☐	☐	☐	☐	☐	☐
g. Enhancing Participant Satisfaction in Meetings	☐	☐	☐	☐	☐	☐
h. Arranging the Meeting Site for Maximum Effectiveness	☐	☐	☐	☐	☐	☐
i. Scheduling the Optimum Time for Meetings	☐	☐	☐	☐	☐	☐
j. Communicating the Ground Rules for Meetings	☐	☐	☐	☐	☐	☐
k. Assigning Appropriate Roles for Meeting Participants	☐	☐	☐	☐	☐	☐

	No Change	Little Change	Some Change	Signifi- cant Change	Much Change	No Opportunity To Use Skill
l. Reaching Consensus in Meetings When Appropriate	☐	☐	☐	☐	☐	☐
m. Listening Actively to Meeting Participants	☐	☐	☐	☐	☐	☐
n. Encouraging Parti- cipants in Meetings	☐	☐	☐	☐	☐	☐
o. Using Brain- storming in Meet- ings When Appropriate	☐	☐	☐	☐	☐	☐
p. Dealing with Difficult Meeting Participants	☐	☐	☐	☐	☐	☐
q. Providing Feed- back to Meeting Participants	☐	☐	☐	☐	☐	☐
r. Handling Conflict in Meetings	☐	☐	☐	☐	☐	☐
s. Keeping the Meeting on Focus	☐	☐	☐	☐	☐	☐
t. Accomplishing Meeting Objectives	☐	☐	☐	☐	☐	☐
u. Evaluating the Meeting Process	☐	☐	☐	☐	☐	☐
v. Implementing Action Plans	☐	☐	☐	☐	☐	☐
w. Planning a Follow-Up Activity	☐	☐	☐	☐	☐	☐

6. List (3) Effective Meeting behaviors or skills you have used as a result of the program. _____
_____
_____
_____

7. What has changed about your meeting activity profile as a result of this program? (Fewer meetings, fewer participants, shorter meetings, etc.)
_____
_____
_____
_____

8. Please estimate the following monthly time-saving measures. Use the most recent month compared to the month before attending this program. Provide only improvements directly related to this program and only when the time is used productively.

    ☐ Number of meetings avoided each month with
       improved planning and analysis   _____
    ☐ Average time saved per meeting per month (in hours)   _____
    ☐ Number of participants reduced per meeting per month _____

9. What level of confidence do you place on the above estimates? (0% = No Confidence, 100% = Certainty) _____ %

10. Please identify any specific accomplishments/improvements that you can link to this program (on-time schedules, project completion, response times, etc.) _____
    _____
    _____
    _____
    _____

11. What specific monetary value can be attributed to the above accomplishments/improvements? While this is a difficult question, try to think of specific ways in which the above improvements can be converted to monetary units. Along with the monetary value, please indicate the basis of your calculation.

    _____

    Basis _____
    _____
    _____
    _____
    _____

12. What level of confidence do you place in the above estimates? (0% = No confidence, 100% = Certainty) _____ %

13. Other factors often influence improvements in performance. Please indicate the percent of the above improvement that is related directly to this program. _____ %

    Please explain._____
    _____
    _____
    _____

14. Do you think the Effective Meetings program represented a good investment for High Tech, Inc.?   Yes ☐   No ☐

    Please explain._____

    _____

    _____

    _____

15. Indicate the extent to which you think this Effective Meetings program has influenced each of these measures in your work unit, department, or business unit:

	No Influence	Some Influence	Moderate Influence	Significant Influence	Much Influence
a. Productivity	☐	☐	☐	☐	☐
b. Customer Response Time	☐	☐	☐	☐	☐
c. Cost Control	☐	☐	☐	☐	☐
d. Employee Satisfaction	☐	☐	☐	☐	☐
e. Customer Satisfaction	☐	☐	☐	☐	☐
f. Quality	☐	☐	☐	☐	☐
g. Other _____	☐	☐	☐	☐	☐

16. What barriers, if any, have you encountered that have prevented you from using skills or knowledge gained in this program? Please explain, if possible.

    _____

    _____

    _____

    _____

17. What specific suggestions do you have for improving this program?

    _____

    _____

    _____

    _____

18. Other comments:

    _____

    _____

    _____

    _____

Action Plan

Page _____ of _____

Name: _____ Instructor Signature _____

Follow-Up Date _____ Objective: _____

Evaluation Period: _____ to _____

Improvement Measure: _____

Current Performance _____

Target Performance _____

Action Steps

1. _____
_____
_____

2. _____
_____
_____

3. _____
_____
_____

4. _____
_____
_____

5. _____
_____
_____

6. _____
_____
_____

7. _____
_____
_____

Intangible Benefits:

Analysis

A. What is the unit of measure? _____

B. What is the value (cost) of one unit? $_____

C. How did you arrive at this value?_____
_____
_____
_____
_____
_____
_____
_____
_____
_____
_____

D. How much did the measure change during the evaluation period (monthly value)? _____

E. What percent of this change was actually caused by this program? _____%

F. What level of confidence do you place on the above information? (100% = Certainty and 0% = No confidence) _____%

Comments:_____
_____
_____

Statistical Inference

The Hypothesis

An hypothesis is a proposed explanation of the relationship between two or more variables, such as performance and training. An example is: "production employees' performance will improve as a result of the training program." The statement is tested and is either rejected or not rejected based on the evaluation data, the result of the statistical analysis, and a statistical test. (Some individuals prefer to use the terminology "fail to reject" or "not rejected" rather than "accept." The rationale is that in some situations failing to reject the hypothesis on the basis of a single test may not be sufficient to accept the hypothesis.)

The hypothesis differs from a problem statement or objective in that it provides a tentative answer to the problem—that is, the training leads to improved performance. A key point to remember is that when a hypothesis is used, a statistical analysis is necessary. This appendix on statistical inference presents the common types of statistical analyses used in hypothesis testing.

Occasionally a null hypothesis is stated. The null hypothesis states that there is no improvement as a result of an HRD program. If the evaluation data and analysis prove otherwise, then the null hypothesis is rejected. The conclusion: there is improvement caused by something other than chance, probably the HRD program. This conclusion is reached based on a specified confidence level, which is discussed later. This null hypothesis may not be formally stated in an evaluation, but it is assumed and is the basis for performing the statistical analysis.

Errors in Hypothesis Testing

As mentioned previously, in hypothesis testing the HRD program evaluator has two choices: reject the hypothesis, or fail to reject the hypothesis. Depending on the decision, there will be a possible error involved in making either one of those decisions. Figure A7-1 shows the possible combinations. If the hypothesis is false and it is rejected, then it is the correct decision. If, on the other hand, the hypothesis is true and it is rejected, then there is an error, usually called a Type I error. If the hypothesis is not rejected and it is true, then it is a correct decision. However, if the hypothesis is not rejected and it is false, there is another error, usually referred to as a Type II error.

	Hypothesis False	Hypothesis True
Reject Hypothesis	Correct Decision	Type I Error
Do Not Reject Hypothesis	Type II Error	Correct Decision

Figure A7-1. Possible errors in hypothesis testing.

Which error is more serious? It depends on the situation. For example, an organization has a large sales force. Management is considering a proposal to purchase a packaged HRD program that is designed to increase the participants' sales output. A pilot program is planned. If the results of the pilot program are good, the packaged program will be purchased and implemented for the entire sales force. The null hypothesis that forms the basis of the evaluation is: "there will be no increase in sales as a result of the program." Pre-program and post-program measurements are taken, and an analysis is conducted to see if that hypothesis is either rejected or not rejected. A Type I error occurs when the hypothesis is true (there is no increase in sales), yet it is rejected. This means that the program is purchased and all salespersons are trained, although there will be no effect on sales output. This error could be very costly. A Type II error, on the other hand, means that there is an improvement in sales, but the hypothesis is not rejected and the program is not purchased. The substantial expenditure is avoided, yet increases in sales will not be realized. A program is discarded that will increase sales. However, another program will probably be examined or developed if the goal is to try to improve the sales output.

As this example illustrates, there is usually more at risk in the Type I error. The probability of making a Type I error is called the level of significance and has the symbol α. The most common value for the level of significance is .05. This figure means that there is a 5% chance that a Type I error can be made. If everything else is held constant, raising the level of significance will decrease the probability of making a Type II error. Consequently, lowering the level of significance increases the probability of a Type II error.

Statistical Tests

The process of testing an hypothesis involves calculating a statistical test value and comparing a value from an appropriate statistical table, based on a predetermined level of significance. The comparison of these two values determines whether the hypothesis is rejected or not rejected.

The type of test statistic depends on the type of data being compared. To keep the presentation simple, the analysis will be confined to comparisons of mean values, since these are probably the most common types of program evaluation data. Typical comparisons are average values of experimental groups versus control groups or average values before and after a training program for the same group. The formula for the test statistic, t, is as follows:

$$t = \frac{\bar{x} - \mu}{\sigma / \sqrt{n}}$$

where

$\bar{x}$ = sample mean (post-program measurement or experimental group measurement).

μ = population mean (pre-program measurement or control group measurement).

s = population standard deviation. If this value is unknown, the sample standard deviation, s, is used.

n = sample size (number of participants).

The use of this statistic can be illustrated by an example. In the previous example of the packaged program to train salespersons, the null hypothesis, H_0, was that there is no difference in the average sales of participants before and after the program. The alternative hypothesis, H_a, is that the average

H_0 : $\bar{x} = \mu$
H_a : $\bar{x}$ is not equal to μ ($\bar{x} > \mu$)

sales after the program are greater. These are represented in the following way:

This is a one-sided analysis, since the interest is only greater sales. Another alternative hypothesis would be that the average sales after the program are either less than or greater than the average sales before the program. This analysis observes changes on both sides of the pre-program average sales and is shown this way:

H_a : $\bar{x}$ is not equal to μ ($\bar{x} \neq \mu$)

This is called a two-sided analysis. For most evaluation uses, the one-sided analysis is appropriate. The reasoning is simple. If post-program average sales were actually less than pre-program average sales, then the conclusion is that without any statistical analysis, there was no improvement in sales. The interest is only in improvement. Therefore, the alternative hypothesis for most program evaluations involves this one-sided analysis.

As might be expected, the one-sided analysis involves what is referred to as a one-tailed test. The test statistic is compared to a critical value from Table A7-1, which contains values for both the one-tailed and two-tailed test. The critical value selected for the one-tailed test depends on two factors: the degrees of freedom, and the level of significance. The degrees of freedom are one less than the sample size.

$$df = n - 1$$

The level of significance, α, is the probability of a Type I error and is selected based on the confidence desired in the outcome of the analysis. The most common value for α is .05. For example, a sample size of 25 participants and $\alpha = .05$ yields a critical value of 1.711 for a one-tailed test in Table A7-1. If the test statistic, t, calculated from the previous formula is larger than this critical value, then the null hypothesis is rejected. There is an increase in sales caused by something other than chance, usually the HRD program.

This result is shown graphically in figure A7-2. The values of the test statistic greater than the critical value are in what is called the region of rejection. The remaining values are in the non-rejection region.

Detailed Example

This process of statistical tests can be further explained and summarized by presenting a detailed example of a calculation. Refer to the data presented in Table 14-1. This example compares the production output of a group of employees before and after an HRD program. Using that data, determine if the change in average output is the result of the training program or chance. Use a level of significance of .05.

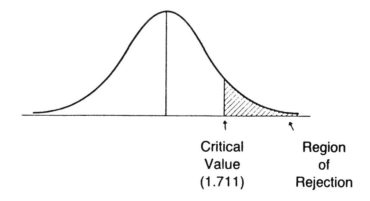

Critical   Region
Value   of
(1.711)   Rejection

Figure A7-2. A one-tailed test.

Setting up the hypothesis:

H_0 : $\mu_a = \mu_b$
H_a : $\mu_a = \mu_a > \mu_b$

where

H_0 = Mean unit hour after training.
H_a = Mean unit hour before training.

This is a one-tailed test, since the interest is only in improvement after training.

Determining the critical value:
There are 15 items in the sample. Therefore, the degrees of freedom are
$df = n - 1 = 14$
The critical value from Table 9-6, based on $\alpha = .05$ is $t_{cv} = 1.761$
$t_{cv} = 1.761$

Calculating the test statistic:
The standard deviation of the post-training data is 7.75, from a previous calculation. This figure can be substituted for the population standard deviation (all production workers), which is unknown. In reality, this may be a known factor. The pre-program mean value is:

$$\mu_b = \frac{\sum xi}{n} = \frac{826}{15} = 55.07$$

The post-program mean (from a previous example) is:

$$\mu_a = \bar{x} = 62.13$$

The test statistic is:

$$t = \frac{\bar{x} - \mu_b}{\sigma / \sqrt{n}} = \frac{62.13 - 55.07}{7.75\sqrt{15}} = \frac{7.06}{2.001} = 3.528$$

The test statistic is larger than the critical value. Therefore, the null hypothesis, H_0, is rejected. The results can be attributed to the HRD program, assuming no other variables entered the picture.

Table A7-1
Critical Values for the t Distribution

df	Level of significance for one-tailed test					
	.10	**.05**	**.025**	**.01**	**.005**	**.005**
	Level of significance for two-tailed test					
	.20	**.10**	**.05**	**.02**	**.01**	**.001**
1	3.078	6.314	12.706	31.821	63.657	636.619
2	1.886	2.920	4.303	6.965	9.925	31.598
3	1.638	2.353	3.182	4.541	5.841	12.941
4	1.533	2.132	2.776	3.747	4.604	8.610
5	1.476	2.015	2.571	3.365	4.032	6.859
6	1.440	1.943	2.447	3.143	3.707	5.959
7	1.415	1.895	2.365	2.998	3.499	5.405
8	1.397	1.860	2.306	2.896	3.355	5.041
9	1.383	1.833	2.262	2.821	3.250	4.781
10	1.372	1.812	2.228	2.764	3.169	4.587
11	1.363	1.796	2.201	2.718	3.106	4.437
12	1.356	1.782	2.179	2.681	3.055	4.318
13	1.350	1.771	2.160	2.650	3.012	4.221
14	1.345	1.761	2.145	2.624	2.977	4.140
15	1.341	1.753	2.131	2.602	2.947	4.073
16	1.337	1.746	2.120	2.583	2.921	4.015
17	1.333	1.740	2.110	2.567	2.898	3.965
18	1.330	1.734	2.101	2.552	2.878	3.922
19	1.328	1.729	2.093	2.539	2.861	3.883
20	1.325	1.725	2.086	2.528	2.845	3.850
21	1.323	1.721	2.080	2.518	2.831	3.819
22	1.321	1.717	2.074	2.508	2.819	3.792
23	1.319	1.714	2.069	2.500	25.807	3.767
24	1.318	1.711	2.064	2.492	2.797	3.745
25	1.316	1.708	2.060	2.485	2.787	3.725
26	1.315	1.706	2.056	2.479	2.779	3.707
27	1.314	1.703	2.052	2.473	2.771	3.690
28	1.313	1.701	2.048	2.467	2.763	3.674
29	1.311	1.699	2.045	2.462	2.756	3.659
30	1.310	1.697	2.042	2.457	2.750	3.646
40	1.303	1.684	2.021	2.423	2.704	3.551
60	1.296	1.671	2.000	2.390	2.660	3.460
120	1.289	1.6958	1.980	2.358	2.617	3.373
∞	1.282	1.645	1.960	2.326	2.576	3.291

How Results-Based Are Your Training and Development Programs?

A Survey for Managers

Instructions. For each of the following statements, please circle the response that best matches the Training and Development function at your organization. If none of the answers describe the situation, select the one that best fits. Please be candid with your responses.

Select the most correct response.

1. The direction of the Training and Development function at your organization:
   a. Shifts with requests, problems, and changes as they occur.
   b. Is determined by Human Resources and adjusted as needed.
   c. Is based on a mission and a strategic plan for the function.

2. The primary mode of operation of the Training and Development function is:
   a. To respond to requests by managers and other employees to deliver training programs and services.
   b. To help management react to crisis situations and reach solutions through training programs and services.
   c. To implement many training programs in collaboration with management to prevent problems and crisis situations.

3. The goals of the Training and Development function are:
   a. Set by the training staff based on perceived demand for programs.
   b. Developed consistent with your organization's human resources plans and goals.
   c. Developed to integrate with operating goals and strategic plans of the organization.

4. Most new training programs are initiated:
   a. By request of top management.
   b. When a program appears to be successful in another organization.
   c. After a needs analysis has indicated that the program is needed.
5. When a major organizational change is made:
   a. We decide only which presentations are needed, not which skills are needed.
   b. We occasionally assess what new skills and knowledge are needed.
   c. We systematically evaluate what skills and knowledge are needed.
6. To define training plans:
   a. Management is asked to choose training from a list of canned, existing courses.
   b. Employees are asked about their training needs.
   c. Training needs are systematically derived from a thorough analysis of performance problems.
7. When determining the timing of training and the target audiences:
   a. We have lengthy, nonspecific training courses for large audiences.
   b. We tie specific training needs to specific individuals and groups.
   c. We deliver training almost immediately before its use, and it is given only to those people who need it.
8. The responsibility for results from training:
   a. Rests primarily with the training staff.
   b. Is a responsibility of the training staff and line managers, who jointly ensure that results are obtained.
   c. Is a shared responsibility of the training staff, participants, and managers all working together to ensure success.
9. Systematic, objective evaluation, designed to ensure that trainees are performing appropriately on the job:
   a. Is never accomplished. The only evaluations are during the program and they focus on how much the participants enjoyed the program.
   b. Is occasionally accomplished. Participants are asked if the training was effective on the job.
   c. Is frequently and systematically pursued. Performance is evaluated after training is completed.
10. New training programs are developed:
    a. Internally, using a staff of instructional designers and specialists.
    b. By vendors. We usually purchase programs modified to meet the organization's needs.
    c. In the most economical and practical way to meet deadlines and cost objectives, using internal staff and vendors.

11. Costs for training and OD are accumulated:
    a. On a total aggregate basis only.
    b. On a program-by-program basis.
    c. By specific process components such as development and delivery, in addition to a specific program.
12. Management involvement in the training process is:
    a. Very low with only occasional input.
    b. Moderate, usually by request, or on an as-needed basis.
    c. Deliberately planned for all major training activities, to ensure a partnership arrangement.
13. To ensure that training is transferred into performance on the job, we:
    a. Encourage participants to apply what they have learned and report results.
    b. Ask managers to support and reinforce training and report results.
    c. Utilize a variety of training transfer strategies appropriate for each situation.
14. The training staff's interaction with line management is:
    a. Rare. We almost never discuss issues with them.
    b. Occasional, during activities such as needs analysis or program coordination.
    c. Regular, to build relationships, as well as to develop and deliver programs.
15. Training and Development's role in major change efforts is:
    a. To conduct training to support the project, as required.
    b. To provide administrative support for the program, including training.
    c. To initiate the program, coordinate the overall effort, and measure its progress, in addition to providing training.
16. Most managers in your organization view the Training and Development function as:
    a. A questionable function that wastes too much of employees' time.
    b. A necessary function that probably cannot be eliminated.
    c. An important resource that can be used to improve the organization.
17. Training and Development programs are:
    a. Activity-oriented (all supervisors attend the "Performance Appraisal Workshop").
    b. Individual results-based (the participant will reduce his or her error rate by at least 20%).
    c. Organizational results-based (the cost of quality will decrease by 25%).

18. The investment in Training and Development is measured primarily by:
    a. Subjective opinions.
    b. Observations by management, reactions from participants.
    c. Dollar return through improved productivity, cost savings, or better quality.
19. The Training and Development effort consists of:
    a. Usually one-shot, seminar-type approaches.
    b. A full array of courses to meet individual needs.
    c. A variety of programs implemented to bring about change in the organization.
20. New Training and Development programs, without some formal method of evaluation, are implemented at my organization:
    a. Regularly.
    b. Seldom.
    c. Never.
21. The results of training programs are communicated:
    a. When requested, to those who have a need to know.
    b. Occasionally, to members of management only.
    c. Routinely, to a variety of selected target audiences.
22. Management involvement in training evaluation:
    a. Is minor, with no specific responsibilities and few requests.
    b. Consists of informal responsibilities for evaluation, with some requests for formal training.
    c. Very specific. All managers have some responsibilities in evaluation.
23. During a business decline at my organization, the training function will:
    a. Be the first to have its staff reduced.
    b. Be retained at the same staffing level.
    c. Go untouched in staff reductions and possibly beefed up.
24. Budgeting for training and education is based on:
    a. Last year's budget.
    b. Whatever the training specialist can "sell."
    c. A zero-based system.
25. The principal group that must justify Training and Development expenditures is:
    a. The Training and Development department.
    b. The human resources function.
    c. Line management.
26. Over the last two years, the Training and Development budget as a percent of operating expenses has:

a. Decreased.
b. Remained stable.
c. Increased.

27. Top management's involvement in the implementation of Training and Development programs:
    a. Is limited to sending invitations, extending congratulations, passing out certificates, etc.
    b. Includes monitoring progress, opening/closing speeches, giving presentations on the outlook of the organization, etc.
    c. Includes program participation to see what's covered, conducting major segments of the program, requiring key executives to be involved, etc.

28. Line management involvement in conducting training and development programs is:
    a. Very minor; only HRD specialists conduct programs.
    b. Limited to a few specialists conducting programs in their area of expertise.
    c. Significant. On the average, over half of the programs are conducted by key line managers.

29. When an employee completes a training program and returns to the job, his or her manager is likely to:
    a. Make no reference to the program.
    b. Ask questions about the program and encourage the use of the material.
    c. Require use of the program material and give positive rewards when the material is used successfully.

30. When an employee attends an outside seminar, upon return, he or she is required to:
    a. Do nothing.
    b. Submit a report summarizing the program.
    c. Evaluate the seminar, outline plans for implementing the material covered, and estimate the value of the program.

Interpreting the Training and Development Programs Assessment

Score the assessment instrument as follows. Allow

1 point for each (a) response.
3 points for each (b) response.
5 points for each (c) response.

The total will be between 30 and 150 points.

The interpretation of scoring is provided below. The explanation is based on the input from dozens of organizations and hundreds of managers.

Score Range	Analysis of Score
120–150	*Outstanding Environment* for achieving results with Training and Development. Great management support. A truly successful example of results-based Training and Development.
90–119	*Above Average* in achieving results with Training and Development. Good management support. A solid and methodical approach to results-based Training and Development.
60–89	*Needs Improvement* to achieve desired results with Training and Development. Management support is ineffective. Training and Development programs do not usually focus on results.
30–59	*Serious Problems* with the success and status of Training and Development. Management support is non-existent. Training and Development programs are not producing results.

Index

415